Constitutional Constraints on Ad Hoc Legislation

Anna Jasiak

Constitutional Constraints on Ad Hoc Legislation

A Comparative Study of the United States, Germany and the Netherlands

intersentia

METRO

Ius Commune Europaeum

Anna Jasiak

Constitutional Constraints on Ad Hoc Legislation

Intersentia Ltd
Trinity House | Cambridge Business Park | Cowley Road
Cambridge | CB4 0WZ | United Kingdom
mail@intersentia.co.uk

ISBN 978-1-78068-017-0
NUR 823

Cambridge – Antwerp – Portland
www.intersentia.com | www.intersentia.co.uk

Cover picture: United States Capitol, Washington, D.C., President's Room, detail of ceiling fresco made in 1850s showing figure symbolizing Legislation, Library of Congress, LC-USZ62-96817

British Library Cataloguing in Publication Data. A catalogue record for this book is available from the British Library.

In memory of Alis Koekkoek

ACKNOWLEDGEMENTS

This book represents my Ph.D. research on ad hoc legislation, I have worked on at Tilburg University in the Netherlands, from a constitutional perspective. It was a special time of discovery. My stay at Georgetown University Law Center in Washington D.C., USA and at the Graduiertenkolleg "Verfassung jenseits des Staates" of Humboldt-Universität in Berlin, Germany have enriched me. It strongly influenced my manner of thinking and doing, and the experiences I gained at the time will always remain with me.

I had help from many people in writing this book, and they all deserve an expression of gratitude. A few of them I would like to mention in particular.

Professors Philip Eijlander and Rob van Gestel supervised this research. They gave me a lot of freedom, and were nonetheless always there for me. Discussions with them were inspiring and energizing. I greatly appreciated their dissatisfaction with what was good and the pursuit of what was better. I also attempted to work in that spirit.

The research periods I spent in America and Germany were meaningful through discussions with many academics and practitioners, and mainly through the discussions with professors Vicki Jackson, Timothy Westmoreland, Nicholas Quinn Rosenkranz, Dieter Grimm and Ulrich Karpen.

I would also like to express a word of thanks to professors Monica Claes, Dieter Grimm, Tim Koopmans, Roel de Lange and Richard Happé (for his last minute involvement) for their willingness to take a seat on my doctoral committee. I appreciate the fact that they read my manuscript so painstakingly and commented on it.

This book would not have materialized, or at any rate not in this form, if I had not gone to work for the late professor Alis Koekkoek as a student assistant. He placed a lot of trust in me and gave me the opportunity to develop academically in Tilburg. He inspired my love of comparative law and American law by quickly involving me in research. I am very grateful to him for this. It is an honor for me to dedicate this book to him.

Anna Jasiak

CONTENTS

ABBREVIATIONS

The United States

A.B.A. J. E-Report	American Bar Association Journal E-Report
AJPS	American Journal of Political Science
Alb. L. Rev.	Albany Law Review
Am. J. Legal Hist.	American Journal of Legal History
Am. L. Reg.	American Law Register
Ariz. L. Rev.	Arizona Law Review
CONG. REC.	Congressional Record
Conn. L. Rev.	Connecticut Law Review
Const. Comment.	Constitutional Commentary
CRS	Congressional Research Service
DePaul J. Health Care L.	DePaul Journal of Health Care Law
Ecology L. Q.	Ecology Law Quarterly
Geo. Immigr. L. J.	Georgetown Immigration Law Journal
Georg. L. J.	Georgetown Law Journal
Geo. Wash. L. Rev.	George Washington Law Review
Harv. Envtl. L. Rev.	Harvard Environmental Law Review
Harv. L. Rev.	Harvard Law Review
Hastings Comm. & Ent. L. J.	Hastings Communications and Entertainment Law Journal
J. Contemp. Legal Issues	Journal of Contemporary Legal Issues
J.L. & Econ.	The Journal of Law and Economics
La. L. Rev.	Louisiana Law Review
Marq. Elder's Advisor	Marquette Elder's Advisor
Mich. L. Rev.	Michigan Law Review
Nw. U.L. Rev.	Northwestern University Law Review
Or. L. Rev.	Oregon Law Review
Priv. L.	Private Law
Pub. L.	Public Law
S. Rep.	Senate Report
Stat.	United States Statutes at Large
St. Thomas L. Rev.	St. Thomas Law Review

Suffolk U. L. Rev.	Suffolk University Law Review
Tax L. Rev.	Tax Law Review
Temp. Pol. & Civ. Rts. L. Rev.	Temple Political and Civil Rights Law Review
Tex. L. Rev.	Texas Law Review
Tul. J. Int'l. & Comp. L.	Tulane Journal of International and Comparative Law
Tul. L. Rev.	Tulane Law Review
U.C.D. L. Rev.	University of California, Davis Law Review
U. Cin. L. Rev.	University of Cincinnati Law Review
U. Col. L. Rev.	University of Colorado Law Review
U. Pa. J. Const. L.	University of Pennsylvania Journal of Constitutional Law
U. Pa. L. Rev	University of Pennsylvania Law Review
U.S.C.	United States Code
U. Tol. L. Rev.	University of Toledo Law Review
Vand. L. Rev.	Vanderbilt Law Review
Wash. U. L. Q.	Washington University Law Quarterly
W. Va.L. Rev.	West Virginia Law Review
Widener J. Pub. L.	Widener Journal of Public Law
Wis. L. Rev.	Wisconsin Law Review
WL	Westlaw
Yale L. J.	Yale Law Journal

Germany

AöR	Archiv des öffentlichen Rechts
BGBl.	Bundesgesetzblat (Federal Bulletin of Acts and Decrees)
BR Drs.	Bundesrat Drucksachen (printed documents, Bundesrat)
BT Drs.	Bundestag Drucksachen (printed documents, Bundestag)
BVerfGE	Bundesverfassungsgericht (Federal Constitutional Court)
BVerwGE	Bundesverwaltungsgericht (Federal Administrative Court)
DÖV	Die Öffentliche Verwaltung
DRiZ	Deutsche Richterzeitung
DVBl.	Deutsches Vervaltungsblatt
FAZ	Frankfurter Allgemeine Zeitung
GG	Grundgesetz (German Basic Law)
GVBl	Gesetz- und Verordnungsblatt
JuS	Juristische Schulung
JZ	JuristenZeitung
MDR	Monatsschrift für Deutsches Recht
NJW	Neue Juristische Wochenschrift
NVwZ	Neue Zeitschrift für Verwaltungsrecht
RGBl	Reichsgesetzblatt
SGB	Sozialgesetzbuch
UPR	Umwelt- und Planungsrecht
U. Toronto L.J.	Univeristy of Toronto Law Journal

VBlBW	Verwaltungsblätter für Baden-Württemberg
ZG	Zeitschrift für Gesetzgebung
ZRP	Zeitschrift für Rechtspolitik
ZZP	Zeitschrift für Zivilprozeß

The Netherlands

AB	Administratiefrechtelijke Beslissingen
ABRvS	Afdeling Bestuursrechtspraak van de Raad van State
Appl. no.	Application number
BNB	Beslissingen in belastingzaken Nederlandse Belastingrechtspraak
CBb	College van Beroep voor het bedrijfsleven (Trade and Industry Appeals Tribunal)
CRvB	Centrale Raad van Beroep (Central Appeals Tribunal for the public service and for social security matters)
ECHR	European Convention on Human Rights
ECtHR	European Court of Human Rights
Eur. J.L. Reform	European Journal of Law Reform
HR	Hoge Raad (the Supreme Court of the Netherlands)
ICCPR	International Covenant on Civil and Political Rights
M&R	Milieu & Recht
NJ	Nederlandse Jurisprudentie
NJB	Nederlands Juristenblad
NJCM	Nederlands Juristencomité voor Mensenrechten
RMThemis	Rechtsgeleerd Magazijn Themis
Stb.	Staatsblad (Stb.) (Netherlands Bulletin of Acts and Decrees)
Stcrt.	Staatscourant
Trb.	Tractatenblad (Trb.) (Netherlands Treaty Series)
VN	Vakstudie Nieuws

TABLE OF CASES

The United States

Antonio v. Wards Cove Packing Co., Inc., 10 F. 3d 1485 (1993)/II.4.3, n.318
Antonio v. Wards Cove Packing Co., Inc., 275 F.3d 797 (2001)/n.318
Apache Bend Apartments Ltd. v. U.S. Through IRS, 964 F.2d 1556 (1992)/II.4.2, n.316
Armstrong v. Manzo, 380 U.S. 545 (1965)/n.327
Allied Structural Steel Company v. Spannaus, 438 U.S. 234 (1978)/n.173
Bartnicki v. Vopper, 532 U.S. 514 (2001)/n.931
Bellsouth Corporation v. FCC, 162 F.3d 678 (1998)/n.221, n.232
Board of Education v. Pico, 475 U.S. 871 (1982)/n.893
Bolling v. Sharpe, 347 U.S. 497 (1954)/n.299
Bowen v. Gilliard, 483 U.S. 587 (1987)/n.309
Brokaw v. Mercer County, 235 F.3d 1020 (2000)/II.1.1.2.1, n.42
Buckley v. Valeo, 424 U.S. 1 (1976)/II.2.3.2, n.177
Burgess v. Salmon, 97 U.S. 381 (1878)/II.3.2.1, n.250
Bush v. Schiavo, 885 So.2d 321 (2004)/n.62, n.65
Calder v. Bull, 3 U.S. 386 (1798)/II. 3.2.1, n.246
Case of Hayburn, 2 U.S. 408 (1792)/II.3.4.1, n.277
Central State University v. American Association of University Professors, 526 U.S. 124 (1999)/n.937
Cherokee Nation v. United States, 270 U.S. 476 (1926)/n.279
Chicago Professional Sports Limited Partnership et al. v. National Basketball Association, 961 F.2d 667 (1992)/n.209
Chicago & Southern Air Lines, Inc., 333 U.S. 103 (1948)/II.3.4.1, n.275
City of Boerne v. Flores, 521 U.S. 507 (1997)/n.931
City of New Orleans v. Dukes, 427 U.S. 297 (1976)/n.314, n.881
City of New York v. Beretta U.S.A. Corp., 401 F. Supp.2d 244 (2005)/n.1007
City of New York v. Beretta U.S.A. Corp. 2008 U.S. App. LEXIS 9309 (2d Cir.)/n.1007
Cmty. Serv. Broad. Of Mid-America, Inc. v. FCC, 593 F2d.1102 (1978)/n.912
Commodity Futures Trading Comm'n v. Schor, 478 U.S. 833 (1986)/n.58
Common Cause v. State of Maine, 455 A.2d 1 (1983)/II.2.2.2, n.125, n.895
Consolidated Edison Co. of New York, Inc. v. Pataki, 292 F.3d 339 (2002)/n.218

Germany

The Netherlands

HR February 20, 1998, *BNB* 1998/207/n.841
HR July 15, 1998, *BNB* 1998/293 (*Autokostenforfaitarrest*)/n.752
HR August 17, 1998, *BNB* 1999/122c/n.762
HR May 12, 1999, *BNB* 1999/271c(*Arbeidskostenforfait*)/n.845
HR February 28, 2001, *BNB* 2001/198c/n.855

ECtHR

Adamogiannis v. Greece (Appl. no. 47734/9) ECHR 14 March 2002/n.837
Anagnostopoulos and Others v. Greece (Appl. no. 39374/98) ECHR 2000-XII/n.823, n.824, n.830, n.835
Ásmundsson v. Iceland (Appl. no. 60669/00) ECHR 2004-IX/n.764, n.938
Brumarescu v. Romania (Appl. no. 28342/95) ECHR 1999-VII/n.852
Brualla Gomez de la Torre v. Spain (Appl. no. 155/1996/774/975) ECHR 1997-VIII/n.858
Bulgakova v. Russia (Appl. no. 69524/01) ECHR 18 January 2007/n.854, n.988
Case "Relating to certain aspects of the laws on the use of languages in education in Belgium" v. Belgium (Appl. nos. 1474/62, 1677/62, 1691/62, 1769/63, 1994/63, 2126/64) (1968) Series A, no. 6/n.747
Chapman v. the United Kingdom (Appl. no. 27238/95) ECHR 2001-I/n.833
Forrer-Niedenthal c. Allemagne (Appl. no. 47316/99) ECHR 20 February 2003/n.826, n.831, n.839
Golder v. United Kingdom (Appl. no. 4451/70) (1975) ECHR Series A, no. 18/n.650, n.857
Gorraiz Lizarraga and Others v. Spain (Appl. no. 62543/00) ECHR 2004-III/n.820, n.833, n.834, n.853, n.989
James and Others v. the United Kingdom (Appl. no. 8793/79) (1986) Series A no. 98/n.833
Levages Prestations Services v. France (Appl. no. 51/1995/557/643) ECHR 1996-V/n.858
Multiplex v. Croatia (Appl. no. 58112/00) ECHR 10 July 2003/n.972
Mellacher and Others v. Austria (Appl. nos. 10522/83; 11011/84; 11070/84) (1989) Series A no. 169/n.833
National & Provincial Building Society, Leeds Permanent Building Society and Yorkshire Building Society v. the United Kingdom, (Appl. nos. 117/1996/736/933–935) ECHR 1997-VII/IV.5.2.2, n.628, n.788, n.798, n.805, n.806, n.808, n.810, n.821, n.823
Ogis Institut Stanislas, Ogec St. Pie X et Blanche de Castille et Autres c. France (Appl. nos. 42219/98 and 54563/00) ECHR 27 May 2004/n.825
Papageorgiou v. Greece, (Appl. no. 97/1996/716/913) ECHR 1997-VI/n.803, n.823
Pravednaya v. Russia (Appl. no. 69529/01) ECHR 18 November 2004/n.852
Pressos Compania Naviera S.A. and Others v. Belgium, (Appl. no. 38/1994/485/567) (1995) Series A no. 332/n.786, n.787, n.808
Ruiz Mateos v. Spain (Appl. no. 12952/87) ECHR 23 June 1993/n.989
Ryabykh v. Russia (Appl. no. 52854/99) ECHR 2003-IX/n.851, n.852, n.982
Scordino v. Italy (Appl. no. 36813/97) ECHR 29 March 2006/IV.5.2.4, n.820, n.827, n.829, n.836, n.837, n.838
Smokovitis and Others v. Greece (Appl. no. 46356/99) ECHR 11 April 2002/n.820, n.823, n.830

Stran Greek Refineries and Stratis Andreadis v. Greece, (Appl. no. 13427/87) (1994) Series A no. 301/IV.5.2.1, n.628, n.797, n.801, n.802, n.804, n.811, n.820, n.893
Stubbings and Others v. United Kingdom (Appl. nos. 36–37/1995/542–543/628–629) ECHR 1996-IV/n.809
Sukhobokov v. Russia (Appl. no. 75470/01) ECHR 13 April 2006/n.988
Zielinski and Pradal and Gonzales and Others v. France (Appl. nos. 24846/94 and 34165/96 to 34173/96) ECHR 1999-VII/IV.5.2.3, n.628, n.799, n.814, n.820, n.822, n.828, n.829, n.967

The Human Rights Committee

Broeks v. The Netherlands, April 9, 1987, Communication no. 172/1984/n.746
Danning v. The Netherlands, April 9, 1987, Communication no. 180/1984/n.746
Gangadin v. The Netherlands, April 4, 2007, Communication no. 1451/2006/n.746

PART I

INTRODUCTION

1. The motivation for this study

The generality of laws prevents the legislature from acting arbitrarily. 'Laws should be general' is therefore a well-known adage of the rule of law. In practice, however, this principle is sometimes an illusory guideline, as legislatures tend to design ad hoc laws for particular cases. This may conflict with the principle of the generality of laws and other constitutional principles such as the separation of powers, legal certainty and equality. Recent developments show how tempting and politically attractive it can be to intervene in predetermined cases. Yet, constitutional principles have continued to resist this.

The 2008 financial crisis is one example of such legislative practice. A number of large companies that were in danger of bankruptcy were bailed out and therefore able to survive the difficult times. This included a huge bailout of the American International Company (AIG) in the United States. The bailout was controversial because it used the money of ordinary taxpayers to cover the losses due to AIG's questionable investments. Even more controversy emerged when the news became public that AIG and other bailed-out companies were paying substantial bonuses to individual employees. The public was furious that these people received huge bonuses, while their tax money was put at risk. The U.S. House of Representatives acted quickly. It addressed the people's dissatisfaction by introducing new legislation. A retroactive tax bill imposing a 90% levy on the bonuses already paid out by these specific firms, and hypothetically by other firms in the future, was meant to calm public outrage. By passing the bill, the House was proud of responding to the peoples' will. Interestingly enough, both the Senate and the U.S. President, Barack Obama, rejected this idea. Together with some legal commentators, Obama cast doubts on its constitutionality. He stated in this context: "As a general proposition, you don't want to be passing laws that are just targeting a handful of individuals. You want to pass laws that have some broad applicability. [...] And as a general proposition, I think you certainly don't want to use the tax code to punish people."[1]

The tax bonus bill was not the only means used by a State power, including the legislature in the United States and in other countries, to respond to great public pressure

1 Interview with U.S. President, Barack Obama, March 22, 2009, on CBS's "60 minutes," <www.cbsnews.com/video/watch/?id=4883409n%3fsource=search_video> (last accessed on June 12, 2011). See also the *Wall Street Journal*'s story at <http://online.wsj.com/article/SB123777236733010369.html> (last accessed on June 12, 2011).

in specific cases. Two landmark end-of-life cases are particularly interesting in this respect. In 2005, the U.S. legislature stepped into the judicial battle concerning the right to die of Terri Schiavo (Chapter II.1.2). In February 2009, a similar case divided public opinion in Italy. Just like Terri Schiavo, the Italian patient Eluana Englaro had been in a coma for many years following a car accident. After a court battle that had lasted years, Eluana's father obtained a court decision that allowed removal of the feeding tube from her body. To prevent the effectuation of this specific court decision, Italian Prime Minister Berlusconi promptly devised a special emergency decree. The Italian president, however, refused to sign it, which made Berlusconi try once again by proposing adequate legislation. Although the new bill was formulated in general terms and thus applied to future cases as well, the focus on Englaro's case was clear. Eluana died, however, before the bill became law.[2]

As regards these two right-to-die cases, the conservative part of public opinion vigorously supported State intervention to prevent the removal of the feeding tubes from the bodies of Terri Schiavo and Eluana Englaro. On the other hand, many legal commentators, but not all,[3] strongly opposed State intervention in specific cases that had been finally decided by the courts in accordance with the existing general laws.[4] In the Italian case, the President's refusal to sign Berlusconi's emergency decree for Eluana Englaro led to a constitutional crisis. President Napolitano based his decision first and foremost on his conclusion that it would be unconstitutional to overrule the final decision of the Italian Supreme Court in the specific case of Eluana Englaro.

Ad hoc legislation as illustrated above is the subject of this book. The examples given above suggest that such laws are controversial in any event. They have both proponents and opponents. On the one hand, from a political point of view, the legislature is forced to act, because it feels obliged to address the public outcry or fulfill other (international) obligations,[5] whereas, on the other, it runs a risk of violating the principles of the rule of law. Although doubts as to their constitutionality have been expressed, a well-founded view on the position of ad hoc laws and the constitutional boundaries of the legislature so far appears to be lacking. Many questions are yet to be answered: Do *all* laws for specific cases pose constitutional problems? Can constitutional burdens be placed on legislatures which might have had politically valid motives to deal with one specific case, for which they nevertheless formulate a law of general applicability? Is it not within the competence of legislatures to deviate from their own previously adopted general rules regardless of whether they do so impulsively and with a focus on individual cases? Should not democratically elected legislatures have the last word, even if this implies overruling specific final judicial decisions? Can the expediency-driven character of ad hoc legislation constitute a violation of the principles of the rule of law?

2 For a description of the case, see R. Donadio, "Death Ends Coma Case That Set Off Furor in Italy," *New York Times* February 9, 2009.

3 See, for example, M.P. Allen, "Congress and Terri Schiavo: A Primer on the American Constitutional Order?," 108 *W. Va.L. Rev.* 309, 321 (2005) and S.G. Calabresi, "The Terri Schiavo Case: In Defense of the Special Law Enacted by Congress and President Bush," 100 *Nw. U.L. Rev.* 151, 164 (2006).

4 See Tribe's comment at <www.pbs.org/newshour/bb/congress/jan-june05/schiavo_3-21.html> (last accessed on June 12, 2011).

5 These are just two conceivable reasons following from the examples given above and later on in Parts II, III, and IV.

2. Defining ad hoc legislation

I define ad hoc laws as discussed in this book as:

> Laws resulting from the legislature's attempt to achieve a particular politically expedient outcome in one specific case by exempting this case from the existing general rules or (unexpectedly) changing the inconvenient rules as such if they stand in the way of that outcome.

It should be emphasized that the term "ad hoc legislation" is not yet established in the legal literature in English. In Dutch, *gelegenheidswetgeving* is a corresponding term, although it seems to have a much broader meaning and is misused nowadays. Since it has a pejorative connotation in the Netherlands, it tends to be used generally by those who disagree with the proposed legislation. Another term one might find attractive, namely "case-specific legislation," is too narrow to cover all characteristics of ad hoc legislation. The following two characteristics can be distinguished. First, ad hoc laws are enacted for the purpose of one particular case or an easily identified group of cases. The legislature's motives are thus directed at one specific case, even though this does not always mean that the law cannot apply to other cases as well. Second, ad hoc laws are usually enacted unexpectedly and sometimes even impulsively.

In general, I will not explicitly discuss certain types of laws which at first sight might seem to be connected with ad hoc legislation. I will do so only when this is necessary to formulate ideas on ad hoc laws. These types include *organizational laws* governing the internal functioning of the State, such as laws on the division of municipalities or creation of specific national institutions, specific *budget laws*, or other *case-specific laws which are permitted on the basis of tradition or a national constitution* (for example, specific amnesty laws laid down in constitutions). Nor will I devote separate attention to *classical emergency legislation*. The broad and autonomous subject of State emergency powers traditionally relates to the possibilities for the government to deviate from its regular powers in the event of an officially announced emergency situation. This is rarely the case in relation to the ad hoc legislation discussed in this book.[6] One of the characteristics of ad hoc legislation is the ordinary nature of cases in which the legislature interferes. The cases of Eluana Englaro and Terri Schiavo, for example, could have been dealt with adequately on the basis of preexisting general rules. Emergency laws in their traditional sense mostly lay down general rules and guidelines for the State to apply in official states of emergency such as war or disasters.

3. Research question

The uncertainty and doubts about the position of ad hoc laws within the framework of the rule of law prompted the following central research question:

6 For clarification of emergency powers in a constitutional system, see e.g., M. Tushnet, "Comparative Constitutional Law," in: M. Reimann & R. Zimmermann (eds.), *The Oxford Handbook of Comparative Law*, Oxford: Oxford University Press 2006, pp. 1240ff.

When do laws enacted to deal with a specific case draw constitutional criticism in the United States, Germany, and the Netherlands, and what constitutional rules and principles primarily determine the legality of such laws?

This central question will be answered by studying the following sub-questions:

1. What types of ad hoc laws can be distinguished?
2. What constitutional rules and principles come to the fore in case law and in the legal literature as regards different types of ad hoc legislation?
3. Do these constitutional rules and principles leave any margin for the justification of ad hoc legislation?

The main research goal is to develop a constitutional framework for the assessment of ad hoc legislation. At the same time I realize that not all conclusions I will reach are necessarily universal, since they are based on my research of three countries. For the above mentioned purpose constitutional principles and rules of hard constitutional law that can limit the legislature's power to adopt ad hoc laws will be identified on the basis of the national constitutions, case law and the legal literature in the United States, Germany, and the Netherlands. To determine the extent to which these principles are of use, the arguments used in the constitutional law of these three countries for the constitutionality of ad hoc laws will be identified and analyzed. I would like to emphasize that this study is in the field of constitutional law rather than legal theory, legal philosophy, or political philosophy. Only limited attention will therefore be paid to the literature in the latter fields. The same holds true for the principles of good quality legislation that are not among the constitutional principles and norms dealt with in this book. Although principles such as, for example, the consistency and clarity of laws, the necessity for new legislation and transparent balancing of interests are relevant in the context of ad hoc legislation, they receive only limited attention, since this is a constitutional study. A more extensive study of other aspects of legislative quality than constitutional ones can be performed in the future.

4. Scientific relevance

The constitutional boundaries of the legislature with regard to ad hoc legislation have not yet been defined, although several publications have paid attention to this subject. Eijlander and Van Gestel were among those who observed this tendency in Dutch legislative practice and addressed possible problems in light of the principles of the rule of law.[7] In Germany, Bücker discussed individual legislation within the German

7 Ph. Eijlander, "Gelegenheidswetgeving. Een rechtsstaat onwaardig," *Ars Aequi*, 2004, pp. 484–491; R.A.J. van Gestel, "De wetmatigheid van wetgeving," *RMThemis* 2005–6, pp. 282ff; R. van Gestel, "Incident- of gelegenheidswetgeving: balanceren op het smalle koord van de trias politica," *Tijdschrift voor privaatrecht* 2004, pp. 1667ff. See also G.J. Veerman, *Over wetgeving. Principes, paradoxen en praktische beschouwingen*, The Hague: SDU Uitgevers 2007, p. 346, who classifies ad hoc legislation as one of the paradoxes of legislation.

constitutional framework. Although his profound work deals with the constitutional position of *Einzelfallgesetze* in Germany, it appears to insufficiently address broader aspects and the complexity of the phenomenon of ad hoc legislation.[8] Moreover, it concentrates on German law only, and the fact that it dates from 1965 raises doubts as to its current value. There are some older publications as well that refer to the general principles of legislation, such as the 1984 dissertation of Van der Vlies.[9] Finally, the principle of the generality of laws has also been discussed in the literature, albeit mostly from the viewpoints of legal philosophy and political philosophy.[10] This study will address this deficiency and extensively discuss the phenomenon of ad hoc legislation from a comparative perspective.

5. Approach

I have conducted a comparative study to answer the research question. It has already been stated that ad hoc laws lead to controversy in various countries and possible boundaries of the powers of the legislatures must still be defined. In the Netherlands, in any event, neither specific doctrine nor case law on this type of legislation exists. Art. 120 of the Dutch Constitution precludes judicial constitutional review of legislation for compatibility with the Dutch Constitution.[11] It states: "The constitutionality of Acts of Parliament and treaties shall not be reviewed by the courts."[12] What is more, the Dutch Supreme Court (*Hoge Raad*) decided that Art. 120 does not only refer to the assessment of legislation within the framework of the Dutch written Constitution but also in light of unwritten principles of the rule of law.[13]

To identify possible conflicts with the principles of the rule of law or even some grounds for justification of the adoption of ad hoc laws, besides the Netherlands, the

8 J. Bücker, *Die Zulässigkeit von Individualgesetzen nach dem Grundgesetz*, Bonn: H. Bouvier u. Co. 1965.

9 I.C. van der Vlies, *Het wetsbegrip en beginselen van behoorlijke regelgeving*, The Hague: Vuga 1984.

10 See, among other publications, Ch. De Secondat Montesquieu, *The Spirit of Laws*, Part II, Book XI, Ch. 6, Berkeley: University of California Press 1977, F. Hayek, *The Political Ideal of the Rule of Law*, Cairo 1955, F. Hayek, *The Road to Serfdom*, London: Routledge & Kegan Paul 1976, J. Raz, *The Rule of Law and Its Virtue*, in: J. Raz, *The Authority of Law*, Clarendon Press: Oxford 1979, L. Fuller, *The Morality of Law*, New Haven: Yale University Press 1974, F. Neumann, *The Rule of Law. Political Theory and the Legal System in Modern Society*, Leamington Spa and Heidelberg: Berg 1986. See also G. Kirchhof, *Die Allgemeinheit des Gesetzes*, Tübingen: Mohr Siebeck 2009 and Ch. Starck, *Die Allgemeinheit des Gesetzes*, Göttingen: Van Den Hoeck & Ruprecht 1987 for a constitutional perspective.

11 No *judicial* review is possible, but legislative proposals can (and should) be subject to constitutional review during the legislative process, R. de Lange, "Constitutionele toetsing van wetgeving in Nederland," *RegelMaat* 2006–4/5, pp. 150–151. See also A.K. Koekkoek, "Constitutionele toetsing door de Eerste Kamer," in: K. Rimanque (ed.), *Het recht op veiligheid*, Antwerp-Apeldoorn: Maklu 2002, pp. 89ff. and M. Claes & G. van der Schyff, "Towards judicial constitutional review in the Netherlands?," in: G. van der Schyff (ed.), *Constitutionalism in the Netherlands and South Africa: A Comparative Study*, Nijmegen: Wolf Legal Publishers 2008, p. 123.

12 The English version of the Dutch Constitution 2008 can be found at www.rijksoverheid.nl/documenten-en-publicaties/publicaties-pb51/the-constitution-of-the-kingdom-of-the-netherlands-2008.html (last accessed on June 12, 2011).

13 *HR* April 14, 1989, *AB* 1989/207 (*Harmonisatiewetarrest*).

United States and Germany have been chosen for comparison. I have also studied the European Convention on Human Rights' law as interpreted by the European Court of Human Rights, insofar as its position on the permissibility of ad hoc laws is concerned.

5.1. Selection of countries

There are several reasons why the United States and Germany were selected for comparison. First of all, the phenomenon of ad hoc legislation can be found in the United States and Germany as well. Both countries have a strong tradition of judicial review of legislation; that of the U.S. is even longer. Both the U.S. Supreme Court and the German Federal Constitutional Court (*Bundesverfassungsgericht*) can be expected to have developed at least several viewpoints that can be helpful in assessing ad hoc legislation, especially in light of the explicit constitutional provisions that prohibit certain types of case-specific laws. In the United States, this is Art. I Sec. 9 and 10 of the U.S. Constitution, which prohibits bills of attainder, while Art. 19 (1) of the German Basic Law (*Grundgesetz, GG*) prohibits *Einzelfallgesetze* that limit basic rights.

Like the Netherlands, both countries are liberal democracies which, as Koopmans concludes, "share some political and ideological traditions, which can briefly be summarized as democracy, rule of law, human rights protection, and open government."[14] As Koopmans further states,[15]

> [e]ach of those traditions implies some of the basic assumptions which determine the working of the constitutional order: the role of representative bodies in legislation; the independence of the judiciary; protection of citizens against arbitrary government acts; participation of citizens in politics by free elections and public debate; autonomy in their own sphere of life.

Although the United States is a common law country, whereas Germany and the Netherlands are civil law countries, a comparison between them is meaningful owing to both the above-mentioned common values in the constitutional orders and a similar economic and social situation. The difference in legal traditions, also with regard to a vision of legislation as such, may also be of particular value for developing fresh ideas on ad hoc laws.

In addition, I have studied the European Convention on Human Rights (ECHR), particularly the case law of the European Court of Human Rights (ECtHR) insofar as it takes a clear position on ad hoc legislation. The case law of the ECtHR is discussed in the Dutch part of this dissertation, since, through Art. 93 of the Dutch Constitution, it has direct effect in the Dutch national legal order. Notwithstanding Art. 120 of the Constitution, Art. 94 allows Dutch courts to review the compatibility of legislation with

14 T. Koopmans, *Courts and Political Institutions. A Comparative View*, Cambridge: Cambridge University Press 2003, p. 7.

15 *Ibid.*, pp. 7–8. For the relevance of historical, political, economic, cultural, and legal factors in comparative law, see O. Kahn-Freund, "On Uses and Misuses of Comparative Law," 37 *Mod. L. Rev.* 1 (1974) and M. Claes, "Comparative Constitutional Law," in: J.M. Smits (ed.), *Encyclopedia of Comparative Law*, Cheltenham: Edward Elgar 2006, pp. 187ff.

the Convention. Dutch courts are thus entitled to check whether parliamentary legislation is in conformity with the international obligations formulated in the ECHR, even if these obligations go beyond those of the Dutch Constitution. It should be noted that the ECHR, including the case law of the ECtHR, is also applicable to the German constitutional order, as Germany is one of the State Parties to the Convention. In Germany, however, unlike in the Netherlands, the Convention is treated as an ordinary law which is solely used by the Federal Constitutional Court to explain the meaning and scope of the provisions of the German Basic Law. If the ECHR conflicts with the German Basic Law, the latter prevails.[16]

5.2. *Method*

The phenomenon of ad hoc legislation and constitutional principles

As already stated, in this comparative study on ad hoc legislation, the legal systems of the United States, Germany, the Netherlands, and the European Convention on Human Rights are compared. The point of departure is ad hoc legislation as such and not any specific legislative rule or provision. To answer the central research question of the constitutional constraints on the legislative branch in enacting ad hoc laws, I have collected and analyzed arguments from these three countries.[17] The phenomenon of ad hoc legislation was examined in light of possible conflicts with the rule of law. The function of the applicable principles in the selected legal systems is similar, namely to limit arbitrary State power, including that of the legislature. This similarity enables meaningful comparative research. In addressing principles of the rule of law that could limit the legislature's actions in specific, predetermined cases, I will focus, for example on the principles of the generality of laws, equality, separation of powers, and legal certainty. In this study, particular attention will be paid to the manner in which they have been translated into positive constitutional law. These principles have been identified on the basis of several high-profile cases in which the legislature was criticized for interfering in particular cases and possibly violating the principles of the rule of law as a result.

Selection of cases

For the Netherlands, I chose the cases of the Licensing of Dredging Act, the Modification of the Dutch Media Act (the so-called BNN Act), and the case of the permanent camera surveillance of Volkert van der G., and in Germany, the cases of the Lex Schörner and the Lex Stendal. In the United States, I selected the intervention of Congress in the case of coma patient Terri Schiavo, the case of Elisabeth Morgan, and the environmental case concerning the northern spotted owl (Northern Timber Compromise). Finally, as regards the law of the European Convention on Human Rights, I devote attention to three of the

16 H. Bethge, "Art. 5," in: M. Sachs, *Grundgesetz. Kommentar*, München: C.H. Beck 2007, p. 276.

17 The comparative study was generally conducted in line with Zweigert and Kötz's comparative method, K. Zweigert & H. Kötz, *An Introduction to Comparative Law*, Oxford: Clarendon Press 1998, pp. 32ff.

most important cases of ad hoc legislation, the *Zielinski* case in France, the *Stran Greek Refineries* case in Greece, and the *Building Societies* case in the United Kingdom. The above-mentioned cases primarily illustrate situations in which the legislature acted impulsively, either deviating from the general, previously enacted rules, or changing these rules for a specific case.

I chose these cases first of all to enable a good understanding of ad hoc legislation in a specific context.[18] Secondly, these cases also help to identify the nature of the criticism they generated, primarily on constitutional issues. I have decided to select only cases which have raised constitutional issues. I describe the above-mentioned cases in detail, because they represent a wide diversity of constitutional aspects. I wish to emphasize that all of them are high-profile cases dating from the twentieth century, which were discussed broadly at national level, usually by legal commentators, but also by the political bodies and the general public. The cases were determined on the basis of the literature and suggestions by experts from the United States, Germany, and the Netherlands, who indicated that these cases were the most important and controversial examples of ad hoc legislation in their native countries. The above-mentioned cases are not the only ones used in this study. Other cases that were particularly interesting in relation to only one aspect of the rule of law are dealt with as well. They are discussed in separate chapters on adequate constitutional principles. It should be borne in mind that all these cases have been used to illustrate the phenomenon of ad hoc legislation and the constitutional problems it causes, rather than as an exhaustive enumeration of ad hoc laws in the three countries.

5.3. *Sources*

To be able to draw sound conclusions on the position of ad hoc legislation within the framework of the rule of law in a comparative perspective, one must first observe and understand this phenomenon in the context of national traditions and the corresponding legal and political systems. Separate attention will therefore be devoted to specific American, German, and Dutch sources. These sources are mainly legal literature, court decisions, and parliamentary documents. Regarding court decisions, the focus in the United States will be on the case law of the U.S. Supreme Court or decisions of other courts insofar as they address constitutional issues that provide insight into the constitutional position of ad hoc laws.[19] In Germany, the decisions of the Federal Constitutional Court (*Bundesverfassungsgericht*) are crucial in this respect, given that this Court is the only court competent to review the compatibility of laws with the German Basic Law, pursuant to Art. 100(1) GG.[20] In the Netherlands, judicial decisions

18 For the value of case studies for qualitative "conceptualized comparison," where the focus is on analytically equivalent phenomena across various contexts, see A.L. George & A. Bennett, *Case Studies and Theory Development in the Social Sciences*, Cambridge: MIT Press 2005, pp. 19ff with references.

19 For both judicial review by federal courts and State court review, see J.E. Nowak & R.D. Rotunda, *Constitutional Law*, St. Paul: Thomson West: 2004, pp. 1ff.

20 Art. 100 (1) GG reads: "If a court concludes that a law on whose validity its decision depends is unconstitutional, the proceedings shall be stayed, and a decision shall be obtained from the *Land* court with jurisdiction over constitutional disputes where the constitution of a *Land* is held to be violated, or

stemming from the lower courts as well as from the Netherlands Supreme Court (Hoge Raad) and the special courts will be cited. The special courts include the Administrative Jurisdiction Division of the Council of State (*Raad van State, Afdeling bestuursrechtspraak*), the Central Appeals Tribunal for public service and for social security matters (*Centrale Raad van Beroep*) and the Trade and Industry Appeals Tribunal (*College van Beroep voor het bedrijfsleven*).[21]

In addition to the official sources, many in-depth discussions were held to obtain information necessary to identify relevant cases of ad hoc legislation, the meaning of constitutional principles, and the legal and political context in which the (federal) legislatures operate. In the United States, conversations with academics at Georgetown University Law Center in Washington, D.C., as well as with experts working for Congress (including the Congressional Research Service), were extremely helpful. In Germany, academics were consulted, mostly from Humboldt University in Berlin, but also from other universities, including those in Hamburg and Göttingen. I also interviewed experts from the *Bundestag*, the *Bundesrat*, and the German Ministry of Justice, as well as Justice Osterloh of the Federal Constitutional Court. The same concept was applied in the Netherlands, where conversations were held with academics and experts from various Ministries, and the Dutch Council of State.

6. The structure of the book

This book is divided into five parts. This introduction is Part I. Next, the phenomenon of ad hoc legislation in the United States (Part II), Germany (Part III), and the Netherlands (Part IV) will be discussed with consistent use of the same structure: I first discuss a few high-profile cases with regard to the purpose for which the legislatures enacted adequate ad hoc laws, and then the constitutional principles that could possibly limit the legislature in this respect. The order in which the countries have been positioned is not random, but corresponds to the order of the actual research. Part V consists of comparison and analysis, including a self-developed typology for ad hoc legislation. I conclude by presenting key conclusions.

from the Federal Constitutional Court where this Basic Law is held to be violated. This provision shall also apply where the Basic law is held to be violated by *Land* law and where a *Land* law is held to be incompatible with a federal law," Basic Law of the Federal Republic of Germany, version of December 2003, published by the German *Bundestag* Administration. See also G. Sturm, "Art. 100," in: M. Sachs, *Grundgesetz. Kommentar*, München: C.H. Beck 2007, pp. 1928ff.

21 For a compact description of the judicial system in the Netherlands, see L. Prakke & C.A.J.M. Kortmann (eds.), *Constitutional Law of 15 EU Member States*, Deventer: Kluwer 2004.

PART II

THE UNITED STATES

Chapter 1

AD HOC LEGISLATION: CASES

Introduction

In this chapter, I discuss three examples of ad hoc, case-specific legislation, namely the Elizabeth Morgan case, the Terri Schiavo case, and the Northwest Timber Compromise case. I first describe the facts of each case and then discuss the legislative intervention. Next, I present the constitutional and other objections to the intervening legislation, followed by concluding remarks.

1.1. The Elizabeth Morgan case

1.1.1. Background

Elizabeth Morgan was a plastic surgeon practicing in Washington D.C. In 1982 she divorced her husband, Dr. Eric Foretich, an oral surgeon. After the divorce, she started judicial proceedings to obtain custody of their baby daughter, Hilary A. Foretich. Morgan succeeded, although broad visitation rights with Hilary were granted to her father. The D.C. Superior Court dealing with this custody dispute found that Foretich had "built a fine home life" for Hilary and had shown, together with his parents, how much love he had for the girl.[22] Morgan challenged and thwarted Foretich's visits. As a result of this negative attitude, the Superior Court formulated a schedule of unsupervised visits, in which Morgan did not have a say.

Shortly afterwards, Morgan accused Foretich of sexual abuse of little Hilary. Besides accusing her ex-husband, she maintained that the girl had also been abused by Foretich's parents and even by the Foretich's expert witness, the president of the American Psychiatric Association.[23] Morgan, however, was never able to convincingly prove these allegations. Foretich had always denied any sexual acts toward Hilary and asserted that Morgan was mentally ill.

22 D.C. Superior Court, *1984 Custody Order*, J.A. 276 as described in *Foretich v. U.S.*, 351 F.3d 1198, 1205 (2003).

23 P. Butler, "Taking Lessons from Elizabeth Morgan. On Congressional Attitudes toward D.C. and the Rule of Law," *Legal Times*, week of June 8, 1998.

But Morgan carried on. She constantly refused to allow Foretich to see Hilary. She also ignored several court orders issued by the D.C. Superior Court to let Foretich exercise his visitation rights. In light of these events and Morgan's insubordination, the D.C. Superior Court held Morgan in civil contempt, and she was sent to jail.[24]

1.1.2. Congress' twofold intervention: The Elizabeth Morgan Acts I and II

The U.S. Congress decided to take action in the Morgan case twice. When Morgan was in jail, Virginia Representative Frank Wolf introduced legislation to overrule the Superior Court's contempt decision and set Morgan free. Morgan would then be able to join her daughter whom, in the meantime, she had sent to New Zealand. The girl lived there with Morgan's parents and was hiding from her father.

The new Act, called the District of Columbia Civil Contempt Imprisonment Limitation Act of 1989,[25] amended the District of Columbia Code and provided it with new procedural rules to shorten the initial length of detention for civil contempt in child custody cases. The statute appeared to be of a general scope, since it did not specifically point to the release of Elizabeth Morgan. Nevertheless, given the timing and the circumstances in which the law was enacted, no one really doubted that it was meant to affect the outcome of the Morgan case. Consequently, Morgan was set free within a couple of days of its enactment.

After she was released from prison, she lived in New Zealand for several years, together with her parents and Hilary.[26] But she also repeatedly admitted that she wished to come back, especially because she was having serious health problems and wished to continue her treatment in the United States under U.S. medical care.[27] Moreover, her daughter desperately wanted to live in the United States again.

But one fundamental problem blocked their return. The D.C. Superior Court's order pertaining to Foretich's initial visitation rights was still in force. This meant that Morgan was still required to comply with the order and let Foretich see his daughter.

Morgan's wish to come back and the same time be exempted from any obligation to put her daughter in contact with Foretich was heard by Frank Wolf, the same Congressman who had introduced the first bill in this case, and two other Congressmen, namely Virginia Representative Thomas M. Davis and Maryland Representative Constance A. Morella. According to Wolf, it was "unconscionable [...] that an American girl is forced to live in exile, away from family and friends, while the courts have failed for nine years to find a solution to this situation."[28] He succeeded in pushing the bill through Congress by positioning it as a small part of a federal transportation spending bill called the 1997

24 For the complete history and background of the Morgan case, see *Foretich v. U.S.*, 351 F.3d 1198, 1204–1209 (2003).

25 Pub. L. 101–97.

26 In the meantime, Hilary had changed her name to Ellen Morgan.

27 J. Groner, "Custody Saga's Latest Twist. Bid to Aid Morgan Hits Home – Rule Snag," *Legal Times*, week of March 4, 1996.

28 D. Skidmore, "Bill Would Let Morgan, Daughter Come Home. Congress OKs Special Custody Measure," *The Washington Times*, September 19, 1996, p. A1.

Department of Transportation Appropriations Act.[29] The Act restricted the jurisdiction of the D.C. Superior Court over the custody case and blocked the existing visitation order that was in favor of Foretich, by amending Title 11 of the District of Columbia Code.[30] The Act determined the circumstances under which a parent had no visitation rights without the child's consent. So the D.C. Superior Court no longer had jurisdiction to make such a decision.[31] Elizabeth and Hilary could now freely come back to the United States without being afraid that Hilary would have to see her father ever again.

The terms of this Act resembled expressions used in the first Elizabeth Morgan Act from 1989 which freed Elizabeth from jail: The 1996 Act contains no names, but the elaborately formulated conditions for the applicability of the Act pointed to its sole usefulness in the Morgan case and its only purpose was keeping Foretich away from Hilary.[32] Moreover, the deliberations on the bill in a House subcommittee focused expressly on the situation of Elizabeth Morgan.

1.1.2.1. Objections, constitutional, and otherwise to the Elizabeth Morgan legislation

The first statute in the Elizabeth Morgan case from 1989 has never been challenged in the courts as violating any constitutional rights of Foretich. He, after all, obtained a valid D.C. Superior Court order that established his visitation rights and the Act did not affect this order. Precisely the converse is true for the second congressional intervention in the Morgan case. The 1996 Act de facto nullified that D.C. Superior Court order and determined that Foretich had no visitation rights. This made a difference and Foretich

29 Pub. L. 104–205, Sec. 11–925.

30 Sec. 11–925 of the Act provided:
"Sec.11–925. Rules regarding certain pending child custody cases.
"(a) In any pending case involving custody over a minor child or the visitation rights of a parent of a minor child in the Superior Court which is described in subsection (b) –
"(1) at anytime after the child attains 13 years of age, the party to the case who is described in subsection (b)(1) may not have custody over, or visitation rights with, the child without the child's consent; and
"(2) if any person had actual or legal custody over the child or offered safe refuge to the child while the case (or other actions relating to the case) was pending, the court may not deprive the person of custody or visitation rights over the child or otherwise impose sanctions on the person on the grounds that the person had such custody or offered such refuge.
"(b) A case described in this subsection is a case in which –
"(1) the child asserts that a party to the case has been sexually abusive with the child;
"(2) the child has resided outside of the United States for not less than 24 consecutive months;
"(3) any of the parties to the case has denied custody or visitation to another party in violation of an order of the court for not less than 24 consecutive months; and
"(4) any of the parties to the case has lived outside of the District of Columbia during such period of denial of custody or visitation."

31 Sec. 11–925 (a)(1).

32 Firstly, the sponsors of the Bill insisted that it was a relief for all women in situations similar to that of Elizabeth Morgan. Jonathan Turley, a professor at George Washington University and later Foretich's attorney, therefore collected the names of women across the country who would potentially qualify for the Bill's application and presented them to Congress. Once confronted with the real existence of cases resembling Morgan's, the Bill's sponsors unambiguously admitted that the Bill was actually intended to apply to the *Morgan* case only, unfortunately for the other cases. See J. Turley, "One American at a Time. Legislating by Bill of Attainder," *Legal Times*, week of February 26, 1996.

challenged the Act. The focus in this Section and in the following chapters will therefore be on the second Elizabeth Morgan Act.

Foretich stated that the Act violated the Bill of Attainder Clause enshrined in Article I, Section 9 of the U.S. Constitution, the doctrine of the separation of powers in Article III, and the Due Process Clause as formulated in the Fifth Amendment to the Constitution. Moreover, the Act was criticized because of the way in which its sponsors attempted to assure its passage. Instead of promulgating it as an autonomous bill, which would have made it more subject to criticism, they attached it to a transportation spending bill, which, as its name suggests, dealt with money rather than substantive legislative changes.

Violation of the Bill of Attainder Clause

Art. I, Sec. 9, Clause 3 of the U.S. Constitution provides that: "No bill of Attainder [...] shall be passed." In *Nixon v. Administrator of General Services*, the Supreme Court described a bill of attainder as "a law that legislatively determines guilt and inflicts punishment upon an identifiable individual without provision of the protections of a judicial trial."[33] Foretich argued that the Elizabeth Morgan Act II constituted a bill of attainder because it singled Foretich out to be punished. In Foretich's opinion, "[i]n a nation of millions of families, Congress imposed [...] deprivations on only one family."[34] Foretich proved that the two requirements of the Bill of Attainder Clause were met. Firstly, the law was specifically tailored to Foretich and the Morgan case, even though no names were mentioned in its text. Given the circumstances in which it was enacted and the fact that the sponsors eventually revealed their real motives, the absence of any names in the statute constituted no obstacle to treating it as specific. Secondly, the law inflicted punishment on Foretich.

Unlike the lower court,[35] the U.S. Court of Appeals agreed with Foretich. It ruled that, without doubt, the law was intended to apply only to the case of Morgan, Foretich and their daughter and that the law punished Foretich. Using a three-pronged punishment inquiry, consisting of a historical, functional, and motivational test,[36] as developed by the Supreme Court in *Selective Service System*,[37] the Court concluded that:[38]

> [b]y singling out Dr. Foretich as virtually the only parent subject to the Act, Congress has permanently associated him with criminal acts of child sexual abuse. The Act memorializes a judgment by the United States Congress that Dr. Foretich is guilty of horrific crimes. Congress reached this determination despite the repeated and unwavering rejection of such claims by every court that considered them. As a result the Act inflicts significant and costly injury to

33 *Nixon v. Administrator of General Services*, 433 U.S. 425, 468 (1977).
34 Brief for the Appellants, D.C. Court of Appeals, No. 02-5224, p. 13.
35 U.S. District Court for the District of Columbia, No. 97cv00929 (2002).
36 These three tests will be discussed in Chapter II.3.1.2.
37 *Selective Service System v. Minnesota Public Interest Research Group*, 468 U.S. 841, 852 (1984).
38 *Foretich v. U.S.*, 351 F.3d 1198, 1223 (2003).

> Dr. Foretich's reputation, while it also takes a significant step toward permanently severing Dr. Foretich's relationship with his own daughter.

The Court of Appeals' decision shows that, at least in this case, the constitutional prohibition of bills of attainder is not only a historical or academic concept, but is still an effective protection against an arbitrary congressional action.

Violation of the separation of powers

Another argument that Foretich used against the Elizabeth Morgan Act, however unsuccessful in the lower court and not discussed in the Court of Appeals was that it violated the principle of the separation of powers. Foretich argued that, by means of the statute, Congress had directed the D.C. Superior Court on how it should decide the particular case of Morgan, Foretich, and their daughter. In this respect, he found Sec. 11–925 (a)(2) of the law decisive. It provided that the Superior Court "may not deprive the person of custody or visitation rights over the child or otherwise impose sanctions on the person on the grounds that the person had such custody or offered such refuge."[39] This part of the law signified, in Foretich's view, that the Superior Court was no longer authorized to decide whether to impose sanctions on Elizabeth Morgan. The Act simply banned the Court from doing so. Moreover, where it is normally within the Superior Court's domain to decide on a custody question in light of a child's best interests, Congress determined by itself that Foretich's visits were not in Hilary's best interest.[40] Such legislative behavior of Congress is normally beyond its legislative competences and encroaches on the domain of judicial power as determined by the Supreme Court in the *Klein* judgment of 1871. At that time, the Supreme Court clearly stated that Congress is allowed to change the existing law underlying the litigation in a pending case but Congress may not direct the courts as to which decision they should reach in a particular case.[41] Foretich's separation of powers argument, as presented above, was also used in the Northwest Timber Compromise case, discussed below.

Violation of due process

Foretich based his due process argument on the *Brokaw v. Mercer County*[42] custody decision, showing that the "interference with or curtailment of a familial relationship can often raise both procedural and substantive due process violations."[43] In summary, Foretich argued that the Elizabeth Morgan Act violated his due process right by manipulating the merits of the pending case and substituting the Court's order, saying that the Foretichs were no danger to Hilary. The Court took this decision into full

39 Brief for the Appellants, D.C. Court of Appeals, No. 02–5224, p. 26.

40 *Ibid.*, pp. 25–26.

41 *United States v. Klein*, 80 U.S. (13 Wall) 128 (1871). See also *Pennsylvania v. Wheeling & Belmont Bridge Company*, 59 U.S. 421 (1855).

42 *Brokaw v. Mercer County*, 235 F.3d 1020 (2000).

43 Brief for the Appellants, D.C. Court of Appeals, No. 02–5224, p. 32.

consideration after receiving evidence, while Congress simply "substituted its evaluation of the charges of sexual abuse for those of the court."[44] In addition, Foretich contested that the Act had been prompted by legitimate governmental interest. There can be no such interest when Congress prevents a court's order from being enforced.[45]

Foretich argued that his right of procedural due process[46] had been violated, because he was deprived of his parental interest, his vested rights of visitation, and his fundamental interest in an independent judiciary, without any procedural safeguards being provided, for example a hearing and the possibility of submitting countervailing evidence.[47]

The Elizabeth Morgan Act as a rider to an appropriations bill

Initially, the 1996 Elizabeth Morgan Bill was not successful in Congress. Davis' attempt to bring it onto the House floor failed. In response, Wolf incorporated it into an omnibus federal transportation appropriations bill. That bill passed without a direct vote, which spared the additional provisions of the Elizabeth Morgan Bill from a direct vote as well.[48]

This cosmetic operation met with severe criticism, as clearly expressed by Representative F. James Sensenbrenner, for example: "It was absolutely inappropriate to attach this to an appropriations bill. [...] This bill has nothing to do with transportation. It is a poster for the line-item veto."[49]

In addition, the bill was placed on, but after strong opposition from a few representatives, quickly removed from the "suspension calendar," which is meant for non-controversial legislative proposals.[50]

1.1.3. Concluding remarks

The case of Elizabeth Morgan clearly demonstrates that Congress was prepared to take sweeping steps to help Morgan win her case, which she had previously lost in court. Although Morgan's allegation that Foretich and his parents had sexually abused Hilary had never been proved in the courts, Foretich was de facto held guilty by the legislative act. This constituted a violation of the Bill of Attainder Clause in the opinion of the Court of Appeals.

Moreover, Foretich did not have any chance to present evidence to the contrary and thus defend himself against Congress (the due process argument). The way the Morgan Bill was presented in Congress raised some criticism as well. The Act was incorporated into the enormous transportation spending bill, although it had nothing to do with money. This made it possible to pass the Morgan Bill without any serious problems.

44 *Ibid.*, p. 33.
45 *Ibid.*
46 The Due Process Clause comprises substantive and procedural due process.
47 Brief for the Appellants, D.C. Court of Appeals, No. 02–5224, pp. 35–38.
48 Ch.W. Hall, "Rep. Wolf Fends Off Criticism after Intervening in Custody Battle," *Washington Post*, September 20, 1996, p. A16.
49 *Ibid.*
50 Groner (1996).

1.2. The Terri Schiavo case

1.2.1. Background

The case of Elizabeth Morgan was not the only long drawn-out and highly publicized dispute for which Congress decided to adopt a legislative measure. An end-of-life case, which caused great commotion not only in the local community, but also throughout the United States, was the case of Theresa Marie (Terri) Schiavo.

Terri was a resident of St. Petersburg in Florida. At the age of 26, while at home, she had a heart attack, as a result of which her brain was deprived of oxygen for a period of time. In the hospital, the doctors who treated her established that she was in a "persistent vegetative state" (PSV).[51] She was not actually in a coma, because she was not asleep, but she was nevertheless unconscious. She could neither eat nor drink by herself. In order to stay alive, she had to be artificially fed.

After eight years of taking care of Terri, and after searching for any existing treatment that would help her regain her former condition, her husband Michael sought a court order allowing him to remove the gastric tube from Terri's body. This would lead to her death. This request was granted by the trial court.[52]

Terri's parents, Robert and Mary Schindler, could not agree with this decision, because they still hoped that some kind of miracle would let Terri recover.[53] As a result of their reiterated appeals, the Florida Court of Appeals issued four decisions following the judgment of the trial court.[54] After a rehearing of the Terri Schiavo case had been denied in the *Schiavo IV* decision, a remarkable action was taken by the then Florida Governor, Jeb Bush.

1.2.2. The Florida legislature's intervention in the Schiavo case: Terri's Law

In conformity with the final judgment in the *Schiavo* case, her feeding tube was removed on October 15, 2003. A few days later, on October 21, 2003, Florida Governor Jeb Bush, signed HB 35-E into law, which clearly intervened in the Schiavo dispute. It authorized the Governor of Florida to issue an executive order preventing the withholding of nutrition and hydration of patients like Terri Schiavo. The law stated that the power to make an executive order would expire 15 days after its enactment. After that time, the Governor would not be able to issue any such order.

Although the law did not specifically refer to the case of Terri Schiavo, all the circumstances in which the law had been passed, and its terms, establishing very narrow requirements which could be met in advance by Terri's parents, indicated its application

51 For more on "persistent vegetative state," see, for example, J.B. Oldershaw et al., "Persistent Vegetative State: Medical, Religious, Economic and Legal Perspectives," 1 *DePaul J. Health Care L.* 495 (1997).

52 *In re Guardianship of Schiavo*, 2000 WL 34546715 (Fla.Cir.Ct. Feb 11, 2000) (No. 90–2908GD-003).

53 The relationship between Michael Schiavo and Terri's parents had already become strained, and the financial claims with regard to Terri's estate drove a wedge between them at the beginning of 1993.

54 *Schiavo I*, 780 So.2d 176 (January 2001), *Schiavo II*, 792 So.2d 551 (July 2001), *Schiavo III*, 800 So.2d 640 (October 2001), and *Schiavo IV*, 851 So.2d 182 (June 2003).

to the Schiavo case only. Moreover, the Act referred literally to the situation of a patient as of October 15, 2003. This raised no doubt as to the intended effect of the law.

On the day the law was enacted, Governor Jeb Bush issued a one-time stay which directed "all medical facilities and personnel providing medical care for Theresa Schiavo, and all those acting in concert or participation with them [...] to immediately provide nutrition and hydration for Theresa Schiavo."[55] Against the final judicial ruling, the feeding tube was surgically reinserted. Schiavo's husband challenged the constitutionality of the Act.

1.2.2.1. Constitutional challenges to Terri's Law

In his petition, Michael Schiavo pointed out several aspects which, according to him, showed that the law violated both the Florida Constitution and the U.S. Constitution as interpreted by the U.S. Supreme Court.[56]

Violation of Terri's privacy right

Firstly, Schiavo argued that Terri's Law violated the constitutional protection of Terri's right to make her own choice pertaining to future medical treatment. Schiavo pointed to Article I, Section 23 of the Florida Constitution. Although the argument involving the right of privacy is of great importance to the alleged unconstitutionality of Terri's Law, the following arguments say more about it by advocating limitations on a legislature that attempts to make ad hoc laws in general.

Violation of the separation of powers

The second challenge to Florida's Terri's Law pertained to its violation of the separation of powers doctrine as guaranteed by the Florida Constitution and the usurpation of the judicial function by the legislature and the executive.[57] In his argument, Schiavo referred mostly to the decisions of the Florida courts, but they, in turn, were often based on the doctrine as applied by the U.S. Supreme Court in its many decisions containing a discussion of this issue. This Court interpreted the separation of powers as representing two different, although related, notions. The first notion is protecting the role of the independent judiciary and the second is preserving the rights of an individual to submit his claim, which are to be decided by an independent judiciary, not influenced by any other government branch.[58]

55 Executive Order 03-201. Petitioner's Brief No. 03-008212-CI-20, *Schiavo v. Bush* (Pinellas County, Fl. Cir. Ct. October 29, 2003), p. 6.

56 Petitioner's Brief No. 03-008212-CI-20, *Schiavo v. Bush* (Pinellas County, Fl. Cir. Ct. October 29, 2003). See also T.C. Marks, Jr., "Terri Schiavo and the Law," 67 *Alb. L. Rev.* 843 (2004).

57 Petitioner's Brief No. 03-008212-CI-20, *Schiavo v. Bush* (Pinellas County, Fl. Cir. Ct. October 29, 2003), pp. 10ff.

58 *Commodity Futures Trading Comm'n v. Schor*, 478 U.S. 833, 848 (1986).

Schiavo argued that Terri's Law could not be viewed as anything but empowering the Executive to exercise the judicial function. After all, the case of Terri Schiavo had already been decided in long-running judicial proceedings. The legislative measure taken by the Florida legislative body allowed the Governor to nullify both factual and legal findings of the Florida Court and replace the judicial determination with his own executive order. In this way, the final judicial decision in a specific case was impudently reversed and the executive took over the judicial function by creating and enforcing its own judgment in one specific case.[59]

Unequal treatment

The next objection to Terri's Law was that it paved the way for unequal treatment. Even if the law did not literally mention the name of Terri Schiavo in either its title or text, the circumstances under which it was hurriedly enacted and the reference to a situation as of October 15, 2003 clearly underline that she was the only addressee of the law. In other words, a totally new legal regime had been created for her, which deviated from the already existing general rules. This would mean that even if, as the Florida Governor insisted, the law was necessary to preserve Terri Schiavo's liberty and privacy rights, such protection would be denied to other individuals who were in a similar situation.

Violation of the Bill of Attainder Clause

According to Michael Schiavo, Terri's Law directly violated Article I, Section 10 of the Florida Constitution and Article I, Section 9, Clause 3 of the U.S. Constitution, which is directed at the states and encompasses a prohibition of bills of attainder, which was the same argument as in the Elisabeth Morgan case. As stated above, no one, including the Governor and the Florida legislature, denied that the bill was tailored to the Schiavo case, even though the classification was drafted in a general way. The element of punishment was seen in the deprivation of Terri's constitutional rights, in particular, the privacy right and due process.[60]

Unconstitutional vagueness

The last problematic issue in Terri's Law was that the law ordered the reinserting of the gastric tube, while there was already a valid final court order authorizing Terri's husband to withdraw the tube. The critics argued that the contradiction between that court decision and Terri's Law was too confusing. Indeed, Michael Schiavo would be acting legally by removing the feeding tube, but at the same time against Terri's Law, and he

59 Petitioner's Brief No. 03–008212-CI-20, *Schiavo v. Bush* (Pinellas County, Fl. Cir. Ct. October 29, 2003), p. 25.

60 This argument was founded in the judgment of the Supreme Court in *Cummings v. Missouri*, 71 U.S. 277, 320 (1866).

could be convicted for this conduct. This resulted in unconstitutional vagueness of Terri's Law, it was argued.[61]

1.2.2.2. The Florida Supreme Court's judgment

Michael Schiavo succeeded in having the Supreme Court of Florida declare the law unconstitutional due to violation of the separation of powers set out in Article II, Section 3 of the Florida Constitution.[62]

The Supreme Court recalled the origins of this doctrine as established by the Founding Fathers. In this respect, the Court pointed to the main idea behind this doctrine, which guaranteed an independent judiciary and prevented Congress from interfering with particular judgments of the courts.[63] This is to serve as protection of individuals' rights. Citing *Plaut*, the Court determined that final judicial decisions could only be reviewed by the judicial, not the legislative branch.[64] According to this line of reasoning, by enacting a statute in a case that had already been finally decided, the Florida legislature acted contrary to the separation of powers doctrine.

The second violation of this doctrine was granting the Governor unlimited power to issue an executive order under certain circumstances, which were described in a very general way. The Florida legislature failed to provide guidelines or standards that could limit the unrestricted power of the Governor in applying the law. Under such circumstances, the situation occurred wherein the Governor was no longer the executor of the law, but its creator.[65] The law was held unconstitutional and Theresa Schiavo's feeding tube was finally removed on March 18, 2005.

1.2.3. Congress' intervention in the Schiavo case: An Act for the relief of the parents of Theresa Marie Schiavo

The battle had not yet been won by Terri's husband, however. In light of the above-mentioned events, the U.S. Congress decided to take action. It intervened in the Schiavo case by passing Public Law 109–3.[66] The Act was entitled an Act for the relief of the parents of Theresa Marie Schiavo, and its central purpose was to confer jurisdiction on a federal court – the District Court for the Middle District of Florida – to review the

61 Petitioner's Brief No. 03–008212-CI-20, *Schiavo v. Bush* (Pinellas County, Fl. Cir. Ct. October 29, 2003), p. 41. Schiavo supported that argument by Florida case law. See, e.g., *Whitaker v. Department of Ins. And Treasurer*, 680 So.2d 528, 531–532 (Fla. 1996).

62 *Bush v. Schiavo*, 885 So.2d 321 (2004).

63 *Ibid.*, p. 330.

64 *Ibid.*, p. 331. See also *Plaut v. Spendthrift Farm, Inc.*, 514 U.S. 211, 227 (1995).

65 For the Court's analysis see *Bush v. Schiavo*, 885 So.2d 321, 332–336 (2004).

66 This was not the first intervention of Congress in the *Schiavo* case to prevent the withdrawal of nutrition and hydration from Terri, but the first one to raise so much controversy and constitutional questions. On the day that Terri's feeding tube was removed, the House Government Reform Committee issued a subpoena for Terri Schiavo and a few other people to testify at a congressional hearing a few days later. The Senate intervened also by inviting Michael Schiavo and his wife to testify, to ensure that the Terri was still kept alive, because only those who are alive may testify.

Schiavo case *de novo*. The law transferred the deliberation of that case from the jurisdiction of the state courts of Florida, where it belonged, to federal jurisdiction. The Act authorized the federal court to:[67]

> hear, determine, and render judgment on a suit or claim by or on behalf of Theresa Marie Schiavo for the alleged violation of any right of Theresa Marie Schiavo under the Constitution or laws of the United States relating to the withholding or withdrawal of food, fluids, or medical treatment necessary to sustain her life.

The Act also provided that the Federal Court had to consider the case *de novo*, which meant "*notwithstanding* any prior State court determination and regardless of whether such a claim has previously been raised, considered, or decided in State court proceedings."[68] The Act therefore indirectly nullified the final judicial determination of the Florida courts.

The Act explicitly declared that it did not create any new substantive rights for Terri Schiavo, nor did it constitute a precedent with regard to future cases and legislation, including private bills. The Act was therefore purely meant to apply to the Schiavo case and no other, even if the same circumstances as in the Schiavo case occurred in other cases as well.[69]

Another remarkable characteristic of the Act, besides its unusual content, was the manner in which it was enacted during a special Sunday session, after Congress was already in Easter recess. That is why it has been called the "Palm Sunday Compromise." Bill S.686 was introduced and passed in the Senate on March 20, 2005. On March 21, 2005, just after midnight, the House of Representatives agreed and President Bush signed it into law. In the Senate, the bill was passed by a unanimous-consent decision of only three senators present. In the House of Representatives, 174 Representatives were absent during the voting.

1.2.3.1. Constitutional objections to the Act

Shortly after the enactment of Pub. L. 109–3, it was criticized on several constitutional points.[70] The criticism related to the separation of powers doctrine, the effect of singling out one person, federalism, and the power of Congress to confer jurisdiction on federal courts.

[67] Pub. L. 109–3, Sec. 1.

[68] Pub. L. 109–3, Sec. 2, emphasis added.

[69] In the Bill itself, however, Congress announced that it would consider a general policy with regard to persons who are incapable of making their own decisions on "the provision, withholding, or withdrawal of foods, fluid, or medical care" Pub. L. 109–3, Sec. 9.

[70] For a short overview, see D.L. Hudson Jr., "Schiavo Law Prompts Constitutional Questions," 4 No. 12 *A.B.A. J. E-Report* 1 (2005).

Violation of the separation of powers

Prescribing a rule of decision

Almost immediately after the Act had been promulgated, the Schindlers filed a petition at the United States District Court for the Middle District of Florida, arguing that the Act gave this Court the jurisdiction to consider their claim.[71] Eventually the relief was denied. In the Court of Appeals decision,[72] Justice Birch delivered an interesting concurring opinion. He argued against any further application of Pub. L. 109–3, because, according to him, it was unconstitutional since it violated the separation of powers doctrine by directing a rule of decision to the court. Birch argued as follows:[73]

> If the Act only provided for jurisdiction consistent with Article III and 28 U.S.C. §1331 the Act would not be in violation of the principles of separation of powers. The Act, however, goes further. Section 2 of the Act provides that the district court: (1) shall engage in "de novo" review of Mrs. Schiavo's constitutional and federal claims; (2) shall not consider whether these claims were previously "raised, considered, or decided in State court proceedings"; (3) shall not engage in "abstention in favor of State court proceedings"; and (4) shall not decide the case on the basis of "whether remedies available in the State courts have been exhausted." [...] Because these provisions constitute legislative dictation of how a federal court should exercise its judicial functions (known as a "rule of decision"), the Act invades the province of the judiciary and violates the separation of powers principle.

Not everyone agrees with this analysis. According to some legal scholars, the Act was solely intended to give the federal courts the chance to review the case, no more than that.[74] Moreover, Congress only established a standard of review, which is the usual pursuance of Congress' authority. However, Justice Birch's main complaint was not that the legislature imposed a review standard on the judiciary in general, but that it did so in a single case.

Reopening of final judgments

Another claim directed against the congressional Act in the Schiavo case, which would constitute a violation of the separation of powers, is that it directed the reopening of the final judgment of the State court. The Act, after all, conferred jurisdiction upon the federal court to hear the case of Terri Schiavo *de novo*, notwithstanding any other prior adjudication in this case. An important decision in this respect is the Supreme Court's

[71] For a detailed description of the procedures in the Schiavo case, see M. Rosenblatt-Hoffman, "The Schiavo Odyssey: A Tale of Two Legislative Reprieves," 7 *Marq. Elder's Advisor* 357 (2006).

[72] *Schiavo ex rel. Schindler v. Schiavo*, 404 F.3d 1270 (2005).

[73] *Ibid.*, pp. 1273–1274.

[74] Allen (2005), p. 321 (2005).

decision in *Plaut*.[75] In *Plaut*, the Supreme Court ruled that once the highest federal court had rendered a final judgment in a specific case, it remained final. A statute that directly ordered the court to hear the claims again that had already been dismissed by the court was declared contrary to this principle, and was therefore held unconstitutional.[76]

Singling out one person

The highly individual character of the Act was its other major problematic feature. As the Act was only effective in the Schiavo case, Justice Birch declared that "it lacked the generality and prospective effect of legislation that comports with the basic tenets of the separation of powers doctrine."[77] Legal scholars had also expressed their concerns about creating new rules only for Terri Schiavo. As Professor Tribe concluded: "Congress would have the power to pass a general law after studying [...] the situation around the country to see of the thousands of tragic cases like this in which families are torn asunder about what should happen." Tribe pointed out the problems in creating a divergent legal regime for just that one case.[78]

Nonetheless, there is no absolute constitutional prohibition of individualized laws. Only punishing bills of attainder are forbidden. The argument used in favor of the Act was that it did not impose any punishment on Terri Schiavo, but, on the contrary, served as protection of her rights.[79] Therefore, as the supporters of the statute contended, the Bill of Attainder Clause from the U.S. Constitution did not apply to this case.

Federalism

The Schiavo case finally brought up questions dealing with the division of powers between the states and the federal government, and the violation of the Tenth Amendment to the Constitution. During the Congressional debate, Representative Honda clearly expressed in this context: "The Schiavo case involves a family dispute over who has final decision-making regarding Terri Schiavo's medical care, and as such falls exclusively under jurisdiction of the State courts. Federal courts do not have any jurisdiction in this case; the U.S. Congress does not have any jurisdiction in this case; only the courts of the State of Florida have jurisdiction here."[80] In the legal comments, the argument of federalism has been rejected by playing with the text of the Constitution. As the pro-Act commentators argue, there is no written limitation in the U.S. Constitution which would

75 *Plaut v. Spendthrift Farm, Inc.*, 514 U.S. 211 (1995). *Plaut* was also invoked by Michael Schiavo when he challenged the constitutionality of the Florida Terri's Law.

76 For arguments that the *Plaut* tenet did not apply to the Schiavo case, because the latter was a state case, see A.M. Samaha, "Undue Process: Congressional Referral and Judicial Resistance in the Schiavo Controversy," 22 *Const. Comment.* 505, 514 (2005).

77 *Schiavo ex rel. Schindler v. Schiavo*, 404 F.3d 1270, 1273–1274 (2005) (Birch, J., concurring).

78 See Tribe's comment at <www.pbs.org/newshour/bb/congress/jan-june05/schiavo_3-21.html> (last accessed on June 12, 2011).

79 Calabresi (2006), p. 164.

80 Mr. Honda in the House of Representatives, 151 CONG. REC. H1731 (March 20, 2005).

prevent Congress from conferring jurisdiction on the lower federal courts. Such a task would be a political one and Congress would have the exclusive right to do so.[81]

1.2.4. Concluding remarks

In this remarkable case of the PSV patient Terri Schiavo, both the Florida State legislature and Congress intervened in the regular court proceedings by enacting two pieces of ad hoc legislation. Both the Florida Terri's Law and the congressional Act were meant to overrule the final adjudication by a Florida State court which authorized Terri's guardian to stop nutrition and hydration. They endeavored to ensure that, despite the final judgment, Terri would still be kept alive.

As described above, there are several serious constitutional objections to both statutes. Some of them, such as singling out Terri as the only addressee of the statutes and overruling the final judicial determination, which can lead to a violation of the separation of powers doctrine, are common to both statutes.

The question of prescribing a rule of decision to the federal court in the Schiavo case and violating state sovereignty by conferring jurisdiction on federal courts to review a case *de novo* that belongs in the state courts was an issue only in the congressional Act. In retrospect, neither of these laws achieved their intended effect. The federal courts refused to yield to political pressure and did not issue an emergency injunction to reinsert Terri's feeding tube, and Terri died.

1.3. The Northwest Timber Compromise

1.3.1. Background

The third case in which Congress enacted a law on an ad hoc basis to intervene in pending litigation and allegedly assure its outcome was the environmental case of the northern spotted owl. This bird is listed as an endangered species[82] and its habitat is the old-growth forests of Washington and Oregon, managed by the United States Forest Service (Forest Service) and the Bureau of Land Management (BLM).[83]

In this case, environmental groups challenged the forests' management by two federal agencies. The first litigation concerned the BLM management policy.[84] In 1988, in the second litigation, which generated ad hoc legislation, the Seattle Audubon Society together with other environmental groups challenged the Forest Service's administrative decision. That decision contained an amendment to the guidelines used by the Forest

81 Allen (2005), p. 324. See the same publication for a detailed description and analysis of the federalism argument.

82 The spotted owl has been listed in the Endangered Species Act since June 1990. Endangered Species Act of 1973, 16 U.S.C. Sec. 1531 *et seq.* (2000).

83 The United States Forest Service manages 13 forests in Washington and Oregon, and the Bureau of Land Management manages forests in western Oregon.

84 *Portland Audubon Soc. v. Lujan*, 884 F.2d 1233 (1989), cert. denied, *Portland Audubon Soc. v. Lujan*, 494 U.S. 1026 (1990).

Service in dealing with the prohibition of timber harvesting in certain areas. The environmental groups contended that the plan provided inadequate protection for the northern spotted owl, even though the plan did not aim to authorize timber harvesting in the owl's habitat areas. One month later, a separate lawsuit was filed by the Washington Contract Loggers Association, which was joined by other industry organizations. They also opposed the plan, but from an opposite angle. They argued that restrictions on the amount of harvesting allowed in the plan would have disastrous consequences for the local economy.

The Seattle Audubon Society invoked a violation of several environmental statutes and in the District Court for the Western District of Washington, 163 of the planned timber sales were preliminarily enjoined.[85]

1.3.2. Congress' intervention: The Northwest Timber Compromise

In light of this ongoing litigation and the preliminary injunctions blocking the proposed timber sales of the old-growth forests, Congress decided to intervene. The Congressmen from Oregon and Washington were the first to introduce legislation after the timber industries asked them for help in reversing the Court's blockade of timber sales. Congress then passed Section 318 of the Department of the Interior and Related Agencies Appropriations Act of 1990,[86] known as the Northwest Timber Compromise.[87] The provisions of Section 318 had limited effects, both temporary and geographical, since it expired at the end of the 1990 fiscal year and governed timber sales in 13 listed national forests in Oregon and Washington. On the one hand, the Compromise directed the Forest Service to offer 7.7 billion board feet of timber from these forests for sale, of which 5.8 billion board feet of net merchantable timber were to be derived from the 13 national forests in Washington and Oregon, known to contain the northern spotted owl.[88] Moreover, the new provisions directed the release of 1.1 billion out of 1.8 billion in board feet of timber sales that the courts had blocked by issuing preliminary injunctions.[89] On the other hand, the Compromise increased the standards for the habitat areas of the northern spotted owl.[90] The Portland Audubon Society and the Seattle Audubon Society directly challenged Section 318 as being unconstitutional.

85 *Seattle Audubon Soc. v. Robertson*, No. 89–160 (WD Wash., March 24, 1989). In May 1989 all timber sales comprising more than 40 acres were preliminarily enjoined. See *Seattle Audubon Soc. v. Robertson*, 931 F.2d 590, 592 (1991), in which the facts of this case are presented. The description of the procedural history in the Portland Audubon Society case and the Seattle Audubon Society case can also be found in *Seattle Audubon Soc. v. Robertson*, 914 F.2d 1311 (1990).

86 Pub. L. 101–121, 103 Stat. 745.

87 The Act was called a Compromise, because it was presented as legislation that attempted to strike a balance between the protection of the endangered species, resolving the timber supply crisis in the Northwest, and preserving important stands of old-growth ecosystems. 135 CONG. REC. S12961 (1989).

88 Pub. L. 101–121, Sec. 318(a)(1).

89 135 CONG. REC. S2961 (October 07, 1989).

90 Sec. 318(b)(3) and (b)(5).

1.3.2.1. Objections, constitutional, and otherwise to the Northwest Timber Compromise

Both environmental groups maintained that the statute, in particular Section 318 (b)(6)(A), violated the separation of powers doctrine. This section provided in part that:[91]

> Congress hereby determines and directs that management of areas according to subsections (b)(3) and (b)(5) of this section on the thirteen national forests in Oregon and Washington and Bureau of Land Management lands in western Oregon known to contain northern spotted owl is adequate consideration for the purpose of meeting the statutory requirements that are the basis for the consolidated cases captioned Seattle Audubon Society et al., v. F. Dale Robertson, Civil No. 89–99 (order granting preliminary injunction) and the case of Portland Audubon Society et al., v. Manuel Lujan, Jr., Civil No. 87–1160-FR.

The groups supported their theory by putting forth three arguments. First, they argued that the contested provision directed the court to reach a certain result in court proceedings by prescribing "a rule of decision." Secondly, they argued that Sec. 318 (b)(6)(A) did not modify the old law, which would be allowed. The last argument concerned the narrow way the section was tailored, which could only point in one direction: the Northern Timber Compromise was undoubtedly meant to intervene in the court proceedings in the two cases of Seattle Audubon and Portland Audubon.[92]

District Courts rejected the claims of both groups and found no constitutional violation of the separation of powers by Sec. 318 (b)(6)(A).[93] In contrast to these decisions, the Court of Appeals for the Ninth Circuit, where the cases were consolidated, declared Sec. 318 (b)(6)(A) to be in violation of the separation of powers by "directing the outcome in pending litigation involving the protection of the northern spotted owl, without any change in the underlying law."[94] The challenges to subsections (b)(6)(A) and the Court of Appeals' and the Supreme Court's responses to them will be discussed below.

Violation of the separation of powers

Prescribing a rule of decision or changing the underlying law?

The main challenge to the Northwest Timber Compromise was that it directed the court to make some factual findings, thereby directing the court to reach a certain result. Such legislative action of Congress had been condemned by the Supreme Court, and the

[91] Moreover, Sec. 318 (b)(6)(A) provided that the new guidelines set out in subsections (b)(3) and (b)(5) "shall not be subject to judicial review by any court of the United States."

[92] See also A.D. Ronner, "Judicial Self-demise: The Test of When Congress Impermissibly Intrudes on Judicial Power After Robertson v. Seattle Audubon Society and the Federal Appellate Courts' Rejection of the Separation of Powers Challenges to the New Section of the Securities Exchange Act of 1934," 35 *Ariz. L. Rev.* 1037 (1993), discussing challenges to the Northwest Timber Compromise.

[93] *Seattle Audubon Soc. v. Robertson*, No. 89–160 (WD Wash., November 14, 1989) and *Portland Audubon Soc. v. Lujan*, No. 87–1160, 1989 WL 155694 (Ore., December 21, 1989).

[94] *Seattle Audubon Soc. v. Robertson*, 914 F.2d 1311 (1990).

origins of the doctrine preventing Congress from controlling litigation through legislation date from 1871, when the Supreme Court issued the *Klein* judgment.[95] The *Klein* decision also supported the arguments in the *Morgan* and *Schiavo* cases referred to above.

To support this argument, the organizations emphasized the imperative language of the statute: "Congress hereby determines and directs ..."[96] and the fact that the statute explicitly referred to the pending cases of the Seattle Audubon and Portland Audubon Societies.

The Court of Appeals concentrated its analysis on the distinction between prescribing a rule of decision and changing the law while relevant cases are pending, as follows from *Klein* and *Pennsylvania v. Wheeling and Belmont Bridge Co.*[97] The Court concluded that the controversial provisions of the Northwest Timber Compromise did not change the previous law and were therefore enacted to assure that the court would give a certain desirable decision. This resulted in a violation of the separation of powers doctrine.

This interpretation was quashed by the Supreme Court. This Court gave the following explanation of how Sec. 318 (b)(6)(A) worked:[98]

> The plaintiffs in both cases alleged violations of MBTA §2, 16 U.S.C. §703, which makes it unlawful to "kill" or "take" any "migratory bird." Before the Compromise was enacted, the courts adjudicating these MBTA claims were obliged to determine whether the challenged harvesting would "kill" or "take" any northern spotted owl, within the meaning of §2. Subsection (b)(6)(A), however, raised the question whether the harvesting would violate different prohibitions-those described in subsections (b)(3) and (b)(5). If not, then the harvesting would constitute "management... according to" subsections (b)(3) and (b)(5), and would therefore be deemed to "mee[t]" MBTA §2 regardless of whether or not it would cause an otherwise prohibited killing or taking.

In other words, if the agencies followed the new requirements of subsections (b)(3) and (b)(5), and logged in the areas described in these sections, they would be deemed to violate neither the Migratory Bird Treaty Act (MBTA) nor the other statutes underlying the litigation.[99]

The Supreme Court, therefore, classified the disputed provisions as modifying the old law, thus changing the standards, which is permissible. In this respect, according to the Court, Congress chose the "operation of the canon that specific provisions qualify general ones," but Congress could also modify the MBTA directly, without enacting an entirely new statute. The argument of the environmental groups pinpointing the imperative tone of Sec. 318 (b)(6)(A) did not achieve its attended effect, either. The Supreme Court considered the provision as being directed to both the courts and the

95 *United Stated v. Klein*, 80 U.S. (13 Wall.) 128 (1871).
96 Brief of Respondents Seattle Audubon Society et al., 1991 WL 521289, p. 34.
97 *Pennsylvania v. The Wheeling and Belmont Bridge Company Co.*, 59 U.S. 421 (1855).
98 *Robertson v. Seattle Audubon Soc.*, 503 U.S. 429, 437–438 (1992).
99 In fact, this would mean that if the agencies operated in the designated areas, they would not "kill" or "take" the northern spotted owl within the meaning of the MBTA, even if they really did.

agencies, and not only to the courts. The argument that Congress intended to direct a rule of decision in a particular case, because the statute explicitly referred to the two pending cases, was also rejected because, as the Supreme Court concluded, reference to the cases was purely meant to identify the five statutes. It was no more than that.

Repeal by an appropriations bill

When discussing the central question whether Sec. 318 (b)(6)(A) of the Northern Timber Compromise prescribed a rule of decision or modified the already existing environmental statutes, the Court of Appeals addressed the issue of repealing or changing the substantive law through an appropriations statute. Such statutes are meant to grant funds to federal agencies to enable them to implement their policies. They are not meant to be a tool for changing substantive laws.

In the Court of Appeals' view, therefore, even if the Northwest Timber Compromise could be considered as changing the previous law (instead of directing the outcome in pending litigation), it would nevertheless be invalid because it was embedded in an appropriations bill.[100]

The Supreme Court responded to this analysis by concluding that the Court of Appeals' interpretation was wrong, because changes to a previous law in an appropriations measure are permissible, provided they are expressly stated in such appropriations bill. It had to be clear that the provisions of an appropriations statute were intended to modify other substantive law.[101]

Sec. 318 (b)(6)(A)'s effect on the cases of the Seattle Audubon Soc. and the Portland Audubon Soc.

The last but not least argument put forth by the Public Citizen on the part of the environmental groups was that even if Section 318 (b)(6)(A) did indeed change the underlying environmental statutes instead of prescribing a rule of decision to the courts, it would still be unconstitutional. Such unconstitutionality would be due to the very narrow scope of the new provisions, so there was (virtually) only one specific situation, namely the pending cases of the Seattle and Portland Audubon Societies, to which the new provisions could be applied. In other words, even if everyone agreed that Congress had changed or repealed the general law in force, such legislative action would still be impermissible as a violation of the separation of powers doctrine, because there were only two specific cases that were affected by the change. "Such a case-specific repeal presents all of the dangers of an explicit legislative direction of the same outcome."[102] It could also be argued that congressional intervention was prompted by the particular interests of a specific litigating party rather than the general governmental interest or purpose that could be achieved by the change or repeal of the existing general rules.

[100] The Court founded its opinion on the Supreme Court's holding in *TVA v. Hill*, 437 U.S. 153 (1978).

[101] *Robertson v. Seattle Audubon Soc.*, 503 U.S. 429, 440 (1992).

[102] On Writ of Certiorari to the U.S. Court of Appeals, Motion of Public Citizen, No. 90-1596, p. 2.

Most unfortunately, the Supreme Court declined to discuss the specificity theory of the Public Citizen, owing to procedural rules.[103]

1.3.3. *Concluding remarks*

In the case of the Northwest Timber Compromise, the controversy centered on the question whether the contested legislation directed the outcome in pending litigation or only modified the general statutes underlying the proceedings. The first action was impermissible, while the second one was an authorized pursuit of legislative powers. Although clear at first sight, this distinction causes more trouble when it is applied. Neither the Court of Appeals nor the Supreme Court was able to provide a clear standard, so the grounds on which they made the decisions remain opaque. The Act was also criticized because it was passed as part of appropriations legislation. The Supreme Court, however, decided that appropriations laws can also modify other substantive law provisions.

1.4. Conclusions

Reasons for enacting ad hoc legislation

The Elizabeth Morgan, Terri Schiavo, and the Northwest Timber Compromise cases are striking examples of the fact that Congress is not reluctant to enact quick-fix impulse legislation for specific cases. It can be argued that Congress acts by means of special legislation in any event in two situations. Firstly, Congress yields to public opinion after courts have upheld the rights of the unpopular party. This is evidenced by the Elizabeth Morgan and Terri Schiavo cases.[104] Secondly, Congress creates ad hoc legislation when it is influenced by special interest groups. In such a situation, Congress may intervene in judicial proceedings to ensure that the court decides in a way which is more favorable for the special interest group involved, or that the government's party wins. This situation occurred in the Northwest Timber Compromise case. In that case, by enacting the Northwest Timber Compromise, Congress ensured that the BLM could proceed with sales, even though the court prohibited certain timber sales as violating federal rules. This was tremendously important for the timber industry in Oregon and Washington. By letting the government (i.e. the BLM) win the case, Congress indirectly favored the timber industry. In all three cases, special impulse statutes attracted similar criticism, which can be divided into two groups: constitutional objections and remarks on the way the statute was drafted and adopted by Congress.

Specificity/Bills of Attainder

As far as the constitutional objections are concerned, all the statutes were criticized because of their specific character. Not every statute used the names of the addressees,

[103] *Robertson v. Seattle Audubon Society*, 503 U.S. 429, 441 (1992).
[104] Brief for the Appellants, D.C. Court of Appeals, No. 02–5224, p. 25.

though. As the case of Elizabeth Morgan shows, the courts were pragmatic in their judgments and paid attention especially to the circumstances in which the Act was adopted and the language of the Act, which is usually so narrowly tailored that only one case or person can qualify. The Supreme Court judgment in *Robertson* differs in this respect. Even though the statute identified specific pending cases by a caption number, the Court did not accept the conclusion that it was enacted solely for the two pending cases.

Separation of powers principle

All three cases were criticized as violating the separation of powers principle. The principle, as argued, was violated because the legislature attempted to dictate to the court how it should decide in a particular case or tried to direct the reopening of closed cases.

The opponents of the Elizabeth Morgan Act argued that the Act directed the Superior Court to find that Foretich's visits to his daughter would not be in the best interest of the girl and rule that Morgan could not be held in contempt for disobeying the court's orders.[105] The arguments against the federal Terri Schiavo Act concerned prescribing a rule of decision to the courts and directing them to reopen the already decided case of Terri Schiavo as well. In giving the court instructions as to how it should decide (*de novo* consideration) and giving the federal court jurisdiction in a case that had already been considered in detail at state level and had been closed by the final judgment of the Florida Supreme Court, Congress encroached on the judicial power of courts and thus violated the separation of powers doctrine.[106]

The main, though unsuccessful, argument against the Northwest Timber Compromise case was also that Congress dictated to the court how it should decide specific pending cases by using the compelling words: "Congress hereby directs..." and pointing very specifically to those cases even by giving them a caption number.

Due process

Another critical remark made in the case of the Elizabeth Morgan Act concerned the arbitrary action of Congress. As Foretich argued, Congress acted arbitrarily and therefore violated his due process right because it had no compelling governmental interest in passing the Elizabeth Morgan Act. Moreover, it deprived Foretich of his rights and interests without offering him procedural guarantees, such as a hearing, which are normally part of judicial procedure.

Equality

The equality argument against congressional intervention in a specific case is the last constitutional argument against ad hoc legislation. The fact that the legislature creates

105 Pub. L. 101–97 (a)(2).

106 It should be noted in this context that others view Terri's Law as a symbolic piece of legislation that was only meant to express a political pro-life statement by Congress and give the case another chance to be decided by a federal court instead of telling the court to decide that Terri should stay alive.

different rules for one case indicates that the other cases are still subject to the old general legal regime. This creates inequality. In the case of Florida's Terri's Law, the counterargument was used that, even if it were true that the law was enacted to preserve Terri's liberties and rights, other individuals in a similar situation would be deprived of such protection.

Legislative riders

The manner in which ad hoc legislation is initiated and eventually passed in the legislative process is also considered problematic. The Elisabeth Morgan Act as well as the Northwest Timber Compromise were enacted as riders to appropriations bills. Such riders are used when legislative proposals are controversial and have little chance of being passed by Congress as autonomous bills. Moreover, especially in the field of environmental law, it is dangerous when Congress changes the substantive environmental policy and makes exceptions to general environmental statutes by attaching riders to appropriations bills. In that case, no experts from the field of environmental law can comment on the rider, since appropriations bills deal with financial matters.

Chapter 2

THE REQUIREMENT OF GENERALITY

Introduction

This chapter devotes attention to the principle of the generality of laws, including the following questions. Do state constitutions and the federal Constitution absolutely require laws to be general in respect of their addressees as well as the interest (public or general v. special) they serve? If so, how strong is the protection against ad hoc legislation guaranteed by such constitutional provisions? To answer these questions, I will first present statements by the U.S. Supreme Court and the state courts. I will then show that state constitutions do indeed prohibit laws that are specific. This is quite interesting given the discrepancy between state and federal law. Next, I will show on the basis of private bills and project laws that the U.S. Constitution does not absolutely require all laws to be general. Nor is there a strict prohibition against serving special interests instead of the public interest. This creates opportunities for pork barrel legislation and special interest legislation.

2.1. Hurtado v. People of State of California

Perhaps the first and also strictest adjudication of the U.S. Supreme Court concerning the requirement of generality was handed down in the nineteenth century. The Court was very outspoken in its position on the role of the legislature and its power to enact legislation in the judgment of *Hurtado v. People of the State of California.*[107] In this case, the violation of due process under the Fourteenth Amendment to the U.S. Constitution was at issue. This Amendment provides that citizens of the United States may not be deprived of their life, liberty or property without due process of law. Explaining the meaning of due process, the Supreme Court referred to its previous decision in which it established that due process does not mean that all American citizens must be subjected to the same rules in every state. Each state legislature may impose certain restrictions on the remedies available to citizens and may create its own "modes of judicial proceedings" independently of the practice in other states.[108] According to the Court, however, such legislative power is not unlimited. There are certain constitutional constraints to be

107 *Hurtado v. People of State of California*, 110 U.S. 516 (1884).
108 *Ibid.*, p. 535, quoting *Missouri v. Lewis*, 101 U.S. 22, 22–31 (1879).

imposed on the legislature, which prevent it from acting arbitrarily. The Court formulated this opinion as follows:[109]

> It is not every act, legislative in form, that is law. Law is something more than mere will exerted as an act of power. It must be *not a special rule for a particular person or a particular case, but … 'the general law,* a law which hears before it condemns, which proceeds upon inquiry, and renders judgment only after trial,' so 'that every citizen shall hold his life, liberty, property, and immunities under the protection of the general rules which govern society,' and thus excluding, as not due process of law, acts of attainder, bills of pains and penalties, acts of confiscation, acts reversing judgments, and acts directly transferring one man's estate to another, legislative judgments and decrees, and other similar special, partial, and arbitrary exertions of power under the forms of legislation. Arbitrary power, enforcing its edicts to the injury of the persons and property of its subjects, is not law, whether manifested as the decree of a personal monarch or of an impersonal multitude. And the limitations imposed by our constitutional law upon the action of the governments, both state and national, are essential to the preservation of public and private rights, notwithstanding the representative character of our political institutions.

By issuing this statement, the U.S. Supreme Court condemned every form of law that creates a special regime or special treatment for a particular case or person. Laws should thus be general in order to be classified as laws and not as arbitrary and despotic acts. In this respect, generality serves as protection of both private and public rights and preserves the liberty of individuals.[110]

The notion of the role of the legislature as one of the three governmental powers setting rules affecting a broad range of people has also been endorsed at state level by the state courts. As the Supreme Court of Florida strongly emphasized, the role of the legislature is nothing but a ruling on future cases, where rules are of a "general and uniform application."[111] Owing to this interpretation of the constraints on the legislature, most states adopted provisions in their constitutions prohibiting the legislature from enacting laws lacking a general scope, which are called special or local laws. At state level,

109 *Hurtado v. People of State of California*, 110 U.S. 516, 535–336 (1884), emphasis added.

110 For another example where the function of the legislature is considered to be to prescribe general rules, see *Fletcher v. Peck*: "It is the peculiar province of the legislature to prescribe general rules for the government of society: the application of those rules would seem to be the duty of other departments," 6 Cranch 87, 136 (1810). In a more recent case, Justice Powell, in his concurring opinion, expressed the view that "[t]he only effective constraint on Congress' power is political, but Congress is most accountable politically when it prescribes rules of general applicability. When it decides rights of specific persons, those rights are subject to 'the tyranny of a shifting majority," *INS v. Chadha*, 462 U.S. 919, 966 (1983). Powell used this argument to support his opinion that the legislative veto, which overturned the administrative recommendation of the Attorney General to suspend deportation of Chadha, was unconstitutional, because it violated the separation of powers doctrine. Chadha was a student from Kenya who was going to be deported after he stayed in the U.S. even though his student visa had already expired.

111 *Ponder v. Graham*, 4 Fla. 23, 1851 WL 1091, 1097 (1851). For a description of legislatures at the state level and their regular usurpation of the judicial function, see W.H. Cowles, "The Distinction Between the Legislative and the Judicial Power," 40 *Am. L. Reg.* 433 (1892).

generality is also seen as a requirement for the legislature to enact laws which serve only a public purpose.

2.2. State level: Special and local laws and public purpose

2.2.1. Special and local laws

Until 1983, a federal uniform law directly barred the American states from passing special or local laws. It is stated in the United States Code that "[t]he legislatures of the Territories of the United States now or hereafter to be organized shall not pass local or special laws [...] granting to any [...] individual any special or exclusive privilege, immunity or franchise whatever." The distinction between special and local laws is that local laws are intended to favor only one part of the state. The idea behind the prohibition of special laws is that of discouraging legislatures from providing benefits to specific individuals, groups of individuals or companies, and protecting the people against "unwise and hasty legislation."[112]

The federal law prohibiting special legislation at state level was repealed,[113] but most of the states had adopted a specific provision in their state constitutions prohibiting special or local laws.[114] The Constitution of Florida, for example, provides that special laws are only permitted if such an intention is first declared by a general law. Nevertheless, there are still some areas where special or local laws are absolutely prohibited.[115]

A frequent provision with regard to special laws is that such laws are prohibited if a general law can be adopted. The existence of a general law that already deals with a specific subject can constitute a serious obstacle for the legislature.[116] This constitutional provision is often invoked when the legislature seeks to ensure a certain (politically preferred) outcome that cannot be achieved if the already existing general rules are applied. Hence, a bill passed by the General Assembly of the State of Colorado that dealt with the "dissolution of towns and annexation thereof by other municipalities" was held invalid because there was already a general law regulating that subject. The law passed by the Colorado legislature pertained to annexation of the town of Glendale, which previously, in conformity with the existing procedures, had twice refused to be annexed. The Colorado Supreme Court did not mince words when it stated that the legislature had

112 S. Rep. No. 49–1327, 1 (1886).

113 Pub. L. 98–213, Sec. 16 (w) to (ee).

114 Except the Constitutions of Connecticut, Massachusetts, New Hampshire and Vermont.

115 State Constitution of Florida, Art. III, Sec. 10 & 11. Among those areas for which it is prohibited to enact special laws are: divorce; rules of evidence in any court; crime or punishment; conditions precedent to bringing any civil or criminal proceedings or limitations of time thereof; disposal of public property, including any interest therein for private purposes; private incorporation and grant of privilege to a private corporation. The Constitution of Alabama contains an impressive list of 31 subjects which the state legislature is prohibited to rule on, including exempting any individual, private corporation, or association from the operation of any general law; fixing the punishment of crime; giving effect to an invalid will, deed or other instrument; and regulating the time within which a civil or criminal action may be begun (Constitution of Alabama, Sec. 104).

116 Nonetheless, the legislature is logically allowed to alter the already existing general provisions in light of new circumstances and developments in other general rules.

attempted to annex Glendale by a special law, because two previous endeavors to do so in accordance with the existing general law had failed. The special law therefore constituted an impermissible exercise of legislative power.[117]

The problem of using special legislation as an instrument to address the particular cases and questions of individuals or companies arose especially in the nineteenth century. At that time, most legislation consisted of special laws, instead of laws that operated uniformly in all territories and applied to all classes of people. For example, as Ireland notes, in 1873, the legislature of New Jersey produced only 100 pages of general public legislation as opposed to 1,250 pages of special legislation.[118] The most obvious reason for the introduction of the ban on special legislation was the constant pressure on the legislators from their constituents to address their particular concerns.

As a result, the considerable number of special legislative bills eliminated any form of deliberative lawmaking. It was simply not possible to pay enough attention to every single bill, because so many were introduced each year. Special legislation was criticized as well for resulting in unequal treatment: unequal protection by the law and unequal rights.[119] It often interfered with judicial proceedings by nullifying judicial adjudications in particular cases or retrospectively validating invalid administrative procedures or previously invalid legislation.[120] The ban on special legislation as guaranteed in the state constitution was meant to prevent this and promote legislation that was founded on general principles rather than on particular concerns of the voters.[121]

2.2.2. *Public purpose*

The state constitutional provisions on special and local laws prohibit such legislation in many different areas. These would be mostly economic areas, in which parties are granted special financial privileges, but could also go beyond that. Examples are granting privileged administrative procedures or exemptions from existing substantive laws.

Regarding the economic sphere alone, the generality requirement at the state level can also be found in the doctrine of public purpose. It refers to the obligation to enact public interest legislation rather than private interest legislation. This doctrine is most meaningful in relation to the expenditure of public money.[122] The requirement of public purpose embodies the idea that the only motivation for the legislative assemblies to enact legislation should be the general, public interest, the common good, and the welfare of

117 *In re Senate Bill No. 95 of the Forty-Third General Assembly of the State of Colorado*, 361 P.2d 350 (1961).

118 R.M. Ireland, "The Problem of Local, Private and Special Legislation in the Nineteenth Century United States," 46 *Am. J. Legal Hist.* 271, 272 (2004).

119 On equality and special laws, see D. Marritz, "Making Equality Matter (Again): The Prohibition Against Special Laws in the Pennsylvania Constitution," 3 *Widener J. Pub. L.* 161 (1993).

120 Ireland (2004), p. 288. Ireland also points out the practical problem of confusion for the people practicing law. It was very difficult, if not impossible, for them to have accurate knowledge of every single special law in existence. Ireland (2004), p. 278.

121 R. Briffault & L. Reynolds, *Cases and Materials on State and Local Government Law*, 6th ed., American Casebook Series, St. Paul, MN: Thomson West 2004, p. 245.

122 W.D. Popkin, *Materials on Legislation: Political Language and the Political Process*, Westbury, New York: The Foundation Press, Inc. 1997, p. 820.

the public at large,[123] rather than particular interests of private individuals or companies.[124] Yet, according to the public purpose doctrine, if the legislature decides to grant specific financial privileges, it is only allowed to do so on one condition: the common good and a general purpose must be served. An important implication of this doctrine is therefore that limits can be set on the powers of the legislature. The mere fact that the majority of the members of the legislative body agreed upon spending money in a particular way does not mean that the legislature is always allowed to act as it sees fit.

State courts used to uphold statutes which, despite being addressed to a specific corporation, contributed to the economic development of certain areas, for example by creating new jobs. The Supreme Court of Maine, for instance, found that bonds issued to a private corporation by state law to support it in developing a dry dock facility at the port of Portland met the requirement of public purpose. The Court considered the project:[125]

> [...] unique in its potential for extensive, long term, favorable economic impact; in the detailed arrangements under which a large private industry has been committed to long-term obligations in support of a major industrial development; and in the expert testimony at trial, tending to show that the project will improve commerce and create jobs, generating sufficient tax revenues to repay the state's investment.

These particulars prevailed over the rather significant fact that the state had paid USD20.1 million of the first USD24.6 million to be spent on the project by the private corporation, without retaining any right to receive the invested money back. The Court was not worried, either, that the benefit for the people of Maine would be indirect.[126]

The courts therefore uphold legislation that encourages "economic development and tourism," reduces unemployment, and "brings needed capital into the state for the benefit and welfare of people throughout the state," even if it means bestowing benefits on a private corporation.[127] Legislative expenditure does not meet the requirement of public purpose "if it is 'clear and palpable' that there can be no benefit to the public."[128] In this respect: "[t]he determination of what constitutes public purpose is primarily a function of the legislative body and as such will not be overruled by this court upon review, except in instances where that determination is 'manifestly arbitrary or unreasonable'."[129]

123 *Kearney v. City of Schenectady*, 325 N.Y.S.2d 278, 280 (1971) as quoted in C.P. Gilette & L.A. Baker, *Local Government Law. Cases and Materials*, 2nd ed., New York: Aspen Law & Business 1999, p. 431.

124 The requirement of public purpose also applies to property rights in the use of eminent domain. It guarantees that private property can only be taken if a public purpose is involved. See O.M. Reynolds, Jr., *Local Government Law*, 2nd ed., St. Paul, Minn: West Group 2001, pp. 498–501.

125 *Common Cause v. State of Maine*, 455 A.2d 1, 20 (1983).

126 *Ibid.*, For a few examples where the public purpose of the state expenses have been questioned, see: *Mc. Nichols v. City & County of Denver*, 280 P.2d 1096 (1955), and recently *Parker v. New Hanover County*, 619 S.E.2d 868 (2005) and *The Board of County Commissioners of Muskogee County v. Lowery*, 136 P.3d 639 (2006). See also Reynolds (2001), p. 355, note 4 citing a large number of cases on the public purpose requirement.

127 *Libertarian Party v. State*, 546 N.W.2d 424, 428 (1996).

128 *State ex rel. Hammermill Paper Co. v. La Plante*, 205 N.W.2d 784, 798 (1973), citations omitted.

129 *Ibid.*

2.3. Federal level: Special laws and public purpose

2.3.1. Special laws

The U.S. Constitution contains no *general* prohibition of case-specific legislation. There is no provision which provides that no special law can be enacted if a general substantive law already exists or can be enacted. Nor does the Constitution list any situations in which special legislation introducing classifications is forbidden. In the first century of the U.S. Constitution, 13 resolutions were introduced in an attempt to remedy this. These proposed constitutional provisions prohibited special and private acts; state constitutions served as examples. Nonetheless, these proposals were not adopted.[130]

The only explicit constitutional prohibition of a *special kind* of case-specific laws is incorporated in Article I, Sections 9 and 10, which prohibits Congress and the state legislatures from enacting Bills of Attainder. In addition to this explicit prohibition of a very particular form of case-specific legislation, a number of other constitutional limitations can be used to constrain the power of the legislature in this respect. The enactment of arbitrary ad hoc laws can be restricted by prohibiting retroactive laws in certain situations. The Equal Protection, the Due Process, and the Ex Post Facto Clauses are also important. They are the explicit constitutional provisions. Addressing retroactivity, the courts also developed criteria to assess legislation that overrules final judicial decisions in particular cases and legislation that intervenes in pending judicial proceedings.

These constitutional constraints will be described in the next chapter. I will now discuss private bills and project laws to show that the requirement of the generality of laws as promulgated so strongly in *Hurtado v. People of the State of California* by the U.S. Supreme Court is not absolute and that the legislature does not always take it into account. The legislature retains the right to grant certain privileges to specific individuals and to divide the collective money among specific projects as well.

2.3.1.1. Private bills

The Encyclopedia of the United States Congress defines a private bill as "a bill that applies only to a named individual (which may be a public body or a corporation), usually granting some benefit from government not otherwise authorized [...]. [W]hen enacted it becomes a private law. Most bear titles declaring them 'for the relief of' the individual, but no authority explicitly defines them."[131] Nevertheless, there are also bills that very distinctly contain the phrase "for the relief of...," but are still enacted by Congress as

130 H. Ames, *The Proposed Amendments to the Constitution of the United States during the First Century of Its History*, New York: Burt Franklin 1970, pp. 252–253.

131 D.C. Bacon, R.H. Davidson & M. Keller, *The Encyclopedia of the United States Congress*, New York: Simon & Schuster 1995, p. 1626. There used to be a federal statute that defined private bills as "[...] bills for the relief of private parties, bills granting pensions, bills removing political disabilities, and bills for the survey of rivers and harbors," 44 U.S.C. Sec.189, as amended 44 U.S.C. Sec. 706 (1968), January 12, 1895, Ch. 23, Sec. 55, 28 Stat. 609; January 20, 1905, Ch. 50, Sec. 2, 22 Stat. 611.

public bills, against all justified expectations of being considered private bills. This was the case in the Terri Schiavo law. Despite the fact that the law was entitled "For the relief of the parents of Theresa Marie Schiavo," Congress passed it as a public law. It remains unclear what drove the legislature to choose this form rather than the private bill, which would be the most appropriate when an individual instead of the general public is the only addressee of the Act.[132]

Equivalents of private bills similar to the Schiavo Act are regularly enacted as a part of public legislation. They, however, are different in the sense that they do not directly bear the names of any of the beneficiaries, but rather describe them. Such undercover private bills benefiting certain individuals have especially come into vogue in tax law.

When enacted, the Tax Reform Act of 1986,[133] for example, contained hundreds of provisions that granted relief from the altered tax provisions. Although these so-called rifle shot provisions mentioned no names, the circumstances and the requirements for the relief created by the law were so specific that there could in fact only be one taxpayer who qualified.[134] A well-known provision that granted tax advantages to only one well-defined taxpayer was the Louis B. Mayer amendment. The amendment afforded favorable tax treatment to a lump-sum distribution received by an employee who could fulfill the following very specific requirements: "1) the distribution resulted from the employee's assignment or release of the right to receive a share of his employer's profit for a period of at least 5 years after his retirement; 2) the employee had worked for the employer for more than 20 years; 3) the employee had held the rights for at least 12 years; 4) the rights had existed before August 16, 1954; and 5) the entire consideration for the assignment or release of the rights had been received in a single taxable year."[135] Not surprisingly, Mayer was the person who could meet these criteria in advance.[136]

132 The federal Schiavo Act was unusual in every facet. One could not immediately determine whether the law deprived Terri of her self-determination right or whether it conferred privileges upon her by giving her one more chance to live. The law actually did not fit into any category: neither the public law form (it was applicable only to her single case instead of providing rules for all persons in a PSV state) nor the private bill form where an individual requests and receives benefits, was appropriate. Mantel justifies the public form for the private nature of the Schiavo Bill by pointing to the language of the Bill, in which Congress declared that "It is the Sense of Congress that the 109th Congress should consider policies regarding the status and legal rights of incapacitated individuals who are incapable of making decisions concerning the provision, withholding, or withdrawal of foods, fluid, or medical care," M. Mantel, "Private Bills and Private Laws," 99 *Law. Libr. J.* 87, 99–100 (2007). Nevertheless, from a substantive viewpoint, Congress still created a divergent legal regime for only one case. That the intention of Congress was to do research on the general policy in the future does not make any difference. It was still only the person of Terri Schiavo to whom the law applied, Mantel (2007), pp. 99–100.

133 Pub. L. 99–514.

134 L. Zelenak, "Are Rifle Shot Transition Rules and other Ad Hoc Tax Legislation Constitutional?," 44 *Tax L. Rev.* 563, 564 (1989).

135 *Ibid.*, note 5. Pub. L. 83–591, Sec. 1240.

136 Classification of a bill as either private or public is thus solely theoretical, since an act officially called a public law can even contain private law provisions. Nevertheless, the distinction is important to determine the choice of the procedure to be followed prior to enactment of the bill. For a description of the private bills procedure, see Mantel (2007), p. 95.

Private bills differ from public bills in the sense that they do not deal with matters of public policy and do not cover the public at large.[137] Such bills in their purest form originate from the idea that the legislature is not always able to foresee the effects that a particular piece of public legislation will have.[138] Sometimes the application of general rules by the administrative bodies or the judiciary can lead to injustice in particular cases. Such injustice needs to be remedied by creating an exception to or exemption from the general rules, when all available means (both administrative and judicial) have been exhausted.[139] Private bills then offer the last chance for individuals who are unreasonably affected by the strict application of general laws or when, at first, there is no remedy at all and where it would be unjust not to provide one.

In the field of immigration law, for instance, extraordinary circumstances which resulted in extreme hardship for aliens seeking relief arose when a mother and her four daughters faced deportation from the United States after having lived there for nine years. They had lost all chance of becoming American citizens, because the father and husband, Mr. Hassan, had been killed. This murder took place only four days after the attacks of 9/11 in 2001, only because Mr. Hassan was a Muslim. At that time, under the current law, if the petitioner for the family's adjustment of status died, the petition was invalid. The USA Patriot Act[140] made an exception to that rule by holding such petitions valid if the petitioner had died in the terrorist attacks of 9/11. This requirement could not save the Hassan family, since Mr. Hassan was not directly killed in the attacks. Yet, his death was closely connected to these events.[141] Those circumstances convinced Congress of extreme hardship which the family would suffer if deported and a private bill granting the women permanent resident status was enacted.[142]

The counterpart of private bills in the tax law benefiting only one taxpayer (see the Mayer amendment) differs from the original form of a private bill (Hassan case as just

137 Hind's definition is: "A private bill is a bill for the relief of one or several specified persons, corporations, institutions, etc., and is distinguished from a public bill, which relates to public matters and deals with individuals only by classes." He, however, is also confused about the proper name for bills containing provisions which are both private and public in nature "and it is perhaps an open question whether they should be placed on the Public or the Private Calendar," A.C. Hinds, *Hind's Precedents of the House of Representatives of the United States*, Vol. IV, Washington D.C.: Government Printing Office 1907, pp. 247–248.

138 E.L. Perris & Ch. Dworin, "Private Immigration and Naturalization Bills – Equitable Safety Valves," 8 *U.C.D. L. Rev.* 263, 264 (1975).

139 Rule 3, Rules of the House Committee on the Judiciary, Subcommittee on Immigration, Border Security and Claims, Rules of Procedure and Statement of Policy for Private Immigration Bills, 109th Congress. See also Rules of Procedure for Private Claims Bills derived from the same Subcommittee. Both can be found at <http://judiciary.house.gov>.

140 Pub. L. 107–56.

141 House Report 108–531, H.R. 867.

142 Priv. L. 108–4 entitled "For the relief of Durreshahwar Durreshahwar, Nida Hasan, Asna Hasan, Anum Hasan, and Iqra Hasan." For an overview of the practice of private immigration bills, see B. Maguire, *Immigration. Public Legislation and Private Bills*, Lanham: University Press of America 1997; R. Hopper & J.P. Osuna, "Remedies of Last Resort: Private Bills and Deferred Action," *Immigration Briefings*, No. 97-6 (Federal Publications, Washington, D.C., June 1997); and K.L. Griffith, "Perfecting Public Immigration Legislation: Private Immigration Bills and Deportable Lawful Permanent Residents," 18 *Geo. Immigr. L. J.* 273 (2004).

described). Even though those tax provisions granted relief from the newly enacted tax rules which turned out to be less favorable, the Mayer amendment raised concerns as to whether this was an equitable reason to favor particular individuals. Another concern was that incorporating such very narrowly tailored measures in a sizable law enabled circumvention of the rules for enacting private bills and therefore kept those measures from transparent public consideration.[143]

Subjects of private bills

What are the areas in which contemporary private bills emerge? Although, formally, no official list of particular topics for private bills exists, the CRS Report for Congress on Private Bills Procedure lists immigration, domestic claims against the government, foreign claims against the government, patents and copyrights, vessel documentation, taxation, public lands, veterans' benefits, civil service status, and medical and armed services decorations.[144]

Although there are no written rules on permitted subjects of private bills, the House Rules determine which type of private bill is prohibited and will therefore not be considered in a committee. House Rule XII, Clause 4, lists the following categories: a bill which authorizes the payment of money for property damages, for personal injuries, or death for which a suit may be filed under the Tort Claims procedure provided in Title 28, United States Code, or for a pension, the construction of a bridge across a navigable stream, or the correction of a military or naval record.[145]

Nowadays, the type of private bills most often requested relates to immigration law as demonstrated above. This type of private bill mainly results in exempting certain aliens from immigration rules and permitting them to stay legally in the territory of the United States, as well as granting individuals waivers of claims by the government.

Congress' authority to enact private bills

Where does the U.S. Congress derive its authority from to grant new remedies to private parties or to grant exemptions from general legislation? It has been averred that the First Amendment to the U.S. Constitution, in particular the last sentence, which states "Congress shall make no law […] abridging the freedom of speech, or of the press […] and *to petition the Government for a redress of grievances*" constitutes a basis for the authority of Congress to pass private acts. However, as once correctly observed, the mere fact that people have the right to seek a remedy for any complaint against the government is insufficient, because it would imply that every petition would eventually have to result

143 As Zelenak shows on the basis of other publications, however, in the case of the Tax Reform Act of 1986, the rifle shot provisions actually contributed to the success of the bill, which would otherwise never have been enacted, Zelenak (1989), p. 566.

144 CRS Report for Congress, R.S. Beth, *Private Bills: Procedure in the House* (2004). For a short description of different types of private legislation, see J. Morehead, "Into the Hopper. Private Bills and Private Laws: A Guide to the Legislative Process," 9 *The Serials Librarian* 3, 116–117 (1985).

145 Rule XI, Clause 4, Rules of the House of Representatives, 110th Congress.

in the enactment of a private bill.[146] This could never have been the purpose of private bills. The power of Congress to enact private bills can therefore be more properly based on Article I of the U.S. Constitution, which deals with the conferral of legislative powers on Congress. Section 8 of this Article provides that Congress has the power to pay the debts of the United States. In 1986, the U.S. Supreme Court for the first time determined that debts within the meaning of this constitutional provision:[147]

> are not limited to those which are evidenced by some written obligation, or to those which are otherwise of a strictly legal character. The term 'debts' includes those debts or claims which rest upon a merely *equitable or honorary obligation*, and which would not be recoverable in a court of law if existing against an individual. The nation, speaking broadly, owes a 'debt' to an individual when his claim grows out of general principles *of right and justice*, when, in other words, it is based upon considerations of a moral or merely honorary nature, such as are binding on the conscience or the honor of an individual, although the debt could obtain no recognition in a court of law.

Whereas general laws are assumed to be suitable to govern all cases, and people and their relationship with the government, a situation could occur in which only one or a few persons are disproportionately harmed. Congress' moral duty is then to remedy wrongs engendered by the application of a general law in a particular case or to provide a remedy if an individual has a claim which would not be satisfied because there are no rules governing the government's liability. In other words, Congress restores justice and equity in specific cases by means of private bills. The question can, however, still be posed whether Congress is the most suitable institution to decide on individual claims. The courts seem to be better equipped to judge whether general rules should be set aside if their application to a particular case results in injustice.

Constitutional objections

Although private bills are often appreciated as being equitable, their individual nature also makes them subject to constitutional challenges.[148] The most obvious challenge involves the principle of equal treatment enshrined in the Equal Protection Clause of the Fourteenth Amendment and the Fifth Amendment. Private bills also raise questions as to the relationship between the legislature and the courts. The latter normally decide on specific cases. The federal case law on the constitutionality of private bills is anything but comprehensive. Nonetheless, in *Paramino Lumber Co. v. Marshall*,[149] the Supreme Court very clearly determined that private bills are not an "excursion of the Congress into the judicial function." Thus, in the eyes of the judiciary, private bills do not violate the separation of powers doctrine.

146 Note, "Private Bills in Congress," 79 *Harv. L. Rev.* 1684, 1685 (1966).

147 *U.S. v. Realty Co.*, 163 U.S. 427, 440 (1896), emphasis added. See also *Pope v. United States*, 323 U.S. 1 (1944) and *Paramino Lumber Co. v. Marshall*, 309 U.S. 370 (1940).

148 See Note, "The Constitutionality of Private Acts of Congress," 49 *Yale L. J.* 712 (1940).

149 *Paramino Lumber Co. v. Marshall*, 309 U.S. 370, 380–381 (1940).

In summary, the courts will not strike down private bills, since they have a long congressional tradition and benefit rather than punish the affected parties. Most of the persons or companies receiving benefits indeed deserve them, but the justification and motivation of a decision to bestow a benefit through a private bill remain obscure.

Decline of private bills

In the First Congress (1789–1791), ten private bills were enacted. Since then the number of private laws enacted has varied.[150] The 109th Congress, however, passed only one private law.[151] Despite this variation, a general tendency can be observed of a decline in the number of private laws since the 1980s.

The process of enacting a bill is lengthy and there is absolutely no guarantee that every private bill introduced will ultimately become a private law. But the advantage of a private bill as a means to provide equity and justice does not compensate the disadvantage of a long and time-consuming process, which serves only the private interest of one individual seeking a remedy. This means that less time can be spent on deliberating over legislation in the public interest and making public policy. Congress took various steps to reduce the considerable workload. The following are the most important. First of all, the U.S. Court of Claims was established.[152] As the U.S. Supreme Court explicitly stated in *Ex Parte Bakelite Corp.*, the Court of Claims (nowadays the U.S. Court of Federal Claims) exercises the power of Congress to pay debts, a function which was delegated to that court by Congress itself.[153] In addition, Congress enacted the Legislative Reorganization Act of 1946.[154] This law helped to make the congressional workload manageable in many respects. Firstly, Section 131 of the Act listed a number of fields in which private bills were prohibited, which immediately reduced the large number of petitions for private bills. Secondly, amendment of the procedural rules that applied to private bills may have reduced the number of requests for private bills. Before the Legislative Reorganization Act was enacted, different committees were responsible for considering private bills. This practice was changed by designating only two of them, namely the Committee on Foreign Affairs and the Committee on the Judiciary, to handle private claims against the government.[155] Thirdly, the Act shifted the responsibility of dealing with private claims against the government from the legislative branch to the

150 As listed in *Guide to Congress*, 5th ed., Vol. 1, Washington, D.C.: CQ Press 2000, p. 526.

151 Betty Dick Residency Protection Act, Pvt. L. 109–1 (2006).

152 Act of February 24, 1855, 10 Stat. 612, Sec. 1.

153 *Ex Parte Bakelite Corp.*, 279 U.S. 438, 452 (1929). For the history and evolution of the claims against the United States, see F. D. Shimomura, "The History of Claims Against the United States: The Evolution from a Legislative toward a Judicial Model of Payment," 45 *La. L. Rev.* 625 (1985) and for the history of the Court of Claims, in particular, see Note, "The Court of Claims: Judicial Power and Congressional Review," 46 *Harv. L. Rev.* 677 (1932–1933) and Comment, "The Distinction between Legislative and Judicial Courts," 43 *Yale L. J.* 316 (1933–1934).

154 Pub. L. 79–601.

155 Pub. L. 79–601, Title I, Sec. 123.

administration[156] and the judiciary.[157] The decline of private bills can be explained further by changes in the law that placed the subjects of private bills under public legislation. This was the case, for example, for quota requirements under immigration law. Until the Immigration and Nationality Act was adopted and supplemented by non-quota status for spouses of American citizens, Asian spouses commonly requested a waiver by way of a private bill.[158] Later, when the legislation was amended under the pressure of the vast numbers of private bills, and the quota status for the spouses of American servicemen was repealed, this type of private bill disappeared.[159]

Another reason for the decline of private bills is linked to the dangers associated with the process in which private bills are initiated. Many scandals, such as the famous Abscam scandal of 1980,[160] accompanying the introduction of private bills made legislators wary of introducing private bills.

Finally, as mentioned by Oleszek, Congressmen hesitate to introduce such bills because it is difficult to explain why benefits should be granted to specific persons by private claim bills, while the budget deficit imposes burdens on everyone else.[161]

Strikingly, the analysis of possible reasons for the diminishing number of private bills does not include any constitutional challenges to such bills. Congress itself does not intend to stop adopting private bills only because they may result in unequal treatment or may encroach on the authority of the judiciary. The main concern of Congress, when it took organizational steps to diminish the number of private bills, was to manage the workload of the lawmakers and make more room for determining public policy.

In spite of these congressional attempts to diminish the number of private bills enacted and ease Congress' workload, private bills will continue to be introduced by Congressmen who see their work as serving their constituents and taking all possible

156 J.S. Hill & K.C. Williams, "The Decline of Private Bills: Resource Allocation, Credit Claiming, and the Decision to Delegate," 37 *AJPS* 1008, 1012 (1993) referring to R.S. Beth, "Trends in Activity on Private Legislation in Congress, 1949–1980," Washington, D.C.: CRS (1982). See also the Federal Tort Claim Act, Pub. L. 79–601, Title IV, Sec. 403.

157 The possibility of suing the government of the United States was established for the first time in 1887, when the Tucker Act was adopted, 24 Stat. 505.

158 See also Note, "Private Bills and the Immigration Law," 69 *Harv. L. Rev.* 1083 (1956) about the quota system and the sort of cases in which private bills, which sought relief from these requirements, tended to be enacted until 1956.

159 Later, the quota status was converted into a non-quota status not only for the spouses of American servicemen, but also for the spouses of all American citizens. T.A. Aleinikoff, D.A. Martin & H. Motomura, *Immigration and Citizenship: Process and Policy*, 4th ed., St. Paul, MN: West Publishing Co. 1998, pp. 787–788, quoting E.J. Harper & R.F. Chase, *Immigration Laws of the United States*, Indianapolis: Bobbs-Merrill 1975.

160 In this case, several lawmakers were accused of taking bribes in exchange for agreeing to introduce private bills for Arab sheiks. The Congressmen involved did not know that the Arab sheiks were in fact FBI agents and that the entire operation was a setup. Countless newspaper articles were published about this high profile case. See, for example, B. Fischkin, "He's the Mastermind behind Abscam," *Boston Globe*, February 12, 1980, "Indictments Expected Soon in Abscam Case," *Boston Globe*, February 29, 1980, "Abscam Trial Opens for Rep. Kelly, First Republican to Face Charges," *New York Times*, December 5, 1980.

161 W.J. Oleszek, *Congressional Procedures and the Policy Process*, 4th ed., Washington, D.C: CQ Press 1996, p. 134.

steps to get re-elected. By introducing a private bill, members of Congress show their care and concern about the people in their districts, which enables them to win the trust of their constituents. It gives them a first-rate opportunity to claim credit, which enhances their possibilities of getting re-elected.[162]

2.3.1.2. Project laws

In addition to private bills, the federal legislature enacts various other laws that are specific, which means they apply to only a specific territory[163] or project (building a specific dam, bridge, or a railroad). In the United States, the legislature decides on the allocation of money for major national projects. The legislature can therefore decide (and has actually done so), for example, that there is a need for a dam on the Tennessee River and provide money for such a project.[164] But such project laws do not deal with financial aspects only. Since the legislature decides on allocating money for specific projects, it is said that the legislature is also allowed to decide on the specific substantive law provisions that will govern such projects.

In such cases, it is not unusual for the legislature to exempt specific projects from the applicability of the general rules, to guarantee that the project can be carried out. The legislature then uses the magic formula "notwithstanding any other provision of law... ,"[165] which literally means that no matter what the general rules say, the project *will* be executed and completed. The legislature clearly expresses its intent in this way.

One of the famous examples where this technique was used is the Tellico Dam project, which will be described in detail in Chapter II.3.4.2. The relevant legislative provision in that case was:[166]

> For the purpose of carrying out the provisions of the Tennessee Valley Authority Act of 1933 [...] *notwithstanding the provisions of 16 U.S.C., chapter 35 or any other law*, the Corporation is authorized and directed to complete construction, operate and maintain the Tellico Dam

162 Hill & Williams (1993), p. 1011.

163 See, for example, Pub. L. 106–291, Sec. 123, that provides specific rules for the Huron Cemetery in Kansas City.

164 The subject of authorization and appropriations legislation will be discussed in Chapter II.6.

165 How popular the magic words "notwithstanding any other provisions of law..." are, is demonstrated in, for example, Pub. L. 108–7: "Notwithstanding any other provision of law, the National Park Service shall not develop or implement a reduced entrance fee program to accommodate non-local travel through a unit" (Division F, Sec. 112); "Notwithstanding other provisions of law, the National Park Service may authorize, through cooperative agreement, the Golden Gate National Parks Association to provide fee-based education, interpretive and visitor service functions within the Crissy Field and Fort Point areas of the Presidio" (Division F, Sec. 120); and "Notwithstanding any other provision of law, the United States Fish and Wildlife Service may use funds appropriated in this Act for incidental expenses related to promoting and celebrating the Centennial of the National Wildlife Refugee System" (Division F, Sec. 129).

166 Pub. L. 96–69, 93 Stat. 449, emphasis added. See also the specific projects concerning three Sisters Bridge, the Potomac River Freeway, the Center Leg of the Inner Loop, the East Leg of the Inner Loop at the Potomac River in the District of Colombia and with regard to the Second World II Memorial Site at the National Mall, Pub. L. 90–495, Sec. 23 and Pub. L. 107–11, respectively.

and Reservoir project for navigation, flood control, electric power generation and other purposes.

In this manner, Congress unceremoniously set aside the general provisions of the Endangered Species Act, thereby guaranteeing the completion of the Tellico Dam project. Such a method of making special rules for a specific project that diverge from the normally applicable general rules in force did not raise any eyebrows. The courts accept it as a power of the legislative branch, which is responsible for political choices, including, among other things, the modification of previously enacted general laws. More examples of special project legislation will be given in one of the following sections dealing with pork barrel legislation and earmarks.

2.3.2. Public purpose

The state doctrine that the state legislature should spend public money only to serve the public purpose, in other words, the general welfare of the whole community, continues to play an important role. Consequently, state courts regularly apply this doctrine when a state law benefiting private entities is challenged. Does this doctrine apply to federal legislation as well?

According to Article I, Section 8, Clause 1 of the U.S. Constitution, "[t]he Congress shall have power to lay and collect Taxes, Duties, Imposts and Excises, to pay the debts and provide for the common Defence and *general Welfare* of the United States; but all Duties, Imposts and Excises shall be uniform throughout the United States."[167] This section of the Constitution establishes the tax and spending power of Congress. Its literal text, however, was subject to different interpretations and to political controversy concerning the boundaries of the legislative powers of Congress in this area. An important issue that needed to be addressed was whether this Constitutional provision vested in Congress the power to make any kind of laws, as long as they served the general welfare, or whether it was restricted to taxation and spending. In his Commentaries on the Constitution, Story expressed his fear of unlimited congressional power if the first interpretation was applied to the clause.[168] In his view, the General Welfare Clause therefore restricted congressional power to tax and spend. In his opinion, no independent power to regulate was conferred.[169] The U.S. Supreme Court adopted this interpretation in *United States v. Butler.*[170] The Court also addressed the contrasting opinions of James Madison and Alexander Hamilton, who disagreed on the interpretation of the Clause. Madison argued that the Tax and Spending Clause empowered Congress to collect taxes and spend federal money only to exercise the powers subsequently listed in Section 8, whereas Hamilton viewed the tax and spending power restrained by the requirement of

167 Emphasis added.

168 J. Story, *Commentaries on the Constitution of the United States*, Durham Carolina Academic Press 1987, p. 330.

169 L.H. Tribe, *American Constitutional Law*, 3rd ed., New York: New York Foundation Press 2000, p. 835. In other words, Congress is not authorized to enact legislation of *any* kind under the guise of being in the general interest.

170 *United States v. Butler*, 297 U.S. 1 (1936).

the general welfare as existing independently and distinctly from other enumerated powers. According to the *Butler* Court, Hamilton was right. The Tax and Spending Clause confers on Congress separate powers to tax and spend money, and its only restriction is that it must provide for the general welfare, as distinguished from the local welfare.[171] The requirement of the general welfare was thus intended to "limit and define the granted power to raise and expend money."[172] Legislation passed on the basis of Congress' power to spend money must, of course, also be reconcilable with constitutionally guaranteed rights. Besides the general welfare requirement for tax and spending powers of the legislature, the U.S. Constitution, as interpreted by the U.S. Supreme Court, sets the requirement of the general interest in the Obligation of Contracts Clause (Art. I, Sec. 10)[173] and the Just Compensation Clause (Fifth Amendment). The Preamble to the U.S. Constitutions mentions the promotion of the general welfare as well, but it is rather a noble idea than a workable requirement.[174]

Although the requirement of general welfare with regard to tax and spending legislation is explicitly provided by the Constitution, its enforcement is not that straightforward. Firstly, to be able to challenge a spending statute, the plaintiff – a federal taxpayer – needs to have standing. Usually, the taxpayer will be adversely affected by the statute together with other taxpayers forming a general group. It would then be quite difficult, if not impossible, to demonstrate the individual character of the challenged effects of legislation in order to obtain standing.[175] Secondly, even more important, the federal courts proved reluctant to enforce the General Welfare Clause. In this respect, the Supreme Court explained in *Helvering v. Davis* that:[176]

> [t]he line must still be drawn between one welfare and another, between particular and general. Where this shall be placed cannot be known through a formula in advance of the event. There is a middle ground or certainly a penumbra in which discretion is at large. The discretion, however, is not confided to the courts. The discretion belongs to Congress, unless the choice is clearly wrong, a display of arbitrary power, not an exercise of judgment. This is now familiar law.

171 At this point, the Supreme Court refers to the Hamilton's Report on Manufacturers.

172 *United States v. Butler*, 297 U.S. 1, 65 (1936). The condition that taxes and spending must be for the general welfare has also been reiterated in, for example, *United States v. Gerlach Live Stock Co.*, 339 U.S. 725, 738 (1950).

173 See *Allied Structural Steel Company v. Spannaus*, 438 U.S. 234, 248–249 (1978), in which the U.S. Supreme Court invalidated a statute which operated as a substantial impairment of contractual obligations because it could "hardly be characterized [...] as one enacted to protect a broad societal interest rather than a narrow class."

174 The Preamble reads: "We the people of the United States, in Order to form a more perfect Union, establish Justice, insure domestic Tranquility, provide for the common Defence, promote the General Welfare, and secure the Blessings of Liberty to ourselves and our Posterity, do ordain and establish this Constitution for the United States of America."

175 See Nowak & Rotunda (2004), pp. 86–91, describing conditions for standing in tax or spending cases prescribed by the Supreme Court in *Frothingham v. Mellon*, 262 U.S. 447 (1923). See also A. Scalia, "The Doctrine of Standing as an Essential Element of the Separation of Powers," 17 *Suffolk U. L. Rev.* 881 (1983).

176 *Helvering v. Davis*, 301 U.S. 619 (1937).

This opinion was later reiterated in other judgments such as *Buckley v. Valeo*[177] and *South Dakota v. Dole*,[178] where the Supreme Court again declared itself not responsible for determining whether the choices made by Congress in relation to its spending power serve the general interest rather than private, particular, or local interests. In *South Dakota*, the Court explicitly cast doubt on the enforceability of the General Welfare Clause: "The level of deference to the congressional decision is such that the Court has more recently questioned whether "general welfare" is a judicially enforceable restriction at all."[179] That is why the assessment of the challenged legislation in that case was very weak. The Court easily concluded that the law was passed to contribute to the general welfare, "especially in light of the fact that the concept of welfare or the opposite is shaped by Congress."[180] This judicial attitude toward the General Welfare Clause shows the Court's reluctance or even refusal to get involved in political decision-making.[181] Tribe made the following comment on this judicial attitude: "[s]uch judicial deference is understandable in an area lacking any coherent and broadly accepted theory of the public good as more than an aggregate of private needs and wants."[182]

2.3.2.1. Pork barrel legislation and earmarks

The non-justiciability of the requirement that the federal legislation passed by Congress in relation to its spending power should be in the general welfare leaves the door wide open for Congress to favor private parties. Congress makes ample use of this possibility given by the Supreme Court by appropriating money for specific projects in the states of Congressmen who introduce their bills for this purpose.[183] Legislation of this kind is called "pork barrel legislation."[184] Closely related to pork barrels are "earmarks," which do not necessarily concern projects in a state represented in Congress by a particular Congressman, but still provide funds for special projects that benefit only particular

177 *Buckley v. Valeo*, 424 U.S. 1 (1976).

178 *South Dakota v. Dole*, 483 U.S. 203 (1987).

179 *Ibid.*, p. 208.

180 *Ibid.*, internal citations omitted.

181 For a description and analysis of the Congressional spending power and the *Dole* doctrine see, for example, D.F. Engstrom, "Drawing Lines Between Chevron and Pennhurst: A Functional Analysis of the Spending Power, Federalism and the Administrative State," 82 *Tex. L. Rev.* 1197 (2004) and B. Galle, "Getting Spending: How to Replace Clear Statement Rules with Clear Thinking About Conditional Grants of Federal Funds," 37 *Conn. L. Rev.* 155 (2004).

182 Tribe (2000), p. 837. See also Chapter II.2.3.2.2 on special interest legislation.

183 The power of Congress to designate a certain amount of money to one specific project is based on its general spending power under Article I, Section 8 of the U.S. Constitution.

184 See also in general J.E. Ransdell, "The High Cost of the Pork Barrel," *Annals of the American Academy of Political and Social Science*, Vol. 64, Public Administration and Partisan Politics (1916), pp. 43–55, K.A. Shepsle & B.R. Weingast, "Political Preferences for the Pork Barrel: A Generalization," *American Journal of Political Science* 25 (1), February 1981, pp. 96–111, S.J. Balla et al., "Partisanship, Blame Avoidance, and the Distribution of Legislative Pork," *American Journal of Political Science*, 46 (3), July 2002, pp. 515–525, and J.A. Ferejohn, *Pork Barrel Politics. Rivers and Harbors Legislation, 1947–1968*, Palo Alto, CA: Stanford University Press 1974.

private parties.[185] Academic earmarks are very popular.[186] The Office of Management and Budget contends that "congressional direction (in bill or report language) circumvents the merit-based or competitive allocation process, or specifies the location or recipient, or otherwise curtails the ability of the executive branch to properly manage funds."[187] It should be noted that the terms "pork barrel legislation" and "earmarks" are often used interchangeably. The third kind of legislation which does not grant money to any particular corporation or project, but benefits the whole industry of a particular sort is called "special interest legislation."

The phrase "pork barrel legislation" dates from the pre-Civil War period and refers to salted pork occasionally received by slaves. The behavior of Congressmen introducing such legislation has been compared to the behavior of the slaves by Safire in his *Political Dictionary*:[188]

> Oftentimes the eagerness of the slaves would result in a rush upon the pork barrel, in which each would strive to grab as much as possible for himself. Members of Congress in the stampede to get their local appropriation items into the omnibus river and harbour bills behaved so much like the Negro slaves rushing the pork barrel, that these bills were facetiously styled 'pork barrel' bills.

Some projects (mostly public projects, such as roads, bridges, dams, and harbors)[189] championed by Congressmen from the same state as the state that will get the federal money make little sense. In the well-known case of the "Bridge to Nowhere," for example, Congress crossed the boundaries of all reason and granted a huge amount of taxpayers' money (more than USD200 million) to a project that became a symbol of "the fiscal irresponsibility of money in Congress."[190] Congress allocated money to a bridge project that would connect the town of Ketchikan in Alaska (8,900 inhabitants) with Gravina Island and its airport. There were only 50 people on the island. The reason for the campaign by Alaska Senator Ted Stevens to obtain congressional money for the construction of a bridge was that some people had complained that the ferry operating between the town and the airport was not optimal: the ferry would not come as often as desired and the car transportation costs were too high.[191] The bridge would replace the "long" ferry trip of less than ten minutes. This earmark received a great deal of criticism centering on the argument that there were other projects that deserved the money more

185 The discussion about what earmarks and other sorts of pork legislation can be, however, is more extensive. See S.A. Frisch, *The Politics of Pork. A Study of Congressional Appropriation Earmarks*, New York: Garland Publishing, Inc. 1998, Ch. 2, who describes different types of earmarks.

186 See J.M. de Figueiredo & B.S. Silverman, "Academic Earmarks and the Returns to Lobbying," 49 *J.L. & Econ.* 597 (2006).

187 Office of Management and Budget, <http://earmarks.omb.gov/> (last accessed on June 12, 2011).

188 W. Safire, *Safire's Political Dictionary*, 3rd ed., New York: Ballantine 1978, p. 553, which was also quoted in *The Guide to Congress* (2000), p. 619.

189 *Ibid.*

190 R.D. Utt, "The Bridge to Nowhere: A National Embarrassment," October 20, 2005, <www.heritage.org/Research/Budget/wm889.cfm?renderforprint=1> (last accessed on June 12, 2011).

191 According to Utt (2005), the waiting time for the ferry service was between 15 and 30 minutes, and the price for car transportation was USD6.

than the Alaska bridge, such as helping to restore areas hit by a hurricane. The "Bridge to Nowhere" is a typical example of pork barrel legislation, which Congressmen use "to bring the pork home."[192]

Why would Congressmen take the risk of being accused of undermining the general interest by wasting their time on undeserving projects or pushing legislation through Congress whose purpose everyone knows is only to enable financial profits for certain industries? In this respect, the cynical idea of a congressional expert reveals the underlying motives of Congressmen: "You thought that there are two parties in U.S. Congress? You were wrong: there is only one party and it is called the Re-election Party."[193] Congressmen's interests lie in getting re-elected and this implies fighting for the welfare of their constituents by putting all their efforts into guaranteeing the largest possible allocation of public money to them.[194]

2.3.2.2. Special interest legislation

In U.S. legal theory, the idea that legislation and administrative regulations serve the general, public interest has been represented by republican and pluralist theories of law. They differed in their views on the manner in which the general, public interest was to be achieved. The republican theory assumed that it was possible for the legislature and the administration to arrive at an autonomous, abstract, general, public interest through an open dialog between those representing different interests or through expertise. The pluralist theory takes its point of departure from the idea that the general, public interest was about balancing special interests. These two theories lost value, and the dominating theory in the United States is nowadays that of public choice. The public choice theory is characterized by a rather cynical view of politics, denying that government officials are aimed at serving the general, public interest. At its heart lies a belief that "all people – including legislators and administrative officials – are rational maximizers of their self interests."[195]

192 The project has been dropped as a result of strong criticism. To enhance the transparency and accountability of the government and to prevent Congress from abusing its spending power by designating money in an irresponsible way, Senators Coburn and Obama introduced the Federal Funding Accountability and Transparency Act of 2006, which president Bush signed into law on September 26, 2006 (Pub. L. 109–282). See also the Chairman's Statement, which clearly explains the purpose of the Act and gives examples of outrageous earmarks: <www.fas.org/sgp/congress/2006/071806coburn.pdf> (last accessed on June 12, 2011).

193 The same congressional expert could also foresee who the authors were of the provisions in a Senate Bill entitled the Iraq Emergency Supplemental Appropriations Act. This Act was originally meant to be an emergency spending bill for the war in Iraq, but was instead loaded with ideas on how much money should be reserved for the recuperation of the strawberries, avocados, and oranges industries by helping affected fruit farmers and with provisions on financial support to the Christmas trees and ornamental shrubs, sugar beet, and fisheries sectors. The House version of the Bill also mentioned shrimps and peanuts. D. Milbank, "Senate's Bold Proposal for Iraq: Sugar Beets and Rural Schools – in the U.S.," *The Washington Post*, March 29, 2007, p. A2.

194 Those who are interested in a theoretical study asserting that the re-election argument does play a tremendously important part, but is not the sole factor, are advised to consult Frisch (1998).

195 For a compilation of the public interest and public choice theories which have been used in this context, see B.Z. Tamanaha, *Law as a Means to an End. Threat to the Rule of Law*, New York: Cambridge

The public choice theory offers a framework for analysis of the practices in the United States, where the influence and the role played by special interest groups, particularly in the legislative arena in Washington D.C., are great. In many if not most cases, they are the driving force behind legislative proposals attempting to ensure a certain favorable outcome. The core of their efforts is, logically, trying to get legislation enacted which will best serve their financial interests. They therefore do not care about the beneficial effects for the public at large and the public welfare. What is more, they sometimes even go against the public interest. This was the case, for example, when the Sports Broadcasting Act was adopted.[196] The main purpose of the Act was to keep the National Football League financially viable. In order to obtain this goal, the statute made an exception to the antitrust laws that were designed to protect the public. In other words, the idea of protecting the public was dropped and lost in the fight against benefiting a big sport industry.[197] Special interest legislation can therefore often be viewed as opposed to general interest legislation and a commentator like Kirchner even skeptically argued that "special interests dominate the public interest in America today."[198]

Benefits

Special interest legislation does not establish a lump-sum distribution of money to special interest groups. The benefits are usually spread over a longer period of time. Licensing laws are an example. Legislative requirements and limitations on entering a certain profession result in benefits in the long run.[199] Nevertheless, Congress has more than once enacted laws that directly and openly benefited specific companies and which were also adopted on an ad hoc basis. This was the case in the 1970s, when Congress provided financial assistance in the form of loan guarantees to the Lockheed Corporation[200] and the Chrysler Corporation.[201] The congressional measures were intended to bail out these two companies, which would otherwise have faced bankruptcy and liquidation. The initiators of the bills invoked the general welfare argument to support these financial plans. They pointed out the potential national disaster if thousands of people were to lose their jobs after the companies' bankruptcy. Moreover, they argued that the bankruptcy would affect "the nation's economy, the Federal budget (and) the balance of payments."[202] It was the unusual nature of the companies' problem that justified such federal financial support. The congressional committees therefore agreed on the proposed legislation only

University Press 2006, pp. 191–195.

196 Pub. L. 87–331.

197 See D.L. Anderson, "The Sports Broadcasting Act: Calling it What It Is – Special Interest Legislation," 17 *Hastings Comm. & Ent. L. J.* 945 (1995).

198 K.P. Kirchner, "Special Interests v. the Public Interest: Money Talks in Environmental Regulation," 25 *Ecology L. Q.* 665, 666 (1999). See also K.P. Philips, *Arrogant Capital: Washington, Wall Street, and the Frustration of American Politics*, Little, Boston: Brown and Co. 1994, referred to by Kirchner.

199 T.J. Zywicki, "Senators and Special Interests: A Public Choice Analysis of the Seventeenth Amendment," 73 *Or. L. Rev.* 1007, 1028 (1994).

200 Emergency Loan Guarantee Act, Pub. L. 92–70 (1971).

201 Chrysler Corporation Loan Guarantee Act of 1979, Pub. L. 96–185.

202 Chrysler Corporation Loan Guarantee Act of 1979, House Committee Report No. 96–690, p. 8.

because of the very special circumstances of these cases and the guarantee that the federal bailouts would not become precedents.[203] These federal bailouts caused a lot of controversy and heated debates. Dissenting Congressmen criticized Congress for going far beyond its constitutional powers under Article I, which under no circumstances authorizes Congress to guarantee loans to private corporations.[204] The Chrysler bailout was also seen as a very explicit form of special legislation, which represented "an outright gift to Chrysler, its stockholders and its bankers." A committee member argued further that "this gift is not available to the people we represent, who have only the pleasure of paying for such special interest legislation as this."[205]

Lobby and the First Amendment

It is general knowledge that in many cases, lobbying is accompanied by the enactment of special interest legislation. It is, however, also viewed as a core, political right of free speech, protected by the guarantees of the First Amendment to the Constitution. Every constituent should have the right to speak freely to his representative about his concerns.[206] It can, however, also be transformed into immoral pressure by offering bribes or threatening to harm the Congressman involved physically or otherwise.[207] Many high profile lobbying scandals, including the recent case of the lobbyist, Jack Abramoff, who tried to influence lawmakers by offering them money and other gifts, led to the introduction of several proposals to avoid such an outrage in the future.[208] Legislators may have contact with their constituents, but such contact is reprehensible when it becomes corrupt.

Special interest legislation and the courts

Although special interest legislation is a cause for concern for many commentators, it has become a part of everyday life in the U.S. Congress. Congress will therefore continue to enact this kind of legislation. It was not the special interest character of the legislation, but rather the way in which it was initiated (bribery) that raised concerns. Not only Congress, but also the federal courts, or at least the U.S. Court of Appeals, seem to have

203 During the deliberations over the Chrysler bailout, the committee was certain that the Chrysler case would not create a precedent, since the financial assistance provided for the city of New York in 1978 and the bailout of Lockheed Corporation in 1971 had not done so either. See New York City Loan Guarantee Act of 1978, Pub. L. 95–339, initially opposed by President Ford, which the *Daily News* illustrated with the famous front-page headline: "Ford to City: Drop Dead," *Daily News*, October 30, 1975.

204 Chrysler Corporation Loan Guarantee Act of 1979, House Committee Report No. 96–690, p. 76.

205 *Ibid.*, p. 65. Cf. the government bailouts which were the government's response to the 2008 financial crisis.

206 See the House Hearing before the Subcommittee on the Constitution of the Committee on the Judiciary in H.R. 4975, No. 109–96, p. 2.

207 Eskridge et al., *Cases and Materials on Legislation. Statutes and the Creation of Public Policy*, St. Paul, Minn.: West Group 2001, p. 268 with references.

208 For a description of the major proposals in the 109th Congress, see B. Griffith, "Lobbying Reform: House-Cleaning or Window Dressing?," 75 *U. Cin. L. Rev.* 863 (2006).

no real problems with legislation which is colored by special interests. When the Sports Broadcasting Act was challenged, the U.S. Court of Appeals observed stoically: "[t]he Sports Broadcasting Act is special interest legislation, a single industry exception to a law designed for the protection of the public" and further: "[w]hat the industry obtained, the courts enforce."[209] The Court thus accepted that industries may obtain certain legislative favors through lobbying and recognized indirectly that Congress is authorized to pass such laws. The Court was not even affected by the fact that special interests suppress the general interest of protecting the public through anti-trust laws. The Court showed its reluctance to assess Congress' legislative action when a choice is involved between special interests and the public interest. Nevertheless, the courts would have a reasonable ground for such an assessment if the violation of a constitutionally guaranteed right is at issue. The most obvious challenge to special interest legislation would be violation of the equal protection right, which, for the federal government, ensues from the Fifth Amendment to the Constitution. However, as will be shown below, special interest legislation is likely to pass constitutional muster because of the less demanding rational basis standard the courts apply to economic legislation in their equal protection analysis.

2.4. Conclusion

The generality of laws requirement can have two perspectives: it can relate to the addressees of laws as well as the nature of laws (the general interest or the public purpose[210]). State constitutions are fairly clear about the generality requirement: they prohibit special laws.

The requirement that legislation must only serve the public interest, and not particular private interests, is still a strict condition and it is quite effectively enforced by the state courts. As far as the public interest requirement at the federal level is concerned, the U.S. Constitution also clearly obligates the legislature to exercise its spending power only for the general welfare. This is set out in Article I, Section 8, Clause 1. Since the courts are reluctant to enforce this constitutional provision, the legislature does not hesitate to enact laws that only benefit particular parties. This is evidenced by the practice of pork barrel or special interest legislation. The U.S. Constitution does not lay down a general prohibition on special legislation in the sense that it should not apply to only one case or person. This is remarkable, given the far-reaching prohibition of special and local laws at the state level. The practice of private bills, where Congress bestows privileges on certain individuals, shows that the generality requirement is not absolute. Although the number of private bills enacted decreases every year, the reasons for this have nothing to do with constitutional concerns about the generality of laws requirement, but are rather dictated by practical considerations.

209 *Chicago Professional Sports Limited Partnership et al. v. National Basketball Association*, 961 F.2d 667, 671 (1992).

210 Both terms are used here interchangeably.

Chapter 3

AD HOC LEGISLATION AND THE U.S. CONSTITUTIONAL PRINCIPLE OF THE SEPARATION OF POWERS

Introduction

In the previous chapter, I showed that most state constitutions clearly provide that special laws are forbidden. The U.S. Constitution does not contain such a direct provision. That is why, for example, private bills are common. Nevertheless, as will be evident from this and the following chapters, the U.S. Constitution contains other provisions that restrict the legislature in enacting ad hoc laws. The federal core limitations are the separation of powers principle, the equality principle, and the Due Process Clause.

I will first discuss the separation of powers, as incorporated in the Bill of Attainder Clause[211] and the Ex Post Facto Clause. I will then focus on congressional interventions in specific cases; cases in which final judgment had already been pronounced or which were still pending. I will explain the Supreme Court's attitude toward such interference in light of the separation of powers doctrine.

3.1. The Bill of Attainder Clause

Article I, Section 9, Clause 3 of the U.S. Constitution prohibits the federal legislature from adopting bills of attainder and ex post facto laws: "No Bill of Attainder or ex post facto Law shall be passed." The same holds for the state legislatures, as provided in Article I, Section 10, Clause 1.

The first relevant question is, of course: What are bills of attainder? Story defines them as "such special acts of the legislature, as inflict capital punishment upon persons supposed to be guilty of high offences, such as treason and felony, without any conviction in the ordinary course of judicial proceedings."[212] If such a bill imposes milder punishment than death, then it is called a bill of pains and penalties, Story explains. The Supreme Court, however, decided in *Cummings v. State of Missouri*: "Within the meaning

[211] Amar argued vigorously that the "nonattainder rule goes much deeper, tapping into basic principles of separation of powers and equal protection," A.R. Amar, "Attainder and Amendment 2: *Romer's* Rightness," 95 *Mich. L. Rev.* 203, 210 (1996).

[212] Story (1987), p. 484.

of the Constitution, bills of attainder include bills of pains and penalties."[213] As a result, the concept of punishment in the Bill of Attainder Clause has a broad scope in a modern analysis. The courts no longer make any distinction between bills of attainder and bills of pains and penalties in their classical meaning.

The main problem accompanying bills of attainder is punishment without a trial. A person "convicted by the legislature" is deprived of any rights to defend himself or herself before an independent court (and jury) in fair judicial proceedings with all necessary guarantees. In England, where the practice of bills of attainder was very common before the enactment of the U.S. Constitution, such bills were even enacted when the person affected was absent and had no opportunity to respond.[214] The English practice of enacting bills of attainder to remove undesired individuals generated the American discussion about the permissibility of this form of legislation. Before the U.S. Constitution was enacted, only four state constitutions paid attention to the bill of attainder. One of them – the Constitution of New York – even explicitly allowed such a mode of legislating.[215]

The Bill of Attainder Clause in the U.S. Constitution serves to protect civil liberties and functions as a bulwark against legislative tyranny. Nevertheless, it may not be regarded as "limiting Congress to the choice of legislating for the universe, or legislating only benefits, or not legislating at all."[216] The Supreme Court declared the Bill of Attainder Clause a guarantee of the separation of powers, because it prevents all power from being concentrated in the legislative branch.[217]

3.1.1. Singling-out effect

A characteristic feature of bills of attainder is that they single out one person or easily definable group of people and subject them to punishment. But the courts also recognized that "protection afforded by the Bill of Attainder Clauses is one of the constitutional rights enjoyed by corporations" as well.[218] So it is not just a guarantee for natural persons.

Singling out needs to be understood in terms of legislative *effect*, rather than legislative language. The names to be deemed specific do not necessarily have to be mentioned explicitly in a contested law, the Supreme Court decided in *Lovett*. It ruled that "legislative acts, *no matter what their form*, that apply either to named individuals or to easily

213 *Cummings v. State of Missouri*, 71 U.S. 277, 323 (1866).

214 J. Reynolds, "The Rule of Law and the Origins of the Bill of Attainder Clause," 18 *St. Thomas L. Rev.* 177 (2005).

215 Reynolds (2005), p. 194.

216 *Nixon v. Administrator of General Services*, 433 U.S. 425, 471 (1977).

217 *United States v. Brown*, 381 U.S. 437, 442–446 (1965). See also Note, "The Bounds of the Legislative Specification: A Suggested Approach to the Bill of Attainder Clause," 72 *Yale L.J.* 330, 343–348 (1962) and F.D. Wormuth, "Legislative Disqualifications As Bills of Attainder," 4 *Vand. L. Rev.* 603 (1951). In the latter article, the object of the separation of powers is explained as "to insure that persons be judged by general and prospective rules." Bills of Attainder punish past conduct, but "under some circumstances a measure penalizing a future act or omission may be a bill of attainder," Wormuth (1951), p. 607.

218 See *Consolidated Edison Co. of New York, Inc. v. Pataki*, 292 F.3d 339, 347 (2002), where an unpopular company became a victim of legislative adjudication.

ascertainable members of a group in such a way as to inflict punishment on them without a judicial trial are bills of attainder."[219] Statutes often describe the addressee. What is important is whether the statute de facto targets a specific person or company. This is an important question, which prevents Congress from omitting the addressee's name in order to claim that the disputed statute is general. Consequently, it was possible for the courts in the Morgan case to argue that, even though the 1996 Elizabeth Morgan Act did not explicitly mention Foretich's or Morgan's name, it was still intended to apply to their case. The requirements for the applicability of the statute were so narrowly formulated that it could be easily and immediately applied to the generally known case of Morgan and Foretich.[220] Although the specificity element in the bill of attainder analysis is an important factor, it does not in itself constitute a prohibited bill of attainder. A second element is needed, namely punishment. The Supreme Court explained the necessity of two components in *Nixon v. Administrator of General Services*.[221] In that case, after he had resigned as President, Nixon agreed with the Administrator of General Services (GSA) that the GSA would store his Presidential materials. They also agreed that both Nixon and the GSA would need each other's consent to access the stored documents. What is more, all materials were to be destroyed after a period of ten years, or sooner, in the event of Nixon's death. After the agreement was announced, the Presidential Recordings and Materials Preservation Bill was introduced and it finally became a public law.[222] Its purpose was to abrogate the agreement and take custody of the presidential materials for their historical value and possible legal proceedings against the Nixon administration.[223] Nixon challenged the Act on the grounds that it violated the constitutional separation of powers and the Bill of Attainder Clause. The Supreme Court ruled, however, that:[224]

> [...] the Act's specificity in referring to the appellant by name does not automatically offend the bill of attainder clause. Since, at the time of the Act's passage, Congress was only concerned with the preservation of appellant's [Nixon's] materials, the papers of former Presidents already being housed in libraries, appellant constituted *a legitimate class of one*

on whom Congress could "fairly and rationally" focus. It is worthwhile noting that the "class of one" represented only by Nixon was closed. The Act was undoubtedly intended to be effective only in Nixon's case, which made the Supreme Court's classification as a "class of one" inappropriate. The Court could only refer to a class, or what is more, of "a legitimate class of one," if the law applied to the materials of future presidents as well. Only then, in my view, could Nixon constitute a "legitimate class of one."[225] But even if

219 *United States v. Lovett*, 328 U.S. 303, 315 (1946).

220 This was the Court of Appeals' line of reasoning in *Foretich v. U.S.*, 351 F.3d 1198, 1217 (2003).

221 *Nixon v. Administrator of General Services*, 433 U.S. 425 (1977). See also *Bellsouth Corporation v. FCC*, 162 F.3d 678, 683 (1998).

222 Pub. L. 93–526.

223 See the syllabus in the *Nixon* decision, 433 U.S. 425, 425–430 (1977).

224 *Nixon v. Administrator of General Services*, 433 U.S 425, 428 (1977), emphasis added.

225 The Court wrongly believed that establishment of "a special commission to study and recommend appropriate legislation regarding the preservation of the records of future Presidents and other federal officials" by Title II of the law made it general.

the Court had recognized things as they were and admitted the real intent of the Act and its focus on Nixon alone, the Court could not have declared the Act a prohibited bill of attainder:[226]

> Congress, by lodging appellant's materials in the GSA's custody pending their screening by Government archivists and the promulgation of further regulations, did not 'inflict punishment' within the historical meaning of bills of attainder.

The Supreme Court decided that the Act was non-punitive and therefore did not fulfill the second essential requirement in the bill of attainders analysis. Accordingly, the Court did not find a violation of the Bill of Attainder Clause. The flagrant specificity of the Act did not lead the Court to draw the opposite conclusion.

3.1.2. Punishment

In *Selective Service System v. Minn. Pub. Interest Research Group*,[227] the Supreme Court developed a three-pronged inquiry test for courts to use when answering the punishment question. It is necessary to inquire "(1) whether the challenged statute falls within the historical meaning of legislative punishment;" (2) whether the statute, "viewed in terms of the type and severity of burdens imposed, reasonably can be said to further non-punitive legislative purposes"; and (3) whether the legislative record "evinces a congressional intent to punish."[228] The three tests represent the historical test, the functional test, and the motivational test, respectively, and they function as indicators. Each test is independent. Yet, the functional test outweighs the two other tests. The Court of Appeals, in the Elizabeth Morgan case, conscientiously pursued the three-step inquiry and reached the conclusion that the Elizabeth Morgan Act was a bill of attainder because it singled out Foretich and inflicted punishment on him.

The historical test

In its historical meaning, punishment in the Bill of Attainder Clause means the death sentence, but it also includes bills of pains and penalties, for example imprisonment or banishment.[229] Imposing the burden of an obligatory oath as a necessary condition to engage in certain professions can be classified as punishment, too.[230] Given this meaning of punishment, the Court of Appeals was forced to conclude that the Elizabeth Morgan Act did not precisely fit this classification. Nevertheless, the Court concluded that the Act was not an "inconsistent extension of the historical category." Moreover:[231]

226 *Nixon v. Administrator of General Services*, 433 U.S 425, 428 (1977).
227 *Selective Service System v. Minn. Pub. Interest Research Group*, 468 U.S. 841, 852 (1984).
228 *Selective Service System v. Minn. Pub. Interest Research Group*, 468 U.S. 841 (1984), quoting *Nixon v. Administrator of General Services*, 433 U.S 425, 473, 475–476, 478 (1977).
229 *Foretich v. U.S.*, 351 F.3d 1198, 1218 (2003).
230 See *Cummings v. Missouri*, 71 U.S. (4 Wall) 277 (1866) and *Garland*, 71 U.S. (4 Wall) 333 (1867).
231 *Foretich v. U.S.*, 351 F.3d 1198, 1220 (2003).

> [...] the burdens imposed on Dr. Foretich under the Act – deprivation of parental rights and the opprobrium of being branded a criminal child abuser – may be of even greater magnitude than many of those at issue in the historical cases.

Apparently, the Court of Appeals did not have much trouble in perceiving a legislative burden on Foretich as a punishment in its historical meaning. The historical category of punishment was quickly expanded and the concept of punishment was given a new, broader interpretation.

The functional test

In the second test, the relevant question is whether the statute in question serves a non-punitive, rational, and fair legislative purpose?[232] If not, then it can be assumed that punishing is its purpose.[233] Furthermore, there needs to be a balance and nexus between the burden placed on the individuals and the purported non-punitive goal of the law in question.

In Foretich's case, the government argued that the Elizabeth Morgan Act's only purpose was to allow Hilary to return safely to the United States, thereby reuniting a family, which was not punitive at all. The burden imposed on Foretich emerged merely as a side-effect. The Court of Appeals took a different view. It elaborated on and dismantled Congress' legislative goal:[234]

> [T]he Government's asserted purposes in this case conveniently beg two telling questions: Why did the protection of Hilary's best interest require this legislation? Why were Dr. Morgan and Hilary unable to return "safely" to this country to reunite with their family before the passage of the Act? The only plausible answer to each question is that Congress believed Dr. Foretich had abused his daughter and posed a continuing threat to her security and well-being. The purposes the Government alleges thus cannot be viewed as nonpunitive.

As a result of the imbalance between the burden imposed on Foretich and the apparently punitive purpose of the Act, the functional test was passed and the punitiveness of the Act established. This conclusion would have been different, the Court stated, if the 'safety standard' in the Act applied to all pending custody cases.

The motivational test

The last question of relevance in determining whether a challenged Act satisfies the requirement of punishment is whether Congress' *intent* was to punish.[235] In this context,

232 *Foretich v. U.S.*, 351 F.3d 1198, 1222 (2003) quoting *Selective Service System v. Minn. Pub. Interest Research Group*, 468 U.S. 841, 845 (1984), *Nixon v. Administrator of General Services*, 433 U.S 425, 483 (1977) and *Bell South II*, 162 F.3d 678, 686–88 (1998).

233 According to *Nixon v. Administrator of General Services*, 433 U.S 425, 476 (1977).

234 *Foretich v. U.S.*, 351 F.3d 1198, 1223 (2003).

235 *Nixon v. Administrator of General Services*, 433 U.S 425, 478 (1977).

the legislative history, timing, circumstances in which the Act was passed and its text are significant.

It is thus not necessary for Congress to *formally announce* "moral blameworthiness or punishment,"[236] which would practically never happen. Therefore, courts are free to use personal statements of Congressmen to evince the intention to punish. In the Elisabeth Morgan case, during the congressional debate, Hilary was depicted as a victim, which was a plausible indication that Congress aimed at condemning Foretich for sexual abuse.[237] During the congressional hearing, the committee members sought to make a deal with Foretich. The Elizabeth Morgan Bill would be withdrawn if Foretich decided to relinquish his parental rights and vacate the D.C. Superior Court visitation order. This gave the Court more reasons to think that the real purpose of the Act was to "assume the role of a judicial tribunal and impose its own determination of who was or was not a fit parent."[238] The Elizabeth Morgan Act fulfilled all the requirements and was therefore a prohibited Bill of Attainder.[239]

3.2. The Ex Post Facto Clause

Although the element of retroactivity comes indirectly to the fore in several constitutional guarantees such as the Bill of Attainder Clause (described above) and the Due Process Clause (discussed later), there is only one constitutional provision that explicitly prohibits the enactment of retroactive laws. It is the Ex Post Facto Clause, which, together with the Bill of Attainder Clause, is laid down in Article I, Section 9, Clause 3.[240] The Ex Post Facto Clause prevents both the federal and the state legislatures from enacting retroactively punishing laws.[241] In *Weaver v. Graham*, the U.S. Supreme Court explained that the Ex Post Facto Clause is meant to prevent arbitrary and vindictive legislation.[242] The Court concurred that the prohibition upholds the separation of powers doctrine by limiting the legislature. When the legislature desires to impose penalties, it may only do so for future cases, while the judicial power and the executive power are only authorized to apply the existing criminal statutes to actual cases.[243] Indirectly, the ex post facto ban guarantees legal certainty, because one of its goals is "that legislative acts give fair warning of their effect and permit individuals to rely on their meaning until explicitly changed."[244]

236 *Ibid.*, p. 480 (1977).
237 *Foretich v. U.S.*, 351 F.3d 1198, 1223 (2003).
238 *Ibid.*, p. 1226.
239 See also J.L. Mascott, "Recent Decisions of the United States Court of Appeals for the District of Columbia Circuit," 73 *Geo. Wash. L. Rev.* 802, 802–815 (2005).
240 For the states, the ex post facto ban is set out in Article I, Section 10, Clause 1, of the U.S. Constitution.
241 Those who are interested in the origins of the Clause in the U.S. Constitution may want to consult D.L. Troy, *Retroactive Legislation*, Washington, D.C: The AEI Press 1998, pp. 47ff. See also L. Ricciardi & M.B.W. Sinclair, "Retroactive Civil Legislation," 27 *U. Tol. L. Rev.* 301 (1996).
242 *Weaver v. Graham*, 450 U.S. 24, 29 (1981).
243 *Ibid.*, with reference to *Ogden v. Blackledge*, 2 Cranch 272 (1804).
244 *Weaver v. Graham*, 450 U.S. 24, 28–29 (1981), with references.

3.2.1. *Retroactivity and punishment*

In the first place, the Ex Post Facto Clause applies to retroactive legislation. The U.S. Supreme Court has repeatedly ruled that the fact that a statute targets past events does not automatically make it retroactive, a classification which is relevant for the purposes of constitutional law. A law is truly retroactive when, in addition, it "attach[es] new legal consequences to events completed before its enactment."[245] In the landmark decision *Calder v. Bull*,[246] the Supreme Court specified the scope of the Ex Post Facto Clause by distinguishing four categories of laws that are subject to the Ex Post Facto Clause challenge. These are:[247]

> 1st. Every law that makes an action, done before the passing of the law, and which was innocent when done, criminal; and punishes such action. 2nd. Every law that aggravates a crime, or makes it greater than it was, when committed. 3rd. Every law that changes the punishment, and inflicts a greater punishment, than the law annexed to the crime, when committed. 4th. Every law that alters the legal rules of evidence, and receives less, or different, testimony, than the law required at the time of the commission of the offence, in order to convict the offender.

In *Weaver v. Graham*, the U.S. Supreme Court held that the laws' *effects* and not their *form* are conclusive in establishing retroactivity within the meaning of the Clause.[248] Considering *effects* instead of the law's language enables the dismantling of true retroactive laws otherwise couched in prospective-sounding terms. The same holds for the second requirement for application of the Ex Post Facto Clause, to wit, *criminal* punishment.[249] In *Burgess v. Salmon*,[250] for example, the Court decided that application of a law that increased the tobacco tax to a tobacco sale that had been completed the morning before the Act was signed by the President (which is a civil rather than criminal measure), violated the Ex Post Facto Clause, because it was *in fact* an "essentially criminal" statute. The Supreme Court, however, does not always act consistently with the *Burgess v. Salmon* ruling. As Tribe demonstrates, the Court refused to invalidate a

245 *Martin v. Hadix*, 527 U.S. 343, 345 (1999) with reference to *Landgraf*, 511 U.S. 244, 270 (1994).

246 *Calder v. Bull*, 3 U.S. 386 (1978).

247 *Ibid.*, p. 390.

248 *Weaver v. Graham*, 450 U.S. 24, 31 (1981).

249 While one of the conditions in the bill of attainder analysis is that such acts inflict punishment, whether criminal or civil, the Ex Post Facto Clause is exclusively limited to criminal punishment. Strasser further explains the relationship between bills of attainder and ex post facto laws in the following way: "In any event, the two have been interpreted in such a way that some laws may violate both clauses, some may violate the Ex Post Facto Clause, without violating the Bill of Attainder Clause, and some may violate the Bill of Attainder Clause without violating the Ex Post Facto Clause," M. Strasser, "Ex Post Facto Laws, Bills of Attainder, and the Definition of Punishment: On DOMA, the Hawaii Amendment, and Federal Constitutional Constraints," 48 *Syracuse L.Rev.* 227, 230 (1998).

250 *Burgess v. Salmon*, 97 U.S. 381 (1878).

number of retroactive statutes which at first sight seemed to be statutes that imposed civil disabilities, but were actually criminal.[251]

3.2.2. *Bill of Attainder Clause or the Ex Post Facto Clause?*

A typical feature of special legislation, cases in point being the Elizabeth Morgan Act, the Terri Schiavo Act, and the Northwest Timber Compromise, is its specificity. Consequently, special laws that intervene in particular disputes and create new, divergent legal regimes for these specific cases would be most subject to the bill of attainder challenge (insofar as the punishment requirement – whether criminal or civil – is also satisfied). But when the bill of attainder claim is likely to fail, particularly when the law intended for one case appears to be generally applicable, the Ex Post Facto Clause may conceivably afford a solution. In such situations, it is essential that the challenged statute fulfills the condition of retrospective criminal punishment. It should be borne in mind, however, that although the Ex Post Facto Clause limits an arbitrary legislature, it appears that the legislature needs to go far beyond its powers in passing retrospective laws to get rapped on the knuckles.

3.3. Congress' intervention in pending cases vs. the judicial branch

The main complaint in the Northwest Timber Compromise case concerned legislative intervention in the pending cases of the environmental groups. It was argued that Congress enacted the intervening law in order to influence the outcome of the dispute. Is the legislature allowed to do that from the point of view of constitutional law?

A long time ago, the Supreme Court determined how courts should respond to legislative changes during pending cases. In *U.S. v. Schooner Peggy*, the Supreme Court explained that, in a situation where a general law has changed subsequent to a judgment already rendered, but before the appellate court has decided the case, the appellate court is obliged to comply with the new rules which govern the case on appeal.[252] One should, however, recognize that the congressional power to change or to repeal laws is not unlimited. When a legislature's intent is to affect the outcome of a specific pending case, it is allowed to do so, except when, in doing so, Congress directs the court as to how it should decide in the specific case. In other words, the legislature may change the law (it is, for example, common practice for Congress to exclude certain classes of cases from the courts' jurisdiction)[253] and may change the applicable standards, but it may not determine the judicial decision without changing the underlying standards.

251 See L.H. Tribe, *American Constitutional Law*, 2nd ed., New York: The Foundation Press 1988, p. 637, with references.

252 *U.S. v. Schooner Peggy*, 5 U.S. 103, 110 (1801).

253 See *Ex Parte McCardle*, 74 U.S. 506 (1868) and W.W. van Alstyne, "A Critical Guide to Ex Parte McCardle," 15 *Ariz. L. Rev.* 229, 232 (1973). The article provides a more extensive analysis of the McCardle case. In *McCardle*, the Supreme Court decided: "We are not at liberty to inquire into the motives of the legislature. We can only examine into its power under the Constitution; and the power to make exceptions to the appellate jurisdiction of this court is given by express words," *Ex Parte McCardle*, 74 U.S. 506, 514 (1868). For a more detailed view on the limitation of courts' jurisdiction, see

In this context, two decisions of the Supreme Court are especially important: *Pennsylvania v. Wheeling & Belmont Bridge Company*[254] and *United States v. Klein.*[255] The Court of Appeals and the Supreme Court mainly used these decisions as guidelines as well in the case of the Seattle Audubon Society in the Northwest Timber Compromise case. Curiously enough, even though both Courts applied the same criteria, they arrived at opposite conclusions.

Both decisions are worth setting forth in full. In the *Wheeling & Belmont Bridge Co.* case, the dispute concerned a bridge on the Ohio River. In accordance with federal law, the bridge was declared to be an obstruction to the public right of free navigation. The Supreme Court decreed that the obstruction needed to be taken away, "either by elevating the bridge or by abatement."[256] Shortly after that decision, Congress enacted a law that legalized the bridges on the Ohio River in the state of Virginia and Ohio in the actual position (location and height were no longer a problem) and made them lawful post roads for the transportation of the U.S. mails. The Act was challenged.

The Supreme Court did not find any unconstitutionality and the argument was rejected. Before reaching this conclusion, the Court clearly presented its position on legislative interference within the judicial purview:[257]

> [I]t is urged, that the act of congress cannot have the effect and operation to annul the judgment of the court already rendered, or the rights determined thereby in favor of the plaintiff. This, as a general proposition, is certainly not to be denied, especially as it respects adjudication upon the private rights of parties. When they have past into judgments the right becomes absolute.

The Court, however, distinguished the Ohio bridge case in the following way. The Court started its analysis of the case by concluding that the right of navigation is a public right common to all people, yet "a private party sustaining special damage by the obstruction may, as has been held in this case, maintain an action at law against the party creating it."[258] In the Court's line of reasoning, a congressional act that would take away such a private right to damages (that may arise from the public right to free navigation) would be beyond Congress' authority. The act, however, did not make such changes. The statute only affected the part of the Court's decree ordering abatement of the bridge, which is a continuing, executory decree. It influenced only the public right of navigation, and it was within Congress' power to regulate commerce.[259] Since the law changed the legal status of the bridge and declared that it no longer interfered with the public right to navigation, the Court's decree ordering abatement of the bridge could no longer be enforced. In

M.S. Gilmore, "Application of Statutory Changes to Cases in Progress: The Crossroads of the Legislative and Judicial Power – An Analysis of Federal and Idaho Law," 34 *Idaho L. Rev.* 571, 540 (1998).

254 *Pennsylvania v. Wheeling & Belmont Bridge Co.*, 59 U.S. 421 (1855).

255 *United States v. Klein*, 80 U.S. (13 Wall) 128 (1871).

256 *Pennsylvania v. Wheeling & Belmont Bridge Co.*, 59 U.S. 421, 429 (1855).

257 *Ibid.*, p. 431.

258 *Ibid.*

259 *Pennsylvania v. Wheeling & Belmont Bridge Co.*, 59 U.S. 421, 431–432 (1855).

summary, the law was not unconstitutional because it did not affect the private rights to damages of the plaintiff and constituted a lawful change of the general rules.[260]

An important variation on that doctrine was formulated in the *Klein* decision. The facts in that case took place in the Reconstruction era after the American Civil War. At that time, a few statutes were enacted by Congress that adversely affected those who had taken part in the rebellion against the United States. The laws particularly affected the American citizens from the Southern states. One of the laws, the 1863 Abandoned Property Collection Act, as the Act's name already reveals, provided for the collection of captured and abandoned property. The Act made recovery by the owners possible even if they had been disloyal and had participated in the rebellion. These owners could get their property back if they had been pardoned by the President. The President had obtained a right to issue pardons for the restoration of property rights by a legislative act of 1862. In 1863, he issued a proclamation in which he pardoned certain individuals on condition that they took a subscribed oath of allegiance and kept it inviolate.[261]

Klein was the administrator of V.F. Wilson, who died after receiving the presidential pardon. In 1865, Klein filed a petition in the Court of Claims, arguing that he was entitled to receive proceeds from Wilson's cotton that had been seized from Mr. Wilson and sold by the Treasury agents. The Court found for Klein, but the government filed an appeal against that decision.[262] While the appeal was pending, Congress enacted an appropriations statute, providing that presidential pardons were inadmissible and could not serve as evidence in the Court of Claims supporting claims against the U.S. government. Such suits, also on appeal, should therefore be dismissed for want of jurisdiction. Moreover, according to the Act, pardons that recited the acts committed in the rebellion and confessed in writing by the person involved, "without express disclaimer and protestation against the fact so recited" constituted evidence that the individual was disloyal and that his suit should therefore be dismissed.[263]

Klein argued that the statute was unconstitutional under the separation of powers principle. On the government's side, the argument was posed that the Act was within congressional legislative powers to regulate the jurisdiction of the Supreme Court. The Supreme Court did not agree with the government. It first explained that if Congress indeed only excluded a certain class of cases from the right of appeal, it would be a constitutional exercise of legislative power.[264] However, the Act effectuated more than that. By directing the courts to dismiss suits on the basis of the ineffectiveness of the presidential pardons, which had first been declared effective by the Court of Claims, Congress directed how the courts should decide in particular cases. Such direction of a rule of decision violated the separation of powers doctrine.[265]

In reaching its conclusion, the Supreme Court distinguished the *Klein* case from the case of *Wheeling Bridge*. As the court explained, unlike the *Wheeling Bridge* case, no new

260 See also G.G. Young, "Congressional Regulation of Federal Courts' Jurisdiction and Processes: *United States v. Klein* Revisited," 1981 *Wis. L. Rev.* 1189, 1243 (1981).

261 *United States v. Klein*, 80 U.S. (13 Wall) 128 (1871).

262 *Ibid.*, p. 133.

263 *Ibid.*, pp. 143–144.

264 *Ibid.*, p. 145.

265 *Ibid.*

circumstances had been created by law in *Klein*. The Court made a distinction between prescribing a rule of decision in pending cases and changing the existing rules. Such changes, even if they affected judicial decisions, were still constitutional because they did not affect private property rights.

As the case of the Northwest Timber Compromise evidenced, the distinction between changing the law, which may affect the outcome of a pending case, and prescribing a rule of decision to the court, which encroaches on the judicial power and therefore violates the separation of powers doctrine, is anything but clear.[266] The Supreme Court decided that the Northwest Timber Compromise set two new environmental requirements and therefore changed the existing general statutes as they applied to the two specific pending cases. Remarkably, the Court of Appeals reached a diametrically opposite conclusion. It concluded that Congress had enacted the Northwest Timber Compromise to tell the courts what decision they should make.

3.4. Finality of final judicial decisions

How final are final judicial decisions? Is the legislature, without violating the separation of powers principle, allowed to replace the final judicial determination in a specific case with its own legislative judgment or ask the court to decide the case again, as Congress did in the Schiavo case? These questions will be addressed in the following sections.

3.4.1. Reopening final judgments

Let us suppose that a specific case has finally been decided by a court and Congress does not agree with the result of the final judicial decision. There could be at least three reasons for Congress' disagreement: 1) "a litigant is unpopular and a court has failed to yield to the popular will,"[267] as maintained by Foretich in the Elizabeth Morgan case, 2) the court's decision is not in keeping with congressional policy, or 3) the court misinterpreted Congress' intention.

Congress can use different techniques to show its disagreement. One of them, also the most disfavored by the judiciary, is that Congress, by subsequent legislation, directs the Supreme Court to reopen final judicial decisions in specific cases and to decide them in conformity with the new legislative standards. Such congressional intervention in specific cases jeopardizes the separation of powers. The Supreme Court has already

266 See also the excellent analysis of the *Klein* judgment in Redish and Pudelski's article that uncovers the vagueness of that decision and tries to understand what the Supreme Court really wanted to say. The authors introduce five possible alternative constructions of Klein: (1) "Congress may not control or direct the Court's interpretation of the Constitution; (2) Congress may not dictate the outcome of an individual litigation, (3) Congress may not dictate the rule of decision in pending cases; (4) Congress may not dictate the rule of decision in cases in which the federal government is a party; and (5) Congress may not alter the substantive law by dictating how a court should weigh competing evidence," M.H. Redish & Ch. R. Pudelski, "Legislative Deception, Separation of Powers, and the Democratic Process: Harnessing the Political Theory of United States v. Klein," 100 *Nw. U. L. Rev.* 437, 447–448 (2006).

267 Brief for the Appellants, D.C. Court of Appeals, No. 02–5224, p. 25.

declared that the legislature *violates* the separation of powers doctrine when it orders the judiciary to reopen and reconsider cases that have already been finally decided.

The Lampf decision

The Supreme Court's opinion mentioned above originated in the *Lampf* decision.[268] In *Lampf*, the Supreme Court ruled that suits pursuant to the Security Exchange Act of 1934 must be brought before a court of law within a reasonable time. In the Court's view, the reasonable time was one year after the facts constituting the violation were discovered and within three years of the violation. After this judgment became final, Congress passed Sec. 27 A(b) of the Securities Exchange Act of 1934 which provided that any action which was found untimely and was therefore dismissed by the courts on the basis of the *Lampf* requirements should be reinstated and treated as being timely filed under the pre-*Lampf* State law. In this way, Congress retroactively corrected the Court's decision and directed the Court to reopen all cases that had previously been dismissed on account of being untimely filed.

The Plaut decision

In *Plaut*,[269] the Supreme Court started its analysis of the constitutionality of Sec. 27 A(b) of the Securities Exchange Act[270] by describing the separation of powers doctrine, to the extent it applied to legislative intervention in final judicial decisions in particular cases. In doing so, it expressly referred to such historical sources as the Federalist Papers and the Supreme Court's decision in *Marbury v. Madison*.[271] As far as the Federalist Papers were concerned, the Supreme Court based its analysis on Hamilton's paper stating that: "[a] legislature, without exceeding its province, cannot reverse a determination once made in a particular case; though it may prescribe a new rule for future cases."[272]

In other words, the legislature's task is to make laws for future cases and cases which are already decided should indeed be final. In its opinion, the Supreme Court also addressed the ideas about the role of the judiciary, as expressed in *Marbury v. Madison*. They stress the function of Article III of the U.S. Constitution, which establishes courts for the purpose of determining what the law is in particular cases and controversies.[273] The Supreme Court described the role of the judiciary as follows: "The record of history shows that the Framers crafted this charter of the judicial department with an expressed understanding that it gives the Federal Judiciary the power, not merely to rule on cases,

268 *Lampf, Pleva, Lipkind, Prupis & Petigrow v. Gilbert Son*, 501 U.S. 350 (1991).

269 *Plaut v. Spendthrift Farm, Inc.*, 514 U.S. 211 (1995).

270 The Act governed the exchange of securities. It "outlawed manipulative and abusive practices in the issuance of securities, required registration of stock exchanges, brokers, dealers and listed securities, and disclosure of certain financial information and insider trading," <www.investorwords.com/4440/Securities_Exchange_Act_of_1934.html> (last accessed on June 12, 2011).

271 *Marbury v. Madison*, 2 L.Ed. 60 (1803).

272 The Federalist No. 81, p. 483, in: C. Rossiter (ed.), *The Federalist Papers*, A Signet Classic: New York 2003.

273 See *Plaut v. Spendthrift Farm, Inc.*, 514 U.S. 211, 218 (1995).

but to *decide* them, subject to review only by superior courts in the Article III hierarchy."[274] This statement, together with the Supreme Court's judgments in *Chicago & Southern Air Lines, Inc.* ("Judgments, within the powers vested in courts by the Judiciary Article of the Constitution, may not lawfully be revised, overturned or refused faith and credit by another Department of Government"),[275] *United States v. O'Grady* ("Judicial jurisdiction implies the power to hear and determine a cause, and [...] Congress cannot subject the judgments of the Supreme Court to the re-examination and revision of any other tribunal or any other department of the government"),[276] and the *Case of Hayburn* ("Such revision and control of we deemed radically inconsistent with the independence of that judicial power which is vested in the courts"),[277] could lead to only one conclusion. The legislature, by retroactively directing the reopening of final judgments, violates the separation of powers principle. Even the general character of the challenged Sec. 27 A(b) of the Securities Exchange Act could not change the Court's determination:[278]

> To be sure, §27 A(b) reopens (or directs the reopening of) final judgments in a whole class of cases rather than in a particular suit. We do not see how that makes any difference. The separation-of-powers violation here [...] consists of depriving judicial judgments of the conclusive effect that they had when they were announced, not of acting in a manner – viz., with particular rather than general effect [...]. To be sure, a general statute such as this one may reduce the perception that legislative interference with judicial judgments was prompted by individual favoritism; but it is legislative interference with judicial judgments nonetheless. Not favoritism, nor even corruption, but *power* is the object of the separation-of-powers prohibition. The prohibition is violated when an individual final judgment is legislatively rescinded for even the very best of reasons, such as the legislature's genuine conviction [...] that the judgment was wrong; and it is violated 40 times over when 40 final judgments are legislatively dissolved.

In summary, the separation of powers principle is violated when the legislature reopens final judicial decisions, regardless of whether the law is general or narrowly tailored to one specific case. Moreover, the Supreme Court accepted no reasons from the legislature that could justify its reopening of final judgments. Although the Supreme Court did not explicitly refer to the general interest as a possible justification, by stating that "even the very best of reasons" cannot justify the legislative reopening of final judicial decisions, it in fact denied that the general, public interest ground could be an effective explanation.

It is worthwhile emphasizing that, although it might appear so, the U.S. Supreme Court did not find that all laws that *affect the outcome of* (*not* reopen in the strict, technical meaning) final judgments impermissibly encroach on the judicial power. Accordingly, subsequent legislation that creates a new forum for a de novo judicial review of financial claims against the United States that were previously denied does not constitute an

274 *Ibid.*, pp. 218–219.
275 *Chicago & Southern Air Lines, Inc.*, 333 U.S. 103, 113 (1948).
276 *United States v. O'Grady*, 89 U.S. 641, 647–648 (1874).
277 *Case of Hayburn*, 2 U.S. 408, 410 (1792).
278 *Plaut v. Spendthrift Farm, Inc.*, 514 U.S. 211, 228 (1995).

impermissible reopening of a final judgment but is viewed as a legitimate change of law.[279] Nor does subsequent legislation that affects the outcome of final judicial decisions by which prospective relief was granted violate the separation of powers principle. Prospective injunctions granted by a final judgment "are subject to modification – and, indeed, must be modified – when Congress changes th[e] law."[280] This is illustrated, for example, by the *Wheeling and Belmont Bridge* case. In that case, the prospective injunction consisted of removing the obstruction created by the bridge by elevating the bridge to a height designated or by abatement. Since the bridge was legalized by subsequent legislation, the prospective injunction could not be enforced. Such legislation, even though it de facto overruled the court's judgment granting the injunction, has been sanctioned by the Supreme Court (also in *Plaut*).

In sum, the significant distinction following from the Supreme Court's case law is between influencing final judgments in which no prospective injunctive relief was granted (this would direct the reopening of final judgments) and influencing judgments by modifying the law underlying the injunction and therefore nullifying the judgment insofar as it grants the injunction (such judgments are not final[281]). In the first case, the legislation would violate the separation of powers doctrine, while in the latter it would not. Rotunda and Nowak put this clearly:[282]

> If the judgment had awarded money damages in action at law instead of a continuing injunction in an action in equity, then that judgment would be final and a latter-enacted federal law could not affect plaintiff's right to those damages.

Some commentators deem the above-mentioned distinction to be decisive in the separation of powers doctrine. Therefore, according to them, the other distinction, the distinction between influencing private or public rights by subsequent legislation as

279 In this respect, the Supreme Court points to the statute in the Sioux case that "notwithstanding any other provision of law" made it possible to "review on the merits, without regard to the defense of res judicata or collateral estoppel" a Sioux tribe claim for just compensation, whilst the Court of Claims had previously rejected such a claim. *Plaut v. Spendthrift Farm, Inc.*, 514 U.S. 211, 230 (1995). See also *United States v. Sioux Nation*, 448 U.S. 371 (1980), *Cherokee Nation v. United States*, 270 U.S. 476 (1926), *Pope v. United States*, 323 U.S. 1 (1944).

280 B.M. Hoffstadt, "Retaking the Field: The Constitutional Constraints on Federal Legislation that Displaces Consent Decrees," 77 *Wash. U. L. Q.* 53 (1999). See also *Miller v. French*, 530 U.S. 327, 344 (2000) quoting *Plaut v. Spendthrift Farm, Inc.*, 514 U.S. 211 (1995) and *Landgraf v. USI Film Products*, 511 U.S. 244, 273 (1994).

281 Nowak & Rotunda (2004), p. 44 saying: "[…] prospective injunctive relief under a continuing, executory decree remains subject to alteration due to changes in the underlying law." So there is no question of a final judgment.

282 Nowak & Rotunda (2004), p. 44 discussing *Miller v.* French, 530 U.S. 327, 344 (2000). See, however, Gerangelos' critical notes addressing the Supreme Court's reasoning in *Miller v. French*. In that case, the Court did not find a violation of the separation of powers principle, even though the statute in question temporarily suspended the prospective injunction relief, regardless of whether or not such relief satisfied new legal standards, P. Gerangelos, *The Separation of Powers and Legislative Interference in Judicial Process. Constitutional Principles and Limitations*, Oxford and Portland: Hart Publishing 2009, pp. 236–246.

distinguished by the Supreme Court in the *Wheeling and Belmont Bridge* case, is unfortunate.[283]

Applicability or inapplicability of Plaut to the Schiavo and Northwest Timber Compromise cases

One of the arguments posed in the Schiavo controversy centered indeed on the violation of the separation of powers doctrine by directing the reopening of final judgments. This argument was based on the fact that Congress conferred new jurisdiction on the federal courts to decide the Schiavo case de novo, notwithstanding the previous final determination by the Florida Supreme Court. This argument, though very reasonable in itself, cannot be accepted, since the Supreme Court's determination in *Plaut* is limited to the relationship between the federal legislature and the federal courts, as established by Article III of the Constitution. The finality argument would have been successful if Congress had directed the federal courts to reopen the final judgment in the Schiavo case which had previously been decided by the federal courts. The federal Schiavo Act, however, carefully avoided such direction. It did not require the federal courts to review their previous judgments, but it changed the law by conferring jurisdiction upon them to decide the Schiavo case. The applicability of the 'finality of judgments doctrine' to the *Northwest Timber Compromise* case is simple. The judgment in that case relates to cases that are still pending, and are consequently not yet finally decided, while *Plaut* relates only to final judicial determinations.

3.4.2. *Overruling specific final judgments*

The guarantee that the legislature is not allowed to order courts to reopen closed cases is a strong protection of the independence of the judicial power. However, to what extent are individuals protected by the *Plaut* judgment, if Congress does not reopen closed cases in the strict sense, but nevertheless tries to annul a specific judicial decision? A popular legislative technique, used particularly in the field of spatial planning and environmental law, is that of amending the law in such a way that a particular court judgment cannot be enforced anymore, as evidenced by the *Wheeling and Belmont Bridge* case discussed above, and even more clearly in the Tellico Dam case.

The Tellico Dam project had a long and tumultuous history. The construction of the dam on the Tennessee River has already lasted years, cost more than USD100 million and was almost finished when a little fish called the snail darter was found in the Little Tennessee River.[284] The fish had in the meantime been listed as an endangered species in the Endangered Species Act (ESA). The environmental activists used this fact to stop the construction work on the dam. The Supreme Court eventually agreed with the environmentalists and decided that the plain language of the ESA and the legislative

283 Hoffstadt (1999), p. 75.
284 The little snail darter is very small: only three inches long.

history left no doubt that Congress not only strongly stressed the protection of certain endangered species, but also made it a priority, no matter what projects would suffer.[285]

The Supreme Court's judgment shocked some groups of the general public and caused profound dissatisfaction among some Congressmen. In particular, the Senator from Tennessee, Howard Baker, could not accept that the Tellico Dam would not be finished. He proposed an amendment to the ESA that established a special commission consisting of experts ("the God Squad") to decide whether certain projects could be exempted from the provisions of the ESA. The Tellico Dam project was, of course, the first one to be discussed. Baker was deeply shocked when the experts decided that the project should be stopped because it was not economically feasible.[286] There were no reasons to finish the dam. The general, public interest was totally lacking.

Eventually, after much effort and Senate (initially uncertain) approval, Baker succeeded in getting an amendment to the ESA passed which directly exempted the Tellico Dam project from the application of the ESA and any other law that could prevent the construction.[287] President Carter, who first fiercely opposed the Tellico Dam project when he was a governor, signed the bill into law. According to some commentators, he did it only because he needed the support of the Senate and Baker on another issue.[288]

The Tellico Dam project explicitly shows how far congressional power reaches. In this case, the legislature directly overruled the Supreme Court's decision which blocked the project, by making a subsequent exception to the general environmental statutes that governed the case.

For the courts, such pursuance of legislative power is not worrisome, since the legislature is primarily responsible for making political choices and is allowed to change the law as long as it does not direct a rule of decision or reopen final cases in the strict sense. In a case following the enactment of the law that exempted the Tellico Dam from the application of any statutes, the Court therefore fully approved the congressional action by declaring that: "[t]here is no question [...] that Congress has the power to make

285 The Act directed the federal agencies executing certain projects "to insure that actions authorized, funded or carried out by them do not jeopardize the continued existence of an endangered species" or "result in the destruction or modification of habitat of such species," 16 U.S.C. Sec. 1536 (1976 ed.) as cited in *Tennessee Valley Authority v. Hill*, 437 U.S. 153, 172 (1978). The contradictory rules laid down by Congress were a problem in the snail darter case. On the one hand, Congress continued to appropriate funds for the construction of the Tellico Dam, but on the other, it enacted the ESA and listed the snail darter as an endangered species, which foreclosed construction. An important question addressed by the Supreme Court was, therefore, whether the appropriation statutes could modify substantive provisions. The Supreme Court was very reserved about such constructions.

286 Z.J.B. Plater, "The Snail Darter, the Tellico Dam, and Sustainable Democracy – Lessons for the Next President from a Classic Environmental Law Controversy," *Boston College Law School Lectures and Presentations* 2000, at <http://lsr.nellco.org/bc/bclslp/papers/4/> (last accessed on June 12, 2011).

287 The Energy and Water Development Appropriations Act of 1979, Pub. L. 96–69, Title IV. The relevant provision stated that "notwithstanding the provisions of 16 U.S.C., Chapter 35 or any other law, the Corporation is authorized and directed to complete construction, operate and maintain the Tellico Dam."

288 O. Houck, "Unfinished Stories," 73 *U. Col. L. Rev.* 867, 938 (2002). The article is a detailed presentation of the facts and the history of the Tellico Dam controversy.

exceptions to rights it or state legislatures have created by statute, as long as such exceptions are not invidiously discriminatory."[289]

The Court of Appeals, after citing the provisions of the Tellico Dam statute, merely emphasized what Congress' will was, without questioning it: "No clearer congressional command is imaginable. No law is to stand in the way of the completion and the operation of the dam."[290] And further: "The only basis upon which the district court or this court would be empowered to enter an order contrary to the express will of Congress is that a violation of the Constitution will result from carrying out the congressional mandate."[291]

3.5. Congress' intervention in pending cases v. the executive branch

If the legislature interferes in specific judicial proceedings in order to ensure a certain outcome, it runs a risk of encroaching not only on the domain of the judiciary but also on the domain of the executive branch. Especially in the field of environmental projects, when general, already existing statutes appear to block projects and interest groups seem to win the case, the legislature does not hesitate to change the rules as it goes along.

Accordingly, when a citizens' interest group was successful in challenging the construction of interstate highway H-3 in Hawaii, Congress enacted the Continuing Appropriations Act for the Fiscal Year 1987[292] which, in Section 114, directed the executive body, namely the Secretary of the United States Department of Transportation, to approve construction of H-3 "notwithstanding section 4(f)."[293] In practice, Section 114 meant that the project had to be approved despite section 4(f), which prohibited approving any project that required the use of any publicly owned land.[294] The purpose of Section 114 was to overturn the Court of Appeals' decision and to ensure that the construction of the H-3 could continue.

The new Section 114 rendered the claims of the citizens' interest organization moot. After its enactment, the organization argued, among other things, that the legislature had violated the separation of powers principle because it had directly ordered the executive body what to do, namely, approve the highway project.[295] The legislature had therefore usurped the executive branch's authority to execute the law.[296]

289 *Sequoyah v. TVA*, 480 F.Supp. 608, 610–611 (1979).

290 *Sequoyah v. TVA*, 620 F. 2d 1159, 1160 (1980).

291 *Ibid.* See also R. Dworkin, *Laws Empire*, Cambridge, Massachusetts: Belknap Press 1986, pp. 20ff on the statutory construction in the Snail Darter Case.

292 Pub. L. 99–500. It is worth noting that substantive changes and decisions are again attached to an appropriations bill.

293 *Stop H-3 Association v. Dole*, 870 F.2d 1419, 1423 (1989).

294 *Ibid.*, p. 1422. In Section 4(f), exceptions to that general rule were made, too.

295 The separation of powers argument makes it seem as if the Secretary had not actually planned to approve the highway. The opposite is true. The Secretary's intention was definitely to approve and proceed with the project, but he did not do so in conformity with the rules (in particular, provision 4(f)). The legislature, de facto, remedied the faults of the Secretary and thus indirectly applauded his wrong application of the rules.

296 *Stop H-3 Association v. Dole*, 870 F.2d 1419, 1433 (1989).

The Court of Appeals concluded that Congress had not violated the separation of powers principle. To underpin its judgment, the Court first made a distinction between two situations: 1) Congress interprets a law that was previously enacted by Congress itself and 2) Congress grants exemptions from already existing general rules for specific projects or cases. The first congressional action, in the Court's opinion, constituted impermissible execution of laws by the legislative power, while the second action was within Congress' competence. The Court decided that, in the H-3 case, the contested "Section 114 [did] not interpret section 4(f)'s requirements but rather exempt[ed] H-3 from them, making section 4(f) irrelevant for purposes of the Secretary's decision to approve construction of H-3."[297] Consequently, the legislature was entitled to change the rules and grant exemptions in specific cases, as long as it did not interpret its own rules.

3.6. Conclusion

The main principle governing ad hoc legislation in the United States is the separation of powers principle. It manifests itself in several Constitutional provisions: the Bill of Attainder Clause, the Ex Post Facto Clause, and Article III and Article II of the U.S. Constitution. The separation of powers principle in Article III has been interpreted by the Supreme Court as proscribing legislative interventions in pending cases by directing the court as to how it should decide or by ordering the court to reopen closed cases. The separation of powers concerning the relationship between the legislative and executive branches allows Congress to grant exemptions from general rules in specific cases or projects, even if such exemptions influence the decision-making power of the executive branch. Congress cannot, however, replace the application of the general rules by the executive branch with its own interpretation and application of the rules in a specific case.

Without doubt, all of the components of the separation of powers doctrine are intended to prevent arbitrary legislation. Nonetheless, only the Bill of Attainder Clause seems to directly protect *individuals* against such legislation. The other components, and especially the courts' explanation of Article III, appear to be a guarantee against congressional intervention in other government branches without providing adequate protection for individuals. Accordingly, the legislature always has the power to influence specific cases and the judicial decisions in these cases. In doing so, it only has to opt for the proper method.

297 *Ibid.*, p. 1434.

Chapter 4

EQUAL PROTECTION

Introduction

The legislature, by passing special rules for a specific case, deprives other similar cases of the same treatment. The argument of equal protection was especially invoked by the opponents of Terri's Law, as signed by the Governor of Florida.

The requirement of equal protection can be found first of all in the Fourteenth Amendment, which provides that no State may "deny to any person within its jurisdiction the equal protection of the laws."[298] This safeguard applies at state level. The prohibition of unequal treatment for the federal legislature ensues from the Due Process Clause of the Fifth Amendment.[299] In this chapter, I will show that even though the requirement of equal treatment is strongly rooted in the U.S. Constitution, it is not always applied effectively to ban arbitrary ad hoc laws.

4.1. Classification

Before proceeding with the question whether the legislature violated the Equal Protection Clause, it must be established that the legislature imposed a classification with regard to certain groups of people, as the equal protection test concerns the question whether the legislative *classification* can be justified. The question therefore arises as to how to deal with ad hoc legislation that addresses particular persons, cases, or companies rather than groups of people on the basis of race or marital status, etc.

The Supreme Court had to deal on several occasions with the issue of the inequality of statutes that explicitly applied to certain companies or persons or that created only a theoretically open group, but that in fact targeted certain individuals. In those cases, the Court just directly applied the equal protection analysis, and as it clearly stated in *Village*

298 Fourteenth Amendment, Section 1.

299 For such a determination by the Supreme Court, see, for example, *Bolling v. Sharpe*, 347 U.S. 497 (1954).

of Willowbrook v. Olech,[300] the Equal Protection Clause also protects individuals that represent a "class of one"[301] and who do not "allege membership in a class or group."[302]

4.2. Strict scrutiny and intermediate tests

The equal protection requirement was originally intended to prohibit racial discrimination and therefore prevent Congress from passing laws that make a distinction between classes on the basis of race.[303] This can be explained by the American history of slavery and racial discrimination in the nineteenth and twentieth century. It is however beyond the scope of this chapter, which focuses on the tests applicable to the assessment of ad hoc legislation as meant in this book, to elaborate on that history.[304] At this point it is sufficient to note that if laws provide such a suspect classification, they are subjected to a high level of scrutiny. The question that courts tend to answer when they assess the constitutionality of such laws is whether they are narrowly tailored to serve a compelling governmental interest. Legislative classifications which are not based on race, but refer rather to such groups as "noncitizens, nonmarital children, and [...] women," are also subject to heightened scrutiny, although not immediately to "strict scrutiny."[305] A test used in such situations may be considered 'intermediate,' which is less demanding than a strict scrutiny test but stricter than the rational basis test described below. The relevant question is then whether "the classification has a 'substantial relationship' to an 'important' governmental interest."[306] When classifications affect fundamental rights, for example, a right to vote, to have an abortion or to speak freely, the courts will mostly use the strict scrutiny test.[307]

4.3. Rational basis test

Overall, it could be said that cases of ad hoc laws, which are the focus of this book, will rarely be a matter of Congressional discrimination against groups or classes on the basis of such fundamental features as race. In assessing ad hoc legislation, courts would therefore often use a less demanding test. The courts would then uphold any law which is

300 *Village of Willowbrook v. Olech*, 528 U.S. 562 (2000).

301 The term "a class of one" has already been discussed in *Nixon v. Administrator of General Services*, 433 U.S. 425 (1977).

302 *Village of Willowbrook v. Olech*, 528 U.S. 562, 564 (2000).

303 Araiza therefore argued for dealing with claims of unequal treatment of 'a class of one' within the Due Process Clause rather than the Equal Protection Clause, because such claims do not involve discrimination on the basis of sex, race, etc., W.D. Araiza, "Irrationality and Animus in Class-of-One Equal Protection Cases," 34 *Ecology L.Q.* 413 (2007).

304 For a compact description of the American history on that point, see Koopmans (2003), pp. 44ff and L.M. Seidman, *Equal Protection of the Laws*, New York: New York Foundation Press 2003, pp. 18ff.

305 Seidman (2003), p. 29, with references to U.S. Supreme Court decisions.

306 Nowak & Rotunda (2004), p. 688.

307 But, according to Nowak & Rotunda, the U.S. Supreme Court sometimes uses the intermediate test when fundamental rights are at stake. It is quite difficult to provide clear guidelines in this regard; see Nowak & Rotunda (2004), pp. 689ff. See also the next chapter on the concept of fundamental rights within the Due Process Clause.

"rationally related to a legitimate state interest." This means that classifications or distinctions made by the legislature must be related to the object of the law and must be relevant to achieving the law's purpose.[308] The Supreme Court explained "the rational basis test" as follows:[309]

> Whether embodied in the Fourteenth Amendment or inferred from the Fifth, equal protection is not a license for courts to judge the wisdom, fairness or logic of legislative choices. In areas of social and economic policy, a statutory classification that neither proceeds along suspect lines nor infringes fundamental constitutional rights must be upheld against equal protection challenge if there is any reasonably conceivable state of facts that could provide a rational basis for the classification [...]. Where there are "plausible reasons" for Congress' action, "our inquiry is at the end." This standard of review is a paradigm of judicial restraint.

And further: "The Constitution presumes that, absent some reason to infer antipathy, even improvident decisions will eventually be rectified by the democratic process and that judicial intervention is generally unwarranted no matter how unwisely we may think a political branch has acted."[310]

As the Supreme Court's decision illustrates, even if the courts do not like certain legislation adopted by the legislature, they are forced to uphold the challenged legislation as soon as they can imagine any plausible reason for its enactment. As a result, legislative bodies are not obliged to explain why certain political choices were made and adopted in concrete legislation. The Supreme Court further suggests that the legislature is even allowed to make distinctions and thus impose unequal treatment when it seeks reforms: "the reform may take one step at a time, addressing itself to the phase of the problem which seems most acute to the legislative mind. The legislature may select one phase or one field and apply a remedy there, neglecting the others."[311] Consequently, experimental laws that, for example, are aimed at solving a problem in one place, leaving the others waiting, would be viewed as a legitimate exercise of legislative power. The Supreme Court is clear about the equal protection guarantee: only laws that are invidiously discriminatory will violate the Equal Protection Clause.

Considering the Supreme Court's view on the function and scope of the Equal Protection Clause, it is interesting to see how the courts respond to specific examples of ad hoc legislation that both provide benefits for certain individuals or companies and except specific persons, companies, or cases from the application of the general legislation that would normally apply to these cases if an explicit exception had not been made.

308 Seidman (2003), p. 46 with references.

309 *FCC v. Beach Communications, Inc.*, 508 U.S. 307, 313–314 (1993) quoting *Sullivan v. Stroop*, 496 U.S. 478, 485 (1990), *Bowen v. Gilliard*, 483 U.S. 587, 600–603 (1987), *United States Railroad Retirement Bd. v. Fritz*, 449 U.S. 166, 174–179 (1980) and *Dandridge v. Williams*, 397 U.S. 471, 484–485 (1970).

310 *FCC v. Beach Communications, Inc.*, 508 U.S. 307, 314 (1993), quoting *Vance v. Bradley* 440 U.S. 93, 97 (1979).

311 *FCC v. Beach Communications, Inc.*, 508 U.S. 307, 316 (1993), quoting *Williamson v. Lee Optical of Okla. Inc.*, 348 U.S. 483, 489 (1955).

As early as 1957, in *Morey v. Doud*,[312] the Supreme Court took a clear position on the legislature's overstepping of its boundaries by enacting legislation for one specific company. In this case, the Court invalidated a statute that favored only one company, the American Express Company, selling and issuing money orders. The Act exempted the company from the requirement that such companies have to obtain a license and submit to state law.[313] The Supreme Court found such legislative determination discriminatory and therefore in violation of the Equal Protection Clause. The Supreme Court, however, reconsidered this judgment in 1976. In that year, it was confronted with a similar law, which permitted two vendors in the New Orleans French Quarter to continue hawking while prohibiting other vendors from engaging in such activities. The Supreme Court upheld the law and made it clear that there are not many possibilities to invalidate economic legislation on equal protection grounds. In doing so, the Court overruled its analysis in *Morey v. Doud* as being erroneous.[314]

In the field of taxation as well, the courts are not willing to invalidate legislation that bestows financial favors on specific persons and companies. The Court of Appeals refused to agree with taxpayers who challenged the constitutionality of the ad hoc 1986 Tax Reform Act's transitional rules that favored only one or a very few specified taxpayers, and obviously not the complaining taxpayers, who were in a similar situation.[315]

The plaintiffs complained that only those taxpayers were favored who had a strong lobby in Congress and that there was absolutely no rational basis for the distinction made by Congress between the favored taxpayers and the rest: "There can never be a legitimate public purpose served by the arbitrary selection of a favored few from the general applicability of a taxing statute."[316] The Court recognized that politics played a significant role when the choice of the favored taxpayers was made by Congress. The Court nevertheless rejected the claims that this choice was arbitrary, especially since there were thousands of applicants seeking exemption from the new tax statute and not receiving it. Moreover, in the Court's opinion, it was the plaintiffs' mistake not to seek transitional relief: "They did not ask for, and therefore did not receive the congressional manna: Congress cannot be expected to search out on its own those taxpayers whose peculiar circumstances give them strong equitable arguments for special relief from general tax provisions; rather, such taxpayers must come to Congress."[317] As the case of *Apache Bend Apartments* shows, the courts give the legislature great latitude for making political choices that serve special interests of powerful constituents with connections in Congress rather than the general, public interest.

In another case, the courts also demonstrated their reluctance to invalidate legislation that seemed to arbitrarily single out one case. In the case of *Antonio v. Wards Cove*

312 *Morey v. Doud*, 354 U.S. 457 (1957).
313 *Ibid.*, p. 458.
314 *City of New Orleans v. Dukes*, 427 U.S. 297 (1976). See also the Court of Appeals' specificity of statutes analysis in *Bellsouth Corporation v. FCC*, 162 F.3d 678, 684 (1998).
315 The plaintiffs alleged violation of the Equal Protection Clause of the Fifth Amendment and violation of the Uniformity Clause.
316 *Apache Bend Apartments Ltd. v. U.S. Through IRS*, 964 F.2d 1556, 1567 (1992).
317 *Ibid.*, p. 1568 (Justice Stevens' concurring opinion).

Packing Co., Inc.,[318] the constitutionality issue centered on Section 402 (b) of the Civil Rights Act of 1991, which exempted one specific pending case from the favorable provisions of the Act.

In the case of *Antonio v. Wards Cove Packing Co., Inc.*, the colored workers working at the Wards Cove Packing salmon cannery brought their case to the court arguing that there was racial discrimination at the company. The Wards Cove Packing Co. discriminated against the non-white workers by preserving separate channels for hiring people for unskilled cannery jobs (held by non-white employees) and for skilled non-cannery jobs (primarily held by white employees) and by providing separate sleeping and eating facilities for them. The non-whites lived and worked in worse conditions than the white workers. Before their case was decided on appeal, the new general Civil Rights Act was passed, from which the workers could benefit. However, the lobbying efforts of the Wards Cove Packing Co. in Congress were successful and an unusual provision was introduced in the Civil Rights Act. The provision excluded the case of the colored workers from the application of the new Act:[319]

> "CERTAIN DISPARATE IMPACT CASES. Notwithstanding any other provision of this Act, nothing in this Act shall apply to any disparate impact case for which a complaint was filed before March 1, 1975, and for which an initial decision was rendered after October 30, 1983."

Although the law did not mention the names of the plaintiffs (Antonio et al.), there seemed to be only one case that qualified for the application of Section 402 (b), as the Court of Appeals observed. Moreover, the legislative history clearly demonstrated that Congress had a specific case in mind when it designed the exception. The legislative history of the Act shows that some Congressmen had problems with the unfairness of the contested provision and saw it as a product of "a high cost lobbying effort" and as the result of a "political deal cut in the Senate."[320]

In its 'after-the-fact' explanation, the government maintained that Congress was aware that this specific case had "consumed enormous time and resources on both sides" and therefore Congress did not want to retroactively bring the provisions of the new general law into the proceedings.[321]

In assessing the constitutionality of Section 402 (b), the Court acknowledged the very specific character of the provision, and that the Congressional Record of the provisions showed that it had been enacted as a result of effective lobbying by the Wards Cove Packing Co. in Congress. Nevertheless, the Court found no violation of the Equal Protection Clause. Applying the "rational basis test," the Court elaborated: "A rational basis need not be one that actually motivated Congress. It is enough that plausible reasons

318 *Antonio v. Wards Cove Packing Co., Inc.*, 10 F. 3d 1485 (1993), cert. denied 115 S.Ct 57, 513 U.S. 809 (1994), affirmed *Antonio v. Wards Cove Packing Co., Inc.*, 275 F.3d 797 (2001).
319 Civil Rights Act of 1991, Section 402 (b).
320 137 CONG. REC. H9516.
321 *Antonio v. Wards Cove Packing Co., Inc.*, 10 F.3d 1485, 1494 (1993).

for Congress exist. Under the minimum standard of rationality, the reason proffered by the Government qualifies as plausible and sufficient."[322]

4.4. Conclusion

The examples described above illustrate that the American judiciary is willing to accept congressional exceptions to the general rules for specific cases, persons, or projects. The courts seem to prefer to watch the political process from a safe distance and intervene in political choices only in very exceptional situations, where it is obvious that the contested legislation is blatantly discriminatory. Apart from deliberate discrimination, if specific exemptions for individual cases arise from a political deliberative process, where the tremendously important role of the lobbies is presupposed and accepted, the courts refuse to take action. At such times, they even appear to be willing to accept an obviously false explanation by the government of the legitimate purpose of a challenged law, as shown in the U.S. Court of Appeals' judgment in the case of the *Wards Cove Packing Co.*

322 *Ibid.*

Chapter 5

THE DUE PROCESS CLAUSE

Introduction

In the three examples of ad hoc legislation (the Elizabeth Morgan case, the Terri Schiavo case, and the Northwest Timber Compromise case), the main problem that bothered the affected parties was that the legislature had acted arbitrarily. As we have seen above, the U.S. Constitution contains several provisions that can limit the legislature in this respect. The last relevant constitutional restriction is the Due Process Clause of the Fifth and the Fourteenth Amendments. Both amendments prohibit the government's deprivation of "life, liberty and property, without due process of law."

5.1. Arbitrariness

What exactly does the due process requirement mean? The Supreme Court addressed this question when it reviewed new general regulations for the public welfare in 1933. According to the Supreme Court, the government is authorized to issue different regulations that are intended to further public welfare. This authority is nevertheless limited by the requirement of due process.[323] In the Court's opinion, "the guaranty of due process [...] demands only that the law shall not be *unreasonable*, *arbitrary*, or *capricious*, and that the *means* selected shall have a *real and substantial relation to the object* sought to be attained."[324] The relationship between the ends, the objective of the law, and the means used is therefore significant, whereby "the reasonableness of each regulation depends upon the relevant facts."[325]

323 *Nebbia v. New York*, 291 U.S. 502, 525 (1934).

324 *Ibid.*, emphasis added. In any event, the law is not reasonable and thus arbitrary if it is not general, but instead created "a special rule for a particular person or a particular case," as suggested by the U.S. Supreme Court in *Hurtado v. People of the State of California*, 110 U.S. 516, 535–536 (1884). However, as we have already seen, the mere fact that the law is case-specific does not automatically render it unconstitutional. See Chapter II.2.1.

325 *Nebbia v. New York*, 291 U.S. 502, 525 (1934).

5.2. Procedural and substantive due process: Threshold question

In the case law, an important distinction has been made between procedural and substantive due process. The threshold question for both types of due process analysis is whether the executive or legislative regulation deprived an individual of his life, liberty, or property. But, as Kaplin states, in procedural due process, this question is much more important than in the substantive due process analysis. While courts put much emphasis on whether or not there has been any deprivation of life, liberty, or property in their procedural due process analysis, they appear to assume such deprivation in the substantive due process test.[326]

5.3. Procedural due process

Procedural due process addresses the issue of whether or not the government offered the individual sufficient procedural guarantees before it rendered a decision. Procedural due process therefore deals with the *application* of the general rules to a specific case. It will be guaranteed if there is a proper hearing. It should be noted that a hearing must be "at a meaningful time and in a meaningful manner."[327] The Supreme Court specified the hearing requirements in *Goldberg v. Kelly*.[328]

As illustrated earlier, the procedural due process analysis is applied in situations of an individualized government action. Kaplin therefore argues that legislative acts are not subject to the procedural due process analysis, since they create a general rule of general applicability:[329]

> If, for example, a legislature promulgates a general rule concerning eligibility for worker's compensation, the procedures for adopting the rule will not be subject to a procedural due process challenge. But if a worker's compensation board applies this eligibility rule to a particular individual and denies or terminates the individual's compensation, the procedures for making the individualized determination may be subject to a procedural due process challenge.

It is fair to question this presupposition. As the Terri Schiavo, the Elizabeth Morgan, and the Northwest Timber Compromise cases show, the legislature sometimes enacts ad hoc laws that are anything but general. In such cases, the procedural due process challenge can legitimately be invoked. The mere fact that the challenged regulation originates from the legislature, which normally enacts general laws, should not stand in the way of a procedural due process challenge when the legislature enacts specific laws. Accordingly, Dr. Foretich opposed the Elizabeth Morgan Act as violating procedural (and substantive) due process. Foretich complained that he had been deprived of his parental custody

326 W.A. Kaplin, *The Concepts and Methods of Constitutional Law*, Durham: Carolina Academic Press: Durham 1992, p. 144.

327 *Armstrong v. Manzo*, 380 U.S. 545, 552 (1965).

328 *Goldberg v. Kelly*, 397 U.S. 254 (1970).

329 Kaplin (1992), p. 143.

rights by the congressional legislation. He argued that he had no real possibility of a meaningful hearing. Nor had he been given the opportunity to provide counter evidence, to cross-examine the witnesses, or to have an impartial decision maker. Finally, he questioned any legitimate governmental interest in the legislation.[330]

5.4. Substantive due process

Unlike procedural due process, substantive due process deals with the *content* of legislative or other regulations.[331] The rules are arbitrary if they are not related to the purpose that the government intends (or says it intends) to achieve. During the assessment of any challenged legislation, the courts will therefore search for a substantive relationship between the means used by the legislature and the objective to be achieved.

Nevertheless, the standard of review in the substantive due process analysis differs according to the type of regulation challenged. While economic legislation is assumed to easily meet the requirement of a rational relationship to any legitimate governmental purpose (rational basis test, presumption of constitutionality), the courts do apply a stricter test when fundamental rights are at stake.[332] They uphold legislation that infringes fundamental rights, only if the legislation serves a "compelling interest" (strict scrutiny test).[333]

5.5. Equal protection and due process

A careful reading of the Equal Protection Clause reveals its close relationship to the due process analysis. In the equal protection analysis as well as in the due process analysis, the courts use the rational basis test to uphold economic legislation, and the strict scrutiny test to assess the constitutionality of legislation which, in general, restricts individual fundamental rights.

Having said that, I now raise the question of the *raison d'être* of these two separate constitutional limitations of the legislative power, since they both operate within a similar framework. Nowak and Rotunda explain this as follows: "When the Supreme Court reviews a law that restricts the liberty of all persons, it will review the law under

330 Brief for the Appellants, D.C. Court of Appeals, No. 02–5224, p. 35. Since the Court of Appeals for the District of Columbia Circuit invalidated the Elizabeth Morgan Act as violating the Bill of Attainder Clause, it did not proceed to examine the due process of law claim. See *Foretich v. U.S.*, 351 F. 3d 1198 (2003).

331 See Tribe (2000), p. 1334.

332 Kaplin (1992), p. 141.

333 The concept of fundamental rights as opposed to non-fundamental rights in the due process analysis is quite vague, since there is no exhaustive enumeration of them. Nonetheless, the courts already distinguished a type of rights that are fundamental in any event. Rotunda and Nowak identify the following: "[...] most of the guarantees of the Bill of Rights, the right to fairness in the criminal process, the right to privacy (including some freedom of choice in matters of marriage, sexual relations and child bearing), the right to travel, the right to vote, the freedom of association, and some aspects of fairness in the adjudication of individual claims against the government (procedural due process rights)," citations omitted, Nowak & Rotunda (2004), p. 456.

due process principles. When the Court reviews a law that classifies persons, it will use equal protection principles."[334]

In summary, the tests used by the courts under the due process and equal protection principles are similar, but the choice to apply the tests to specific legislation depends on whether the challenged legislation imposes classifications.

5.6. Retroactive legislation and due process

Enacting retroactive legislation is one of the methods for the legislature to affect the outcome of specific cases that are politically unpopular. As we have seen before, the Ex Post Facto Clause of the U.S. Constitution clearly prohibits retroactive laws that impose criminal punishment. Other retroactive laws, however, are outside the scope of that provision. Such laws may therefore be subjected to a due process analysis. Does this mean that due process prevents the enactment of all retroactive legislation?

Nowak and Rotunda distinguish four categories of cases in which retroactive laws have hitherto been challenged on the basis of the Due Process Clause. These categories are: "(1) cases that involve emergency retroactive legislation; (2) cases that challenge the constitutionality of curative statutes; (3) cases that involve the constitutional merits of retroactive taxing legislation; and (4) cases that contest the constitutionality of retroactive general legislation."[335]

Despite a general presumption against the retroactivity of statutes, the Supreme Court does not treat retroactive legislation that is not punishing within the meaning of the Ex Post Facto Clause with any special care and applies the ordinary rational basis test to decide on its constitutionality.[336] In *Usery v. Turner Elkhorn Mining Co.*[337] (general retroactive legislation) and *U.S. v. Carlton*[338] (retroactive tax legislation), the Supreme Court stressed that a burden "is met simply by showing that the retroactive application of the legislation is itself justified by a rational legislative purpose."[339] Such a relationship was easily found, as the courts had repeatedly refused to judge the wisdom and fairness of legislative choices. The same holds for retroactive emergency legislation (where the Court recognizes the importance of public interest involved[340]) and curative legislation[341]

334 *Ibid.*, p. 452.

335 Nowak & Rotunda (2004), p. 486.

336 In this respect, see Ricciardi and Sinclair's dissatisfaction with this Court's attitude in Ricciardi & Sinclair (1996).

337 *Usery v. Turner Elkhorn Mining Co.*, 428 U.S. 1 (1976).

338 *U.S. v. Carlton*, 512 U.S. 26 (1994).

339 *Ibid.*, p. 31, quoting *Pension Benefit Guaranty Corporation v. R.A. Gray & Co.*, 467 U.S. 717, 730 (1984).

340 See, for example, the case of *Veix v. Sixth Ward Building and Loan Association of Newark*, 310 U.S. 32, 38–39 (1940), where the Court upheld economic depression emergency legislation, and recognized that the public interest is not limited to "health, morals and safety," but "[i]t extends to economic needs as well," with references.

341 Curative legislation or remedial legislation is meant to cure statutory errors or to validate otherwise ineffective administrative proceedings. By means of curative statutes, the legislature cures mostly technical mistakes suggested by the judiciary and thereby serves "the public interest in the smooth functioning of government." In general, curative laws are viewed as a legitimate exercise of legislative power, but this authority is not unlimited. The legislature is, among other things, allowed to change the

(which by definition serves the public interest because it will "remove unintended flaws in existing legislation and help give full effect to the legislative intent behind the initial legislation"[342]), which will usually meet the rationality requirement and therefore pass constitutional muster.[343]

5.7. Conclusion

The purpose of the Due Process Clause is to prevent government acts, including legislation, that are capricious. Although this is not yet an established view, it appears that ad hoc laws which in fact apply to one specific case should be subject to procedural due process, because they resemble specific administrative decisions rather than general statutes. Ad hoc laws which nevertheless take the form of general statutes will normally be governed by the regime of substantive due process. An important question that must then be asked is whether the legislature chose adequate means to achieve a legitimate purpose, a test that does not appear to provide serious guarantees. This test becomes tougher when legislation encroaching on individual fundamental rights is at issue. In that case, the government must prove the compelling government interest that demands passage of that legislation. Interestingly, retroactive legislation is not treated in a different, sterner way in the due process analysis than prospective legislation.

law retroactively using a curative act only when it does not impair private rights that were already vested before the law was enacted. The Supreme Court, however, usually denies vested rights protection if they arose from defective legislation or a government action. The Supreme Court argued in this respect: "Where the asserted vested right, not being linked to any substantial equity, arises from the mistake of officers purporting to administer the law in the name of the Government, the legislature is not prevented from curing the defect in administration simply because the effect may be to destroy causes of action which would otherwise exist." According to the Supreme Court, when the remedy can be applied without injustice, it is allowed. *Graham v. Goodcell*, 282 U.S. 409, 429 (1931). Public rights (rights that are statutorily granted by the legislature) may easily be affected and even reversed by a curative act. See *Hodges v. Snyder*, 261 U.S. 600 (1923) and Ch.B. Hochman, "The Supreme Court and the Constitutionality of Retroactive Legislation," 73 *Harv. L. Rev.* 692, 703–706 (1960).

342 Nowak & Rotunda (2004), p. 489.

343 For more examples of case law in the four categories mentioned by Nowak and Rotunda, see Nowak & Rotunda (2004), pp. 487–494, and Hochman (1960).

Chapter 6

AD HOC LEGISLATION AND DELIBERATIVE DEMOCRACY

Introduction

Hitherto, I have discussed the possible constitutional limitations on the legislature when it enacts laws for particular occasions and cases where the application of the general rules would result in a politically undesirable decision. Besides constitutional implications, an interesting point that deserves more attention is the manner in which such impulsive ad hoc legislation has been enacted. Strikingly, in two of the three examples, the Elizabeth Morgan case and the Northwest Timber Compromise case, substantive rules were designed and adopted for specific cases, without the important safeguard of a deliberative process. Both Acts were passed as small riders to appropriations bills: the Elizabeth Morgan Act constituted one of the sections of the 1997 Department of Transportation Appropriations Act,[344] while the Northwest Timber Compromise was embedded in the 1990 Department of the Interior and Related Agencies Appropriations Act.[345] As will be shown, appropriations bills give Congressmen a great opportunity to push a controversial bill through Congress; a bill that would otherwise fall in the battle to become a law. This may jeopardize democracy.

6.1. Appropriations bills and legislative riders

What are appropriations bills and what is their real purpose? Substantive governmental programs require authorizing legislation. Such authorization is the first step in making the program successful. The second and essential step to make the program work concerns funds that need to be allocated. Such funds are granted by appropriations bills.[346] Once enacted, authorizing legislation does not have to be enacted every year to remain in force. By contrast, there is a real pressure to allocate funds annually to federal programs by means of appropriations acts. Congressional failure to grant money may in

344 Pub. L. 104–205, Sec. 11–925.

345 Pub. L. 101–121, Sec. 318.

346 H.H. Bruff, *Balance of Forces. Separation of Powers Law in the Administrative State*, Carolina Durham, North Carolina: Academic Press 2006, p. 247.

practice lead to frustration of the federal government.[347] The absolute necessity to allocate money in a timely fashion gives some determined Congressmen an opportunity to attach substantive ad hoc provisions to appropriations bills[348] that are controversial and would otherwise "lack the political momentum (or even majority support) necessary for passage."[349] In that way, they can be sure that these proposals will be passed, since the whole appropriations bill *must* and *will* be passed. Such ad hoc rules are called appropriations riders or legislative riders.

For example, the technique of legislative riders was a very attractive tool in the hands of the Republican Congressman who pleaded for Elizabeth Morgan's return to the Unites States without any legal repercussions. The Elizabeth Morgan Bill was a fairly small amendment to the annual appropriations bill, and the chance that the complete appropriations bill would be rejected because of this rider was minimal if not unreal. No Congressman would dare to frustrate the annual appropriations process that simply must be completed within a certain time and under great political pressure, because of one small rider.

The subjects of appropriation riders may vary greatly (the Elizabeth Morgan rider shows how exotic they can be) but they are, in any event, popular in the field of environmental law, where they are "used with particularly destructive effect to circumvent longstanding environmental policies," as Zellmer argues.[350]

6.2. Objections

Appropriations riders are objectionable, and, in Lazarus' opinion, have "serious implications for the transparency of the lawmaking process as well as for the degree to which interested members of the public may both participate in and influence the legislative outcome."[351] Lazarus supports this view by explaining both the procedural differences between the authorizing legislation and appropriations bills, and their substantive repercussions.

347 If Congress does not provide the federal government with money on time, the programs may in fact cease to operate, which can have a great impact on constituents making use of the program. See R.J. Lazarus, "Congressional Descent: The Demise of Deliberative Democracy in Environmental Law," 94 *Georg. L. J.* 635 (2006).

348 Such substantive rules that de facto change substantive laws are often attached to appropriations bills, despite the House and Senate rules that put limitations on policy changes through the use of appropriations bills. See House Rule XXI(2) ("A provision changing existing law may not be reported in a general appropriations bill") and Rule XVI (4) of Standing Rules of the Senate ("On a point of order made by any Senator, no amendment offered by any other Senator which proposes general legislation shall be received to any general appropriation bill, nor shall any amendment not germane or relevant to the subject matter contained in the bill be received; nor shall any amendment to any item or clause of such bill be received which does not directly relate thereto…"), at <www.gpoaccess.gov/hrm/index.html>.

349 Lazarus (2006), p. 635.

350 S.B. Zellmer, "Sacrificing Legislative Integrity on the Altar of Appropriations Riders: A Constitutional Crisis," 21 *Harv. Envtl. L. Rev.* 457 (1997).

351 Lazarus (2006), p. 652.

6.2.1. *Procedural aspects*

As far as procedural differences are concerned, he demonstrates that, despite the common and general label of "law," authorizing legislation is different from appropriations legislation. He summarizes the differences in the following way. Unlike authorizing legislation, which is considered by experts on the subject of authorizing laws, appropriations bills (and thus also legislative riders) are handled by the appropriations committees that usually deal with budget and spending rate issues. In such a committee, there is little knowledge about the substantive issues included in legislative riders. Moreover, the members of the authorization committees formally have no competences to discuss the rider.[352] The technique of appropriations riders also frustrates transparency and the deliberative process, since the appropriations committees are not formally subject to rules that promote such ideals. As Lazarus illustrates, for example, it is not required for the appropriations committees to publicly announce the date, time, and subject matter of legislative hearings.[353]

Outside the appropriations committees, there is little meaningful debate on the small legislative riders, and sometimes none at all. The reason is that the riders are embedded in omnibus appropriations bills having hundreds or even thousands of pages. Since the riders do not appear in the tables of contents of appropriations bills, it is impossible to track them down.[354] An interested Congressman would then have to go through the whole bill (it is no secret that legislators do not do so), firstly to find it and secondly to initiate a debate on it that could influence congressional voting on the entire appropriations bill. In practice, only very controversial riders that receive a great deal of publicity will be discussed, but the question is still whether they would substantively influence the passage of the entire act.

6.2.2. *Substantive result*

The use of legislative riders has significant substantive consequences, as Lazarus illustrates by way of the Congressional enactments of legislative riders in the field of environmental law.[355] Most importantly, legislative riders help to destroy substantive legislative policy which was first developed in the course of extensive research, after years of experience and compromises between different parties. Such long-term policy is easily damaged when legislators agree on ad hoc rules that often serve special interests and are generated by short-term thinking.[356] The resulting laws lack any coherency and systematic approach to environmental law issues:[357]

352 *Ibid.*, pp. 654–655.
353 Standing Rules of Senate, Rule XXVI(1)-(4), Lazarus (2006), p. 655.
354 Lazarus (2006), p. 660.
355 The objections apply to non-environmental riders as well.
356 Lazarus (2006), pp. 661–664.
357 *Ibid.*, p. 662.

There is no particular resulting policy coherence in the final product, which represents an expedient amalgam of individual legislative preferences sharing in common only the simple fact that each is tied to the same bill. It is literally akin to a Christmas tree on which enough members of Congress have hung their favorite ornaments with little regard (or perhaps even knowledge) of what else is on that same tree.

6.3. Appropriations riders and the Supreme Court

Initially, the Supreme Court regarded repeals or changes by appropriations bills with suspicion. In the *Tellico Dam* case, which has already been mentioned several times, the Supreme Court rejected the idea that substantive law provisions can be implicitly changed or repealed by an appropriations bill.[358] In the Supreme Court's view, the mere fact that the legislature constantly allocated funds for the continuation and ultimately completion of a certain project does not mean that it also intended to exempt the project from the well-considered general substantive legislation that represents the long-term policy. The Supreme Court supports this conclusion by referring to the specific character of appropriations legislation. The Court recognized that both the substantive legislation (in the *Tellico Dam* case, it was the Endangered Species Act) and the appropriations legislation are "Acts of Congress," "but the latter have the limited and specific purpose of providing funds for authorized programs."[359] In its decision, the Supreme Court endorsed the substantive objections against the repeal or change of substantive legislation by appropriations bills, using the argument that it would be surprising if legislation that deals with money could implicitly repeal a substantive law prepared by experts in the relevant field, and in a long and conscientious process.[360]

The converse is true for the *explicit* statement of the legislature in an appropriations statute that aims at changing the substantive legislation for one case or exempting the case from the applicability of such rules. If the legislature makes such a determination in an appropriations act in a "clear and manifest"[361] way, the Supreme Court will accept it. Following this line of reasoning, the Supreme Court approved the legislative rider in the Northwest Timber Compromise. The Court decided: "First, although repeals by

358 *TVA v. Hill*, 437 U.S. 153 (1978). This Supreme Court judgment refers to the appropriations legislation that allocated money to the Tellico Dam project and therefore violated the Endangered Species Act, which in fact prohibited the completion of the dam. This judgment does not deal with the appropriations rider that was enacted subsequent to the Supreme Court's judgment to accomplish the completion of the dam.

359 *TVA v. Hill*, 437 U.S. 153, 190 (1978).

360 *Ibid.*, p. 191. McCubbins and Rodriguez have problems with this approach. According to them, appropriation bills are the most suitable type of legislation to make changes in substantive legislation. They argue: "Legislative changes subsequent to the original enactment are to be encouraged; they represent legislative appreciation of the role of changed circumstances (or, in some instances, changed politics). Legislative changes through the appropriations process may well ease these changes; they enable Congress to limit the scope and reach of a legislative policy without dismantling the policy altogether; they permit a greater range of discretion by providing a more finely tuned instrument of revision and change." M.D. McCubbins & D.B. Rodriguez, "Canonical Construction and Statutory Revisionism: The Strange Case of the Appropriations Canon," 14 *J. Contemp. Legal Issues* 669 (2005).

361 *TVA v. Hill*, 437 U.S. 153, 190 (1978), quoting *Wood v. United States*, 10 L.Ed. 987 (1842).

implication are especially disfavored in the appropriations context [...] Congress nonetheless may amend substantive law in an appropriations statute, as long as it does so clearly [...]. Second, because subsection (b)(6)(A) [challenged provision] provided *by its terms* that compliance with certain new law constituted compliance with certain old law, the intent to modify was not only clear, but express."[362] Deciding in this way, the Supreme Court unambiguously approved the practice of changing substantive legislation by legislative riders embedded in omnibus spending bills (such riders are usually clear enough), thereby unfortunately ignoring the procedural differences between the enactment of substantive legislation and appropriations legislation, as described in subsection 6.2.1.

6.4. Conclusion

The absence of a firm constitutional provision prohibiting legislation by appropriations bills makes it easy for legislators to get legislation passed which is fairly controversial and probably would not get sufficient political support if it were subjected to the regular democratic process. Despite objections to the method of inserting substantive legislative provisions into appropriations bills, the main criticism being that it frustrates the democratic process, legislators make extensive use of it. This method guaranteed enactment of the ad hoc provisions of the Elizabeth Morgan Act and the Northwest Timber Compromise.

362 *Robertson v. Seattle Audubon Soc.*, 503 U.S. 429, 440 (1992).

IN SUM

Legislative policy often originates from actual events and specific cases.[363] As the cases of Terri Schiavo, Elisabeth Morgan, and Northwest Timber Compromise illustrate, specific cases may sometimes become the sole focus of legislative acts. Based on the previous description of the phenomenon of ad hoc legislation in light of constitutional limitations, I can make the following final remarks.

Phenomenon of ad hoc legislation

While studying ad hoc legislation in United States practice and constitutional law at Georgetown Law Center in Washington, D.C., I regularly spoke to law school professors and congressional experts. During the first meetings, when I explained my research subject, asking about the occurrence of ad hoc laws in the United States, the American experts spontaneously tended to ask: "What exactly is your problem? This is how we do it in the United States." In many cases, this is true. Laws that are enacted for a specific case are not unusual, which is evidenced by a long tradition of private bills and special interest legislation that includes privileges for specific individuals or corporations. In the field of environmental law, legislation for specific infrastructural projects can be found as well.

Although such laws are accepted as such in the everyday legislative arena, this does not mean that they are not criticized. For example, particular concerns have arisen about private bills resulting from bribery. Legal scholars who commented on special interest legislation pointed out the negative effects for the general, public interest, and the public at large. In addition, there are case-specific laws that generate serious criticism from the constitutional point of view as evidenced, most explicitly, in Chapter II.1.

Constitutional constraints

This study shows that there are a number of constitutional constraints that can be imposed on a legislature when it acts in specific cases. One of the main principles is the separation of

363 Wise gives an example of a former basketball player who was found dead two days after he had appeared at a press conference. He died from a drug overdose. Because the case attracted media attention and was subject to a broad public debate on the drug crisis, the legislature decided to act. Anti-drug bills were swiftly introduced and six months after the incident, a new Anti-Drug Act was enacted. C. Wise, *The Dynamics of Legislation*, San Francisco, Oxford: Jossey-Bass Publishers 1991, p. 3.

powers, which applies to legislation that interferes with pending cases or directs the reopening of finally decided cases. They also include the prohibition of bills of attainder and ex post facto laws. Other constraining principles are equal treatment and due process.

First of all, it is striking that the U.S. Constitution does not contain any general prohibition of laws which are not generally applicable. On the one hand, this is not strange, since private bills are part of a deep-rooted tradition. On the other, it is at least remarkable, because the state constitutions do generally prohibit special legislation. Although proposals to insert such a prohibition in the federal Constitution have repeatedly been put forth, there has been no political will to support such a broad limitation of the legislative power of Congress. Nevertheless, lessons have been learned from English practice, and bills singling out one specific person or an easily defined group of persons for punishment are absolutely prohibited by the U.S. Constitution.

Besides the Bill of Attainder Clause, several other constitutional principles can limit legislative power, but whether or not they apply to ad hoc laws depends on their effects rather than their case-specific character. Neither case-specific motives of the legislature, nor case-specific application are significant for the courts when they examine the contested legislation in light of the constitutional principles of ex post facto, equal treatment, due process, or the separation of powers. With the exception of the separation of powers principle and the prohibition of retroactively punishing laws, which appear to be more absolute in nature, a decisive question for the permissibility of ad hoc laws is whether they can be justified. These principles do not stand in the way of ad hoc legislation relating to a legitimate government interest.

In general, it can be stated that federal courts, when they are not directly affected by the contested ad hoc statute themselves and that statute does not infringe fundamental rights or make a distinction on the basis of such characteristics as race, rather defer to the political choices of Congress. Particularly with regard to economic legislation, the courts conclude that constitutional provisions do not give them "a license [...] to judge the wisdom, fairness of logic of legislative choices."[364] Except for the Bill of Attainder Clause, the applicable constitutional principles *as applied by the courts* in many cases prove not to offer a strong constitutional guarantee in the context of ad hoc legislation.

Deliberative democracy

Although the primary focus of ad hoc legislation in the United States was on constitutional principles, it should be emphasized that ad hoc legislation is also problematic from the point of view of deliberative democracy. The manner in which the political process of legislating in the United States is arranged makes the introduction of ad hoc laws attractive and their passage rather easy. The ad hoc laws in two of the three high-profile cases described in Chapter II.1 were enacted as riders to omnibus appropriations bills. The absence of a constitutional provision prohibiting legislating by substantive riders to appropriations bills and the inability of Congress to enforce its own internal rules limiting the political process make this method an attractive tool for Congressmen to push difficult and controversial bills through Congress.

364 *FCC v. Beach Communications, Inc.*, 508 U.S. 307, 314 (1993), quoting *Vance v. Bradley*, 440 U.S. 93, 97 (1979).

PART III

GERMANY

Chapter 1

AD HOC LEGISLATION: CASES

Introduction

In Chapter III.1, I discuss two examples of ad hoc legislation, namely, the Lex Schörner and the Lex Stendal.[365] In each case, I describe the facts and then discuss the legislative intervention. Afterwards, I present the constitutional and other objections to the intervening legislation, and offer conclusions.

1.1. The Schörner case

1.1.1. Background

The case of Ferdinand Schörner recalls the difficult history of Germany and the Second World War in particular. As a successful, but ruthless field marshal, Schörner was a very controversial person. He served as a soldier in both the First and the Second World War, but the broad criticism is especially directed at his attitude in the last phase of the Second World War. At that time, he was a passionate national socialist. He was one of Hitler's best commanders. Hitler even appointed him as a Commander-in-Chief of the army for the northern and middle division. Among the other soldiers, Schörner had a reputation for cruelty, which earned him nicknames like "terror flyer" (*Terrorflieger*) and "bloodhound" (*Bluthund*).[366] He earned the most disrespect, however, when he abandoned his troops on May 9, 1945, after the capitulation of Germany and, pretending to be a civilian, tried to escape by plane to Austria.[367] Eventually, he was arrested by the Americans who handed him over to the Russian authorities. In the USSR, he was sentenced to twenty-five years in prison, but his sentence was reduced and he was able to return to Germany in 1955, after the Federal Chancellor negotiated the release of 9,626

[365] For the selection of cases, see Chapter I.5.2.

[366] B.O. Manig, "Der Bluthund ist zurück," *Zeit Online*, no. 37, 2005, p. 90 <www.zeit.de/2005/37/A-Sch_9arner_neu> (last accessed on June 12, 2011).

[367] P. Steinkamp, "Generalfeldmarschall Ferdinand Schörner," in: G.R. Ueberschär, *Hitlers militärische Elite. Bd. 2 Vom Kriegsbeginn bis zum Weltkriegsende*, Darmstadt: Primus Verlag 1998, p. 238. This episode has also been described in detail by Kaltenegger in his biography of Schörner: R. Kaltenegger, *Schörner. Feldmarschall der letzten Stunde. Biographie*, München, Berlin: Herbig 1994, pp. 305–316.

war prisoners from Russian captivity. As a result of these successful negotiations, the Chancellor's popularity grew enormously[368] and everyone was happy with the release of the soldiers, with one exception. Schörner's return led to a lot of controversy and public debate. One of the most discussed issues was the fact that, according to the general laws existing at that time, Schörner, like other officers of Hitler's regime, was entitled to a state retirement pension and could therefore spend a carefree old age in Germany.[369] This was unacceptable, not only to the public at large, but also to the various military organizations and political parties, which were of the opinion that Schörner did not deserve a state pension.

1.1.2. The Lex Schörner

Under public pressure, Schörner was subjected to a disciplinary procedure, because he had abandoned his troops and had tried to escape to Austria. During this procedure, the German Parliament enacted a law that addressed the problem of pensions for, among other persons in public service, officers who had returned from foreign captivity. The law added a new provision to a criminal statute. The first paragraph provided the following:[370]

> (1) Wird gegen eine Person, auf die Kapitel I oder §62 des Gesetzes zur Regelung der Rechtsverhältnisse der unter Artikel 131 des Grundgesetzes fallenden Personen Anwendung findet, wegen eines vor dem Inkrafttreten des Gesetzes begangenen Dienstvergehens oder einer vor Inkrafttreten des Gesetzes begangenen, als Dienstvergehen geltenden Handlung das förmliche Disziplinarverfahren nach §9 des Gesetzes eingeleitet, so gelten die nach dem Gesetz zu zahlenden Bezüge in voller Höhe als einbehalten. Die Einleitungsbehörde kann jederzeit zur Vermeidung besonderer Härten die Einbehaltung der Bezüge anderweit regeln.

Accordingly, once a disciplinary procedure had been initiated, the person subjected to this procedure lost the full amount of his pension money, except in cases of extreme hardship.

The law, generally called "Lex Schörner," was given retroactive effect as of January 1, 1953, and was immediately invoked by the Federal Minister of Domestic Affairs in Schörner's case.

368 According to Manig (2005).

369 By granting these officers a state pension, the German government gave them an opportunity to integrate into the new society.

370 Sec. 1 (2) of the Gesetz zur Ergänzung des Gesetzes zur Änderung und Ergänzung des Dienststrafrechts of August 5, 1955. BGBl. I S. 497. The provision refers to persons called "131-ers." This designation refers to Art. 131 of the German Basic Law which required that the legal position of persons who were public servants at the time of the German capitulation in the Second World War was to be regulated by law.

1.1.2.1. Objections, constitutional, and otherwise to the Lex Schörner

The law was not only a cause of concern for other officers and persons in public service, who were afraid of losing their own pension rights, but was also criticized by academics, who argued that the law was incompatible with the German Basic Law. Eventually, the Federal Disciplinary Court requested the Federal Constitutional Court (*Bundesverfassungsgericht*) to pass judgment on the constitutionality of the Lex Schörner. The major[371] constitutional objections to the law as put forward in that Court were directed at the problems of the specificity of the Act, its retroactivity, the equality principle, and the separation of powers principle.

Violation of the prohibition of special laws (Einzelfallgesetze)

Art. 19 (1) of the Basic Law prohibits case-specific laws that limit individuals' rights. In other words, if the legislature intends to restrict individuals' rights, it is only allowed to do so by means of a general law: "Insofar as, under this Basic Law, a basic right may be restricted by or pursuant to a law, such a law must apply generally and not merely to a single case."[372] The argument put forward in the academic debate about the Lex Schörner pointed to the possible violation of that prohibition. A detailed analysis of the Lex Schörner in light of that prohibition can be found in Krüger's work. Her scientific exploration eventually led to the conclusion that Lex Schörner was incompatible with Art. 19 (1) GG.

Krüger began her analysis by stating that Art. 19 (1), as it protects individuals against decisions of the majority, is one of the most important norms of the constitutional order: in a conflict situation between democracy and the rule of law, the rule of law prevails.[373] In her interpretation, Art. 19 (1) prohibits individual laws (*Individualgesetze*) that apply to a single case and requires general and abstract laws (they must be repeatedly applicable) if they restrict civil rights.[374]

The author analyzed the parliamentary history of the Lex Schörner, as it could be helpful to answer the question whether the Lex Schörner was a prohibited case-specific law. More surprisingly perhaps, the Schörner case was not mentioned as such during the debates in the *Bundestag*, in contrast to the debates in the *Bundesrat*.[375]

As stated by a parliamentary commission working on civil servants law, the bill in question was generated by the fact that in the application of the existing law a few gaps

371 The most important criticism from the academic debate will be presented here. Not all constitutional challenges put forward by the Disciplinary Court will be discussed. The reason is that some of them are very complicated and very closely connected to the national rules, for example the principle of the professional civil service, which requires that civil servants must be guaranteed the necessary financial support for the period that they were active as civil servants (Art. 33 Sec. 5 GG).

372 Art. 19 (1) of the Basic Law for the Federal Republic of Germany, version of December 2003, published by the German *Bundestag* Administration. Henceforth, this document is referred to whenever provisions from the German Basic Law are cited in English.

373 H. Krüger, Die Verfassungswidrigkeit der lex Schörner, *DVBl.* 1955, p. 760.

374 *Ibid.*, p. 762.

375 *Bundesanzeiger* (the Official Gazette of the German Federal Agencies) No. 141, July 26, 1955, p. 6.

had been found that needed to be closed. The commission pointed to the fact that it would be unreasonable if a person who was suspected of committing serious acts that led to a disciplinary procedure should nevertheless have a right to receive a state pension.[376]

The question is, however, whether it is pure coincidence that the Act was proposed at the time the disciplinary procedure against Schörner was initiated, in the wake of a fierce public debate about Schörner's pension rights.[377] For Krüger, it was not: she calls the law "a disguised case-specific law" (*getarntes Individualgesetz*), the sole purpose of which was to affect the outcome of the Schörner case. Its general wording did not make any difference.[378]

Retroactivity of the Act and the equality principle

Krüger also argued that Lex Schörner was void because it violated the constitutional prohibition of retroactive legislation. She connected the case specificity to the retroactive character of the Lex Schörner. In her view, the specificity of the law was clearly demonstrated by its retroactive effect. If the law only applied to future cases, one could say that the Schörner case only gave *cause* for new legislation. The retroactive effect of the law, however, left no doubt that its purpose was to provide rules specifically for Schörner's case:[379]

> Da das allgemeine Gesetz ein hypothetisches Urteil über zukünftiges Verhalten vor Rechtssubjekten ist, ist das rückwirkende Gesetz kein allgemeines Gesetz, denn es regelt eine bestimmte zählbare Anzahl von bereits vor Erlaß des Gesetzes vollendeten Tatbeständen. Wie deutlich wird das bei der lex Schörner! Ohne Rückwirkung wäre der Fall Schörner nur der

376 Schriftlicher Bericht des Ausschusses für Beamtenrecht, BT Drs. 1545: "Bei der Anwendung der Bundesdisziplinarordnung sind zwei Lücken hervorgetreten, die eine Ergänzung des Gesetzes notwendig machen. [...] Bei dem Vorliegen ernster Verfehlungen wäre es nicht zu verantworten, wenn den belasteten Personen Rechte nach dem Gesetz zu Art. 131 GG zuerkannt und Bezüge angewiesen würden, die ihnen im Disziplinarverfahren wieder aberkannt werden müßten. Der Gesetzentwurf [...] sieht deshalb vor, daß mit der Einleitung des Disziplinarverfahrens die nach dem Gesetz zu zahlenden **Bezüge in voller Höhe** als **einbehalten** gelten."

377 The bill was proposed on March 31, 1955, which was exactly the same day on which a disciplinary procedure against Schörner was started by the Federal Ministry of Domestic Affairs, BVerfGE 7, 129 (132). Moreover, the subject of Schörner's pension was discussed in the Cabinet meeting, where not only different federal ministers, but also the Federal Chancellor stressed that Schörner should not receive any payments from the State: "Zu der Entlassung des ehem. Generalfeldmarschalls Schörner bemerkt der Minister, Schörner dürfe mit Rücksicht auf seine Vergangenheit unter keinen Umständen eine Pension erhalten" and "[d]er Bundeskanzler betont, daß Zahlungen an Schörner unbedingt vermieden werden müßten," M. Hollmann & K. Von Jena, *Die Kabinettsprotokolle der Bundesregierung*, Vol. 8, 1955, München: R. Oldenbourg Verlag 1997, pp. 124–125.

378 Krüger (1955), p. 762. She argues: "Alle auf den Einzelfall oder gegen die Einzelperson gemünzten Gesetze, seien sie konkrete oder abstrakte-"getarnte"-Individualgesetze, wollte Art. 19 Abs. 1 S 1 GG treffen." She stresses therefore that it should not be the form that makes the law a prohibited case-specific law, but the purpose (and the legislative intention that generates the purpose) of the Act, which is to provide rules for a specific case or person (*ibid.*, p. 794).

379 Krüger (1955), p. 795.

> Anlaß für das Gesetz vom 5.8.1955 gewesen (…). Aber durch die angeordnete Rückwirkung ist der Fall Schörner Ziel und Zweck des Gesetzgebers geworden.

Moreover, she argued that retroactive legislation in general violates the equality principle.

Scheerbarth considered the retroactive character of a law in relation to the equality principle rather than to the generality principle. In his analysis, he distinguished two groups of retroactive laws: 1) laws which provide legal rules for future cases and also subject past cases to the new regime, and 2) retroactive laws that apply exclusively to past facts and are meant as measures: instead of providing legal norms for past situations (laws which can be called *Ordnungen*); they provide measures that are meant to achieve a certain purpose. In Scheerbarth's view, the Lex Schörner was a special measure law (*Maßnahmegesetz*). He argued that measure laws are unconstitutional only if they violate the equality principle. This principle is violated if the legislature's intention is to govern one specific case. According to Scheerbarth, Lex Schörner was such a special measure law which was meant for the Schörner case. It therefore violated the equality principle.[380] In the view of the Federal Disciplinary Court, the legislation retroactively imposed punishment, which is forbidden by Art. 103 §2 of the Basic Law. The Lex Schörner was thus unconstitutional.

Separation of powers principle

The Lex Schörner was also criticized for its possible conflict with the principle of the separation of powers. This argument addressed the separation between the legislative and the executive branches. Different commentators concluded that the Act in fact constituted an executive order, by means of which the legislature decided on a specific case.[381] Krüger even called it an abuse of the instrument of legislation to govern specific cases (*Formenmißbrauch*)[382] and concluded that the law was therefore unconstitutional. Schultz doubted whether the Act was unconstitutional as a result of a violation of the separation of powers principle, since it was written in general terms and therefore applied to future cases as well. Nevertheless, he found the way the legislature had acted worrying, especially because the rights of other persons involved in a disciplinary procedure would be limited only for the sake of Schörner's case.[383]

The ad hoc character of the law

Objections that had been expressed in the academic literature addressed not only the problem of the constitutionality or unconstitutionality of Lex Schörner, but also the

[380] H.W. Scheerbarth, "Zur 'Rückwirkung' von Gesetzen, insbesondere der 'Lex Schörner'," *DVBl.* 1956, p. 399.

[381] See, for example, W. Gross, who addressed the problem of separation of powers: W. Gross, "Die Entwicklung des öffentlichen Rechts," *DVBl.* 1955, p. 390.

[382] Krüger (1955), p. 792.

[383] G. Schultz, "Rundschau. Blick in die Zeit," *MDR* 1955, p. 337.

manner in which the legislation had been proposed and enacted. Gross and Schultz pointed out the impulsive character of Lex Schörner. Gross was seriously concerned about the way the German *Bundestag* had acted. In his view, the *Bundestag* had overreacted. Moreover, he concluded that Lex Schörner was a matter of *voluntas* and not *ratio*, thereby diminishing the value of the Act.[384] Schultz similarly criticized the expediency, emotions, and suspected reasons in relation to the law's enactment.[385]

1.1.2.2. The *Bundesverfassungsgericht's* judgment

The Federal Constitutional Court rejected all constitutional objections to the Lex Schörner and found no violation of the Basic Law. As far as the argument that the law infringed Art. 19 (1) was concerned, the Court ordered that it could be true that the new legislation was generated by the case of Fieldmarshal Schörner. It was that case which made the legislature realize that there were gaps in the old law. The specificity of the intention, however, did not automatically mean that the law was to be classified as a forbidden *Einzelfallgesetz* within the meaning of Art. 19 (1). Laws enacted in response to a specific case which are nevertheless general are not problematic.[386]

> Aber selbst wenn man unterstellt, daß der "Fall Schörner" den Anstoß zur gesetzlichen Regelung gegeben habe, so folgt daraus doch nur, daß sich der Gesetzgeber erst aus Anlaß dieses Einzelfalles dessen bewußt geworden ist, daß die ursprüngliche Regelung eine Lücke aufwies, die auszufüllen war.

The retroactivity of the law was also justified in the Court's view. It decided that when the legislature enacts a complicated and extensive law, the law may have certain gaps or (technical) errors that manifest themselves at a later stage. Subsequent legislative corrections of these errors which have a retroactive effect are desired under certain circumstances, namely when allowed on the grounds of equity.[387] Such corrections are also allowed if some individuals unintentionally benefited from the original law's mistakes. The Court argued further: it would even contradict the principle of the social State[388] if the legislature were prohibited from correcting mistakes that are disadvantageous to the public at large, and some persons receive undeserved profits from public resources.[389] The Court was also aware that retroactive legislation may threaten the principle of legal certainty. Retroactive corrections of legislative acts are not problematic, however, if such corrections are not contrary to the system of the law to be changed and if they are in harmony with the original meaning and object of the law. Conversely, if the legislature pretended to complement the law, but it in fact created new

384 Gross (1955), p. 390.
385 Schultz (1955), p. 336.
386 BVerfGE 7, 129 (150–151).
387 BVerfGE 7, 129 (152).
388 The principle of social state belongs to the constitutional law of Germany. It includes a state which is based on the principles of social justice and social security, see, Art. 28 (1) GG.
389 BVerfGE 7, 129 (152).

rules that had little to do with the original meaning, it would infringe the principle of legal certainty:[390]

> Ergänzende gesetzliche Regelungen, die solche Irrtümer nachträglich beseitigen und Lücken schließen wollen, sind jedenfalls dann nicht zu beanstanden, wenn sie sich ohne Bruch dem ursprünglichen System des Gesetzes, seinem Sinn und Zweck harmonisch einfügen, wenn sie nicht in sich Verfassungsverstöße enthalten und wenn es sich auch nicht etwa darum handelt, daß der Gesetzgeber unter dem Anschein einer nachträglichen Ergänzung in Wahrheit eine wesensfremde Gesetzesänderung lediglich für den Rest der nachträglich noch zu regelnden Fälle vornehmen will.

In the Court's opinion, such a false legislative motive was not present in the case of Lex Schörner.

This line of reasoning, ending with a conclusion that the Lex Schörner was in keeping with the original meaning and object of the previous law, and had been enacted on the basis of neutral and just reasons, was used in the Court's analysis of the equal protection claim as well. This led to the conclusion that Lex Schörner did not infringe the equality principle of Art. 3 of the Basic Law. This principle neither requires the reopening of definitively decided cases nor prevents the legislature from correcting legislative errors if this is fully in line with the original meaning and purpose of the legislation.[391]

1.1.3. Concluding remarks

The case of Ferdinand Schörner shows that one controversial case can motivate the legislature to change a general piece of legislation. Although it was clear to the public that the law was in fact meant to prevent Schörner from receiving his state pension (the Act was nicknamed "Lex Schörner" as a result), the *Bundestag* tried very carefully to avoid the name Schörner during the preparation of the Act. The result was a general law, through which the legislature was even prepared to sacrifice the rights of other civil servants only to obtain a certain, politically desired result in the individual case of Ferdinand Schörner.

The academic world was shocked and sharply criticized the new piece of legislation. Legal scholars not only accused the legislature of acting unprofessionally by letting public opinion direct the legislative agenda, but they also put forth several constitutional objections which, in their view, made the Act unconstitutional. Unexpectedly, the *Bundesverfassungsgericht* disagreed with the critics and found no violation of the Basic Law.

390 BVerfGE 7, 129 (152) with reference to BVerfGE 4, 219 (243–246).
391 BVerfGE 7, 129 (153–154).

1.2. Südumfahrung Stendal

1.2.1. Background

West and East Germany were reunified in 1990. As a result, much new investment was required, especially in the economy and the infrastructure. New transportation connections that would facilitate the connection between West and East Germany were either lacking or not functioning properly, which was particularly problematic for economic development in East Germany. The federal government addressed this problem in a project called "*Verkehrsprojekte Deutsche Einheit*" (German Reunification Infrastructural Projects).[392]

The government, however was most concerned about difficult and time-consuming administrative procedures that normally had to be followed for each new infrastructural project. It takes many years for the plans to be officially approved, the environmental impact assessments made, private and public interest groups consulted, licenses granted, and any expropriations to be executed.[393] Possible judicial procedures may be an important factor holding up the execution of a project or even making it impossible. To shorten this long period, several pieces of legislation were enacted at the beginning of the 1990s:[394] the *Verkehrswegeplanungsbeschleunigungsgesetz* of 1991,[395] the *Planungsvereinfachungsgesetz* of 1993,[396] the *Magnetschwebebahnplanungs-gesetz* of 1994,[397] and the *Genemigungsverfahrensbeschleunigungsgesetz* of 1996.[398]

1.2.2. Accelerating legislation

The laws listed above were aimed at shorter periods and easier procedures for administrative decision-making on the infrastructural projects in the former states of the German Democratic Republic and in other important parts of the western states.[399] Especially the first Act (*Verkehrswegeplanungs- beschleunigungsgesetz*) represented a new

392 B. Stüer, "Investitionsmaßnahmegesetze als Verfassungsproblem," *DVBl.* 1991, p. 1333. See also the information about the project on the website of the Federal Ministry of Transport, Building and Urban Affairs at <www.bmvbs.de>.

393 At the beginning of the 1990s, the average period for bigger infrastructural projects from the moment of the first initiative to the moment of factual realization was estimated to be between 10 and 20 years. See W. Blümel, *Verkehrswegeplanung in Deutschland*, Forschungsinstitut für öffentliche Verwaltung, Speyer 1991, p. 137.

394 Blümel strikingly describes the reaction to the reunification of East and West Germany as acceleration euphoria (*Beschleunigungseuphorie*).

395 Gesetz zur Beschleunigung der Planungen für Verkehrswege in den neuen Ländern sowie im Land Berlin of December 6, 1991, BGBl. I S. 2174.

396 Gesetz zur Vereinfachung der Planungsverfahren für Verkehrswege of December 17, 1993, BGBl. I S. 2123. See also M. Ronellenfitsch, "Neues Verkehrswegeplanungs-recht," *DVBl.* 1994, pp. 441–449.

397 Gesetz zur Regelung des Planungsverfahrens für Magnetschwebebahnen of November 23, 1994, BGBl. I S. 3486 November 23, 1994, BGBl. I S. 3486.

398 Gesetz zur Beschleunigung von Genehmigungsverfahre*n* of September 12, 1996, BGBl. I S. 1354.

399 Sec. 1 (1) 5 of the Verkehrswegeplanungsbeschleunigungsgesetz. See also Gesetz zur Beschleunigung von Planungsverfahren für Infrastrukturvorhaben of December 9, 2006, BGBl. I S. 2833.

development in administrative law. The law was criticized, however,[400] because it limited both the requirement of an environmental impact assessment and the opportunity of the public to be consulted and to put forth objections. It was even suggested that the law might therefore violate the European Directive requiring the Member States of the European Union to make an environmental impact assessment for infrastructural projects.[401] Finally, the limitation of legal protection to only one authority, namely the Federal Administrative Court (*Bundesverwaltungs-gericht*), was considered inadequate and problematic.[402]

Serious constitutional objections first arose when, in addition to this general accelerating law, the legislature started to enact additional specific laws in which it decided on the permissibility of individual infrastructural projects in East Germany.[403] These individual laws, called "special measure laws" (*Investitionsmaßnahmegesetze*) could be viewed as aimed at accelerating the construction of such infrastructural projects. The first project to be regulated by a legislative act was one section of the railway connection between Berlin and Hannover, which was commonly called Südumfahrung Stendal.[404]

1.2.3. The Südumfahrung Stendal Act

The Act determined the permissibility of a new piece of the Federal Railways as a part of the railway connection between Berlin and Oebisfelde. The construction was to be carried out according to the plan appended to the Act *and* irrespective of any other administrative rules and procedures that normally apply to infrastructural projects. No administrative licenses were required:

> Weitere behördliche Entscheidungen, insbesondere öffentlich-rechtliche Genehmigungen, Verleihungen, Erlaubnisse, Bewilligungen, Zustimmungen und Planfeststellungen sind nicht erforderlich.

400 See, for example, W. Brohm, "Beschleunigung der Verwaltungsverfahren-Straffung oder konsensuales Verwaltungshandeln?," *NVwZ* 1991, pp. 1025–1033.

401 *Ibid.*, p. 1027, referring to Council Directive 85/337/EEC.

402 It is fair to question the extent to which the new law indeed accelerated the procedures for the infrastructural projects, as the Federal Administrative Court had already issued more than 30 decisions generated by the application of that law in the first few years after it was enacted. See, S. Paetow, "Rechtsprechung zum Verkehrswegeplanungsbeschleunigungsgesetz," *DVBl.* 1994, pp. 94–100.

403 J. Würtenberger, " 'Maßnahmegesetze' zur Beschleunigung der Verkehrsplanung?," *VBlBW* 1992, pp. 1–4.

404 Gesetz über den Bau der "Südumfahrung Stendal" der Eisenbahnstrecke Berlin-Oebisfelde of October 29, 1993, BGBl. I S. 1906. The second special measure law was the Gesetz über den Bau des Abschnitts Wismar West-Wismar Ost der Bundesautobahn A 20 Lübeck-Bundesgrenze (A11) of March 2, 1994, BGBl. I S. 734. The enactment of special measure laws in order to realize the "German Reunification" project was proposed by the government: *Beschlußvorlage zur Kabinettvorlage. Entwurf eines rechtlichen Grundgerüstes für Investitionsmaßnahmegesetze zur Umsetzung der Verkehrsprojekte "Deutsche Einheit." Anlage 3 zur Kabinettsache des BMV*, August 20, 1991.

Moreover, all legal relations in the sphere of public law between the federal railway company which became responsible for the plans and others affected by the plans were to be governed by the Act.[405] The Federal Secretary of Transport was further authorized by that Act to change or supplement the plans, if necessary.[406]

1.2.3.1. Constitutional challenges

This special measure law (*Maßnahmegesetz*) was strongly criticized during the parliamentary process, and constitutional objections were eventually raised in the Federal Constitutional Court. In the *Bundesrat*, the representatives of the State of Hessen could not agree on the bill. They argued that it was unconstitutional for at least the following reasons.

Violation of the separation of powers principle

According to the argument, the legislature had violated the constitutional principle of the separation of powers, since it in fact took over the functions of the executive. It is among the competences of the executive power to decide on the permissibility of individual projects, on the basis of general legislation. In the view of the government of the State of Hessen, by taking measures for a specific project, the legislature had in fact applied the general laws. The legislative decision replaced the required administrative decision-making and therefore left no more margin for administrative bodies to apply general laws to specific projects.[407]

Critics argued that, even if the separation of powers principle in a democratic *Rechtsstaat* cannot be viewed as a mechanical separation between the three State powers, but should rather be viewed as a division of different functions, that principle would still be violated. Ronellenfitsch argues that, if the legislature did take over the administrative function, it would still be subject to the conditions connected with that function. In other words, if the legislature grants licenses by a legislative act for individual projects, then it is bound by the general legislation that applies to these projects: building regulations, environmental laws, etc. In such situations, no margin of appreciation exists for the legislature: when the requirements of the generally applicable laws are met, the licenses must be granted. Vice versa: no licenses may be granted if not all obligatory conditions are fulfilled. Such bound decision-making is alien to the democratic legislature, which operates according to the majority principle, Ronellenfitsch argues. He also doubted the capability (the required expertise, time, etc.) of the legislature to perform the executive function:[408] "Maßnahmegesetze im engeren Sinne für Straßen- und Bahnvorhaben würde die Planung und Realiserung der Vorhaben zur Aufgabe des Parlaments machen. Das will wohl niemand ernstlich, ganz absehen davon, daß die

405 Sec. 1 (2) of the *Südumfahrung Stendal* Act.

406 Sec. 2 (1) of the *Südumfahrung Stendal* Act.

407 BR Drs. 513/2/92, pp. 2–3.

408 M. Ronellenfitsch, "Maßnahmegesetze zur Beschleunigung von Verkehrsprojekten," *DÖV* 1991, pp. 779–780.

Parlamente gar nicht in der Lage waren, diese Aufgabe wahrzunehmen. Der erstrebte Zeitgewinn erweist sich als Utopie."[409]

Violation of the right of self-government of municipalities

The sovereignty of the municipalities and their right to self-government is regulated in Art. 28 (2) of the Basic Law:

> Municipalities must be guaranteed the right to regulate all local affairs on their own responsibility, within the limits prescribed by the laws. Within the limits of their functions designated by a law, associations of municipalities shall also have the right of self-government according to the laws.

In the view of the government of Hessen, this constitutional provision protects the sovereignty of municipalities in the sphere of planning. Any interference with this principle requires at least sufficient compensation, such as the legislature's involvement of the municipalities in the planning process. The government of Hessen argued that the individual special measure laws did not provide such sufficient compensation.[410]

Violation of the guarantee of effective legal protection

Art. 19 (4) of the Basic Law provides:

> Should any person's rights be violated by public authority, he may have recourse to the courts. If no other jurisdiction has been established, recourse shall be to the ordinary courts.

This provision guarantees individuals' right of legal protection if their rights have been violated by a public authority. The term "public authority" refers to executive bodies. The legislature falls outside its scope.[411] In consequence, individuals cannot claim comparable legal protection against legislation, as they can in the case of administrative acts. When administrative acts are examined, all circumstances of the individual case and all general rules that apply to that case are included in an extensive review. By contrast, legislative acts can only be examined in one respect: only the violation of constitutional provisions can be invoked. The argument against the *Südumfahrung Stendal* Act centered on this distinction. Because the federal legislature, rather than the administration, decided on the permissibility of one specific railway project, individuals were deprived of effective legal protection: "Die Möglichkeit der Verfassungsbeschwerde ergänzt folglich den Individualrechtsschutz ohne ihn zu ersetzen. Sie allein garantiert noch keinen effektiven

409 *Ibid.*, p. 780 with references.
410 BR Drs. 513/2/92, p. 7.
411 BVerfGE 24, 33 (49).

Rechtsschutz."[412] Art. 19 (4) of the Basic Law was therefore violated, according to the argument.

1.2.3.2. The *Bundesverfassungsgericht's* judgment

The Südumfahrung Stendal Act survived in the course of the review of its constitutionality by the Federal Constitutional Court. The *Bundesverfassungsgericht* found no violation of any constitutional principle. The Court started its analysis by discussing the constitutional principle of the separation of powers. This principle can be found in Art. 20 (2) GG. The Court argued that this principle centers on the organization and the distribution of State functions, thereby moderating State power.[413] Its purpose is also to ensure that State decisions are made by these bodies which, given their organization, structure, function, and the type of procedures they apply, are best equipped for the task. But the German Basic Law does not prescribe any strict separation of different functions. It is rather about mutual control, constraints, and moderation of the State's powers to prevent one of those bodies from getting the upper hand. The core function of each State body, which for the legislature is to enact general rules and for the executive to enforce these general rules, cannot, however, be changed.[414] Planning is an exceptional case. It can be strictly allocated to neither the executive nor the legislative branch. There are situations in which the legislature adopts a plan, for example, the budgetary plan, for a certain period of time. More detailed plans can also be included in a legislative act.

In the Court's view, the German Basic Law does not prescribe that the legislature must enact general laws alone. It is true that Art. 19 prohibits individual laws (*Einzelfallgesetze*), but this prohibition concerns only laws that restrict basic rights. Moreover, the German Basic Law makes it possible to decide on expropriations by means of legislation.[415] It follows that the legislature does not necessarily infringe on the function of other State powers in an impermissible manner when it issues a plan for one project.

The *Bundesverfassungsgericht* admits that, in conformity with general laws that apply to spatial planning (for example, transportation planning), the executive branch is

412 Ronellenfitsch (1991), p. 780. Complaining about the reduction of legal protection by the Stendal Act, the government of Hessen invoked the judgment of the *Bundesverfassungsgericht* concerning expropriation by a legislative act. Normally, executive bodies have the authority to decide on expropriations. When the legislature usurps that function, it de facto makes an executive decision, which, however, cannot be subjected to extensive judicial review, because it takes the form of a legislative act: "Wählt der Gesetzgeber an Stelle der Enteignung durch Verwaltungsakt die Enteignung durch Gesetz, so schließt er damit den nach Art. 19 Abs. 4 GG garantierten Rechtsweg zu den zuständigen Gerichen aus [...]. Die richterliche Prüfung, ob die Enteignung gegenüber dem einzelnen Grundrechtsträger zulässig ist, ist damit nicht möglich. Wird aber berücksichtigt, daß die Legalenteignung wesenmäßig "Verwaltung" durch Gesetz ist und daß es gerade die Aufgabe des Art. 14 Abs. 4 GG ist, Exekutivakte einer effektiven gerichtlichen Kontrolle zu unterwerfen, so wird damit die Abwehrmöglichkeit des Grundrechtsträgers in einem wesentlichen Punkt verkürzt." These reflections led the Federal Constitutional Court to conclude that expropriations by means of legislation can be justified only in a few very exceptional situations. BVerfGE 24, 367 (401ff.). BR Drs. 513/2/92.

413 BVerfGE 95, 1 (15).

414 BVerfGE 95, 1 (15).

415 The case of legal expropriations by the *Deichordnungsgesetz*, BVerfGE 24, 367.

primarily competent: executive bodies are simply better equipped. They have the required administrative machinery and the necessary knowledge. This means that the legislature is only allowed to decide on spatial planning matters by a legislative act under one condition: it must have *good reasons* (*gute Gründe*) for doing so. Such good reasons exist, for example, when fast execution of the plans is particularly important in the public interest, the common good (*Gemeinwohl*). As the *Bundesverfassungsgericht* already decided, the legislature has much freedom to decide what constitutes good reasons required by the public interest.[416]

The *Bundesverfassungsgericht* applied this exception to the case of the Südumfahrung Stendal railway connection and concluded that the German legislature indeed had *good reasons* to take over the function of the executive in that specific case and decide on the individual project. These good reasons were to speed up the construction of the railway connection in East Germany, which was required after the reunification of the Eastern and Western territories. The Court concluded that the mere application of the new, general accelerating legislation would not result in such a great gain in time as would be possible under the Lex Stendal.

The Court observed that the Lex Stendal was indeed necessary; otherwise the construction of the project would take many years. This was all the more so because many private and public interests were involved in the area where the railway connection was to be built, and the city of Stendal had already announced that it would try to block the project because of its great ecological harm to the environment.[417]

The federal legislature had investigated the interests involved in an adequate and reliable way, and given the public sufficient opportunity to respond to the plans: "Darüber hinaus gibt es keine Anhaltspunkte dafür, daß der Gesetzgeber seine Pflicht, die Ermittlungen vollständig und zuverlässig durchzuführen, verletzt hat. [...] Das Gesetz stützt sich auf eine umfassende und nachvollziehbare Abwägung aller in Rede stehenden Belange."[418]

The executive branch normally has the authority to decide on expropriations. The Südumfahrung Stendal Act, however, affected the way the expropriations procedures took place and diminished the legal protection of the owners of the parcels involved. According to the *Bundesverfassungsgericht*, this is only allowed when planning by means of an administrative decision would be disadvantageous to the general interest, and could therefore be effected only by means of a legislative act:[419]

> Eine Legalplanung hat vor der Verfassung jedenfalls dann Bestand, wenn eine mit ihr verbundene Enteignung nicht nur – wie jede Enteignung – im Sinne des Art. 14 Abs. 3 Satz 1 GG zum Wohle der Allgemeinheit erforderlich ist, sondern auch triftige Gründe für die Annahme bestehen, daß die Durchführung einer behördlichen Planfeststellung mit erheblichen Nachteilen für das Gemeinwohl verbunden wäre, denen nur durch eine gesetzliche Regelung begegnet werden kann.

416 BVerfGE 95, 1 (17).
417 *Ibid.*, p. (19).
418 *Ibid.*, p. 25.
419 *Ibid.*, p. 22.

In the eyes of the *Bundesverfassungsgericht*, there were sufficient grounds to justify the legislative measure: the reunification of East and West Germany created an exceptional situation and the law was necessary to speed up improvements of the infrastructure and for economic development.[420] This purpose could not be achieved through administrative procedures, because administrative decision-making takes much more time. This exceptional situation therefore justified the unequal treatment of the Berlin-Oebisfelde railway route in comparison with other infrastructural projects that were normally governed by administrative decision-making.[421] The legislature eventually proved not to have violated the principle of self-government of municipalities because the interests of the municipalities had been taken into consideration during the legislative decision-making process.[422]

The *Bundesverfassungsgericht*'s judgment on the constitutionality of Lex Stendal had the following tenor: the legislature is in principle prohibited from enacting individual project laws, thereby in fact taking over the powers of the executive in the sphere of spatial planning, unless there are special, good reasons that can justify such action.[423]

1.2.4. Concluding remarks

The Südumfahrung Stendal Act (Lex Stendal) was a reaction to the sudden developments in East Germany that led to the reunification of the eastern and the western part of that country in the early 1990s. After the reunification, new infrastructural projects needed to be executed in order to make the connection between the western and the eastern states possible. This was crucial for the economic development of East Germany. Owing to the very long process of administrative decision-making, the federal legislature cleverly enacted a few ad hoc legislative acts that decided on the permissibility of individual projects. The first one was the Südumfahrung Stendal Act. Although this law was strongly criticized by both the government of Hessen (during the parliamentary process) and academics, the *Bundesverfassungsgericht* found no violation of any constitutional principle. It allowed the legislature to decide on the Südumfahrung Stendal project, because the ordinary process of administrative decision-making would have taken too many years. This was a good reason, in the Court's view.

1.3. Conclusion

The two cases described above give the following reasons for, characteristics of, and objections against ad hoc legislation.

420 BVerfGE 95, 1 (23).
421 BVerfGE 95, 1 (26).
422 *Ibid.*
423 The judgments of the *Bundesverfassungsgericht* have been discussed in, for example, Ch. Schneller, "Gewaltenteilung und Rechtsschutz in der objektbezogen Legalplanung," *ZG* 1998, pp. 179–191; H.J. Pabst, "Das Investitionsmaßnahmegesetz 'Südumfahrung Stendal' vor dem BVerfGE," *UPR* 1997, pp. 284–286, and U. Hufeld, "Anmerkung," *JZ* 1997, pp. 302–305.

Reasons for enacting ad hoc legislation

The German federal legislature seems to be vulnerable to public commotion, which is evidenced by the Lex Schörner. In that case, the legislature acquiesced to public opinion, which could not accept that one of Hitler's former generals, particularly known for his extreme cruelty towards the German soldiers, would return from Russian captivity after the war and enjoy a peaceful life with a state pension. The legislature responded to that situation by retroactively changing the applicable general rules in order to affect the outcome of Schörner's case.

The second reason for the legislature to enact ad hoc laws can be found in external events which, in contrast to the Schörner case, are not followed by any intense and emotional public debate. It is rather a matter of the political will to improve the infrastructure and thereby the economy, as illustrated by the Lex Stendal.

Ad hoc legislation for one person or one case/project

Both cases show that ad hoc legislation, which was viewed as problematic in Germany, can concern not only an individual person but also a specific project. Both Acts were criticized for violating the prohibition of *Einzelfallgesetze* in Art. 19 (1) GG.

Separation of powers principle

The arguments put forward against the Lex Schörner and the Lex Stendal addressed the problem of the separation of powers between the executive and the legislative branches. By legislating in specific cases, the legislature in fact executed general laws, a task which is normally reserved for the executive bodies. This argument was most explicit in the case of the Lex Stendal, where there was no doubt that the legislature had taken over the executive function and left no margin for usual administrative decision-making, including granting necessary licenses for the Südumfahrung Stendal project. In the eyes of the *Bundesverfassungsgericht*, nonetheless, such usurpation of executive power does not always violate the separation of powers principle. If the legislature has good reasons for acting as the executive, it is allowed to do so, especially in the field of planning. In the opinion of the *Bundesverfassungsgericht*, these good reasons lay in the acceleration of the improvement of the infrastructure between East and West Germany.

Equality

When a divergent legal regime is created for one case, it can be argued that other cases are consequently treated unequally. The case of Südumfahrung Stendal clearly illustrates this. While the project of the railway connection between Berlin and Oebisfelde received special treatment, the other projects continued to be governed by the old general, administrative, and environmental laws. This meant longer procedures and stricter environmental requirements to be met. According to the *Bundesverfassungsgericht*, however, such unequal treatment was justified by the exceptional situation that arose from the reunification of the eastern and the western part of Germany.

Legal protection

A serious problem that arose as a result of legislation which, in fact, constitutes executive decisions was the diminished legal protection of individuals. Whereas individuals have a right to extensive examination of any administrative decision in concrete terms, i.e. in relation to the individual him or herself, once an administrative decision has been made in the form of a legislative act, the only possible objection concerns the unconstitutionality of the act. In the last case, judicial review is abstract and less extensive: it involves only the provisions of the Basic Law. The *Bundesverfassungsgericht* agreed on that but found justification for the legislative regulation in the Südumfahrung Stendal case. It argued again that the exceptional situation arising from the reunification of Germany required an administrative decision in a legislative act.

Legislative irrationality

The legislature has been accused of acting irrationally, especially in connection with the Lex Schörner. The legislature acted impulsively in response to great public commotion about the return of Schörner and the fact that he would receive a state pension. The emotions of the legislature adversely affected the quality of Lex Schörner, in critics' minds.

Chapter 2

THE REQUIREMENT OF GENERALITY

Introduction

The generality of laws as such is an old concept, and, as Schneider states, it stems from Roman times.[424] It is beyond the scope of this chapter to go so far back in time, however interesting it may be to do so. In this chapter, the focus will be only on major points of the German discussion of the requirement of the generality of laws. This discussion is about laws in the formal and in the material sense, the prohibition of special laws (*Einzelfallgesetze*) in Art. 19 (1) GG, the phenomenon of special measure laws (*Maßnahmegesetze*), and the requirement of the general, public interest (*Gemeinwohl*).

2.1. Two concepts of laws: Laws in the formal and laws in the material sense

In German constitutional law theory, a distinction has been made between laws in the formal sense and laws in the material sense.[425] Laws in the formal sense ("*Gesetze im formellen Sinne*") are all laws enacted in a legislative process as prescribed by the German Basic Law.[426] Laws in the material sense (*Gesetze im materiellen Sinne*) refer to laws containing legal norms that have external effect and bind individuals.[427] These two categories do not have to exclude each other. Many laws which are enacted by Parliament contain legal norms and are therefore both: laws in the formal and in the material sense. Classic examples of laws which belong to the category of laws in the formal sense only are budget laws (Art. 110 [2]GG) and laws that approve international agreements (Art. 59 [2]

424 Schneider goes back to the times of Papinian and Ulpian: H. Schneider, *Gesetzgebung*, Heidelberg: C.F. Müller Verlag 2002, pp. 22ff. See also a more extensive exploration about the historical aspects of the generality requirement: Kirchhof (2009), p. 69ff, H. Hofmann, "Der Postulat der Allgemeinheit des Gesetzes," in: Ch. Starck, *Die Allgemeinheit des Gesetzes*, Göttingen: Van Den Hoeck & Ruprecht 1987, pp. 15ff, and C. Schmitt, *Verfassungslehre*, München und Leipzig: Duncker & Humblot 1928, pp. 139ff.

425 For the development of the ideas on the concept of legislation, see E.W. Böckenförde, *Gesetz und gesetzgebende Gewalt*, Berlin: Duncker und Humblot 1958.

426 It is a generally accepted definition, Ch. Starck, *Der Gesetzesbegriff des Grundgesetzes*, Baden-Baden: Nomos 1970, p. 21. See also R. Schmidt, *Staatsorganisationsrecht*, Grasberg: Rolf Schmidt Verlag 2008, p. 70.

427 Starck (1970), p. 21.

GG). Such laws are declaratory or organizational. A large number of laws which contain legal norms do not originate from Parliament. These are laws in the material sense only.

The question is, however, whether the legislature is bound by any special requirements as regards the content of these externally binding legal rules. Opinions differ on this point. Mayer states:[428]

> Über das Wesen der Gesetzgebung besteht Meinungsverschiedenheit. Ziemlich allgemeine Übereinstimmung herrscht darüber, daß es die Aufgabe der Gesetzgebung ist, Rechtssätze aufzustellen. Streitig ist dagegen, ob ein Rechtssatz bzw. ein Gesetz eine allgemeine Regel enthalten muss.

Mayer refers to laws in the material sense when he describes the State function as being divided into legislation and administration in a broad sense (including the administration of justice). He assumes that the object of legislation is general or abstract legal rules, as opposed to the object of administration, which is about rulings on individual or specific matters:[429]

> 1. Die Tätigkeit des Staates zerfällt in die Gesetzgebung, welche den Erlass von allgemeinen oder abstrakten Vorschriften (Rechtssätzen), und die Verwaltung im weiteren Sinne, welche die Regelung individueller oder konkreter Angelegenheiten zum Gegenstand hat.

Laband, on the other hand, agrees with the concept of legislation in the material sense but does not see the requirement of generality as a necessary condition of legal norms. In his opinion, legal norms are general by nature, rather than it being essential for legal norms to be general:[430]

> Es gehört zum Begriff des Gesetzes im materiellen Sinne des Wortes, daß dasselbe einen Rechtssatz aufstellt; aber nicht, daß dieser Rechtssatz eine allgemeine Regel enthält, welche auf viele, oder auch nur auf eine unbestimmte Anzahl von Fällen anwendbar ist. Zwar liegt es in der Natur des Rechts, daß dasselbe gewöhnlich solche Regeln bildet, welche in allen Fällen Anwendung finden sollen, in denen bestimmter Tatbestand gegeben ist, und da das Gesetz eine Rechtsquelle ist, so hat es gewöhnlich dieser Natur des Rechtes entsprechend, einen allgemeinen Rechtssatz zum Inhalt. Allein dies ist eben nur ein Naturale, nicht ein Essentiale des Gesetzesbegriffes.

In his view, there are a few exceptional situations that justify individual legislative acts, for example, a situation where a Regent must be appointed if the monarch is not able to

428 G. Mayer, *Lehrbuch des deutschen Staatsrechts*, 1919, Berlin: Duncker & Humblot 2005, p. 27. See also Starck (1970), p. 21: "Was die Kriterien des Rechtssatzes (= Satz des objektiven Rechts) sind, ist nie eindeutig und unbestritten geklärt worden." He concludes, however, that "[ü]berwiegend hält man den Rechtsatz, somit das Gesetz im materiellen Sinne, für eine 'allgemeine' Norm" but "[was] allgemein, generell oder abstract bedeutet, ist wiederum höchst umstritten, so daß der Ausdruck 'allgemeines' Gesetz verschieden gedeutet wird."

429 G. Mayer (1919), p. 27.

430 P. Laband, *Das Staatsrecht des Deutschen Reichs*, Tübingen: J.C.B. Mohr 5th ed. 1911, Vol. 2, pp. 2ff.

fulfill his function or where the working period of a parliament must be prolonged due to war.[431] These are indeed extraordinary situations, and legislation then serves as a guarantee against the abuse of power. Such laws, however, should be distinguished from laws which are directly binding on individuals, put certain obligations on them, and are not formulated in general and abstract terms. This could result in tyranny.

It is exactly this abuse of power that Carl Schmitt tried to eliminate by arguing in favor of the requirement of the generality for legislation. He argued for a concept of legislation that incorporates the principles of the rule of law and the freedom of people (*der rechtsstaatliche Gesetzesbegriff*). Only legal norms that possess certain qualities can be distinguished from arbitrary orders of a monarch or any arbitrary measures.[432] Schmitt concluded that the supremacy of legislation as opposed to the supremacy of the people and their will can only be achieved if the legislature is bound by these laws itself. However, such a commitment makes sense only if legislation is rational and fair. These features are closely connected with the feature of generality:[433]

> Die Bindung des Gesetzgebers an das Gesetz ist aber nur so lange möglich, als das Gesetz eine Norm mit gewissen Eigenschaften ist: Richtigkeit, Vernünftigkeit, Gerechtigkeit usw. Alle diese Eigenschaften setzen voraus, daß das Gesetz eine generelle Norm ist. Ein Gesetzgeber, dessen Einzelmaßnahmen, Spezialanweisungen, Dispense und Durchbrechungen ebenso als Gesetze gelten, wie seine generellen Normierungen, ist in keiner denkbaren Weise an sein Gesetz gebunden; die "Bindung an das Gesetz" ist für diejenigen, die beliebig "Gesetze" machen können, eine bedeutungslose Redensart.

Schmitt positioned his concept of legislation to correspond with the principles of the rule of law, against a political concept of legislation. While the first concept concerns the rule of law, the latter considers politics as specific will and order.[434]

Schmitt not only argues for generality, he also explains what generality means. In his view, the requirement of the generality of laws is an essential element of the separation of powers principle. He argues that this principle can only be useful if legislation is understood as general norms. Otherwise, there will be no distinction between the legislative, administrative, and judicial powers. He therefore rejects a purely formal concept of legislation: "Ein bloß formeller Gesetzesbegriff: Gesetz ist das, was die gesetzgebenden Stellen im Wege des Gesetzgebungsverfahrens anordnen, würde aus der Herrschaft des Gesetzes einen Absolutismus der Gesetzgebungsstellen machen und jede Unterscheidung von Gesetzgebung, Verwaltung und Justiz beseitigen."[435] It is this very

431 *Ibid.*, p. 3.

432 Schmitt (1928), p. 138. See also D. Grimm, "Stufen der Rechtsstaatlichkeit," *JZ* 2009/12, p. 596, who views the generality of laws as an essential element of the *Rechtstaat* as well: "Zum Begriff der Regel gehört es, dass sie nicht auf einen Einzelfall bezogen ist, sondern für eine Vielzahl künftiger Fälle gilt, dass sie nicht im laufenden Vollzug geändert wird und dass sie auf alle, die in der gleichen Situation sind, auch gleichmäßig angewendet wird. Regelhafte Herrschaft ist das Gegenteil von Willküricher Herrschaft."

433 Schmitt (1928), p. 139.

434 *Ibid.*, p. 146.

435 *Ibid.*, p. 151.

distinction between the general norm and the application of this norm by administrative bodies and courts that guarantees the freedom of people. In this respect, Schmitt focuses on the issue of expropriation. He argues that freedom is only guaranteed when expropriation takes place on the basis of general rules and conditions that are applied by the administration and the judiciary to a specific expropriation case. Schmitt also sees a problem with the equality principle. It is at risk if the legislature acts by means of individual orders and measures. Schmitt cannot understand how such specific legislative orders can help to promote equality:[436]

> Wo Spezial-Befehle oder bloße Maßnahmen getroffen werden, liegt infolgedessen kein Gesetz und keine Gleichheit vor. Die Anordnung: Herr X wird des Landes verwiesen, ist nichts, demgegenüber man vernünftigerweise von "Gleichheit" sprechen könnte; sie trifft nur eine individuell bestimmte Person, einen einzelnen Tatbestand und erschöpft sich in diesem Befehl. Es ist ganz unsinnig zu sagen, vor dem konkreten Befehl, daß Herr X. des Landes verwiesen wird, könnten alle Deutschen gleich sein. Weder Herr X., den dieser Befehl trifft, noch irgendwelche anderen Personen, die nicht von ihm betroffen werden, können hier "gleich" genannt werden.

Lastly, Schmitt deals with the principle of the independent judiciary. Independence means that judges should be free from individual legislative orders and special wishes of the legislature. This guarantee can only be achieved when laws are general.[437]

An interesting question now is what position the German Basic Law takes on laws in the formal and in the material sense, and whether it requires every legislative act to be of a general and abstract nature. The German Basic Law starts from a concept of laws in the formal sense. This means that it is focused on the legislative process and on procedures in which a legislative act is to be adopted.[438] If these procedures have been taken into account, the legislative product must be seen as valid law. Nevertheless, it is still possible to challenge such a legislative act if the law is suspected of violating any of the Basic Law's provisions.

As far as the contents and the quality of legislative acts are concerned, including the generality requirement, the Basic Law does not pass any judgments. It is left to the political process to make these decisions,[439] with one exception, however: individual and specific laws that restrict fundamental rights are prohibited on the basis of Art. 19 (1) GG, which will be discussed below.

436 *Ibid.*, p. 155.

437 *Ibid.*

438 Chapter VII of the Basic Law.

439 E. Benda, W. Maihofer & H.J. Vogel, *Handbuch des Verfassungsrechts der Bundesrepublik Deutschland*, Berlin, New York: Walter de Gruyter 1983, p. 1099. Some authors believe that, since the Basic Law works with the formal concept of legislation, the distinction between laws in the formal sense and laws in the material sense has become obsolete. See, for example, Ch. Degenhart, *Staatsorganisationsrecht*, Heidelberg: Müller 2007, p. 51.

2.2. Special laws: Individual laws and project laws

2.2.1. Art. 19 (1) GG

The first sentence of the first paragraph of Art. 19 (1) of the German Basic Law reads:

> Insofar as, under this Basic Law, a basic right may be restricted by or pursuant to a law, such law must apply generally and not merely to a single case.

This provision was introduced relatively late in the preparation of the Basic Law after the Second World War, and the motives for its inclusion remain unclear. From the debates in the general commission where it was discussed, however, it can be concluded that the prohibition of special laws can be viewed as a restriction of the legislative branch.[440] In the literature, the *ratio* of Art. 19 (1) has been discussed on several occasions.

2.2.1.1. Ratio

Prohibition of special laws as a principle of the Rechtsstaat

Krüger, who devoted special attention to this provision in relation to the Lex Schörner, attributed a special meaning and function to Art. 19 (1). In her view, the prohibition of special laws was one of the most important norms of the rule of law. Its importance could be found particularly in its function in deciding between the rule of law and democracy in conflict situations. In such a conflict situation, Art. 19 (1) provides that the rule of law and the protection of an individual against a special Act prevail, even though the Act was passed in a democratic process.[441]

Prohibition of special laws and the separation of powers

Krüger, among other authors, was also convinced that the prohibition of special laws in Art. 19 (1) is narrowly connected with the principle of the separation of powers. It prohibits administrative acts in the form of legislative acts.[442] The Federal Constitutional Court rejected such a strict interpretation of Art. 19 (1). In the case of Südumfahrung Stendal, as described above, the *Bundesverfassungsgericht* decided that the legislature does not automatically impermissibly encroach on other State powers when it provides rules for a single case. The German Basic Law does not impose a total prohibition of

440 A description of the discussion in the commission working on the Basic Law can be found in: K. Stern, *Des Staatsrecht der Bundesrepublik Deutschland*, Vol. III/2, München: Beck 1994, p. 713. See also P.M. Huber, "Art. 19," in: H. v. Mangoldt, F. Klein & Ch. Starck, *Kommentar zum Grundgesetz*, München: Franz Vahlen 2005, p. 1719.

441 Krüger (1955), p. 760.

442 *Ibid.*, p. 791. This view can also be found in R. Herzog, "Art. 19," in: Th. Maunz/Dürig, *Grundgesetz. Kommentar*, Vol. III, München: C.H. Beck 1981, no. 27.

special laws. Only special laws in Art. 19 (1) which restrict fundamental rights are prohibited.[443]

Prohibition of special laws in relation to the equality principle

Art. 19 (1) is often linked with the equality principle, as laid down in Art. 3 of the Basic Law. It is also said that the prohibition of special laws qualifies the equality principle and therefore has no autonomous meaning.[444] But not everyone shares this view which, as Huber argues, is inconsistent with the Basic Law: why would the Basic Law provide two different rules if both were to have the same meaning? The meaning of the prohibition of special laws should therefore be understood in light of the concept of legislation, rather than in light of the equality principle, according to Huber.[445] Arguments have been raised in favor of the equality principle as the only touchstone for special laws.[446] Although the function of this principle is to prevent legislative arbitrariness, its effectiveness in relation to special laws has been questioned. According to Schneider, it could not be effective because the equality principle makes it possible to treat special cases in a special way:[447]

> Sicherlich verbietet der Gleichheitsgrundsatz, daß in Fällen, in denen gleichartige Tätbestande vorliegen, nur ein bestimmter Fall herausgegriffen und einer gesetzlichen Lösung zugeführt wird. Davon abgesehen bietet jedoch das Gleichheitsprinzip keine wirksame Schranke vor Einzelfallgesetzen, denn es gestattet ja gerade, daß etwas Einmaliges und Einzigartiges seiner Besonderheit entsprechend behandelt wird.

If it is assumed that *all* special laws should be forbidden, it could indeed be said that the equality principle would not work, but if it is assumed that only special laws which are arbitrary must be eliminated, then nothing stands in the way of applying the equality principle.[448]

In the meantime, it had become clear that the *Bundesverfassungsgericht* leans towards the equality test of arbitrariness (*Willkür*) in Art. 3 of the Basic Law, when it applies Art.

443 BVerfGE 95, 1 (17).

444 See, e.g., H. Jarass & B. Pieroth, *Grundgesetz für die Bundesrepublik Deutschland. Kommentar*, München: C.H. Beck 2006, p. 420.

445 K. Huber, *Maßnahmegesetz und Rechtsgesetz*, Berlin: Duncker & Humblot 1963, p. 132.

446 K.M. Meessen, "Maßnahmegesetze, Individualgesetze und Vollziehungsgesetze," *DÖV* 1970, p. 317.

447 H. Schneider, "Über Einzelfallgesetze," in: H. Barion, E. Forsthoff & W. Weber, *Festschrift für Carl Schmitt*, Berlin: Duncker & Humblot 1959, p. 171 with references.

448 As far as the equality principle can be seen in connection with the concept of legislation in the material sense, Zahn would not be satisfied with this view. He concluded that the requirement of generality of legislation cannot be substituted by the equality principle, because then no distinction could be made between the different state powers: "Diese auch heute noch gültige Forderung nach Unterscheidbarkeit der Gewalten ignoriert aber Leibholz, wenn er die Zugehörigkeit der Gleichheitsidee zum Rechtssatzbegriff einfach damit begründet, was willkürlich, also Unrecht, Nicht-Recht sei, könne nicht Gesetz im materiellen Sinne genannt werden. Rechtmäßige Entscheidungen zu fällen, ist die oberste Pflicht *aller* Gewaltenträger. Sie unterscheidet nicht den einen vom anderen," K.Ch. Zahn, *Gesetz und Einzelakt*, Göttingen 1963, p. 101.

19 (1). In the famous case of the Rheinstahl Company, the Court addressed the view of some members of the Senate that the prohibition of special laws from Art. 19 (1) was nothing more than a qualification of the equality principle. Although the Court did not confirm this view directly, it did so indirectly: it found that the prohibition of special laws from Art. 19 (1) prevented the legislature from singling out one case and subjecting it to *arbitrary* treatment. Consequently, Art. 19 (1) is not violated if there is only one case governed by the law at the time, and the law is formulated in an objective (non-arbitrary) way.[449] This resembles the equality test.

2.2.1.2. A catalog of fundamental rights in Art. 19 (1) GG

It should not be overlooked that Art. 19 (1) of the Basic Law only prohibits special laws that restrict basic rights, but which rights are "basic rights"? The first chapter of the Basic Law includes a catalog of 17 basic rights with such subjects as human dignity; personal freedoms; equality before the law; freedom of faith, conscience and creed; freedom of expression; protection of marriage and the family; school education; freedom of assembly; freedom of association; privacy of correspondence, posts, and telecommunications; freedom of movement; occupational freedom; compulsory military or alternative service; inviolability of the home, property, inheritance; rules on expropriation, socialization, citizenship, extradition; right of asylum and right of petition. Besides these freedom rights, the Basic Law guarantees other rights, such as: political rights, the right to run for elections and a right to an independent judiciary. It follows from the purpose of Art. 19 (1) that not only basic rights that represent freedoms of individuals, but also that second category of rights is protected against special violations by the legislature.[450]

Special attention should, however, be devoted to the right of the inviolability of property and expropriation, which can be found in Art. 14 (3): "Expropriation shall only be permissible for the public good. It may only be ordered by or pursuant to a law that determines the nature and extent of compensation." The *Bundesverfassungsgericht* already decided that Art. 14 (3) is governed by a regime of its own and that restrictions of that right by special expropriation laws are not in keeping with the meaning of 'restriction' as referred to in Art. 19 (1).[451]

The restriction of the prohibition of individual laws to laws that limit basic rights is an extremely important element of Art. 19 (1) GG. In German history, there are several examples of laws that have been labeled as case-specific and have received a lot of criticism from a political point of view. Nevertheless, these laws were not subject to constitutional challenges under Art. 19 (1) GG, because they did not restrict anyone's rights. A prominent example is the Lex Naumann. This statute changed previous law, making it possible for Federal Chancellor Schröder's favorite, Michael Naumann, to become the *Staatsminister* for Culture.

According to the general law, only Parliamentary Secretaries could be appointed as *Staatsminister*. However, a title and position of a Parliamentary Secretary could only be

[449] BVerfGE 25, 371 (399).
[450] Stern (1994), pp. 727–728.
[451] BVerfGE 24, 367.

held by someone who was a Member of Parliament, and Naumann was not. To remedy this deficiency, the government proposed an amendment that made exceptions to this rule possible. From then on, people who were not members of Parliament could also be appointed as Parliamentary Secretary. The amendment eliminated a serious obstruction for Naumann to become a *Staatsminister*.[452] Although the law was criticized because it was obviously enacted for the Naumann case,[453] it was still beyond the scope of Art. 19 (1) GG, because it did not restrict Naumann's rights.

2.2.1.3. Individual laws (*Einzelfallgesetze*)

For a further elaboration on the prohibition of special laws, it is essential to understand what constitutes a special law within the meaning of Art. 19 (1) GG in German doctrine and case law.

Schneider presented an interesting view on what laws should be classified as special laws. In his contribution to the *Festschrift für Carl Schmitt*, he paid special attention to case-specific laws, thereby distinguishing between, on the one hand, organizational laws and individual laws that are enacted because the Constitution or tradition impose such obligation on the legislature,[454] and, on the other, special laws that create an exceptional legal regime for an individual case. He is mainly interested in the last category of laws which breach the general legal order. While discussing individual laws, Schneider, unlike other authors,[455] does not make any distinction between individual laws that are addressed to certain persons (*Einzelpersonengesetze*) and laws that address individual cases (*Einzelfallgesetze*). The *Bundesverfassungsgericht* does not make this distinction, either.

In Schneider's opinion, the generality of laws requires that legislative acts provide rules for an indefinite number of cases – so not the number of cases affected by the law, but their indeterminacy is decisive. Accordingly, if only one case is addressed by the law when it is enacted, but there is a possibility that other cases will be governed by the law in the future, the law must still be considered general law:[456]

> Ein Gesetz, welches die Amtsbezüge des Staatsoberhauptes regelt, mag nur für eine Person anwendbar sein, aber da es für jeden künftigen Inhaber dieses Amtes gilt, nicht nur für ein Individuum als solches, besitzt es Allgemeinheit.

452 Gesetz zur Änderung des Gesetzes über die Rechtsverhältnisse der Parlamentarischen Staatssekretäre of January 15, 1999, BGBl. I S. 10.

453 "Was nicht paßt, wird angepaßt" became a popular adage in response to the Naumann legislation. Some members of Parliament called the legislative proposal a "trick" to enable Naumann to become a minister of state, BT 14. Wahlperiode, 8. Sitzung, November 19, 1998, pp. 468ff. See also *FAZ* October 6, 1998, no. 231, p. 16.

454 These laws hardly contain any legal rules as such, Schneider (1959), p. 163.

455 Krüger designated the Lex Schörner as an *Einzelpersongesetz*, Krüger (1955), p. 761. See also H. Bauernfeind, "Zum Verbot von Einzelfallgesetzen gemäß Art. 19 I GG," *DVBl.* 1976, pp. 193–198.

456 Schneider (1959), p. 160.

This view was shared by the Federal Constitutional Court.[457] For the *Bundesverfassungsgericht*, such indeterminacy played the most important part. The Court explicitly expressed this view in the Rheinstahl case. In that case, under pressure from the labor unions, the federal legislature retroactively changed the law on the structure of the supervisory board in companies in the mining, and iron and steel industries. This law was changed when it appeared that the Rheinstahl Corporation no longer met the law's conditions and was therefore no longer required to compose its supervisory board in a manner which was favorable for the employees. The Court upheld the Act despite the criticism expressed during the parliamentary debates and constitutional challenges which especially concerned the case-oriented character of the law and its sole purpose to prevent the Rheinstahl Concern from dropping out of the old regime of the structure of the supervisory board.[458] The *Bundesverfassungsgericht* held that the law was general and not special, because it was written in general terms and made repeated application to future cases possible. The Court defined a general law in the following way:[459]

> Eine Norm hat den Character eines für eine unbestimmte Vielzahl von Fällen geltenden generellen Rechtssatzes – und ist also kein Einzelfallgesetz –, wenn sich wegen der abstrakten Fassung des gesetzlichen Tatbestandes nicht genau übersehen läßt, auf wieviele und welche Fälle das Gesetz Anwendung findet [...], wenn also nicht nur ein einmaliger Eintritt der vorgesehen Rechtsfolge möglich ist [...].

Schneider divides special laws into explicitly (*offenen*) and implicitly (*verdeckten*) individual laws. Open laws are laws that clearly demonstrate their individual character. Laws concerning the prolongation of specific offices and the working period of the legislature, laws that establish a special legal status for explicitly named persons or companies, and laws that occasionally exempt specific legal persons from general rules are explicitly individual laws.[460] Most of the laws, however, especially when they are

457 BVerfGE 85, 360 (374).

458 "Die Vorschrift sei allein geschaffen worden, um zu verhindern, daß die Rheinischen Stahlwerke mit Ablauf des 31. Dezember 1966 aus der qualifizierten Mitbestimmung ausschieden. Die gesetzliche Regelung erschöpfe sich in dieser Maßnahme. Bei der Verabschiedung des Änderungsgesetzes sei lediglich für die Rheinischen Stahlwerke erkennbar gewesen, daß die Umsätze der nicht-mitbestimmten Konzernunternehmen diejenigen der mitbestimmten Unternehmen im zweiten Jahr übersteigen würden," BVerfGE 25, 371 (377). See also the parliamentary debates and the words of Representative Wilhelmi: "Aber es ist immer ein schlechtes Ding, wenn man bei seinem politischen Tun auf einen bestimmten Fall abstellt; das wissen wir alle. [...] So, wie das praktisch gelaufen ist, käme durchaus in Frage, daß das Verfassungsgericht sagt: Offensichtlich ist das alles auf einen Fall zugeschnitten, und schon deshalb ist es verfassungswidrig." BT 5. Wahlperiode, 98. Sitzung, March 15, 1967, p. 4517. The participation of the employees in the mining, and iron and steel industry has a long history. After the Rheinstahl case, the law was changed a few times for other companies as well. The last change focused on the Mannesmann company: BVerfGE 99, 367. See also the Volkswagen law, which pertains directly to the Volkswagen Company, BGBl. I S. 585–587, as amended by BGBl. I S. 1195 and BGBl. I S. 461.

459 BVerfGE 25, 371 (397) with references.

460 A few examples cited by Schneider are: the Act for the exemption of President Von Hindenburg from taxes for the Neudeck manor (Gesetz über die Befreiung des Reichspräsidenten von Hindenburg von Reichs- und Landessteuern für das Rittergut Neudeck) of August 27, 1933 (RGBl. I S. 595), and the Act

controversial, will not explicitly state that they were enacted for the purpose of one case, also given the possibility of nullification by the *Bundesverfassungsgericht* during assessment in light of Art. 19 (1) GG. Schneider called such laws that are abstractly formulated but in fact aimed at one specific case or cases implicitly individual laws (*verdeckte Einzelfallgesetze*).[461] A law that is often discussed, and is designated as an implicitly special law apparently formulated in general terms was the amnesty law for the persons involved in the Platow Affair. Platow was a journalist who regularly provided subscribers of smaller newspapers with confidential economic news. He obtained this news, however, by bribing people in public service. Such activities are punishable in Germany. To guarantee that individuals who were involved in the affair (about 40 people) would not be punished, the German Parliament enacted a law which granted a general pardon to these people.[462] The law, however, referred only indirectly to the "Platow-Komplex." It guaranteed amnesty for persons who had committed a certain type of prohibited acts, but the deadline set could only refer to the Platow affair. The law was sharply criticized in Parliament. Some members of Parliament were ashamed of its reprehensible course of action and stressed the infringement of the Constitution. The general character of the law did not help, since it was in fact restricted to the journalists and civil servants involved in the Platow Affair, according to critics:[463]

> Das Schlimmste: wenn der Gesetzgeber glaubt, er könne in der Form des Gesetzes alles beschließen. […] Das Gesetz, das wegen meines Widerspruches nicht verkündet wurde, über Straffreiheit für 40 Journalisten und Beambte – Platowkreis – in Form eines allgemeinen **Straffreiheitsgesetzes** verstößt gegen Grundsätze der Verfassung, aber auch gegen Grundsätze des Rechtes, gegen den Grundsatz der Gleichheit vor dem Rechte. […] Wir haben einen besseren Bundestag gewählt.

And:

> Ich habe diese Platow-Amnestie nicht ausgefertigt, weil ich sie für verfassungswidrig halte. […] Ich bin der Ansicht, daß die Verfassungswidrigkeit auch nicht dadurch beseitigt würde, daß diese "Amnestie" in ein allgemeines Amnestiegesetz, aber doch wieder auf diese Fälle beschränkt, eingebaut würde.

In its judgment in the Platow case, the *Bundesverfassungsgericht* also addressed the problem of implicitly individual laws. In the Court's view, implicitly individual laws are laws made by a legislature that wants to influence only one specific case or a defined group of cases, and this intention is couched in seemingly general and abstract rules

on Restructuring of the pension fund for the German Railways and trams (Gesetz zur Neuordnung der Pensionskasse der Deutschen Eisenbahnen und Straßenbahnen) of March, 5, 1956 (BGBl. I S. 101).

461 Schneider (1959), p. 165. See also Krüger (1955), p. 762, who termed the Lex Schörner an implicitly individual law (*getarntes Einzelfallgesetz*).

462 Gesetz über den Erlaß von Strafen und Geldbußen und die Niederschlagung von Strafverfahren und Bußgeldverfahren (*Straffreiheitsgesetz* 1954), of July 17, 1954, BGBl. I S. 203.

463 See, e.g., the reaction of Dehler, BT 2. Wahlperiode, 4. Sitzung, October 28, 1953, p. 54 and BT 2. Wahlperiode, 12. Sitzung, February 4, 1954, p. 352.

which, in fact, could only be applied to one specific case or group of cases. In this specific decision, the *Bundesverfassungsgericht* thus attributed significant importance to the motives of the legislature. On the other hand, it applied the criterion of the objective content of a law (general or specific) to define the subjective intention of the legislature. The long and the short of this vision is that, even though the legislature's motive is to influence a specific case or a group of cases, and it nevertheless provides general rules that can be applied in an undefined number of cases, the legislation will still be considered general and not individual. As a result, the meaning and importance of the "motives criterion" seems to be negligible, because the objective content of the law prevails. The *Bundesverfassungsgericht* seems to have understood this fallacy: in later judgments, it never explicitly investigated the motives of the legislature, but it only assessed whether a law was written in general terms and was therefore suitable to govern future cases as well. Applying the "motive criterion" to the Platow Amnesty case, the Court held that the controversial amnesty law was general, because it was suitable for application to future cases, even though the Platow Affair gave the impetus for its enactment.

2.2.1.4. Individual legislation (*Einzelfallgesetzgebung*) vs. case-generated legislation (*Anlassgesetzgebung*)

The *Bundesverfassungsgericht* makes a distinction between individual laws that are enacted for a specific case or group of cases and laws that are enacted as a reaction to a specific case. The second type of laws can be classified as general, although a specific case was the reason for the legislature to propose it. The amnesty law in the Platow case could be seen as case-generated legislation, in the Court's view. It is true that the Platow Affair served as a model for the legislature. At the time of the law's enactment, the Platow case(s) was the only case to which it could be applied, to the knowledge of the legislature. The law, however, was formulated in neutral terms, was applicable to future cases as well and was therefore general and not problematic in light of Art. 19 (1) GG, in the opinion of the *Bundesverfassungsgericht*.[464]

A recent example of legislation where the federal legislature quickly responded to one specific case can be found in the field of social security. In 2003, the popular German paper *Bild* published an item about a German citizen who lived in Florida where he received his social security benefits. In Germany, people were shocked that this man, soon called "Florida-Rolf," apparently lived under the palm trees in Miami and enjoyed financial support from the German government. In no time, to prevent the abuse of the old legal regime,[465] the German government proposed new legislation that prohibited payment of social security benefits to German citizens living abroad, unless there were very exceptional circumstances.[466] The law was obviously generated by the reports

464 BVerfGE 10, 234 (243).

465 On the legal aspects of the old and the new regimes, see F. Baur, "Sozialhilfe für Deutsche im Ausland (Sec. 24 SGB XII)," *NVwZ* 2004, pp. 1322–1325.

466 Art. 1 of Sec. 24 of the *Sozialgesetzbuch* (SGB) Zwölftes Buch (XII), BGBl. I S. 3022. See also <www.abendblatt.de/daten/2003/09/03/203759.html?prx=1> (last accessed on June 12, 2011). The law had an unintended effect: persons who lived in less wealthy countries and received their social security benefits there, which were lower due to the lower costs of living in that country, had to come back to Germany.

concerning the case of "Florida Rolf" in the media, but was also clearly applicable to other cases as well.

Rather surprisingly, the *Bundesverfassungsgericht* never declared a law a prohibited *Einzelfallgesetz*. In every case in which it was obvious that the legislature had enacted a law to touch one specific case, the Court decided that such a case was rather the motive for the legislation than its only target.[467]

2.2.2. *Project laws or special measure laws (Maßnahmegesetze)*

A special category of laws which is treated by the Federal Constitutional Court with less scrutiny, or which is even considered acceptable and not problematic, are *Maßnahmegesetze* (here referred to special measure laws or project laws). The concept of special measure laws was firstly systematically discussed by Forsthoff. He positioned the special measure laws against the classical form of general laws.[468] In contrast to classical general norms, special measure laws are ad hoc measures and specific orders.[469] They are not enacted to have a long-lasting effect in a certain area, such as classical general laws have (for example, in the field of civil law). They can be seen as an *actio* and are characterized by a special relationship between the means and the purpose. Special measure laws are intended for a specific purpose and prescribe appropriate means to achieve that purpose.[470] Their value is strongly connected to their aim, while classical laws have an intrinsic value.[471] This is also evident from the fact that they cease to operate when the aim becomes invalid or when it has been achieved.

The specificity of special measure laws comes to the fore in their relationship to a specific situation[472] giving rise to or necessitating specific measures, but, as a rule, special measure laws are general in nature. This means that they pertain to an undefined number of cases. Nevertheless, special measure laws that are similar to individual laws within the meaning of Art. 19 (1) GG are not uncommon either. Forsthoff illustrates this with the example of the Platow Amnesty Act referred to above: the law had the specific aim of protecting the people involved in the Platow Affair. It was an action of the legislature (unlike classical legislation) to benefit a narrowly defined group of persons.[473] Schneider formulated the relationship between special measure laws and individual laws within the meaning of Art. 19 (1) GG as follows: Every special law is a special measure law, but not every special measure law relates to a single case.[474]

From then on, they had to be paid by German standards, which was more expensive for the German State than just continuation of payment abroad.

467 For a recent example, see the decision of the *Bundesverfassungsgericht* of March 12, 2008, 2 BvF 4/03.

468 Cf. K. Zeidler, *Maßnahmegesetz und «klassisches» Gesetz*, Karlsruhe: C.F. Müller 1961, pp. 77 ff.

469 E. Forsthoff, "Über Maßnahme=Gesetze," in: E. Forsthoff, *Rechtsstaat im Wandel*, Stuttgart: W. Kohlhammer Verlag: 1964, p. 81.

470 *Ibid.*, p. 83.

471 *Ibid.*, p. 84.

472 *Ibid.*, p. 85.

473 *Ibid.*, p. 86.

474 Schneider (2002), p. 144. See also Ch.F. Menger, *Das Gesetz als Norm und Maßnahme*, Berlin: Walter de Gruyter & Co. 1957, p. 21.

The *Bundesverfassungsgericht* has already declared special measure laws irrelevant for the purposes of constitutional law. It appears that the Court uses the word "irrelevant" as a synonym for "permissible."[475] This classification seems to be correct. Special measure laws, mainly economic ones, by the legislature trying to achieve a certain goal, are very common nowadays.[476]

More interesting than the problem of the permissibility of special measure laws in general,[477] however, is the question of the permissibility of special measure laws by which the legislature tries to achieve a certain aim in a specific case. Three famous cases were the motivation to answer this question: the Platow Amnesty case, the Lex Rheinstahl case, and the Südumfahrung Stendal, which have already been described. In the first two cases, the *Bundesverfassungsgericht* rejected the claim that the acts were individual and the Lex Rheinstahl was explicitly designated a special measure law, which the Court considered an irrelevant concept from a constitutional point of view. In the third case, the constitutional claims centered on the character of the Act as a special measure, which the legislature had used for a single railway project near Berlin. In its decision on Südumfahrung Stendal, the Court could not ignore the specific character of the special measure law.[478] It held, however, that, especially in the field of spatial planning, the legislature may enact a specific project law if there are good reasons (*gute Gründe*) to do so. It has often been said that the *Bundesverfassungsgericht* delivered that decision while experiencing "reunification euphoria." It is unclear whether that Court would approve any other project law providing executive measures in order to accelerate the decision-making process with regard to major infrastructural projects nowadays. One thing is clear: the federal legislature is not interested in finding out. Other important infrastructural projects, for example the construction of Berlin Brandenburg International Airport (BBI), were governed by an administrative decision-making process.[479]

2.3. The general interest requirement

The general discussion about the requirement that legislation and law should serve the general interest (*Gemeinwohl*) in Germany can be positioned within the subject of the targets, purposes, and legitimacy of State action. There are different theories about this, for example, the ethical theory, the religion theory, and the theory of the liberal State but, as Katz shows, all these theories have a common element. They all presuppose that the

475 P. Kunig, "Einzelfallentscheidungen durch Gesetz," *Jura* 1993, p. 308.

476 See W. Thiele, "Vom Wandel des Gesetzesinhalts," *DVBl.* 1978, pp. 901–903.

477 The subject of special measure laws was a very popular topic of discussion in the 1960s. See, e.g., Zeidler (1961), Huber (1963), and L. von Westerholt, *Neugliederungsgesetze als Maßnahmegesetze und generelles Landesplanungsrecht in Nordrhein-Westfalen*, Münster 1976.

478 About the special measure character of the Lex Stendal and the decision of the Federal Constitutional Court, see Hufeld (1997), pp. 302–305.

479 See the spatial planning decision (Planfeststellungsbeschluss – Entscheidungsgründe Ausbau Verkehrsflughafen Berlin-Schönefeld) at <www.mil.brandenburg.de/sixcms/media.php/4055/PFSB_283-350.pdf> (last accessed on June 12, 2011).

basic purpose of the State is to promote the common good, the common interest.[480] In addition to State purpose theories, the concept of general interest in Germany can be found in the sphere of fundamental rights and limitations of these rights by the State.

But what is actually the general interest that should be furthered? The general interest is sometimes understood as the common interest that can be derived from united private and public interests.[481] These two kinds of interests differ, but the difference has nothing to do with the personal entity representing the interests, for example, private groups representing the public interest (e.g., an environmental interest) and public bodies that do not always have the will or intention to serve the public interest.[482] Public interest can be viewed as directly intended to further the general interest.[483]

The definition of the general interest given above appears to be quite vague. Moreover, it is not the only definition of the general interest, and some German authors doubt whether a uniform definition will ever be found. The distinction between the "public interest" (*öffentliche Interesse*) and the "general interest" (*Gemeinwohl*) is also unclear, so arguments have been raised to use the terms as synonyms.[484]

But others had more hope and took up the challenge to concretize the concept and to give it more content. Brugger, for example, views the concept of *Gemeinwohl* as an integrated concept of legal certainty, legitimacy, and efficacy. In his opinion, legal certainty means formal rationality and legal coherence, which requires clarity of legal norms, stability, distinction of State functions, and certainty of compliance with legal rules. Legitimacy is about substantive rationality and the promotion of good and fair purposes, while efficacy stands for empirical coherence and the rationality of the purpose.[485] As Brugger admits himself, these three pillars of the general interest still need to be concretized. For that purpose, he developed three procedures: 1) a legal discourse concerning the determination and the organization of State bodies, competences, procedural rules etc., which determines what the law should be, 2) a political and moral discourse, including an open and public debate before just rules can be defined, and 3) social-scientific discourse of experts who can calculate the effects of rules in society.[486] Brugger admits, however, that legal rules cannot always realize these three elements of the general interest at the same time, since they will sometimes contradict each other.[487]

480 A. Katz, *Staatsrecht*, Heidelberg: C.F. Müller Verlag 2007, p. 21. For the different legitimacy theories from a historical perspective, see Th. Würtenberger, "Legitimationsmuster von Herrschaft im Laufe der Geschichte," *JuS* 1986, pp. 344ff.

481 H.J. Wolff, O. Bachof & R. Stober, *Verwaltungsrecht*, München: Beck 1999, Vol. 1, p. 424.

482 E. Schmidt-Aßmann, *Das allgemeine Verwaltungsrecht als Ordnungsidee*, Berlin, Heidelberg: Springer 2004, p. 151. Cf. the lively discussion in the U.S. about special interest legislation.

483 Schmidt-Aßmann (2004), p. 151.

484 See, for example, Th. Brandner, *Gesetzesänderung*, Berlin: Berliner Wissenschafts-Verlag 2004, p. 337. Uerpmann already uses these two concepts interchangeably: R. Uerpmann, *Das öffentliche Interesse*, Tübingen: Mohr Siebeck 1999, p. 37.

485 W. Brugger, "Gemeinwohl als Integrationskonzept von Rechtssicherheit, Legitimität und Zweckmäßigkeit," in: W. Brugger, S. Kirste & M. Anderheiden, *Gemeinwohl in Deutschland, Europa und der Welt*, Baden-Baden: Nomos 2002, p. 23.

486 Brugger (2002), pp. 23–34.

487 Brugger (2002), p. 38.

Another attempt to concretize the concept of the general interest was made by Koller and Uerpmann. Koller formulated three requirements legislation has to meet to be considered in the general interest. Firstly, there must be a universal benefit (*Gemeinwohl als allseitiger Vorteil*). Actions of individuals that promote short-term interests and benefits would sometimes have to be curtailed so that long-term universal benefits could be provided for everyone. Koller takes traffic regulations as an example of this requirement. The limitation of individuals' freedom to drive as fast as they wish and to park and pass other cars wherever they want contributes to the general benefit of safety on the road for everyone.[488] Secondly, society is sometimes justified in imposing obligations and limitations on individuals if they are necessary to achieve common purposes, even if not everyone in society will directly benefit from these purposes (*Gemeinwohl als allgemeines Interesse*). In this regard, compulsory purchase for the purposes of a new road or a railway comes to mind. Thirdly, Koller views the general interest in terms of collective benefits (*Gemeinwohl als kollektive Nützlichkeit*). This third meaning presupposes a collective identity of a society. A rule promotes the general interest of a society if it increases the collective benefits of that society.[489]

Uerpmann argues for understanding the concept of general interest as the consideration and balancing of different interests. He states that endeavors to find out what the general interest is, at least in the field of law, are only meaningful in the context of a specific situation or a specific case.[490]

The next question is whether the concept of general interest is used in German positive constitutional law and whether constitutional law limits the legislature to acting only in the general interest, or whether it might obligate the legislature to promote the general interest.

First of all, let us take a look at the German Basic Law. The text itself comprises several provisions that either use the concept of the general interest or name other interests that correspond to the general interest. The following examples can be given: Art. 14 (3), which provides that expropriation is only permissible for the public good; the legislature's obligation to protect the environment as set out in Art. 20a; peace and security in Art. 24 (2)[491] and Art. 38 (1), which indirectly requires the legislators to serve the general interest of the whole society.[492] But first and foremost, the requirement that laws should serve the general interest follows from fundamental rights and the principle of the rule of law (*Rechtsstaat*), as formulated in Art. 20 (3) ("The legislature shall be bound by the constitutional order, the executive and the judiciary by law and justice").[493] These

488 P. Koller, "Das Konzept des Gemeinwohls," in: Brugger, Kirste & Anderheiden (2002), p. 58.

489 Koller (2002), p. 68.

490 Uerpmann (1999), p. 26. In the same key, BVerfGE 93, 319 (350) and BVerfGE 93, 121 (148): "Der abstrakte Rechtsbegriff des Gemeinwohls deckt eine Vielfalt von Sachverhalten und Zwecken; er bedarf daher der Konkretiserung im einzelnen Fall." For an extensive treatment of the general interest, see M. Anderheiden, *Gemeinwohl in Republik und Union*, Tübingen: Mohr Siebeck 2006.

491 M. Anderheiden, "Gemeinwohlförderung durch die Bereitstellung kollektiver Güter," in: Brugger, Kirste & Anderheiden (2002), p. 434, with more examples.

492 The second sentence of Art. 38 (1) GG reads: "They shall be representatives of the whole people, not bound by orders or instructions, and responsible only to their conscience."

493 Schmidt-Aßmann deduces the normative effect of the concept of the general interest not only from Art. 20 III, but also from Art. 1 of the Basic Law (human dignity), Schmidt-Aßmann (2004), p. 153.

concepts serve as a limitation on the legislature. The *Bundesverfassungsgericht* could not be clearer about it:[494]

> Für die Bestimmung des Verhältnisses von Staat und Religionsgesellschaften nach dem geltenden Verfassungsrecht ist grundlegend, daß das Grundgesetz [...] der staatlichen Gewalt prinzipielle Grenzen setzt. Dies folgt aus der normativen Bedeutung der Freiheitsrechte des Grundgesetzes. Das Grundgesetz hat nicht eine virtuell allumfassende Staatsgewalt verfaßt, sondern den Zweck des Staates materialiter auf die Wahrung des Gemeinwohls beschränkt, in dessen Mitte Freiheit und soziale Gerechtigkeit stehen.

Consequently, legislative constraints on fundamental rights are allowed if they are inspired by the general interest. A few examples of such justifying interests are: prevention of the evasion or abuse of laws,[495] efficiency of collective agreements' norms and safeguarding of legal relationships,[496] public health,[497] the public food supply,[498] or protection of the public against further criminal acts.[499]

Nonetheless, the fact that the legislature provides benefits for a certain group of people or a certain industry does not automatically mean that the law furthers special interests rather than the general interest. This follows from the decision of the Federal Constitutional Court in the case of water legislation in Hessen. The legislature in Hessen enacted a law establishing a levy for taking groundwater. The levy varied from 0.20 DM/m3 to 0.50 DM/m3, but the fisheries industry could benefit from a lower rate of 0.10 DM/m3. These financial benefits were one of the reasons why the law was challenged in the courts as violating, among other constitutional provisions, the principle of equality. In the *Bundesverfassungsgericht*'s view, the legislature is generally allowed to provide benefits for one person, one company, or an industry without violating the principle of equality if such a distribution of collective resources is not arbitrary. No arbitrariness will be found if there are objective grounds (*sachliche Gründe*) for the unequal distribution, and it can be justified by general interest arguments. The *Bundesverfassungsgericht* accepted the argument of the Hessen legislature that the general, problematic competitive position of the fisheries industry justified the privilege.[500]

It is among the competences of the legislature to define the general interest which it aims to promote:[501]

> Die Ausrichtung an dem jeweils zu konkretisierenden Gemeinwohl ist zwingendes Erfordernis jeder rechtsstaatlich gebundenen Gesetzgebung (vgl. BVerfGE 50, 50 [51]). Dies gilt auch,

494 BVerfGE 42, 312 (331–332). See also BVerfGE 44, 125 (141).
495 BVerfGE 78, 249 (278).
496 BVerfGE 72, 141 (152), 77, 84 (107), 78, 77 (85). These and other examples can be found in: Stern (1994), pp. 353ff.
497 BVerfGE 7, 377 (414).
498 BVerfGE 25, 1 (16).
499 BVerfGE 35, 185 (190ff.). For more examples, see Uerpmann (1999), p. 63.
500 BVerfGE 93, 319 (350). See also BVerfGE 80, 360 (364) for the justification of social privileges, for example to secure jobs and avoid unemployment.
501 BVerfGE 59, 216 (229).

> wenn der Gesetzgeber eine Namensgebung im Zusammenhang mit der kommunalen Neugliederung nach wenigen Jahren wieder ändern, also das Neugliederungsgesetz selbst korrigieren will. Es obliegt allerdings in erster Linie dem Gesetzgeber, zu entscheiden, ob eine bestimmte normative Ausgestaltung eines Lebenssachverhalts im Interesse des gemeinen Wohls liegt; im Rahmen der verfassungsrechtlichen Bindungen kommt dabei dem Gesetzgeber ein Einschätzungs- und Bewertungsvorrang zu, den das Bundesverfassungsgericht zu beachten hat.

The courts are very reserved in this respect, and they will only declare the law unconstitutional if the general interest as set out by the legislature is obviously not the real interest that the legislature seeks to serve. The real intention of the legislature is decisive in this respect, as can be demonstrated by the case of passenger transportation.

After the Second World War, new transportation agencies were established that helped to bring private car drivers into contact with private persons who wished to travel in the same direction. This was a new phenomenon. Private passengers were to pay the driver for a ride in a car, but the costs were not higher than the real operating costs, in addition to a fee charged by the transportation agency for its service. In conformity with the old legal regime, the agencies were not required to have any administrative transportation permission. They only needed to be registered. The German legislature, however, changed the transportation law[502] and required that, from then on, drivers had to have a license if transportation of private persons was arranged through an agency or by means of advertising. Otherwise, they risked criminal prosecution or civil penalties.[503] The legislature justified the legislative change by invoking the general interest of road safety and the protection of private passengers. The *Bundesverfassungsgericht* found this reason questionable. The judges could not understand how road safety could be achieved by obligating the drivers to get a license if transportation is arranged by an agency, and why the passengers making use of transportation arranged by an agency should be protected more than passengers where no such arrangement had been made. The *Bundesverfassungsgericht* therefore searched for the real motives of the legislature. Given the legislative history of the new bill and the fact that the German public transportation company (*Deutsche Bundesbahn*) had agitated against the private transportation agencies, it was clear to the Court that the only reason to enact the new provision was to protect and favor the *Deutsche Bundesbahn* by hindering the activities of the private agencies, the ultimate purpose being to stop these activities completely.[504] The Court termed this abuse of legislative power and accused the legislature of hiding the real legislative motives by pretending that the general interest of road safety and protection of passengers was to be promoted. Consequently, the *Bundesverfassungsgericht* found that the law was incompatible with the principle of the rule of law (*Rechtsstaatlichkeit*).[505]

502 Sec. 1 (2), No 1 PBefG (*Personenbeförderungsgesetz*).

503 BVerfGE 17, 306 (312).

504 After enactment of the law, the agencies brought 2,000 drivers into contact with private passengers. None of these drivers had a license to carry passengers, as required by the new law. Surprisingly, it was not these drivers who were prosecuted, but the transportation agencies. These agencies were accused of helping the drivers to commit the crime of not having a license, BVerfGE 17, 306 (310).

505 BVerfGE 17, 306.

Legislation must serve the general interest, and the legislature itself is, at least in the eyes of the *Bundesverfassungsgericht*, the guardian of the general interest and not of special interests.[506] As stated above, however, only the legislature determines what the general interest is. In practice, the influence of lobby groups is significant in this respect. It has even been said that the role of Parliament in making political choices is diminishing, since the policies are prepared and decisions made in other places, such as the ministries, where the lobby groups have much influence. Parliament would only have to ratify what had already been decided.[507]

The role of the lobby groups in the legislative process in Germany is taken for granted, since it has been institutionalized. Sec. 41 and 47 of the Federal Government's Joint Rules of Procedure (*Gemeinsame Geschäftsordnung der Bundesministerien*) provide for consultation of the interest groups in the process of preparing a bill.[508] This, however, does not mean that this influence of interest groups is always welcomed. In the literature, concerns are regularly expressed about the diminishing amount of legislation that is enacted on neutral grounds to solve real problems and therefore the general interest instead of special interests. Von Hippel, for example, gives the example of the tobacco and alcohol industry lobbies. Despite the fact that a great number of people die in Germany because of tobacco usage and alcohol abuse every year, the State, strongly influenced by these two lobbies, has not succeeded in reducing alcohol and tobacco abuse.[509] In general, lobbying is seen as a threat to democracy, because only groups that are strong and individuals who are represented by these strong groups have the possibility to influence the legislature to promote these interests. As Leif and Speth observe, small interest groups nowadays have no chances to influence the German Parliament in such a way that it will enact legislation that serves the particular interests of these groups.[510]

2.4. Conclusion

A discussion about the generality of laws in Germany can be viewed from different angles, namely, the concepts of laws in the formal and in the material sense, the prohibition of individual laws that restrict individuals' basic rights, the concept of special measure laws, and the requirement of general interest. As far as the normative framework

506 BVerfGE 33, 125 (159), in which the *Bundesverfassungsgericht* calls the legislature "Hüter des Gemeinwohls gegenüber Gruppeninteressen."

507 Th. Leif & R. Speth, *Die Stille Macht: Lobbyismus in Deutschland*, Wiesbaden: VS Verlag 2003, p. 25.

508 *Gemeinsame Geschäftsordnung*, version of June 1, 2009 at <www.bmi.bund.de/cln_095/SharedDocs/Downloads/DE/Veroeffentlichungen/ggo.html?nn=267412> (last accessed on June 12, 2011).

509 E. von Hippel, "Machtmißbrauch der Lobby als Herausforderung," in: S. Brink & H.A. Wolf, *Gemeinwohl und Verantwortung*, Berlin: Duncker & Humblot 2004, p. 81. As Hippel states, the most popular area for lobbying is tax law.

510 Leif & Speth (2003), p. 27. For the influence of the lobby groups, see also K. Von Beyme, *Der Gesetzgeber: der Bundestag als Entscheidungszentrum*, Opladen: Westdeutscher Verlag 1997, p. 149, and A. Gutersohn, "Gruppeninteresse und Allgemeinwohl," in: H.J. Pleitner & K.H. Schmidt, *Grundlagen und Grundfragen der gewerblichen Wirtschaft*, Berlin/München/St. Gallen: Duncker & Humblot 1984, pp. 3–32. Cf. P. Lösche, "Demokratie braucht Lobbying," in: Th. Leith & R. Speth, *Die fünfte Gewalt Lobbyismus in Deutschland*, Bonn: Bundeszentrale für politische Bildung 2006, pp. 53–69, who confirms this general view, but finds the risks of lobbying for democracy exaggerated.

of the Basic Law is concerned, no distinction is made between laws that are general and those that are case-specific. Irrespective of these characteristics, every legislative act that has been adopted in the procedure dictated by the Basic Law itself is seen as a valid source of law. Case-specific laws that limit individuals' basic rights are an exception in this respect. Apart from this, several constitutional principles can be invoked to restrict the legislature when it acts by means of ad hoc laws. In that case, however, the mere fact that a law is case-specific will hardly justify the violation of any of the constitutional norms, as will be shown in the next chapters.

Chapter 3

EQUAL TREATMENT

Introduction

It has often been argued that the equality principle, which can be found in Art. 3 of the Basic Law,[511] presupposes the generality of laws. As far as the equality principle is concerned, the legislature should be prevented from creating exceptional regimes for specific persons and cases.[512] Both favorable and unfavorable exceptions to the general rules should be prohibited.[513] Owing to this line of reasoning, both the Lex Stendal and the Lex Schörner were criticized because the legislature had exempted the Südumfahrung Stendal project from the "inconvenient" general rules and created an exceptional, disadvantageous regime for Ferdinand Schörner, according to critics.

Although true in general, that argument appears insufficient for the Federal Constitutional Court to invalidate an ad hoc law in light of Art. 3 GG, only because it treated a single case differently. For the Court, the deciding factor is whether the legislature acted arbitrarily. At the beginning of the 1980s, the *Bundesverfassungsgericht* developed a second test (*die neue Formel*), which centered on the question whether the differences between two cases (or groups) were of such a nature and importance that the differentiation could be justified.

511 Art. 3 of the Basic Law states:
"(1) All persons shall be equal before the law.
(2) Men and women shall have equal rights. The state shall promote the equal implementation of equal rights for women and men and take steps to eliminate disadvantages that now exist.
(3) No person shall be favored or disfavored because of sex, parentage, race, language, homeland and origin, faith, or religious or political opinions. No person shall be disfavored because of disability."

512 For the relation between the generality of laws and the equality principle, see G. Dürig, "Art. 3" in: Th. Maunz & G. Dürig, *Grundgesetz: Kommentar*, München: Beck 1958–2003, pp. 13ff. The equality principle applies to persons. Art. 3 GG expresses this idea clearly, but it does not require that these persons must be directly affected to be able to challenge a law. Unequal treatment of cases and situations can indirectly impose unequal treatment on people as well. See L. Osterloh, "Art. 3," in: M. Sachs, *Grundgesetz. Kommentar*, München: C.H. Beck 2007, p. 183.

513 The Federal Constitutional Court already decided that not only legislation which is disadvantageous but also legislation which provides benefits is governed by Art. 3 GG: BVerfGE 79, 1 (17).

3.1. The arbitrariness test (*Willkürverbot*)

A decision of the Federal Constitutional Court from 1951 gave rise to the interpretation of the German equality principle in Art. 3 GG as a prohibition of arbitrary action by the legislature. In that decision, the *Bundesverfassungsgericht* decided in what circumstances the legislature is likely to violate Art. 3:[514]

> Der Gleichheitssatz ist verletzt, wenn sich ein vernünftiger, sich aus der Natur der Sache ergebender oder sonstwie sachlich einleuchtender Grund für die gesetzliche Differenzierung oder Gleichbehandlung nicht finden läßt, kurzum, wenn die Bestimmung als willkürlich bezeichnet werden muß.

Accordingly, a legislative act will survive the arbitrariness test of Art. 3 GG if the differentiation made by the legislature is objective (*sachlich*) and it arises from the nature of the case. The terms 'objective' or 'neutral' are used here as the opposite of individual or personal classification.

In the early 1950s (and as complemented in 1960), the federal legislature enacted a law that governed the closing hours of shops at railway stations. The law provided exceptional closing times for pharmacies. In contrast to other shops, they were not allowed to be constantly open. The owner of a pharmacy in Frankfurt, which happened to be the only pharmacy at any federal railway station, complained before the court that he was the only target of the new disadvantageous rules and that he was being discriminated against by the legislature in comparison to other shops. The *Bundesverfassungsgericht* decided that the challenged differentiation made by the legislature was justified, as it ensued from the special nature of pharmacies. Since they had a special task of providing people with medication, they could be treated differently from other commercial shops at railway stations.[515]

The test of arbitrariness does not impose a heavy burden on the legislature, because only legislation that differentiates in an *evidently* unobjective way (*unsachlich*) will violate Art. 3 GG.[516] Unobjectivity in this context is associated with evident injustice.[517] The new justification test requires more.

3.2. The justification test (*die neue Formel*)

According to the new version of the equality test, Art. 3 GG is violated if the legislature treats two groups of addressees differently, and there are no differences between these groups whose nature or importance could justify unequal treatment:[518]

514 BVerfGE 1, 14 (52). See also BVerfGE 33, 367 (384) and BVerfGE 54, 11 (25).
515 BVerfGE 13, 225.
516 See, for example, BVerfGE 12, 326 (333).
517 Osterloh (2007), p. 171.
518 BVerfGE 55, 72 (88).

> Demgemäß ist dieses Grundrecht vor allem dann verletzt, wenn eine Gruppe von Normadressaten im Vergleich zu anderen Normadressaten anders behandelt wird, obwohl zwischen beiden Gruppen keine Unterschiede von solcher Art und solchem Gewicht bestehen, daß sie die ungleiche Behandlung rechtfertigen könnten.

The central issue here is therefore the justification issue. There must be sufficient reasons to justify unequal treatment. In its review, the Federal Constitutional Court does not examine whether the differentiating rule is the fairest or the most functional one.[519]

The exceptional situation of the reunification of East and West Germany very often provided such a ground for justification, for example in the case of the closing of the Academy of Sciences of the German Democratic Republic. After the reunification, the federal law ordered the dissolution of the employment contracts of people working for the Academy. The German legislature saw this as a necessary condition for the reorganization and renewal of the scientific scene in the newly reunited Germany. Several employees of the Academy opposed the law, claiming, among other things, that it violated the equality principle. They complained that they were put at a disadvantage in comparison to other employees in public service. The Federal Constitutional Court rejected this claim. It considered the need to reorganize the Academy of Sciences in East Germany after reunification (which was not necessary for the Western academic institutions) and decided that the unequal treatment was therefore justified.[520]

3.3. The relationship between the two tests

The new justification test developed by the Federal Constitutional Court in the 1980s is clearly more rigorous than the arbitrariness test. It requires reasons that justify the differentiation, whereas the arbitrariness test only requires objective grounds for differentiation. Not every objective differentiation will provide sufficient grounds for justification.[521]

There are thus two tests, but does this mean that they can both be used, and if so, in what circumstances? Or is it rather correct to say that the arbitrariness test has been replaced by the new justification review? The Federal Constitutional Court has already decided that both tests are still useful. This is clear, but it is less clear which test should be used and when. The Court has attempted to clarify this issue on several occasions. The answer seems to depend on a number of factors. Osterloh[522] ranges these factors as follows. Firstly, the Court relates the new justification test to the group of people. It prescribes a more stringent review of legislation that differentiates on the basis of personal characteristics rather than on the basis of neutral features or situations. Secondly, the question of the consequences of the unequal treatment for civil liberties and rights

519 BVerfGE 68, 287 (301).
520 BVerfGE 85, 360 (383).
521 A.R. Maaß, "Die neuere Rechtsprechung des BVerfGE zum allgemeinen Gleichheitssatz – Ein Neuansatz?," *NVwZ* 1988, 21.
522 Osterloh (2007), pp. 185ff.

(*Freiheitsgrundrechte*) plays an important role.[523] The more negative consequences differentiating legislation has for the constitutionally protected freedoms, the stricter the test it applies. Finally, and most unclear, is the meaning of the principle of the social State based on the principles of social security and social justice, for review in light of Art. 3 GG. As Osterloh observes, while the Court gives the legislature much freedom in relation to the labor market, and social and economic policy, it does not hesitate to apply a more rigorous test when the legislative measures in these fields restrict civil rights and liberties.[524] In any event, fiscal ends alone do not provide sufficient grounds for justification of unequal treatment.[525]

It is interesting to observe how the Federal Constitutional Court applied the equality principle to the Südumfahrung Stendal railway connection case. On the one hand, the Court's assessment in light of the equality principle seemed not to be extremely strict. This would point to the application of the arbitrariness test. On the other hand, the Court paid attention to the unusual and exceptional nature of the project and the circumstances (reunification of western and eastern Germany) which points more in the direction of the new 'justification test.'

3.4. The consistency of the legal system and the equality principle

The examples of ad hoc legislation in Germany show that the legislature does not hesitate to provide exceptional rules for a specific case or situation and therefore to deviate from the general system of legal rules in one specific field. The Lex Stendal illustrates this most explicitly. Whereas a decision making-process concerning specific infrastructural projects is mainly one of the competences of the executive branch of government, the legislature was guilty of breaching this system by providing rules for Südumfahrung Stendal on its own. The *Bundesverfassungsgericht*, however, did not address the inconsistency in the Südumfahrung Stendal case. It did so in other cases, including the case of the Lex Schörner.

The principle of legislative consistency (*Systemgerechtigkeit*) concerns the legislature's commitment to the reasonableness criteria and to evaluations it previously made.[526] This means that the legislature is in principle bound by its previous choices, unless there are sufficient and convincing reasons to justify changes or deviations from previously adopted general rules.[527] The *Bundesverfassungsgericht* explained this principle understandably in its judgment in the Lex Schörner case, on the basis of retroactive, curative legislation. In the Court's view, legislation correcting errors or closing gaps in earlier legislation is not constitutionally problematic, as long as it does not upset the

523 See, e.g., BVerfGE 82, 126 (146).

524 BVerfGE 89, 365 (376).

525 See, e.g., BVerfGE 93, 386 (402).

526 Ch. Starck, Art. 3, in: H.V. Mangoldt, F. Klein & Ch. Starck, *Kommentar zum Grundgesetz*, München: Franz Vahlen 2005, p. 307.

527 BVerfGE 13, 331 (340): "'[S]achlich hinreichend gerechtfertigt' im Sinne der Judikatur des Bundesverfassungsgerichts (BVerfGE 9, 20 [28] und 201 [207]) ist eine Abweichung jedoch in einem Falle, in dem das Steuergesetz die von ihm selbst statuierte Sachgesetzlichkeit aufgibt, nur dann, wenn sie von überzeugenden Gründen getragen ist." See also BVerfGE 85, 238 (247) with references.

original system of the law, and is in line with its purpose and meaning.[528] In later judgments, the *Bundesverfassungsgericht* connected the principle of legislative consistency to the equality principle and refused to treat it as an independent ground for the assessment of legislative changes: violation of the consistency principle does not automatically result in violation of the Constitution: "Das *Bundesverfassungsgericht* kann eine Regelung nur nach den Maßtäben der Verfassung, nicht aber unter dem Gesichtspunkt der Systemwidrigkeit für verfassungswidrig erklären."[529] Nevertheless, the inconsistency of new legislation can be an indication that the equality principle of Art. 3 GG is violated.[530]

In the literature, many academics applauded the principle of legislative consistency, as formulated by the Federal Constitutional Court. They also vigorously argued that transparency and rationality of legislative choices be understood as constitutional principles.[531] These principles are especially threatened when the legislature acts impulsively as a reaction to specific situations or cases:[532]

> Der Gesetzgeber schuldet Rationalität im Verfahren. Gerade in Bereichen sich ausweitender, anlaßbezogener Gesetzgebung gehen Mängel in der rechtsstaatlichen-distanzschaffenden Funktion des Verfahrens typischerweise einher mit einer Schwächung materieller rechtsstaatlicher Funktionen der Gesetzgebung. Dies gilt für die Begrenzung staatlichen Handelns, dies gilt für das freiheitssichernde Postulat der Rechtssicherheit, der Unverbrüchlichkeit der Rechtsordnung. In zweifacher Hinsicht bedarf dieses Postulat verstärkter Hervorhebung – es richtet sich zum einen auf Klarheit und Konsequenz im Rahmen der bestehenden Ordnung, hat zum andern aber neben dieser gleichsam statischen Dimension eine dynamische Komponente, gerichtet auf zeitliche Kontinuität.

In line with this view, although the consistency principle has generally been applauded, the case law of the Federal Constitutional Court has been criticized. Making the consistency of legislative changes subject only to the equality rule in Art. 3 GG was seen as problematic. This limitation was believed to inadequately address the larger aspects of legislative consistency, such as legal certainty (in connection with reliability) and continuity of legislation.[533]

[528] BVerfGE 7, 129 (152). Besides, repairing legislation is also seen as problematic if it pretends to repair faults, but it in fact makes odd changes in a law.

[529] BVerfGE 76, 130 (140). See also Brandner (2004), p. 313 for further references.

[530] See, e.g., BVerfGE 59, 36 (49).

[531] See an overview of several academic opinions made by U. Battis, "Systemgerechtigkeit," in: R. Stödter & W. Thieme (eds.), *Hamburg, Deutschland, Europa. Festschrift für Hans Peter Ipsen*, Tübingen: J.C.B. Mohr 1977, p. 17.

[532] Ch. Degenhart, "Gesetzgebung im Rechtsstaat," *DÖV* 1981, p. 486.

[533] Ch. Degenhart, *Systemgerechtigkeit und Selbstbindung des Gesetzgebers als Verfassungspostulat*, München: C.H. Beck 1976, pp. 27–28.

3.5. Legal protection

A common claim in Germany with regard to legislative acts that are de facto in the nature of case-specific administrative acts is that they diminish legal protection and thus violate the guarantee of effective legal protection set out in Art. 19 (4) GG. Complaints are regularly made that legislatures act opportunistically. This depends on how controversial the situation or case to be governed is and what instrument would guarantee a successful remedy. If a case is hardly controversial or not at all, it will be regulated by an administrative decision. If it is contentious and the possibility that it will be challenged in court is great, a legislative act will be chosen as an instrument. Because the judicial review of a legislative act is less extensive, since only constitutional arguments can be raised in court, the legislative act is more likely to survive. A judicial review based on constitutional arguments is therefore perceived as an ineffective guarantee of *individual* legal protection.[534]

In the literature, this phenomenon has been called *Formenmißbrauch*,[535] which can be translated as abuse of form. The most prominent case of legislation criticized for abuse of form at the federal level is the Südumfahrung Stendal case. At the *Länder* level, such legislative practices appear as well. In Hamburg, for example, the legislature decided by a legislative act to reorganize the school system at one specific school, namely the Wilhelmsburg Gymnasium. The legislature decided to enact a specific legislative measure after the administrative regulation of the same matter was annulled in provisional judicial proceedings. The administrative courts in Hamburg strongly criticized the Act. In their view, legislatures act arbitrarily and therefore violate the equality rule of Art. 3 GG if the provision of exceptional legal regimes for one case is expediency-driven and its only purpose is to avoid strict judicial review. The Federal Constitutional Court took the same view in another case from Hamburg, where controversial construction plans were laid down in a legislative instead of an administrative act:[536]

> Eine derartige Abgrenzung mit der Folge, daß in ein und demselben Bundesland [...] der Rechtsschutz gegen bestimmte Bebauungspläne eröffnet, gegen andere – und zwar gerade die möglicherweise besonders kontroversen – dagegen verschlossen ist, erweist sich, nachdem der Bundesgesetzgeber der verwaltungsgerichtliche Normenkontrollverfahren gegen Bebauungspläne [...] gerade bundesweit eröffnet hat, als nicht sachgerecht im Sinne des Art. 3 Abs 1 GG.

534 Meessen (1970), p. 319 with references. Ronellenfitsch views the judicial assessment of constitutional challenges as an important supplement, rather than as a replacement of effective individual legal protection: Ronellenfitsch (1991), p. 780.

535 See, for example, H. Goerlich, "Formenmißbrauch-Einzelfallgesetz-Gewaltenteilung," *DÖV* 1985, pp. 945–953, and Ch. Pestalozza, *"Formenmißbrauch" des Staates*, München: C.H. Beck 1973.

536 BVerfGE 70, 35 (57). In that case, the claims were nevertheless rejected by the *Bundesverfassungsgericht*, which decided that the legislative act from Hamburg, given its administrative character, could be challenged in a normal administrative procedure as well. Both cases have been discussed by Goerlich (1985), pp. 945–948.

Nevertheless, the legislature is not always prohibited from reducing the possibilities of legal protection. In a specific expropriation case where the legislature had used a legislative act, the *Bundesverfassungsgericht* reflected on the problem of legal protection and formulated grounds for justification of expropriations by legislation. In the *Bundesverfassungsgericht*'s opinion, the legislature cannot be accused of *Formenmißbrauch* if the circumstances are so exceptional that they require a legislative act instead of an administrative one, even though the extent of the legal protection is diminished. In that specific case, the exceptional situation that justified a legislative measure was the flood disaster in 1962. The legislature had to respond quickly by constructing new dykes and strengthening the old ones. This would have been impossible if the traditional way of administrative decision-making with the possibility of administrative judicial review had been followed.[537]

In light of this case law of the Federal Constitutional Court, it was difficult for some legal commentators to understand that the same Court had treated the Lex Stendal in the Südumfahrung Stendal case so mildly. There the Court did not require any exceptional and urgent situation to justify the reduction of legal protection: good reasons (*gute Gründe*) sufficed.[538]

It is interesting to note that, although the guarantee of legal protection can be found in Art. 19 (4) GG, the Court often decides the issue by applying the equality test of Art. 3 GG. This is inspired by the fact that, as the Court decided earlier, Art. 19 (4) GG does not apply to legislative acts[539] and it does not require the legislature to choose a form beforehand that guarantees the best possible legal protection.[540]

3.6. Conclusion

Although the general purpose of the equality principle of Art. 3 GG is to prevent the arbitrary unequal treatment of similar cases by the legislature, several different types of arguments can be dealt with within its scope. Those of particular importance for ad hoc legislation are the arguments of legislative inconsistency and diminished legal protection. The *Bundesverfassungsgericht* is willing to uphold any legislative act that deviates from the established legal system and diminishes the possibilities of judicial control if the circumstances that forced the legislature to take extraordinary action are of an exceptional nature and the differentiation made is objective. To the dissatisfaction of academics, who argued for the broader meaning of the principle of legislative consistency and its independent status in constitutional law, the *Bundesverfassungsgericht* refused to impose such far-reaching limits on the legislature.

537 BVerfGE 24, 367 (403).

538 W. Blümel, "Fachplanung durch Bundesgesetz (Legalplanung)," *DVBl.* 1997, p. 211.

539 BVerfGE 24, 33.

540 BVerfGE 70, 35 (56).

Chapter 4

LEGAL CERTAINTY (*RECHTSSICHERHEIT*) AND THE PROTECTION OF LEGITIMATE EXPECTATIONS (*VERTRAUENSSCHUTZ*)

Introduction

One of the most important legal principles of German constitutional law centers on legal certainty and the protection of individuals' legitimate expectations with regard to the existing legal order. This chapter will focus on this issue, but not every aspect of legal certainty and protection of legitimate expectations will be discussed. Rather than such aspects as clearness and definiteness of legislative rules, attention will be paid to the retroactivity of laws, and the aspect of stability and durability of legal norms.[541] These are the points on which ad hoc laws are criticized in Germany. Retroactivity was apparently one of the most significant problems in the case of the Lex Schörner. The criticism was directed at the fact that the legislature suddenly changed the existing statute, thereby acting emotionally rather than rationally. The case of the Südumfahrung Stendal railway connection went even more deeply into the problem of the stability of laws: how stable are general administrative laws if they can be changed every time they appear to be inconvenient to reach short-term governmental goals?

4.1. Retroactive legislation

Retroactive legislation may sometimes threaten individuals' expectations about the continuity of legislation and cause uncertainty about their legal position if the existing rules change. As the famous case of the Lex Schörner illustrates, however, this does not necessarily imply that every law in which legal consequences are attached to past events is prohibited or that every form of expectations must be protected. Hence, the Federal Constitutional Court dismissed the claims in the case of Ferdinand Schörner, although legal scholars were convinced that the Lex Schörner was unconstitutional.

The Federal Constitutional Court has already convincingly declared that the principle of protection of legitimate expectations stems from the rule of law (Art. 20 GG), although

541 The focus in this Chapter will be on changing legislation, although *Vertrauensschutz* can be found in other specific constitutional provisions as well, for example the guarantee of property. For an overview, see B. Pieroth, "Die neuere Rechtsprechung des Bundesverfassungsgerichts zum Grundsatz des Vertrauensschutzes," *JZ* 1984, pp. 974–976.

the German Basic Law makes an explicit reference to retroactivity of legislation in criminal law only. In that field, the legislature is absolutely prohibited from giving retroactive effect to legislation, pursuant to Art. 103 (2) GG: "An act may be punished only if it was defined by a law as a criminal offence before the act was committed." To define the limits of legislative changes that affect past events in other areas, the Federal Constitutional Court distinguished between real and pseudo-retroactive legislation.[542] Each of these two forms is subjected to a more or less stringent assessment. It should be mentioned here, however, that the principle of the retroactivity of laws, including the presumption against retroactivity is particularly meaningful for retroactive laws that are disadvantageous for their addressees. Laws that retroactively benefit individuals are not prohibited in principle.[543]

*4.1.1. Real retroactivity (*echte Rückwirkung*)*

The *Bundesverfassungsgericht* defined real retroactive laws as laws that intervene in matters that were completed and settled before the law was enacted.[544] Laws in this category are fundamentally prohibited, unless an exceptional ground for justification can be found.

4.1.1.1. Grounds for justification

The Federal Constitutional Court classified the possible grounds for justification which it considered to have stemmed from the principle of the *Rechtsstaat*[545] in several categories.[546] Retroactive legislation will not be invalidated if individuals could have foreseen that the law would change,[547] their rights were unfairly obtained, the existing rules were unclear or defective, any unconstitutional legislation was replaced, retroactivity was required for compelling reasons of the general interest, the legislature had tried to avoid certain effects that the promulgation of new legislation would have had, or the damage caused by the law's retroactivity was insignificant.[548] The exceptions that justify the use of real retroactive laws do not form any exhaustive list. They are subject to further development.[549]

542 In the academic literature, the distinction between real and pseudo retroactive legislation has not always been found that clear and has therefore often been criticized. See, for example, K. Quack, "Die Rückwirkung belastender Gesetze," *DVBl.* 1962, p. 290, and J. Iliopoulos-Strangas, *Rückwirkung und Sofortwirkung von Gesetzen*, Baden-Baden: Nomos 1986, pp. 76ff.

543 See BVerfGE 30, 367 (386), in which the *Bundesverfassungsgericht* explained what laws can be seen as disadvantageous.

544 BVerfGE 11, 139 (145ff.).

545 BVerfGE 13, 261.

546 BVerfGE 18, 429.

547 BVerfGE 13, 261 (273ff.), BVerfGE 72, 200 (261ff.).

548 For a more detailed list of exceptional grounds for justification, see Iliopoulos-Strangas (1986), pp. 54ff., and Th. Berger, *Zulässigkeit der Rückwirkung von Gesetzen*, Frankfurt am Main: Peter Lang 2002, pp. 92ff.

549 BVerfGE 72, 200 (258).

Foreseeability of amendment

The Federal Constitutional Court decided what time is decisive to conclude that it was foreseeable for the public that the existing legislation would change. From the time the *Bundestag* agrees on legislative changes, in conformity with the legislative procedure as formulated in Art. 77 (1) GG, individuals' expectations that the old legal regime will continue are no longer legitimate and therefore no longer protected.[550] In formulating this rule, the *Bundesverfassungsgericht* attempted to strike a balance between individual and government interests, as Berger observes. It is in the interest of individuals to be able to act according to the existing legal rules, until new legislation has definitively been declared binding and they have had sufficient opportunity to study it. On the other hand, it is the government's interest to limit individuals' chances to evade the new legal regime. The government would therefore prefer the time of the legislative proposal's submission to be decisive, rather than the time of the Act's official promulgation.[551] As a compromise, the Federal Constitutional Court chose the middle ground.

Avoiding the effect of the law's announcement

The Court did allow for the fact that special circumstances may justify an exception to the rule formulated above. The legislature is permitted to give new legislation retroactive effect, not only from the time the *Bundestag* has agreed on legislative changes, but even from the time the legislative proposal is announced.[552] This exception is meaningful, especially when the new legal regime is less favorable for the addressees than the old one. The risk would be that individuals will take steps, as a result of which the new legislation can never achieve its intended effect. The *Bundesverfassungsgericht*'s decision in a case concerning social housing illustrates this idea:[553]

> Mit dem 31. Dezember 1989 hat der Gesetzgeber keinen zu frühen Stichtag für die Rückwirkung gewählt. Grundsätzlich wird das Vertrauen in den Fortbestand einer gesetzlichen Regelung zwar erst mit dem Änderungsbeschluß des Bundestags zerstört (vgl. BVerfGE 72, 175 [200]), der hier am 29. März 1990 gefaßt wurde. Dieser Gesichtspunkt hat aber insbesondere dann weniger Gewicht, wenn es darum geht, einen Ankündigungseffekt zu vermeiden, der die beabsichtigte Wirkung der Gesetzesänderung ganz oder zum Teil zunichte zu machen droht. Ein solcher Fall lag hier vor. Das Wohnungsbindungsänderungsgesetz hätte sein wohnungspolitisches Ziel nicht im geplanten Umfang erreichen können, wenn zahlreiche Eigentümer von Sozialwohnungen die bevorstehende Verlängerung der Wohnungsbindung und die ungünstigere Berechnung der Kostenmiete zum Anlaß vorzeitiger Rückzahlung genutzt hätten.

550 BVerfGE 72, 175 (200), BVerfGE 76, 256 (351).

551 Berger (2002), pp. 93–94.

552 For sharp criticism on this point, see R. Gerhardt, "Veröffentlichung von Gesetzesvorhaben und Rückwirkung von Gesetzen," *ZRP* 1973, pp. 81–84.

553 BVerfGE 95, 64 (88–89).

Reparation of defective legislation

Situations are conceivable in which the legislature attempts to correct errors in existing legislation. According to the Federal Constitutional Court, however, even though such rectifications are understandable, the legislature is not always allowed to implement them if, by doing so, it intervenes in closed cases and past events. The *Bundesverfassungsgericht* has regularly decided that such legislative reparations are only allowed when errors result in decidedly unclear rules and objective lacunas or when the rules are unfair or contrary to the law's system, so that serious doubts as to whether they are in accordance with the Basic Law are justified.[554] But it will not always be easy to draw a distinct line between the efforts of the legislature to clarify the original rules and the legislature's intentions to change the rules, thereby imposing new obligations on the addressees of the law. Regarding taxation, for example, the *Bundesverfassungsgericht* is exceptionally skeptical about so-called curative legislation, which in fact leads to tax increases for fiscal years that have already been closed. If retroactive curative legislation actually changes the content of the original legislation instead of merely clarifying it and filling in the gaps, it will be invalidated.[555] In particular, the *Bundesverfassungsgericht* prohibits legislation that, according to the legislature's explanation, is intended to clarify past rules when it in fact attempts to correct a final decision by the highest court, which had already clarified it:[556]

> Der Gesetzgeber durfte nicht angesichts der klaren Rechtslage die zutreffende Rechtsprechung rückwirkend korrigieren und sie "gleichsam für die Vergangenheit ins Unrecht zu setzen" versuchen [...].

And:[557]

> Der Versuch des Gesetzgebers, die Rechtsprechung rückwirkend zu korrigieren, sie gleichsam für die Vergangenheit ins Unrecht zu setzen, gibt keinen Anlaß, den Bereich einer verfassungsrechtlich zulässigen Rückwirkung belastender Gesetze zu erweitern.

Unfairly obtained rights

Retroactive interference by the legislature in legal status and rights obtained by individuals in the past is justified if these rights were obtained unfairly. This was especially clear in the period of the German reunification, when the reunified country had to deal with property issues from the period of the German Democratic Republic (DDR). During that painful period, the properties of people who left East Germany for the western part were confiscated by the public authorities and later sold to private persons. At some point, these persons were forced to return the properties to the previous and legitimate

554 BVerfGE 13, 215 (224).
555 BVerfGE 13, 261 (273). See also BVerfGE 30, 367 (389).
556 BVerfGE 30, 367 (389). See also BVerfGE 13, 39 (45ff.).
557 BVerfGE 18, 429 (439).

owners. Legislation that regulated this issue was challenged on constitutional grounds. The Federal Constitutional Court decided, however, that the rights of the plaintiffs had been obtained unfairly, so they could not expect these rights to be guaranteed. The Court explained this issue in the following way:[558]

> Eine echte Rückwirkung liegt vor, wenn ein in das Grundbuch eingetragener Käufer nach den Bestimmungen der §§3 Abs. 1, 4 Abs. 2 VermG dem früheren Eigentümer oder dessen Rechtsnachfolger das bereits erworbene Eigentumsrecht zurückübertragen muß. Dies ist der Fall, wenn der Käufer entweder unredlich erworben hat oder wenn der Kaufvertrag erst nach dem 18. Oktober 1989 angebahnt und abgeschlossen worden ist. In beiden Fallgruppen durfte der Gesetzgeber eine Regelung mit echter Rückwirkung treffen.

Replacement of unconstitutional or invalid legislation

In the *Bundesverfassungsgericht*'s opinion, the legislature is allowed to replace legislation or regulations which were found invalid or unconstitutional, giving it not only a possibility to work prospectively, but also to give it retroactive effect. A case in point is the one from Hamburg, where every owner of a watchdog was obliged to pay tax for each dog he owned. In addition, a special administrative regulation required the owners to pay for every certificate of tax payment: a dog license disk. During the judicial proceedings, the administrative regulation was invalidated. The Administrative Court in Hamburg decided that there was no legal basis in a legislative act for such regulation. In response to this ruling, the legislature enacted a law that provided such a basis. The law had retroactive effect and was therefore challenged by one of the dog owners as violating the prohibition of retroactive legislation. The *Bundesverfassungsgericht* found no violation of any principle of the rule of law.[559]

> Die Rückwirkung ist auch in der Sache begründet. Es handelt sich darum, daß die vergangenen Lebensverhältnisse selbst einer gesetzlichen Regelung bedurften, nachdem das Urteil des Oberverwaltungsgerichts ergangen war. Da der Staat mit der Gebühreneinnahme gerechnet hatte, war die Schaffung einer Rechtsgrundlage anderer Art für diese Einnahme nunmehr sachgerecht. [...] Auch soweit die Unzulässigkeit der Gebührenerhebung rechtskräftig festgestellt war, verletzt die Rückwirkung der Steuererhöhung den Grundsatz der Rechtsstaatlichkeit nicht. Das Prinzip der Rechtssicherheit, soweit es in der Rechtskraft ausgeprägt ist, wendet sich primär gegen die erneute Aufrollung der entschiedenen Sache vor den Gerichten. Es kann einer späteren gesetzgeberischen Regelung des Lebenssachverhalts, über den entschieden worden ist, nicht schlechthin entgegengesetzt werden: Gerade die rechtsstaatliche Prüfung der Verfassungsmäßigkeit von Gesetzen und der Gesetzmäßigkeit der Verwaltung, die das Grundgesetz in so weitgehendem Umfange verwirklicht, führt notwendig dazu, daß der Gesetzgeber Verhältnisse, die er oder die Verwaltung gesetzlich geregelt glaubte, auf Grund gerichtlicher Entscheidung nicht oder anders geregelt findet, als er

558 BVerfGE 101, 239 (266–267).
559 BVerfGE 7, 89 (93–94). See also BVerfGE 13, 261 (272).

annahm; gerade die Rechtsstaatlichkeit kann so den Gesetzgeber zu rückwirkenden Regelungen veranlassen.

The *Bundesverfassungsgericht* thus decided that the principle of legal certainty is not violated if the legislature retroactively provides a legal basis for administrative rules that were invalidated by the administrative court due to the absence of such a basis. As the legislature was unaware of this lack of a legal basis and since its original intention was to regulate the obligation to pay for dog license disks anyway, which did not change after the administrative court invalidated the administrative regulation, the legislature had every right to provide a retroactive legal basis for the regulation.

This, however, would have been different if the legislature had in fact made no attempt to give full force to its original intention but had instead attempted to provide a legislative basis for the arbitrary action of the executive, thereby approving it: "Dem werden äußerste Schranken entgegenstehen, wenn es sich etwa darum handle, daß Willkür, z. B. in der Verwaltung, gesetzlich sanktioniert werden soll."[560]

Compelling grounds of general interest

Probably the most insubstantial exception serving as a basis for justification of the legislature's intervention in past events is the compelling ground of the general interest.[561] When the Federal Constitutional Court applies this test, it considers the interests involved: individuals' interest in legal certainty and respect for their expectations of the legal status quo, and the general interest. Only if the general interest the legislature attempted to serve by way of the retroactive legislation is compelling and therefore prevails will the impugned legislation pass constitutional muster.[562] At this point, it must be concluded that this "compelling grounds of general interest test" is more rigid than the general interest test as applied to the assessment of pseudo-retroactive legislation. Enacting pseudo-retroactive legislation, as will be discussed later on, is simply about striking a balance between the damage to the individual's expectations and the protection of the general interest.[563]

The judicial test of compelling grounds of general interest in the case of real retroactivity involves all the circumstances and facts of a specific case. Nevertheless, the case law of the Federal Constitutional Court provides the opportunity to deduce more general rules as to what could and what could not be invoked as justifying compelling

560 BVerfGE 7, 89 (94).

561 BVerfGE 13, 261 (272) with reference to BVerfGE 2, 380 (405): "Schließlich können zwingende Gründe des gemeinen Wohls, die dem Gebot der Rechtssicherheit übergeordnet sind, eine Rückwirkungsanordnung rechtfertigen."

562 Berger (2002), p. 105 with references.

563 BVerfGE 30, 367 (390–391): "Es ist schließlich nicht ersichtlich, daß zwingende Gründe des gemeinen Wohls, die dem Vertrauensschutz vorgehen, die Rückwirkung hier rechtfertigen könnten (vgl. BVerfGE 13, 261 [272]). Dafür gelten strengere Voraussetzungen als im Falle einer unechten Rückwirkung, bei der lediglich die Anforderungen des Gemeinwohls mit dem Ausmaß des Vertrauensschadens abzuwägen sind," with references.

grounds of general interest.[564] It is interesting to mention here that the *Bundesverfassungsgericht* tends to include the other grounds for justification it had already formulated in its final conclusion on compelling grounds of general interest. This was the case, for example, when the Court connected the presence of compelling general interest to the opportunity of the legislature to retroactively repair gaps and errors in the existing legislation. In one tax case, the Court concluded that there were no compelling grounds of general interest that could justify the retroactive legislative intervention, because the legislature was not allowed to correct legislative errors:[565]

> Die rückwirkende Erhöhung des Steuersatzes ist auch nicht durch zwingende Gründe des gemeinen Wohls, die dem Gebot der Rechtssicherheit übergeordnet sind, zu rechtfertigen. Daß der Gesetzgeber ein ihm bei der Gesetzesfassung unterlaufenes Versehen berichtigen will, berechtigt ihn noch nicht, dies für einen vergangenen Veranlagungszeitraum zu tun. Nur wenn sein Versehen zu erheblichen Unklarheiten oder zu objektiven Lücken in der ursprünglichen gesetzlichen Regelung geführt hätte, wäre eine Rückwirkung ausnahmsweise zulässig [...]. Hier jedoch war trotz des Versehens des Gesetzgebers eine Regelung entstanden, die als sinnvoll und als vom Gesetzgeber gewollt erscheinen konnte.

In other words, the arguments of compelling grounds of general interest are most likely to be accepted if the legislature, in conformity with its original intention, attempts to clarify, correct, or complement existing legislation which would otherwise contain serious gaps and errors. Justification of real retroactive legislation will be accepted as well if the legislature makes efforts to correct unfair and erroneous laws, either because individuals unfairly acquired certain rights and privileges or because the previous law created unjustifiable inequalities.[566]

The *Bundesverfassungsgericht* also indicated what reasons are unlikely to be acceptable as compelling grounds of general interest. In this context, Berger mentions changing views on certain legal concepts, especially when they are indefinite[567] and merely fiscal aspects resulting in retroactive changes.[568] Significant financial interest of the State can, however, make a difference. This criterion seems to raise more questions than it answers, because it is still unclear what financial interest would be seen as "significant."

No significant damage

A criterion of "significance" also appears in the last ground for justification of real retroactive legislation discussed in this chapter. The Federal Constitutional Court decided that individuals' expectations that the current legal norms will remain unaltered are not protected if the retroactive legislation that changes these norms causes no or only negligible damage to the law's addressees. The Court stated that the principle of legal

564 Berger (2002), pp. 104ff.
565 BVerfGE 13, 261 (273), internal citations omitted.
566 BVerfGE 13, 261 (273). See also BVerfGE 72, 200 (260).
567 Berger (2002), p. 106 with reference to BVerfGE 2, 380 (395ff., 405).
568 Berger (2002), p. 106 with reference to BVerfGE 22, 330 (349).

certainty does not protect individuals against every disappointment. This principle is only effective if legal rules are of such a nature that they are able to bring about or influence decisions and actions of individuals, and these decisions prove to be disadvantageous after the law's retroactive change.[569]

As stated above, although the Lex Schörner was sharply criticized, especially in the academic literature, the Federal Constitutional Court found no violation of the prohibition of real retroactive laws. The Court held that, by means of that Act, the legislature had repaired errors in the law and had therefore satisfied the true and original intention of Parliament.[570]

*4.1.2. Pseudo-retroactivity (***unechte Rückwirkung***)*

While real retroactivity is characterized by legislative intervention in closed cases, and past facts and situations, pseudo-retroactivity is involved when the legislature intervenes in present situations and continuing cases that originated in the past. The interfering legislation is thereby meant to act for now and for the future.[571] As a rule, such pseudo-retroactive legislation is not problematic from the point of view of constitutional law. The Federal Constitutional Court did, after all, decide that it is inherent to the legislative function to change laws for the present, thereby subjecting individuals to a new legal regime.[572] If the legislature provides new rules (there are no existing rules on this subject yet) for situations that originated in the past and regulates issues that have hitherto not been governed by any legal rules, individuals are not able to invoke the principle of legal certainty in any way.

In summary, pseudo-retroactive legislation is generally not problematic. Occasionally, however, individuals may challenge such legislation, asserting that it impermissibly interferes with the principle of legal certainty. During the assessment, the task of the judiciary is to balance the interests involved. The significance of the new rules for the general interest will then be positioned against the individuals' interest consisting of the expectation that the law will remain unaltered and the damages sustained as a result of the legislative changes. Pseudo-retroactive legislation will be invalidated if individuals' interests outweigh the State's interest in changing the law.[573] Moreover, the law will be invalidated if it is not proportional, which means that it is not suitable or necessary to achieve the intended effect.[574] The principle of proportionality and the protection of legitimate expectations require further that the legislature enacts transition rules to lower the burden for those persons who relied on the durability of the law and followed incitements given by the legislature.[575] The test of balancing interests is not stringent. It is much less rigorous than the test the *Bundesverfassungsgericht* applies to real retroactive

569 BVerfGE 30, 367 (389).
570 BVerfGE 7, 129 (152).
571 BVerfGE 11, 139 (146). See also BVerfGE 22, 241 (248).
572 BVerfGE 48, 403 (415). No general expectation that the law will remain unaltered can be protected, either. See BVerfGE 105, 17 (40).
573 BVerfGE 97, 378 (389).
574 BVerfGE 97, 271 (286).
575 See, e.g., BVerfGE 67, 1 (15).

legislation when it decides whether compelling grounds of general interest justify intervention in closed cases, and past facts and situations. In that test, it is much more difficult to justify legislative changes than it is in the balancing test.[576] The Federal Constitutional Court already indicated that, for example, the general interest in overcoming the financial costs of the reunification of West and East Germany is more important than claimants' individual interests. The same is true for the State interest of compensating unexpectedly diminished revenues or correcting certain effects of fiscal legislation. However, the State interest to simplify the fiscal system or the mere purpose to simply obtain more revenues cannot in itself justify retroactivity, when an individual legitimately trusted that the rules would not change.[577]

4.1.3. *Retroactive legislation and final judicial decisions*

Prospective overruling of court decisions by the legislature is quite common in Germany. In particular, the legislature regularly decides to overrule decisions of the highest court in the field of taxation if they have serious implications for State finances (*Nichtanwendungserlasse* or *Nichtanwendungsgesetze*). This type of legislation is viewed as suspect in the literature, but its prospective nature makes it more subject to criticism from a legal policy than from a constitutional law point of view. In this respect, the diminishing quality of legislation, restraints put on the dogmatic development of law, and the psychological effects of overruling laws on single taxpayers have been pointed out.[578] Retroactive intervention in closed cases may be more problematic.

In most cases of retroactive legislation, the legislature will make legislative changes that leave finally decided cases untouched. It is clear that the Federal Constitutional Court prefers this approach. In such circumstances, the Court operates from "the viewpoint of a decided case" (*der Gesichtspunkt der 'entschiedenen Sache'*). As a result, the Court will usually uphold retroactive legislation that does not apply to cases already conclusively decided by the courts. Unless the legislature acts arbitrarily,[579] no violation

576 BVerfGE 70, 69 (84 f.). See also BVerfGE 71, 255 (273).

577 See, e.g., BVerfGE 105, 17 (44ff.).

578 J. Lang, "Reaktion der Finanzverwaltung auf mißliebige Entscheidungen des Bundesfinanzhofs," *DRiZ* 1992–10, p. 370. Cf., however, G. Crezelius, "Rechtsprechungüberholende Gesetzgebung und gesetzesüberholende Rechtsprechung," in: D. Carlé, K. Korn & R. Stahl, *Herausforderungen-Steuerberatung im Spannungsfeld der Teilrechtsordnungen*, Köln: Otto Schmidt 1989, pp. 37–54, and F. Ossenbühl, "Die Bindung der Verwaltung an die höchstrichterliche Rechtsprechung," *AöR* 1967–92, pp. 478ff.

579 BVerfGE 1 BvR 4/01: "Allerdings ist die Rechtskraft richterlicher Entscheidungen ein Element der Rechtssicherheit, die ebenso wie die materielle Gerechtigkeit wesentlicher Bestandteil des Rechtsstaatsprinzips ist (vgl. BVerfGE 7, 194 <196>). Funktion der Rechtskraft ist es, durch die Maßgeblichkeit und Beständigkeit des Inhalts der Entscheidung über den Streitgegenstand für die Beteiligten und die Bindung der öffentlichen Gewalt an die Entscheidung die Rechtslage verbindlich zu klären und damit dem Rechtsfrieden zwischen den Beteiligten zu dienen, ihnen insbesondere zu ermöglichen, ihr Verhalten gemäß dieser Rechtslage auszurichten (vgl. BVerfGE 47, 146 <161>). Das Prinzip der Rechtssicherheit kann mit der Forderung nach materieller Gerechtigkeit in Widerstreit liegen, wobei es in erster Linie Aufgabe des Gesetzgebers ist, einen solchen Widerstreit nach der einen oder anderen Seite zu entscheiden. Geschieht dies ohne Willkür, ist dies verfassungsrechtlich nicht zu beanstanden."

of the principle of equal treatment will be ascertained. This principle is often invoked when the legislature exempts finally decided cases from new, disadvantageous legislation.[580] In the opinion of the Federal Constitutional Court, the principle of legal certainty will mostly be violated if the retroactive legislation does not take final judicial decisions into account.[581]

In summary, retroactive legislation that does not affect finally decided cases is encouraged. Conversely, retroactive laws that do not take final judicial decisions into account may be problematic. In this respect, the Federal Constitutional Court warns for a possible conflict with the constitutional principle of the separation of powers:[582]

> Bedenklich, weil an den Grundsatz der Gewaltenteilung rührend, wäre es eher im umgekehrten Fall gewesen, wenn das Gesetz rückwirkend in die Rechtskraft von Entscheidungen eingegriffen hätte.

Retroactive nullification of final judicial decisions by the legislature must therefore be avoided because of possible conflict with the principles of the separation of powers and legal certainty.[583]

Besides the retroactive overruling of final judicial decisions, the legislature may use another technique to affect the outcome of a judicial decision in a specific case at short notice. It may adopt a pseudo-prospective law that formally does not reopen any final judicial decision, but renders its enforcement practically impossible. A German case concerning the placement of billboards on railroad bridges is illustrative. After the court's decision imposing an obligation on the authorities of the city of Hamburg to grant permits for such billboards to a specific applicant and the authorities' persistent refusal to do so, the legislature enacted a statute pertaining to the placement of billboards on various bridges, including railway bridges. The only provision of the statute prohibited such activities.[584] The Act was challenged by the applicant in the administrative court on the basis of its incompatibility with constitutional law. The Federal Administrative Court (*Bundesverwaltungsgericht*) eventually decided that the law was not problematic from a constitutional law point of view. According to the Court, the legislature did not abuse the instrument of a legislative act (the Court referred to *Formenmißbrauch* in this context) to render enforcement of the court's judgment impossible, since the original intention of the legislature was to prohibit the placement of billboards on the bridges. This intention became even clearer after the court's decision. The *Bundesverwaltungsgericht* held that the situation would have been different if the law had had a *Kampfcharakter*. In other words, if the legislature deliberately challenged the rights and claims as established by

580 See BVerfGE 29, 413 (432) and BVerfGE 19, 150 (166).

581 BVerfGE 15, 167 (205ff.), BVerfGE 48, 1 (22), BVerfGE 72, 302.

582 BVerfGE 72, 302 (328).

583 B. Grzeszick, "Art. 20, VII," in: T. Maunz, *G. Dürig* & R. Herzog (eds.), *Grundgesetz: Kommentar*, München: Beck 1958-(2006), p. 39, and W. Habscheid, "Urteilswirkungen und Gesetzänderungen," *ZZP* 1965–6, p. 428.

584 *Gesetz über Außenwerbung an Brücken* of October 1, 1957 (GVBl. S. 442) is fairly unambiguous: "An Brücken, die über öffentliche Straßen, Plätze, Grünanlagen, Wasserläufe und sonstige öffentliche Flächen führen, dürfen Werbemittel nicht angebracht werden."

the court in a specific case and attempted to annul them, the law would be more suspicious. In conclusion, it appears that this administrative Court attaches consequences to the specific intention of the legislature to affect the outcome of a judicial decision in a specific case. If, however, the law has a general character and is enacted to fulfill the original intention of the legislature, no constitutional principle will obstruct it:[585]

> Unter Umständen könnte sogar gerade eine Klausel, die für den einzelnen, zuvor ausgeurteilten Fall eine nunmehr allgemein verbotene Leistung oder Maßnahme noch zuließe, als Einzelfall- oder Maßnahmegesetz bedenklich erscheinen. Daher geht das Verlangen der Rev. Fehl, in das Brückenwerbungsgesetz zwecks verfassungskonformer Auslegung eine solche Klausel hineinzudeuten. Ihr Fehlen stellt jedenfalls die Gültigkeit des Gesetzes nicht in Frage. Die Kl. kann also nicht damit durchdringen, daß sie dem BrückenwerbungsG einen Kampfcharacter in dem Sinne beilegt, der Gesetzgeber habe das Urt. v. 10.7.1954 oder ihr in diesem Urt. gutgeheißenes Einzelfallbegehren bekämpf. Ein Formmißbrauch des Gesetzgebers, ein Einbruch in die richterliche Gewalt, ein Richten in eigener Sache oder eine Entziehung des gesetzlichen Richters liegen nicht vor.

4.2. Impulsive legislative changes and legal certainty

Although the Federal Constitutional Court has argued that the legislature has an undisputable general right to change the legal regime for the future,[586] some academics have raised doubts. Degenhart, for example, particularly questions legislation which is hastily enacted in reaction to a specific case or situation. In his view, such impulsive legislation results in instability of the legal system and therefore leads to legal uncertainty.[587] Brandner agrees with the idea that it is the function of the legislature to change the actual legal rules, but he argues in favor of limitations of such freedom. In his opinion, these limitations should be the legislature's obligation to explain (*Begründungspflicht*). This obligation means that each time the legislature intends to alter the existing rules, it must give sufficient reasons beforehand. It is then crucial to explain why the legislature decided that the existing legal rules are no longer in accordance with the general interest, and why such legislative changes are required:[588]

> Die Rechtssicherheit zwingt den ändernden Gesetzgeber vielmehr dazu, nicht nur sich selbst, sondern auch der Öffentlichkeit gegenüber Rechenschaft darüber abzulegen, warum und inwieweit die alte Regelung nicht (mehr) "gemeinwohlrichtig" ist und er deswegen im Interesse

585 BVerwGE *NJW* 1962, 12, p. 554. The case has also been discussed in light of the possible abuse of power by the legislature in Pestalozza (1973). See also BVerwGE VII B 28/67, *DÖV* 1969, p. 431, Bayerischer Verfassungsgerichtshof, Vf. 20-VII-83, and H. Goerlich, *"Formenmißbrauch" und Kompetenzverständnis*, Tübingen: Mohr 1987.

586 See, however, the legislature's obligation to provide transitional rules, as expressed in, for example, BVerfGE 51, 356 (368) and BVerfGE 75, 40 (72).

587 Degenhart (1981), p. 483.

588 Brandner (2004), pp. 354–355. See also Sec. 43 of the *Gemeinsame Geschäftsordnung*, version of June 1, 2009 at <www.bmi.bund.de/cln_095/SharedDocs/Downloads/DE/Veroeffentlichungen/ggo.html?nn=267412> (last accessed on June 12, 2011).

des Gemeinwohls eine Änderung für angezeigt hält. Das Gebot der Rechtssicherheit beinhaltet insofern eine Begründungspflicht des ändernden Gesetzgebers. Er ist frei, die fragliche Norm zu ändern, doch er schuldet eine Begründung dafür, warum er es tut. In diesem eingeschränkten Umfang gilt für die Abgeordneten des Deutschen Bundestages das Gesetz, welches *Mephistopheles* zufolge die Teufel und Gespenster bindet: „Das Erste steht (ihnen) frei, beim Zweiten sind (sie) Knechte."

As far as the extent and the intensity of the obligation to give reasons is concerned, the reason why the legislation must be changed is decisive. The obligation to explain will, for instance, be minimal if the legislature is forced to change the existing rules as a response to higher international or European law or to the decisions of the European Court of Justice and the *Bundesverfassungsgericht*. Brandner argues that the same holds for the legislature's corrections of erroneous legislation.[589] In other situations, where the legislature designs new policy and creates new substantive rules or changes the existing ones, the obligation to explain would be much stronger.[590]

4.3. Conclusion

The principle of legal certainty and protection of legitimate expectations plays the most important role when the legislature imposes retroactive obligations on individuals, as shown by the case law of the Federal Constitutional Court. That Court is especially critical when the legislature intervenes in cases and situations that had been closed before the enactment of a new piece of legislation. Only a few exceptional circumstances, for example, correction of obviously technical errors and nullification of unfairly obtained rights, will justify real retroactive legislation. In the literature, the need for a broader concept of legal certainty has been advocated. The necessity of sudden legislative changes should at least be convincingly justified by the legislature, in the commentator's view.

[589] It seems that the obligation to explain in the event of defective legislation will not always be that minimal, as Brandner suggests. As was shown by the case of Ferdinand Schörner, the German legislature presented the formulation of new rules as a correction of erroneous legislation. Nevertheless, the circumstances in which the legislation was enacted made its enactment at least suspicious. The critics argued that the law provided new retroactive rules to influence only the case of general Schörner, instead of correcting the errors in the previous legislation. It appears therefore that only legislation that clearly corrects technical errors will be exempted from the extensive obligation to explain.

[590] Brandner (2004), pp. 357–358.

Chapter 5

PROPORTIONALITY

Introduction

In German constitutional law, the principle of proportionality (*Verhältnismäßigkeit* or *Übermaßverbot*)[591] of State action became an important element of the judicial check of State action, including legislation. The proportionality principle is strongly related to the prohibition of arbitrary acts of the State.[592] It also plays an important part at the federal government departments – at the federal Department of Justice in particular – which are responsible for assessment of the compatibility of legislative proposals with the German Basic Law.[593] The principle of proportionality curbs State power[594] and expresses the idea that the State may interfere with the freedom of individuals, their rights, and their legal status, which are protected by various laws, only if such intervention is necessary to protect the general interest.[595] The *Bundesverfassungsgericht* declared this principle to be rooted in the principle of the rule of law (*Rechtsstaatsprinzip*):[596]

> [...] die Grundsätze der Verhältnismäßigkeit und des Übermaßverbotes, die sich als übergreifende Leitregeln allen staatlichen Handelns zwingend aus dem Rechtsstaatsprinzip ergeben und deshalb Verfassungsrang haben.

To assess this proportionality, the *Bundesverfassungsgericht* formulated several criteria. The preliminary question (i.e. step 0) is whether the government's purpose the legislature attempts to achieve when it limits individuals' fundamental rights is legitimate. In this context, a legitimate purpose means a purpose which is not prohibited by the German

591 These two terms are used interchangeably, but some authors are in favor of using the term *Übermaßverbot* only as part of the judicial three-step check, Stern (1994), p. 763.

592 "Das Verhältnismäßigkeitsprinzip gibt dem Bundesverfassungsgericht einen Kontrollmaßstab allen staatlichen Handelns, auch und vor allem der Gesetzgebung, der dem Prinzip der praktischen Vernunft entspricht." K.A. Schachtschneider, *Prinzipien des Rechtsstaates*, Berlin: Duncker & Humblot 2006, p. 342.

593 See the *Gemeinsame Geschäftsordnung*, version of June 1, 2009, Annex 6 about the constitutional check of legislative proposals at <www.bmi.bund.de/cln_095/SharedDocs/Downloads/DE/Veroeffentlichungen/ggo.html?nn=267412> (last accessed on June 12, 2011).

594 Stern (1994), p. 762.

595 Schmidt (2008), p. 80, with reference to BVerfGE 19, 342 (348). See also BVerfGE 77, 84 (106).

596 BVerfGE 23, 127 (133).

Basic Law, including the principle of the rule of law (*Rechtsstaat*). At this stage, the Court does not investigate the importance of the government's interest.[597] According to Grimm, it is highly unusual that any law will fail to meet the preliminary requirement: "[c]ases in which the legislature pursues a constitutionally prohibited purpose (*e.g.*, racial discrimination) are extremely rare."[598] When the preliminary question is answered in the affirmative, the *Bundesverfassungsgericht* will investigate 1) the suitability of the chosen measures, 2) the necessity of these measures and, 3) their proportionality in a stricter sense. A description of these three elements follows.

5.1. Suitability (*Geeignetheit*)

The principle of proportionality requires that measures chosen (or legislation, which is the focus here) are suitable to achieve the legitimate aim. Or, in other words, it prohibits legislation that is not suitable for the purpose that the legislature wants to achieve. At this point, it should be noted that the *Bundesverfassungsgericht* does not require that the purpose has indeed been accomplished by these means. A theoretical possibility is sufficient as such.[599] A natural situation in which the means used by the legislature to achieve a specific purpose are not suitable would be when the legislature in fact tries to hide its real motives, and the purpose that is made public is not the real one.[600] It is conceivable that the legislature would do this when it expects that the real purpose of the legislation, if revealed, would be controversial. The case of the private transportation agencies described in Chapter III.2.3 addresses this problem. In that case, the legislature purported that it wanted to promote road safety and protect the position of the passengers who had been brought into contact with a private driver by a private transportation agency. In fact, the legislature wanted to get rid of these agencies in order to protect the position of the public transportation company. Exploring the circumstances in which the legislature enacted the controversial provision, the *Bundesverfassungsgericht* found that road safety could not be promoted by requiring private drivers to obtain a license for transportation if the connection between the driver and the passenger was brought about by a private transportation agency. The means chosen was therefore unsuitable.[601]

5.2. Necessity (*Erforderlichkeit*)

The second requirement is that the suitable means chosen must be necessary to achieve the goal. The means are necessary when it is impossible for the legislator to choose other equally effective means that restrict individuals' rights less:[602]

597 D. Grimm, "Proportionality in Canadian and German Constitutional Law," 57 *U. Toronto L.J.* 388 (2007).

598 *Ibid.*

599 BVerfGE 67, 157 (175).

600 See, in this respect, P. Lerche, *Übermaß und Verfassungsrecht*, Goldbach: Keip Verlag 1999, pp. 45ff.

601 BVerfGE 17, 306 (316).

602 BVerfGE 63, 88 (115).

> [E]s [das Mittel] ist erforderlich, wenn der Gesetzgeber nicht ein anderes, gleich wirksames, aber das Grundrecht nicht oder doch weniger fühlbar einschränkendes Mittel hätte wählen können (BVerfGE 30, 292 [316]).

The requirement of necessity is therefore also called the principle of the mildest means.[603] However, means that cause less damage to the addressee of the law, but are extremely harmful to the State in general (*Allgemeinheit*), also financially, cannot be considered alternative means.[604] During the assessment of the suitability and the necessity of the legislative measures, the Court leaves a great margin of appreciation to the legislature, because, as it decided, it is not the role of judiciary to check whether legislative acts are the wisest, fairest, or most efficient:[605]

> Das Bundesverfassungsgericht kann dessen Entscheidung nicht darauf prüfen, ob er die zweckmäßigste, vernünftigste oder gerechteste Lösung gefunden hat; es hat lediglich darüber zu wachen, daß die Strafvorschrift materiell in Einklang mit den Bestimmungen der Verfassung steht und den ungeschriebenen Verfassungsgrundsätzen sowie Grundentscheidungen des Grundgesetzes entspricht (vgl. BVerfGE 80, 244 [255] m.w.N.).

In relation to the economy and the labor market in particular, the legislature has the most freedom to judge which means are the best.[606]

5.3. Proportionality *sensu stricto* (*Angemessenheit*)

The third element of the proportionality principle is proportionality in the narrow sense. The central question here is whether there is a fair balance between the State action that restricts individuals' rights, the urgency that possibly justifies this intervention, and the importance (*Gewicht und Bedeutung*) of the right that the State violates.[607] In other words, the harm caused to individuals and restrictions of individuals' rights may not be disproportional to the purpose the State endeavors to achieve; again, there must be a fair balance between the interests involved. The question of the proportionality of the State action in its narrow sense must be decided anew for every single case, since it depends on the circumstances of that case. The *Bundesverfassungsgericht* already held that it is a matter of weighing the individual's interests against the general interest.[608] It is exactly this vagueness of the proportionality principle in its narrow sense that has mostly been criticized.[609]

603 Grzeszick (2006), p. 44.

604 BVerfGE 88, 145 (164).

605 BVerfGE 90, 145 (173), citations omitted.

606 The Bundesverfassungsgericht calls this the *Einschätzungs- und Prognosevorrang*, BVerfGE 103, 293 (307). See also BVerfGE 81, 156 (193).

607 H. Schulze-Fielitz, "Art. 20," in: H. Dreier, *Grundgesetz Kommentar*, Tübingen: Siebeck Mohr 2006, pp. 258ff.

608 BVerfGE 92, 277 (327).

609 See, for example, R. Dechsling, *Das Verhältnismäßigkeitsgebot*, München: Verlag Franz Vahlen 1989, pp. 17ff and F. Ossenbühl, "Der Grundsatz der Verhältnismäßigkeit (Übermaßverbot) in der

In the academic literature on the quality of legislation, a general "*Pflicht des Gesetzgebers zu intensievem Nachdenken*" (the legislature's obligation of careful consideration) has been deduced from the proportionality principle.[610] According to Hoffmann, the legislature is able to satisfy the above-mentioned conditions included in the proportionality test only if it actually did something to find out what instrument would be the most suitable and what alternative would be the least burdensome.[611]

5.4. Conclusion

The principle of the proportionality of State action and the proportionality of legislation in particular forms an interesting tool for the assessment of legislation in the abstract. This principle allows a judicial check of the rationality of political choices, since it requires that the means chosen by the legislature are suitable and necessary to achieve a certain legitimate purpose promoted by the legislature (particularly steps 1 and 2). In principle, in doing so, it allows the true intentions of the legislature to be revealed, as evidenced by the judgment of the Federal Constitutional Court in the transportation agencies case. This, however, appears to be the only case in which the Court went so far in assessing the true intentions of the legislature so explicitly. Finally, it should be emphasized that the principle of proportionality does not apply to every kind of legislation. It constrains only a legislature that restricts fundamental rights of individuals. Ad hoc legislation that might be expediency-driven, but that does not restrict fundamental rights is therefore unlikely to be governed by the regime of the proportionality principle.

Rechtsprechung der Verwaltungsgerichte," *JURA* 1997, pp. 619ff.

610 G. Hoffmann, "Das verfassungsrechtliche Gebot der Rationalität im Gesetzgebungsverfahren," *ZG* 1990–2, pp. 97ff. In Germany, the obligation of careful consideration must be positioned within a broader discussion of the rationality of legislation. See, for example, A. Burghart, *Die Pflicht zum guten Gesetz*, Berlin: Duncker & Humblot 1996, H. Schulze-Fielitz, *Theorie und Praxis parlamentarischer Gesetzgebung*, Berlin: Duncker & Humblot 1988, pp. 480ff, and H. Schneider, "Der Niedergang des Gesetzgebungsverfahrens," in: Th. Rittersbach & W. Geiger (eds.), *Festschrift für Gebhard Müller*, Tübingen: J.C.B. Mohr 1970, pp. 421ff.

611 Cf. Ch. Gusy, "Das Grundgesetz als normative Gesetzgebungslehre," *ZRP* 1985–11, pp. 291ff.

Chapter 6

AD HOC LEGISLATION AND THE GERMAN CONSTITUTIONAL PRINCIPLE OF THE SEPARATION OF POWERS

Introduction

The criticism of ad hoc legislation often concentrates on the violation of the separation of powers principle. The federal legislature was criticized for acting as the executor and not the maker of laws when it adopted the Lex Stendal and the Lex Schörner. In the critics' view, Parliament thereby usurped the executive power, thus violating the principle of the separation of powers between the legislative and the executive branches. The separation between the legislature and the judiciary can be at issue as well. In Germany, it has been argued (not very often, though) that in adopting an ad hoc law, the legislature attempts to influence the outcome of specific pending cases. In this chapter, the separation of powers principle in Germany will be discussed in relation to ad hoc laws.

6.1 Ad hoc laws and the separation of powers between the legislature and the executive

The separation of powers idea can be found in Art. 20 (2) of the Basic Law which reads: "All state authority is derived from the people. It shall be exercised by the people through elections and other votes and through specific legislative, executive, and judicial bodies." However, the strict division of powers between the legislative branch and the executive branch in particular has never been fully realized in Germany, given, for example, the simple fact that the government, as part of the executive branch, is involved in the decision-making process of Parliament. The Federal Constitutional Court has repeatedly explained that the German conception of this constitutional principle entails the organization and division of tasks, rather than a strict separation.[612] It is nevertheless quite obvious that the State function of legislating and creating rules is a power of the democratic Parliament, and the bodies of the executive branch, as the name itself suggests, must execute rules enacted by Parliament.[613] But the principle of the separation of powers also entails restraints and mutual control to prevent one of the State branches

612 BVerfGE 3, 225 (247).
613 BVerfGE 34, 52 (59), BVerfGE 49, 89 (124ff.).

from predominating and acting arbitrarily.[614] The core of each State function must be guaranteed. Although, at first sight, the drafting of individual rules by the legislature seems to imply that the legislature simultaneously creates and executes laws, thereby encroaching on the domain of the executive power, the Federal Constitutional Court disagreed. In the Südumfahrung Stendal case, it acknowledged that the legislature does not violate the separation of powers in relation to the executive automatically, when it enacts a project-specific law. If the legislature can explain why a law is reasonable and necessary (i.e., not arbitrary), the constitutional principle of the separation of powers will not be at risk.[615]

6.2 Legislative intervention in pending cases and the separation of powers between the legislature and the judiciary

Situations in which the federal legislature interferes with pending judicial proceedings to ensure a certain (politically desired) outcome in specific cases are rare in Germany. Nevertheless, a few striking examples can be pointed out: the Flick affair and the Platow Amnesty case. These cases concern legislative plans to pardon a certain group of people accused of crimes, while judicial criminal proceedings against them had already been initiated.

The Flick affair concerned a political scandal in the early 1980s about secret financial donations to particular members of several political parties by a private company owned by Flick.[616] Its managers transferred substantial amounts of money to political parties for the "besondere[n] Pflege der Bonner Landschaft" ("for the cultivation of the political landscape"), as one of Flick's managers put it. In fact, the donations were meant to influence the decision-making process in specific ministries and induce the responsible Minister of Economic Affairs to issue particular certificates to the Flick company, as a result of which the company would be exempted from considerable tax obligations. At some point, the accounting records of the Flick company, including the secret payments, were discovered and the Flick managers and politicians involved were charged with tax evasion and bribery. Moreover, in response to that case, the German Parliament

614 BVerfGE 9, 268 (279), BVerfGE 22, 106 (111), BVerfGE 34, 52 (59).

615 In a similar key, J. Bücker, *Die Zulässigkeit von Individualgesetzen nach dem Grundgesetz*, Bonn: H. Bouvier u. Co. 1965, pp. 66–67. See also the case of the Großer Erftverband, where the *Bundesverfassungsgericht* answered claims that the legislature had deviated from the general rules and had opportunistically created an ad hoc law by stating that the law was necessary and not arbitrary, BVerfGE 10, 89 (103). Moreover, the German Basic Law does not reserve a general, well-defined area of competences for the executive branch that are free from legislative interference (*Verwaltungsvorbehalt*). In this connection, see B. Grzeszick, "Art. 20, VI," in: T. Maunz, *G. Dürig* & R. Herzog (eds.), *Grundgesetz: Kommentar*, Beck: München 1958-(2007), p. 54.

616 The case was broadly discussed in the literature and in the media. See, for example, H. Leyendecker, M. Stiller & H. Prantl, *Helmut Kohl, die Macht und das Geld*, Göttingen: Steidl 2000, "Flick – ein Mann kauft die Republik," *Der Spiegel* 1984–44, pp. 26ff., D. Werthmüller, *Junge Wissenschaft. Schriften der Hochschule für Politik München*, Vol. 1, München: Ernst Vögel 1990, Th. Bartholmes, *Die „Flick-Affäre"-Verlauf und Folgen*, Speyer 2003, Th. Ramge, *Die großen Polit-Skandale. Eine andere Geschichte der Bundesrepublik*, Frankfurt/New York: Campus 2003, pp. 153ff., O. Schily, "Wie der Flick-Konzern in Bonn Politik machte," *Blätter für deutsche und internationale Politik* 1986–4, pp. 436ff.

promulgated an Act which entered into effect on January 1, 1984, aimed at strengthening and clarifying the rules on financial donations to political parties.

While the criminal cases were pending, the parliamentary coalition of CDU (Christian Democratic Union)/CSU (Christian Social Union) and FDP (Free Democratic Party) introduced an interesting legislative proposal. The bill's purpose was to dismiss all pending proceedings against persons involved in suspect donations and to prevent any new trials. Although the bill itself did not mention any names, it was clear that the legislature had the Flick affair in mind.[617] The bill, popularly known as "*Parteispenden-Amnestiegesetz*" was hotly debated and greatly criticized. The general public was furious and accused its initiators of, among other things, pleading their own case, since many politicians from the political parties that initiated the amnesty law were involved in the Flick scandal as well.[618] Moreover, not only newspapers, but also various public organizations and the German association of judges (*Deutscher Richterbund*), sharply criticized the legislature for encroaching on the domain of the judiciary by deciding on its own the guilt of persons accused of criminal acts in the sphere of financial donations to political parties:[619]

> Auf das Schärfste und mit Empörung verurteilt der deutsche Richterbund die Absicht der Regierungskoalition, eine Amnestie für Verstöße gegen Steuergesetze im Zusammenhang mit Parteispenden zu erlassen. Der Verstoß von CDU/CSU und F.D.P. will das Recht zur Disposition einzelner Interessengruppen stellen. Das ist der Anfang des Verfalls der Rechtskultur. [...] In der Sache fügen die Amnestiepläne dem Rechtsbewußtsein der Bevölkerung schwersten Schaden zu. Es ist ein Skandal, wenn der Generalsekretär der CDU in diesem Zusammenhang davon spricht, es gehe darum „unbescholtene Bürger" nachträglich straflos zu stellen. Hier werden die Dinge auf den Kopf gestellt. In Wahrheit geht es offensichtlich darum, den Parteien die Gunst potenter Spender zu erhalten. *Es ist Sache der Gerichte und Staatsanwaltschaften festzustellen, inwieweit Betroffene, zu deren nachteil Verfahren eingeleitet worden sind, als "unbescholten" gelten können.*

The opposition in Parliament criticized the proposal in a similar way. One of the arguments of the SPD (Social Democratic Party) was that the bill was improper and was a brute encroachment on the administration of criminal justice, because the legislature took over the function of the judiciary by deciding a few specific cases.[620]

In the literature, it was suggested that the proposal could lead to violation of the separation of powers principle, since the legislature had attempted to interfere with pending judicial proceedings.[621] Attention has also been paid to the possible violation of the prohibition of individual laws, as set out in Art. 19 (1) of the Basic Law. The conclusion

617 For the proposal's text and the explanatory memorandum see BT Drs. 10/1421.

618 Thanks to this serious criticism, the legislative proposal never became a law.

619 Deutscher Richterbund, press release, no. 5/84, May 4, 1984 in: Werthmüller (1990), p. 108, emphasis added. For a more detailed description of the legislative history and the references with regard to the criticism which the legislative proposal received, see Werthmüller (1990), pp. 37ff.

620 Werthmüller (1990), pp. 51–52.

621 B. Schünemann, "Amnestie und Grundgesetz. Zur Verfassungswidrigkeit einer Amnestie in der Parteispendenaffäre," *ZRP* 1984–6, p. 138, and Schmidt (2008), p. 69.

was eventually reached that even though, if enacted, the legislative proposal would immediately benefit a specific group of politicians involved in the Flick affair, it was still phrased in general terms. Given the established case law of the Federal Constitutional Court on this point, the *Parteispenden – Amnestiegesetz* could therefore not be condemned as an individual law prohibited by Art. 19 (1) GG.

The established case law referred to above concerns the decision of the Federal Constitutional Court in a comparable case, where the federal legislature interfered with pending judicial proceedings in another scandal, called *Platow Amnestie* (Chapter III.2.2.1.3). The case concerned similar attempts by the legislature to drop the criminal proceedings against a group of persons involved in a bribery affair. In that case, the *Bundesverfassungsgericht* clearly emphasized the relationship between the generality of laws and the legislature's power to encroach on the judicial power to both dismiss pending criminal proceedings and prevent the execution of penalties. The legislature is allowed such intervention only when the interfering legislation is general, which means that it applies to an indefinite group of persons:[622]

> Zur Errichtung eines Hindernisses für die Strafverfolgung oder die Strafvollstreckung durch ein Gesetz ist der Bundesgesetzgeber dann befugt, wenn nicht nur die Straffolgen von Einzelfällen, sondern von einer "unübersehbaren und unbestimmten, nach Typen gekennzeichneten Zahl von Straftaten" geregelt werden (BVerfGE 2, 213 [222]).

Although the Federal Constitutional Court made it clear that legislation which mentions no names can still prove to be a disguised individual law (*verdecktes* or *getarntes Individualgesetz*) if the legislature's motives were to touch a specific case or group of cases, it found the *Amnestie Gesetz* to be a general, and therefore permitted law.[623]

The *Platow Amnesty* judgment reflects the Federal Constitutional Court's view on legislative interventions in pending criminal cases. The question therefore remains whether the legislature is allowed to enact legislation that interferes with other than criminal pending cases in order to influence the outcome of a specific case or group of cases. It is fair to assume that the same question will then be posed: is the law general or is it in fact tailored to a specific case or group of cases? Legal commentators, in the main, agree that the generality of the law will be decisive in answering the question whether the legislature encroached on judicial power and therefore violated the principle of an independent judiciary (Art. 97 GG).[624] They argue that judicial independence is threatened if the legislature influences the outcomes in *specific* judicial proceedings: "[V]or allem aber darf der Gesetzgeber keinen unmittelbaren Einfluß auf die Entscheidungen **im konkreten** laufenden **Verfahren** durch Einzelfallgesetze nehmen."[625]

622 BVerfGE 10, 234 (238–239).

623 The "motives criterion" in the *Amnesty Platow* case, as explained and applied by the Federal Constitutional Court appears to be a logical error. See the description of the case and the accompanying remarks in Chapter III.2.

624 The principle of an independent judiciary is considered an aspect of the principle of the separation of powers.

625 H. Schulze-Fielitz, "Art. 97," in: H. Dreier, *Grundgesetzkommentar*, Tübingen: Mohr Siebeck 2000, p. 490 with references.

Herzog qualifies this view by adding that such laws are not unconstitutional because they *could* influence the outcome of a specific pending case, but rather when they are enacted with the express purpose of effecting a judicial decision which is opposite to the expected decision.[626]

> Beide Möglichkeiten sind nach hier vertretener Auffassung nicht schon deshalb unzulässig, weil sie die gerichtliche Entscheidung im konkreten Einzelfalle beeinflussen können. Art. 97 I [...] [macht] den gesetzgeberischen Gebrauch von diesen Möglichkeiten aber jedenfalls dann verfassungswidrig, wenn er **gerade dazu dienen soll**, im konkreten, bereits anhängigen Einzelfall eine andere Entscheidung als nach der normalen Rechtslage herbeizuführen.

Herzog seems to apply a kind of a motive test (Was the law meant to influence the outcome of a specific case?), without giving further specifications.

Moreover, the legislature would be allowed to steer the outcome of judicial proceedings of the same type in a certain desired direction which is opposite to the direction taken by the existing case law by means of general and abstract legislative changes of laws underlying the pending cases. Such pseudo-retroactive laws are valid as long as they respect the rules governing the doctrine of the retroactivity of laws. This implies that legislation that is changed during the pending proceedings can nevertheless be invalidated if the individuals' expectations concerning the continuation of the old regime weigh more heavily than the State's interest in changing the law.[627]

One should not forget, however, that despite German doctrine, the German legislature is bound by higher international law, including the European Convention on Human Rights and the case law of the European Court of Human Rights, in particular. The ECtHR developed a sophisticated view on how to assess legislative interventions in pending cases.[628] This doctrine is discussed in the Dutch part.

6.3. Conclusion

The German constitutional law idea of the separation of powers focuses on the checks and balances, and the limitation of the State power rather than the strict separation of three State functions. Having this point of departure in mind, the *Bundesverfassungsgericht* refused to automatically declare the Lex Stendal unconstitutional. The fact that the legislature occasionally takes over the function of the executive power does not immediately render it unconstitutional, the Court decided. Grounds for justification can be found in "good reasons."

626 R. Herzog, "Art. 97," in: Th. Maunz, G. Dürig & R. Herzog, *Grundgesetzkommentar*, München: C.H. Beck 1997, p. 11.

627 Schulze-Fielitz (2000), p. 490. See also BVerfGE 24, 33 (55).

628 The key judgments with respect to this doctrine are *Stran Greek Refineries and Stratis Andreadis v. Greece*, (Appl. No. 13427/87) (1994) Series A no. 301; *National & Provincial Building Society, Leeds Permanent Building Society and Yorkshire Building Society v. the United Kingdom*, (Appl. nos. 117/1996/736/933–935) ECHR 1997-VII; and *Zielinski and Pradal and Gonzales and Others v. France* (Appl. nos. 24846/94 and 34165/96 to 34173/96) ECHR 1999-VII.

As far as the relationship between the legislature and the judiciary is concerned, the German Parliament will not often decide to interfere with the administration of justice. Such legislative attempts may be expected to lead to much criticism of possible violation of the principle of judicial independence, within the broader idea of the separation of powers.

IN SUM

Legislation designed for one specific case is not part of everyday practice in Germany. Nevertheless, there are cases in which the German legislature could not resist the political pressure to act in specific cases. Resulting ad hoc laws attracted much criticism, which was most devastating on constitutional points. With regard to the phenomenon of ad hoc legislation and the constitutional boundaries of the German legislature, the following conclusions can be drawn.

Phenomenon of ad hoc legislation

Direct responses which I received from German scholars when I explained to them the object of this study speak volumes. Understanding the problem and the possible conflicts of laws designed for particular, pre-determined cases, they denied that such laws are common legislative practice. This can be seen as confirmation that the German tradition is one of a civil law country operating on the basis of general laws which form a systematic and coherent unity. This explains why ad hoc legislation designed to govern specific cases received sharp criticism, which concerned constitutional aspects and other aspects of the quality of legislation.

The cases of ad hoc legislation that can nevertheless be found in Germany at the federal level show that there are at least four reasons why the legislature decides to act contrary to the agreed legal order. These are 1) public pressure (Lex Schörner), 2) fast improvement of the infrastructure (Lex Stendal), 3) personal preferences of politicians (Lex Naumann), and 4) protection of members of Parliament against criminal prosecution (Platow Amnesty). These different reasons can, however, be reduced to one overarching motive: the regular general laws that could be applied to the cases that gave rise to the legislative response could not guarantee the outcome desired by the politicians. The criticism of ad hoc legislation related to a number of constitutional principles, which in the critics' view were intended to limit the legislature.

Constitutional principles and limitations

The most natural principle often connected with ad hoc legislation is that of the generality of laws. One must, however, conclude that no such general requirement for the legislature can be found in German positive constitutional law. Despite the extensive discussion on laws in the formal and in the material sense and the fervent arguments in the academic literature on the importance of the generality of legal norms, the German Basic Law sees every Act of Parliament as valid if it is enacted in a certain procedure, which is laid down in the Basic Law, regardless of its inner characteristics. Even though no general prohibition of case-specific laws exists, the German Basic Law prohibits individual laws (*Einzelfallgesetze*) which *limit individuals' basic rights* in Art. 19 (1) GG. In other words, the legislature is allowed to limit basic rights only by means of general laws. It seems that the Federal Constitutional Court is somehow uncomfortable with Art. 19 (1) GG. Despite the fact that the claims pointing out the specific character of legislation (in combination with the limitation of basic rights) have been raised many times in the past, the *Bundesverfassungsgericht* refused to invalidate any law in light of that provision. Not a single legislative act was specific in the Court's eyes, as they were all written in general terms and were thus potentially applicable to future cases as well. Even though there was only one popularly known case that existed at the time of the law's enactment and it was the first one to be governed by the law, it was not impossible that there would be more, similar cases in the future, the Court argued.[629] Although the Court developed a concept of a 'disguised special law' as well, it never applied it effectively to invalidate a piece of ad hoc legislation. At a quite early point, this Court abandoned the idea that the motives of the legislature to affect the outcome of one specific case could be decisive to declare a law a disguised individual law. This reluctance can most likely be explained by the Court's respect for the legislature's political choices, a body which, unlike the Court, is democratically chosen. On the contrary, the Court seems to be particularly critical of retroactive legislation that is disadvantageous for individuals, because it is most likely to violate the principle of legal certainty. The presumption against the retroactivity of laws as a part of the principle of legal certainty is particularly important in German constitutional law.

There seems to be a striking discrepancy between the critical comments on ad hoc legislation in the literature and their assessment by the Federal Constitutional Court. The academic discussion involves the broader rationality of legislation aspects and it appears to suggest that the interpretation of the traditional, above mentioned principles should be expanded to the quality aspects. In the literature, the concepts of the abuse of form (*Formenmißbrauch*), legislature's obligation to give reasons and explain the need for legislative changes, the legislation's obligation of careful consideration,[630] and the consistency of legislation have been discussed in a normative sense. The *Bundesverfassungsgericht* was less willing to broaden the meaning of the constitutional principles. As regards the principle of legal consistency, for example, this Court refused to treat it as an independent basis for the assessment of the constitutionality of the impugned statute. According to the Court, the inconsistency may *indicate* the violation of equal treatment. This does not mean that a statute which is inconsistent with the laws' system automatically violates the principle of equal treatment. Reiterating the previous argument: the Court is reluctant to go far in its assessment of legislative products, because it takes the special position of a democratic legislature into account. By contrast, academics are allowed more freedom in criticizing the legislative function of Parliament.

629 Sometimes it seems to be a theoretical possibility only.

630 This concept, however, is not unanimously accepted in the academic literature. For critical comments, see K. Meßerschmidt, *Gesetzgebungsermessen*, Berlin: Nomos 2000, pp. 780ff.

PART IV

THE NETHERLANDS

Chapter 1

AD HOC LEGISLATION: CASES

Introduction

The debate on ad hoc legislation in the Netherlands arose especially at the beginning of the 1990s after the Licensing of Dredging Act (*Vergunningwet Westerschelde*) in the Western Scheldt (River) case had been enacted by the Dutch Parliament. Later, several other expediency-driven pieces of legislation were enacted, of which the most prominent were the Modification of the Dutch Media Act (the so-called BNN Act), in the case of the popular public broadcasting association BNN, and the modification of the ministerial regulation concerning the requirements for equipping the cells in penitentiary institutions with permanent camera surveillance. Although the latter case concerned a ministerial regulation instead of an Act of Parliament, it still is an important example of changing the general rules for a specific case. The heated debate and criticism regarding the individual focus of the regulation also apply to ad hoc legislation as enacted by Parliament. This first chapter contains a description of the above-mentioned cases, including the legislative interventions and corresponding criticism in the media, literature, and parliamentary debates.

1.1. The Western Scheldt (River) case

1.1.1. Background

In 1995, the Dutch State and its southern neighboring State, the Flemish region of Belgium, agreed on deepening and widening the fairway in the Western Scheldt (River) in order to enable the larger ships to reach the harbor of Antwerp. To give full effect to this bilateral treaty,[631] the Dutch government was obliged to issue all (environmental) licenses which were necessary to start the operations. The Dutch Minister of Transport and Public Works granted, among other licenses, an environmental license on the basis of the Pollution of Surface Waters Act (*Wet verontreiniging oppervlaktewateren*).

631 *Tractatenblad* (*Trb.*) (Netherlands Treaty Series) 1995, 51. See also *Staatsblad* (*Stb.*) (Netherlands Bulletin of Acts and Decrees) 1996, 332.

1.1.2. *The decision of the Dutch Council of State*

Various environmental groups had campaigned against the license granted by the Minister. They invoked diverse arguments addressing the possible threat of the dredging operations to the environment. The highest administrative Court in the Netherlands, the Administrative Jurisdiction Division of the Council of State (*Raad van State*), however, did not get around to discussing these substantive claims. It started and ended its analysis by addressing the procedural errors in the Minister's decision-making process.

The Council of State explained that the license pursuant to the Pollution of Surface Waters Act alone did not suffice. The Minister had unfortunately overlooked that dredging operations were of such a nature that a license pursuant to the Dutch Environmental Management Act (*Wet Milieubeheer*) was required as well. The Council had already decided a few similar cases in the same key.[632] Next, the Council pointed to the coordination regime as provided for in the Dutch Environmental Management Act, in conformity with which applications for licenses under the Pollution of Surface Waters Act can only be considered if an application for the licenses pursuant to the Dutch Environmental Management Act has been filed.[633] In short, the license on the basis of the Pollution of Surface Waters Act, if already granted, was void. Applying this regime, the Council of State concluded that the Minister had erroneously taken the application for the first license into consideration.[634] The license already granted was therefore to be considered as never having existed.

1.1.3. *The legislative response: The Licensing of Dredging Act*

The final decision of the Council of State overwhelmed the government and jeopardized the construction of the project and therefore the fulfillment of the bilateral agreement with Belgium within the agreed time schedule. Its factual implications were that the entire administrative procedure with regard to the required licenses had to be repeated and started again concerning the license for which no application had been filed. Moreover, an obligatory, time-consuming environmental impact assessment had to be made.

The relations between the Dutch and Belgian governments concerning the agreements on significant (infrastructural) projects had already been difficult in the past.[635] The Dutch government feared that these relations would deteriorate even further if it did not do anything to overcome "the Western Scheldt deadlock." To avoid the inconveniences

632 See ABRvS December 20, 1995, *AB* 1996/139 and ABRvS December 21, 1995, E03.94.1381.

633 Art. 7b, par. 3a of the Pollution of Surface Waters Act.

634 ABRvS June 14, 1996, *M&R* 1996, p. 247.

635 The problems related to the so-called "water management agreements" and their execution date from the beginning of the 1970s. At some point, the negotiations were developing so slowly that they were even broken off until the 1980s. The "water management agreements" were not the only reason for the difficult relationship between the Dutch and the Belgian governments. It cooled again as a result of the difficulties in agreeing on the high-speed train link (HSL) between Antwerp (Belgium) and Rotterdam (Netherlands). For an outline of the problems, see *Kamerstukken II* (Parliamentary Papers II) 1996/1997, 24 451, no. 3, pp. 1–2.

and to guarantee that the time schedule for the work as agreed with Belgium would not suffer from the decision of the Council of State, the government devised a creative solution.[636] It proposed an exceptional bill, which was eventually passed by the Dutch Parliament. The law took effect only one year after the decision of the Council of State and after just a few months of preparation and consideration in Parliament. It was called the Licensing of Dredging Act (*Vergunningwet Westerschelde*).[637] It concerned a specific legislative license to the Flemish region for the dredging operations in the Western Scheldt (River), thereby de facto overruling the final decision of the Council of State.

The Act was extraordinary in several aspects. It granted one general license to the Flemish region, thereby setting aside all general statutes and their requirements which were normally applicable to the Western Scheldt project:[638]

> Without prejudice to the provisions of Article 1, second paragraph, the statutory regulations pursuant to which a license is required are not applicable to the Works and dumping of sediment referred to in Article 1 unless a license has been granted with application of those regulations through one or more decisions that have become final and conclusive before the entry into force of this Act.

By way of this technique, the legislature de facto usurped the power of the administrative bodies to grant licenses. It also deviated from the substantive provisions of the general (environmental) statutes that set out substantive standards and requirements which must be satisfied in order for applications for licenses to be successful. The separate standards that the Act itself introduced were less stringent, especially since the environmental impact assessment was no longer required.

1.1.3.1. Objections, constitutional, and otherwise to the Act

Serious objections were already expressed during the preparation of the Act and the first review by the Division of the Council of State responsible for advice on bills to be introduced in Parliament. Later, when the bill nevertheless became law, it was fiercely debated in the academic literature. The discussion and criticism centered on the concept of legislation and a possible violation of the principles of the separation of powers, legal certainty, equality, and legal protection. A violation of European law has also been invoked.[639]

636 In the explanation accompanying the bill, the motives for nullifying the unfavorable decision of the Council of State and trying to speed up the administrative licensing were explicitly mentioned. The renewed administrative decision-making with regard to the new licenses was estimated at about 15 months plus the possible judicial proceedings. *Kamerstukken II* 1996/1997, 25 187, no. 3, pp. 1–2.

637 *Stb.* 1997, 258.

638 Art. 2 of the Licensing of Dredging Act. All translations are mine.

639 For a summary of the arguments, see J. Verschuuren, "De formele wetgever als uitvoerder: de Vergunningwet Westerschelde en het streven naar een integrale afweging," *Bouwrecht* 1998–5, pp. 361–367.

The concept of legislation/generality of laws

The Council of State based its advice on the response of the National Commission for Water Legislation (*Staatscommissie voor de Waterstaatswetgeving*).[640] First of all, the Commission criticized the legislature for providing rules for one specific case by means of a statute. In the Commission's view, the theory of legislation presupposes that legislation is meant to contain general rules instead of specific ones.[641] In the literature concerning the Licensing of Dredging Act, on the other hand, it has been said that it is not a firm requirement that every legislative act must contain general rules only. Drupsteen, for example, referred in this regard to a statute passed by the legislature which, in the past, had regularly been used in cases of expropriations.[642] Nowadays, the Dutch Expropriation Act (*Onteigeningswet*) requires a statute in the event of expropriation of patents in the public interest.[643] Drupsteen, however, points to the specific character of expropriations. In that case, the choice to use an Act of Parliament instead of an administrative decision was made very consciously. This choice was based on the idea that expropriations put such a great burden on individuals that the highest body, namely the legislature, should decide on them. The form of a statute can then be seen as a strong safeguard for those subject to expropriation. Unlike a case-specific expropriation act, the case-specific Licensing of Dredging Act was passed to overcome an administrative impasse, as Drupsteen observed. He condemned the ad hoc character of the Act and argued that it is not the function of legislation to solve such problems by deviating from prior general statutes.[644]

The separation of powers principle

As regards the separation of powers argument, the Council invoked the strong reservation of the Commission, which was convinced the legislature had acted in conflict with the separation of powers principle: "Furthermore, the Government Commission points out that, by granting the license itself, the legislature acts contrary to the principle of the separation of powers (according to which granting licenses belongs to the competence of administrative bodies)."[645] For the Commission, the separation of powers principle was violated because the legislature had granted an administrative license for a specific project. On the basis of the general laws, the executive branch and administrative bodies (alone) are competent to grant licenses. In addition, the relationship between the legislature and the judiciary had suffered from the Act. The Commission called the way the legislature had acted "inappropriate" toward the judiciary, given that the legislature had overruled the judiciary by acting on mere expediency-driven grounds.

640 Van Buuren doubted, however, whether the Council of State would indeed adopt the criticism of the National Commission integrally, or whether it would just repeat it, P.J.J. van Buuren, "Vergunningwet Westerschelde niet voor herhaling vatbaar," *M&R* 1997–6, p. 123.

641 *Kamerstukken II* 1996/1997, 25 187, A, p. 2.

642 Th. Drupsteen, "Kroniek van het milieurecht," *NJB* 1997, p. 1492.

643 Art. 98 of the Dutch Expropriation Act.

644 Drupsteen (1997), p. 1492.

645 *Kamerstukken II*, 1996/1997, 25 187, A, p. 2.

The same concerns about the balance (or lack of it) between the legislature and the judiciary have been expressed in the literature. Tak even called this abuse of the instrument of a legislative act. In his opinion, the only reason to use a legislative act was to be able to overrule the final decision of the highest administrative court in the specific case of the Western Scheldt project. This was necessary to comply with the "deal," as he called it, which the Dutch government had made with the Belgian government. The deal involved an exchange of favors: the Dutch government promised it would grant all necessary licenses for the dredging operations in the Western Scheldt River, which would enable bigger ships to reach the harbor of Antwerp and thereby contribute to the economic development in Belgium, while Belgium would fully cooperate in the Dutch project of the high-speed train line (HSL).[646]

Legal certainty

The Licensing of Dredging Act also jeopardized legal certainty, according to critics. Legal certainty no longer exists if the legislature deviates from the general statutes and from the entire administrative/environmental system it had previously designed in a careful legislative process. In the case of the Licensing of Dredging Act, the particular concerns were the fact that the legislature replaced the legal rules it had created itself to protect the environment by a few vague ad hoc rules in a special Act, which were much easier to satisfy. The question is whether the environmental interest would ever be able to prevail in such a situation. Verschuuren was afraid that this interest would unfortunately always be treated as of secondary importance.[647]

The equal treatment principle

Another criticism of the Act implicitly concerned the problem of (un)equal treatment. Both the Council of State and legal commentators discussed and condemned the fact that the legislature had deviated from the general rules and statutory requirements concerning environmental issues, whereas these rules remained in effect for other similar projects. These projects were still required to make a complicated and time-consuming environmental impact assessment, which remains a constitutive requirement for licensing. The National Commission for Water Legislation concluded that the legislature had acted contrary to the legal order: "The legislature clearly attempted to neutralize the effects of the judicial decision, *while the applicable law continues to be in force for future cases. With the solution chosen, the government places itself above the law.*"[648]

Legal protection

Another, even more serious problem that had been identified, was diminished legal protection and possibilities for individuals and interest groups to participate in the

646 A.Q.C. Tak, "Misbruik van wetgeving," *Openbaar bestuur* 1997–12, pp. 7–9.

647 Verschuuren (1998), p. 364.

648 *Kamerstukken II* 1996/1997, 25 187, p. 2. See also Drupsteen (1997), p. 1492.

decision-making process as regards the specific license for the Western Scheldt project. By granting an environmental license to the Flemish region by a statute instead of an administrative decision, the legislature had de facto annulled the standard administrative procedures that normally apply to such licenses. Not only were individuals deprived of a possibility to present their objections against the proposed license[649] but they could not challenge it in any administrative court either, since it was not a typical administrative decision. Moreover, Art. 120 of the Dutch Constitution excludes the possibility of judicial review of legislation in light of its compatibility with the Constitution. Art 120 reads: "The constitutionality of Acts of Parliament and treaties shall not be reviewed by the courts." In this respect, the Council of State addressed the possible violation of Art. 6 of the European Convention on Human Rights (ECHR), which is binding on the Dutch State as one of the contracting parties. Art. 93 of the Dutch Constitution guarantees its direct application in the Dutch legal order. Art. 6, paragraph 1 of the ECHR entails a right to a fair trial, including a right of access to independent courts:

> 1. In the determination of his civil rights and obligations or of any criminal charge against him, everyone is entitled to a fair and public hearing within a reasonable time by an independent and impartial tribunal established by law.

Addressing the absence of a possibility of administrative judicial review of the dredging license, the Council of State doubted whether the legislative action was compatible with the international right to a fair trial. This question was even more relevant since the European Court of Human Rights (ECtHR) had decided already in 1975 that the right of access to a court does not depend on whether or not the national law of the contracting States allows this.[650]

Van Buuren indicated the possibility of judicial review by a civil court as a substitute for the administrative court procedure but, as he rapidly concluded, such review would provide only a less stringent assessment. Moreover, the financial burden of applying to the civil court would be greater than that of administrative court proceedings.[651]

European law

The last argument concerned the possible incompatibility with the European environmental directives and the obligation of the Dutch government to carry out an environmental impact assessment, given the nature of the dredging operations. The Minister, however, argued that this obligation had been fulfilled. He supported this claim by referring to his own report on the Western Scheldt (River) case. But Verschuuren was

[649] The government argued that such a possibility was given during the consideration of the license granted earlier on the basis of the Pollution of Surface Waters Act (*Wet verontreiniging oppervlaktewateren*), which had eventually been invalidated by the Council of State. Besides, the government argued that another procedure with broad participation of interest groups in light of the second license which had erroneously not been considered would not have made any difference; *Kamerstukken II* 1996/1997, 25 187, no. 3, p. 7.

[650] *Golder v. United Kingdom* (Appl. no. 4451/70) (1975) ECHR Series A no. 18.

[651] Van Buuren (1997), p. 124.

not entirely convinced that the data contained in the report reflected the data obtained in a regular environmental impact assessment, if carried out.[652]

The government persistently justified the extraordinary form of environmental license by pointing out the exceptional circumstances that required the enactment of the Licensing of Dredging Act. The Act, as the government explained, was an inevitable response to the judgment of the Council of State which created uncertainty about the entire project, which could adversely affect the already difficult relations with the Belgian State. For the sake of "good neighborliness," the Dutch Parliament was forced to grant a license for this one specific project:[653]

> The much broader scope linked to the Treaty which, in the light of the improvement of Dutch-Flemish relations in general, as well as the fact that the Netherlands and Flanders, in a spirit of good neighborliness, have meanwhile succeeded in reaching an arrangement on a number of issues, of which the deepening of the Western Scheldt is a vital element, suggests to the government that the special circumstances of this case justify the granting of licenses by the primary legislator. In this way, the procedure can be expedited and the above-mentioned uncertainty is removed.

The Council of State reassured the government that it had indeed understood these reasons, but considered the serious complaints to be of much greater importance.[654] Van Buuren, by contrast, considered the exceptional circumstances and the interest of good relations with the neighboring country, Belgium, legitimate, but he advocated a sporadic use of such ad hoc laws: "The Licensing of Dredging Act is therefore not a disaster, but it must remain a unique event."[655]

1.1.4. Concluding remarks

The government and the legislature considered the Licensing of Dredging Act to be a special kind of emergency legislation the authorities needed to avoid a dilemma. They decided to set aside the generally applicable rules, including the requirement of an environmental impact assessment and the possibilities of participation and judicial review, in order to fulfill the conditions they had agreed on with the Flemish region. The bill and later on the Act received fundamental criticism from a constitutional law point of view. Legal scholars and advisory bodies agreed that the legislature should no longer legislate by means of such specific, expediency-driven acts. It appears that the legislature has taken these remarks seriously. A similar Act, granting licenses to specific projects in deviation from the general rules, has never been enacted since.

652 Verschuuren (1998), p. 365.
653 *Kamerstukken II* 1996/1997, 25 187, A, p. 3.
654 *Ibid.*
655 Van Buuren (1997), p. 124.

1.2. Modification of the Media Act – the BNN Act

1.2.1. Background

Dutch broadcasting associations that want to join the public broadcasting system have to receive accreditation from the Dutch Minister of Education, Culture, and Science.[656] The main requirement, which is also the most difficult to fulfill, concerns the number of members they must have in order to obtain accreditation.[657] Until the year 2000, the minimum quantity of broadcasting time they could receive from the Dutch government depended on the number of members. Broadcasting associations having 450,000 members were classified as group A, those with 300,000 to 450,000 as group B, and those having 150,000 to 300,000 members were in group C. Provisional accreditation could already be obtained by candidate broadcasting associations having 60,000 members. In the year 2000, this differentiated system was deliberately changed by Parliament. The new system did not make a distinction between different groups, but introduced a fixed criterion of 300,000 members as a requirement to be part of the public broadcasting system. The threshold for candidate broadcasting associations to receive a provisional accreditation (and later on full accreditation with 300,000 members) was lowered to 50,000 members.[658]

The State Secretary for Education, Culture, and Science supported the abolition of differences between groups A, B, and C by addressing the need for cooperation rather than competition among the different broadcasting associations. The State Secretary said that by fixing the number of 300,000 members as a requirement to stay in the public broadcasting system, he was anticipating modern trends, meaning that young people would become members of a broadcasting association. In his view, this number could not be lowered again, because the number of members was still an important indication of whether a broadcasting association had broad support in society and therefore deserved to be part of the public broadcasting system:[659]

> The required number of members must not be lowered to 100,000, for example, as requested by the members of GroenLinks. After all, the new system is still grounded on the aforementioned principle that the broadcasting associations that appeal to an important part of the population should form the basis of the public broadcasting system. Lowering the membership threshold would be inconsistent with this. A consequence of the principle that the number of members is meaningful, and an essential element of the legitimization of the broadcasting system is that a broadcasting association that no longer has the required number of members cannot continue to be part of the broadcasting system.

656 Accreditation was given once every five years for a period of five years.

657 A person is a "member" of a broadcasting association if he or she is older than 16 years of age, lives in the Netherlands, and pays the minimal contribution of EUR5.72 a year, according to Art. 2.24 of the Dutch Media Act of 2008.

658 The Concessions Act (*Concessiewet*), *Stb.* 2000, 138.

659 *Kamerstukken II* 1999/2000, 26 660, no. 7, p. 52.

Nevertheless, the State Secretary was willing to introduce a transitional regime for one new and dynamic broadcasting association, namely BNN, which attracted especially young people.[660] BNN could obtain accreditation for five years if it only had 100,000 members.[661] Eventually, it was obligated to recruit 300,000 members; otherwise it would fall outside the public broadcasting system, as the State Secretary sternly concluded:[662]

> If BNN does not succeed in recruiting a sufficient number of members, then it's curtains for BNN and it will no longer be accredited as of 1 September 2000. It cannot be justified to again include a further provision in case BNN does not reach the threshold. [...] A very flexible transitional arrangement was already created for BNN and, moreover, I am of the opinion that if this broadcasting association cannot meet the lower requirements either, the programming probably has too little appeal to draw an audience of such a size that its continued participation in the system is justified.

Furthermore, the State Secretary argued that BNN had sufficient opportunities to grow and eventually reach the number of 300,000 members. The relevant provisions of the Act, it must be said, did not mention the name of BNN at all. The focus on BNN, by contrast, was the subject of parliamentary debates and can be regularly found in the official preparatory documents.

1.2.2. The BNN Act

Only two years after the Concessions Act of 2000 had been enacted, the new State Secretary for Education, Culture, and Science proposed amending it.[663] She argued that the public broadcasting system as designed in 2000 imposed too heavy a burden, particularly on candidate broadcasting associations. The State Secretary was concerned about the fact that these associations had to grow from 50,000 to 300,000 members in a period of five years. This was difficult if not impossible: membership recruitment was very expensive and the young candidate broadcasting associations could not afford it, according to the State Secretary. Moreover, these broadcasting associations generally did not publish any special magazine for members that could have a uniting effect on them.[664] For these reasons, the requirements for candidate broadcasting associations as established in 2000 were disproportionate, in the State Secretary's view. The remedy she proposed concerned the lowering of the standard from 300,000 to 150,000 members. This proposed amendment was eventually enacted and was due to sunset after September 1, 2008.[665]

660 "BNN" stands for "Barts Neverending Network."

661 Art. V, Sec. 2 of the Concessions Act (*Wet van 23 maart 2000 tot wijziging van de Mediawet in verband met de invoering van een vernieuwd concessiestelsel voor de landelijke publieke omroep*), *Stb.* 2000, 138.

662 *Kamerstukken II* 1999/2000, 26 660, no. 7, p. 21. See also *Kamerstukken II* 1998/1999, 26 660, no. 3, p. 52.

663 For the history, see G. Schuijt, "Kroniek van het Nederlandse mediarecht 2001–2006," *Auteurs & Media* 2006-3, pp. 238–256.

664 *Kamerstukken II* 2002/2003, 29 030, no. 3, p. 2.

665 *Stb.* 2004, 668, and *Stb.* 2004, 669. The criterion of 150,000 members has meanwhile become permanent. See Art. 2.25 of the Media Act, *Stb.* 2008, 583 and *Stb.* 2008, 584.

1.2.2.1. Objections to the Act

Even before enactment, the bill received much substantive criticism.

Specificity of the Act

During the parliamentary debates, several political parties criticized the bill, labeling it a special kind of ad hoc expediency-driven legislation. They dealt with the fact that the only purpose of the bill was to benefit a specific candidate broadcasting association (BNN) by preventing it from dropping out of the public broadcasting system (as a result, the bill was nicknamed the BNN Act). This was a real possibility, since it turned out that BNN would not reach the number of 300,000 members required for ministerial accreditation. The governing body of NOS[666] expressed this concern in a letter to the State Secretary of Education, Culture, and Science, who had initiated the bill. In the Dutch Parliament, the ChristianUnion (*ChristenUnie*) was a major opponent of the proposed legislation:[667]

> The question about this law occupying the ChristianUnion is whether it is in fact ad hoc legislation. [...] We are inclined to answer this question in the affirmative. Why else would it be necessary to decide on a relatively radical change of the Media Act at this time without very detailed substantiation? We can think of only one reason for this, an ad hoc reason: BNN must remain in the public broadcasting system at all costs.

The Dutch Council of State, which had given advice on the bill, responded in a similar way. It found that a more profound explanation of the proposed change must be given:[668]

> In the light of the parliamentary history of the Media Act [...], any choice of a lower membership threshold requires more solid motivation. The proposed solution must be prevented from having, however inadvertently, the nature of ad hoc legislation favoring BNN.

Another political party, the Socialist Party (SP), also observed that the bill was meant to make it possible for BNN to stay in the public broadcasting system. The SP, however, did not immediately conclude that it was consequently an objectionable proposal. The SP looked beyond the benefits BNN would receive, and saw the broader purpose of the Act, which could only be achieved by lowering the required number of members:[669]

> Is the proposed lowering of the required number of members from 300,000 to 150,000 an ad hoc statute? Yes, it is. [...] Is it a proposal to keep BNN within the system? Yes, that too is the case. Is the proposal to lower the membership threshold therefore a bad proposal? No, not in

666 Netherlands Broadcasting Corporation (*Nederlandse Omroep Stichting*).
667 *Handelingen II* 2003/2004, no. 42, p. 2980.
668 *Kamerstukken II* 2002/2003, 29 030, A, p. 3.
669 *Handelingen I* 2003/2004, no. 36, p. 1929.

> the opinion of the SP, in any case. Lowering the required number of members keeps the public broadcasting system open to newcomers. Moreover, my party is afraid that, after the monopoly on the program schedule has ended, many more broadcasting corporations with fewer than 300,000 members will emerge so that soon there will be nothing to see on television or hear on the radio but the commercial channels.

The State Secretary for Education, Culture, and Science explained that BNN was not the only focus of the bill. This specific candidate broadcasting association had merely inspired the legislation, which in fact had a general character and was applicable to future cases as well.[670] It was the case of BNN that made it clear to the State Secretary that the requirement of 300,000 members was disproportionate and should therefore be lowered. This would serve the greater general interest of providing openness and continuity in the national public broadcasting system.

Not every political party was satisfied with this line of reasoning. The Christian Democratic Appeal (CDA) argued that it was already known in 2000, when the public broadcasting system was changed and the threshold of 300,000 members was introduced, that young broadcasting associations were having difficulty in recruiting new members. The difficult situation of BNN was also known at that time. Nonetheless, the government had firmly stated that the number of 300,000 members could not be lowered, even if it would lead to BNN's removal from the public broadcasting system.[671]

Sudden policy changes

Precisely this sudden change in the policy gave the critics a reason to think that the precarious position of BNN was the only purpose of the legislative proposal. But this sudden change in itself was also an independent point of criticism. The government, and later on the legislature, were accused of acting impulsively and changing the rules that had previously been enacted in a careful legislative process. The members of the Christian Democratic Appeal could not understand what new developments in society had taken place in the three years after the new public broadcasting system was introduced in 2000 that could justify the policy change:[672]

> When the State Secretary [...] states that the present motion anticipates a social development and that BNN is a symbol of that social development, the members of the CDA wonder exactly what changes in social development took place in the past three years (since the Concessions Act took effect in September 2000) that make the present motion urgent.

The CDA advocated a careful use of legislation, which should be preceded by consistent substantiation.

670 *Handelingen II* 2003/2004, no. 42, p. 2991.

671 *Kamerstukken I* 2003/2004, 29 030, A, p. 2.

672 *Kamerstukken I* 2003/2004, 29 030, A, p. 2. See also Van Gestel (2005), p. 284.

1.2.3. Concluding remarks

The changes in the Dutch Media Act met with a great deal of criticism due to the alleged special interest effect of the modified provision. At the time the law was introduced, it was public knowledge that the BNN broadcasting association would not meet the requirements of the existing law for permanent accreditation. The State Secretary who sponsored the bill even frankly announced that this fact had been a reason for the introduction of the bill, but she refused to acknowledge that the new provisions were intended to bestow privileges on BNN only. She argued that the general terms of the bill created an opportunity (even if only a theoretical one) for future broadcasting associations to benefit from the new law. To avoid the impression that the only reason for modification of the public broadcasting system was the position of BNN, the Christian Democratic Appeal and the Council of State argued for better motivation of a sudden policy change.

1.3. Volkert van der G. and permanent camera surveillance

1.3.1. Background

The year 2002 was one of the most remarkable years in the modern history of the Netherlands. In that year, Pim Fortuyn, a Dutch politician, was assassinated. Such an event is a highly unusual occurrence in the Netherlands and it therefore shocked entire Dutch society.

Pim Fortuyn stood for a new development in the Dutch political landscape at the beginning of the 21st century. He symbolized the rise of political populism and was especially known for his hostile attitude toward Islam and the Muslim community in the Netherlands. He particularly criticized Islam for discriminating against minorities such as homosexuals (he was gay himself) and for undermining the liberal tradition characterizing Dutch society in general. He vigorously advocated a rigorous immigration policy with regard to Muslims.

After leaving a political party called Livable Netherlands (*Leefbaar Nederland*) due to several conflicts stemming from his controversial ideas, he founded his own party in February 2002 and simply named it Pim Fortuyn List (*Lijst Pim Fortuyn*). In the meantime, his popularity grew enormously and his party was expected to gain a significant number of seats in the Lower House of the Dutch Parliament during the elections of May 2002.

But not everyone agreed with Fortuyn's political ideas. Volkert van der G., a Dutch animal rights activist, believed that Fortuyn represented a threat to Dutch democratic society and especially to the minority groups. He decided to murder Fortuyn just a few days before the elections took place.

Volkert van der G. was arrested almost immediately after his deed. Responding to the great consternation in society and the political pressure to prevent Van der G. from committing suicide before being tried, the director of the penitentiary where Volkert van der G. was kept in custody decided to place him under permanent camera surveillance.

According to the applicable legal regime at that time, special, important requirements had to be met to make such surveillance possible. Art. 33, Sec. 1 and 2 of the relevant ministerial regulation on disciplinary and isolation cells provided:[673]

> 1. The director may decide, if necessitated by the physical or mental condition of the detainee, that the detainee will be monitored day and night by a camera.
> 2. Before deciding to do so, he shall seek the advice of the detention center's medical officer, unless urgency precludes this. In that case, the director shall consult with the medical officer as soon as possible after his decision.

Accordingly, given the far-reaching effect of permanent camera surveillance, it was only permitted if it was necessary in view of the exceptional physical or mental condition of the detainee. A medical report about a detainee evidencing the risk of committing suicide or escaping from custody was indispensable in this respect. Moreover, the detainee concerned had to be placed in a special disciplinary or isolation cell. Volkert van der G. challenged the decision of the director of the penitentiary and complained that he was not suicidal and that his condition was thus not of such a nature that permanent camera surveillance was justified. The Appeals Commission appointed by the Council for the Administration of Criminal Justice and Protection of Juveniles (*Raad voor Strafrechtstoepassing en Jeugdbescherming*), which dealt with Van der G.'s complaint, agreed by concluding that no detailed report existed, and ordered by means of a preliminary judgment on Thursday July 4, 2002, that the cameras had to be removed from Van der G.'s cell.[674]

This decision was completely unacceptable to the Dutch Minister of Justice, who would be under tremendous political pressure in the event Van der G. nevertheless escaped or committed suicide. To prevent the decision of the Council of Thursday July 4, 2002 from taking effect, he preferred to overrule it by a new amendment to a general regulation. Just one day after the decision of the Council was issued, on Friday July 5, 2002, he promulgated an amendment to the Regulation on the requirements for accommodations in penitentiaries and introduced a new possibility for placing cameras in detainees' cells for the purpose of permanent surveillance. From then on, permanent camera surveillance became possible in case great public unrest would arise if a detainee were not able to stand trial because he committed suicide, harmed himself, or escaped from prison.[675] Not surprisingly, this new provision was immediately invoked and

673 *Regeling straf- en afzonderingscel penitentiaire inrichtingen* of June 15, 1999, no. 762711/98/DJI.

674 Decision of the Council for the Administration of Criminal Justice and Protection of Juveniles of 4 July 2002, no. 02/1292/SGA, unpublished.

675 Art. 10b of *Wijziging regeling eisen verblijfsruimte penitentiaire inrichtingen in verband met cameraobservatie*, July 5, 2002, no. 5175032/02/DJI, Government Gazette, (*Staatscourant*, hence *Stcrt.*) 2002, 127, p. 8. Art. 10b, Sec. 1 provided the following:
1. The director may decide that a detainee who has been placed under an individual regime [...] or who has been placed in a high-security prison [...] shall be monitored day and night by a camera:
a. if this is necessary in the interest of maintaining the order or security in the institution,
b. if this is necessary for an undisturbed execution of the deprivation of liberty,
c. if this is necessary in connection with the mental or physical condition of the detainee,

applied by the director of the penitentiary where Volkert van der G. was staying. Van der G. was again placed under permanent camera surveillance.[676]

1.3.2. *Objections, constitutional. and otherwise to the ministerial regulation*

The new regulation was by no means uncontroversial[677] and it received a lot of attention, especially in the media. The criticism focused on the expediency-driven, case-oriented character of the regulation, the place of the regulation within the system of relevant legislation, and the irrationality of the ministerial choices.

Case-specific character

In the media, no doubts remained about the reason why the Minister had introduced the amendment. The national newspapers unanimously spoke about the case of Volkert van der G. as being the only reason for the new rules. The commentators based their argument on the circumstances in which the new rules had been enacted. It was just one day after the uncomfortable judgment of the Council for the Administration of Criminal Justice and Protection of Juveniles that the Minister came up with the new rules. This exceptional timing made it very unlikely that this was a coincidence:[678]

> Minister Korthals (Justice) arranged for around the clock use of the surveillance cameras in Volkert van der G.'s cell, even though the Council for the Administration of Criminal Justice and Protection of Juveniles is of the opinion that there was no longer a need to do so. In order to ensure that constant camera surveillance could continue, the Minister introduced a new criterion: the risk of "great public unrest."

With reference to the American prohibition of bills of attainders, the individual focus of the Dutch regulation was not only considered an unwelcome development but also a possible problem of constitutional law:[679]

> And this is a form of regulation that is generally disapproved. General rules must not be inspired by the issue of the day. In the case of measures against particular persons, there are even constitutional objections to ad hoc legislation. For example, the American Constitution

d. if, in the event of escape or of damage to the health of the detainee, great public unrest would arise or if this would cause serious harm to the relations of the Netherlands with other states or international organizations.

676 The case of Volkert van der G. including the ministerial intervention(s) has accurately been described by Van der G.'s advocate, B. Böhler, *Crisis in de rechtsstaat*, Amsterdam: De Arbeiderspers 2004, pp. 109–146.

677 The Minister knew that his plans were controversial. He probably therefore did not consult the Council for the Administration of Criminal Justice and Protection of Juveniles, while such a consultation usually takes place during the preparation of new regulations of this kind. The Minister justified this omission by citing the need for immediate action.

678 F. Kuitenbrouwer, "Gelegenheidswet voor Volkert van der G.," *NRC Handelsblad* July 9, 2002.

679 *Ibid.*

> contains an explicit prohibition of bills of attainder. This is a legislative act, in whatever form, aimed at explicitly named persons or easily identifiable members of a group, in order to impose punishment on them without the benefit of trial.

The Minister of Justice was also asked critical questions about the sudden amendment and its focus on the specific case of Volkert van der G. by the members of the Lower House of Parliament: "Does not the amendment effected by you rather have the character of ad hoc legislation and thus of arbitrariness?"[680] The Minister stuck to the explanation that he had not acted arbitrarily, since the preparation for the amendment had already been going on a long time before the Council for the Administration of Criminal Justice and Protection of Juveniles ordered the director of the penitentiary where Volkert van der G. was staying to remove the cameras.[681] Indirectly, however, the Minister admitted that the case of Volkert van der G. had accelerated its enactment, although he resisted the conclusion that the new regulation was tailored to the case of Van der G.:[682]

> By the time the president of the Appeals Commission rendered his decision, the draft of the regulation referred to had almost been completed. Given the necessary speed with which the regulations were to take effect, consultation with the Council for the Administration of Criminal Justice and Protection of Juveniles, which, incidentally, is not mandatory, did not take place.

And:

As is shown by the answers to questions 2 and 3, [...] regulations were already being prepared for situations in which 24-hour camera surveillance was deemed necessary. Therefore, the new regulations were not tailored to the case of Mr. Van der G. only.

Place of the regulation

The new authority to place cameras in a detainee's cell was given a remarkable place in the system of relevant criminal regulations. The Minister had chosen to incorporate a far-reaching authority of permanent camera surveillance, directly infringing detainees' privacy rights, in a regulation concerning the minimal equipment of prison cells. The new rules concerning the placement of cameras were introduced in Arts. 10a-10c of that regulation, right after Art. 10, which stipulated the minimal requirements for the furniture and equipment of a prison cell. The new rules had a paradoxical effect. From then on, besides a mirror, closet, table, chair, bulletin board, bed, and two wall sockets, which served as a minimum guarantee for prisoners (Art. 10), a surveillance camera could be installed. This ministerial trick was strongly criticized. Legal scholars were

680 *Kamerstukken II* 2001/2002, Appendix 1469, p. 3119.

681 The Council for the Administration of Criminal Justice and Protection of Juveniles had no idea that the Minister was already working on such a regulation, according to the media, "Camera blijft in cel V.d. G. via noodwet," *NRC Handelsblad* July 9, 2002, p. 1.

682 *Kamerstukken II* 2001/2002, appendix 1469, p. 3120.

convinced that neither the parliamentary history nor the wording of the regulation on the furniture and equipment of the cell itself was meant to open the possibility of such far-reaching authority to order permanent camera surveillance.[683] They argued that a legal basis for such far-reaching authority therefore did not exist and that the Minister had acted against the principle of legality (*legaliteitsbeginsel*).[684]

Legal certainty

The new regulation was criticized further from the perspective of the principle of legal certainty. The problem pointed out was the rush with which the new provisions had been pushed through. Fiselier, a professor of penitentiary law, put it as follows:[685]

> This smacks of ad hoc legislation, which is an improper tool. That is not the way to deal with the law. The law is not a trick to quickly fix a problem. Nor are the regulations elegant from a legal certainty point of view. What used to be the law yesterday is no longer the law today.

Impulsivity

Lastly, the Minister was criticized for acting impulsively, being swayed by the issues of the day. This resulted in a premature regulation, nevertheless with far-reaching consequences. The Minister should have provided better justification for the necessity of the sudden change to the permanent camera surveillance regime.[686]

Volkert van der G.'s rights of privacy

On the basis of the ministerial regulation as amended by the Minister of Justice on July 5, 2002, Volkert van der G. was again placed under permanent camera surveillance. Before the European Court of Human Rights (ECtHR), he complained that his right of privacy, as guaranteed by Art. 8 of the European Convention on Human Rights, had been violated. The ECtHR examined the interference with Volkert van der G.'s right and concluded that the measure served a legitimate aim of prevention of disorder and public safety. Moreover, the Court considered such surveillance necessary in a democratic society, stating the following reasons:[687]

> The Court acknowledges that the applicant's detention placed an exceptionally heavy responsibility on the penitentiary authorities to prevent the applicant from escaping or from

683 J. uit Beijerse & W. Bos, "Camera's in de cel om het publiek gerust te stellen?," *NJB* 2002–29, p. 1414.

684 The Dutch principle of legality implies that the government may infringe or limit individual freedom or property only when there is a legal basis in legislation, see F.J. van Ommeren, *De verplichting verankerd. De reikwijdte van het legaliteitsbeginsel en het materiële wetsbegrip*, Zwolle: W.E.J. Tjeenk Willink 1996, p. 13.

685 "Juristen: camera in cel Van der G. is onaanvaardbaar," *Volkskrant* July 10, 2002, p. 2.

686 Van Gestel (2005), p. 283.

687 ECtHR, Decision as to the admissibility, Appl. no. 8704/03.

> being harmed [...]. This responsibility stemmed directly from the fact that the Netherlands authorities rightly considered it to be of the utmost importance that, in order to prevent the great public unrest caused by the killing of Mr Fortuyn, the applicant be brought to trial.

The ECtHR thus directly sanctioned the permanent camera surveillance of Volkert van der G. Continuing this line of argument, it could also be argued that in doing so, the Court indirectly approved the ad hoc amendment to the ministerial regulation on which the executive measure was based.

1.3.3. Concluding remarks

The Minister of Justice decided to intervene in the specific case of Volkert van der G. after he had experienced strong political pressure to do everything in his power to prevent Pim Fortuyn's murderer from committing suicide or escaping from prison. The realistic fear of public unrest if Volkert van der G. could not be brought to trial motivated the Minister to act. By changing the applicable rules, he reassured that Volkert van der G. could be subject to permanent camera surveillance, despite the fact that the Council for the Administration of Criminal Justice and Protection of Juveniles had ordered the removal of the cameras just one day earlier. The criticism of the new regulation was mainly directed at the impulsiveness of the Minister's action and its focus on the case of Volkert van der G., as well as the suspect way it was introduced. The Minister decided to insert the new rules in a regulation in which it in fact did not belong, because they would then be easier to pass.

1.4. Conclusion

The cases of the Licensing of Dredging Act, the BNN Act, and the Regulation allowing permanent camera surveillance show that the Dutch legislature (or, in the latter case the Minister of Justice) is willing to interfere in specific cases to obtain a politically desired outcome. What exactly are the reasons for such an action and what are the points of criticism?

Reasons for enacting ad hoc legislation

The three cases show three different reasons for impulsive legislation. It can be the political will to fulfill bilateral (international) obligations, especially in light of a difficult relationship with a neighboring country, as illustrated by the case of the Licensing of Dredging Act or the legislative will to benefit a specific body (in the case of the BNN Act: a broadcasting association). In the case of Volkert van der G., the great public commotion and the political pressure the Minister experienced were clear reasons to amend the rules on permanent camera surveillance.

Legislation for one case

A Dutch counterpart of the term "ad hoc legislation" as used throughout this book is the term *gelegenheidswetgeving*. This term has a strongly negative connotation in the Netherlands and it is mostly used to criticize a legislative action that has one specific case in mind. It should be noted, however, that "a case" has a broad meaning in this respect. The cases of ad hoc legislation as described above show that "a case" can be understood as a case of one person (Volkert van der G.), one organization/company (the broadcasting association BNN) or one project (the dredging operations in the Western Scheldt [River]). In all three cases, the specific motives of the legislature were pointed out and criticized, but the specific motives did not always coincide with the unrepeatable application of the new rules in all these cases.

Specificity

Both the specific motive of the legislature and the specific character of the laws in terms of their specific application have been criticized. As far as the specific motive is concerned, the criticism focused on the irrational, impulsive way in which the legislature acted and the fact that the legislature had allowed specific cases to dictate the legislative agenda. Moreover, as the case of the BNN Act showed in particular, the legislature was criticized for acting in the specific interest of one broadcasting association, since it had insufficiently justified why the existing rules for the public broadcasting system needed to be altered just two years after they were enacted.

The criticism regarding the application of the law in one specific case was linked to the concept of legislation in the material sense and the requirements legislative acts should meet, one of them being generality. This type of criticism was expressed by the National Commission for Water Legislation in the case of the Licensing of Dredging Act. The Commission stated that the legislature's power is restricted to acts of general application only.

Generality of laws, separation of powers, equality, legal protection

In the line of the National Commission for Water Legislation's reasoning, legislation that grants licenses to specific projects usurps the executive function, violating the separation of powers principle. It also circumvents the administrative rules concerning the possibilities of individual legal protection. Moreover, the legislature creates inequality if it treats one project as an exception. These rule of law arguments were used only in the case of the Licensing of Dredging Act, where the case-specific motives of the legislature were equal to the case-specific application of the Act.

Legislative irrationality

Regarding the legislative changes of general rules for the sake of one specific case, the legislature was criticized for acting irrationally. In the case of BNN, this criticism came particularly clearly to the fore after the Dutch Council of State required the government to give a better explanation of the necessity of the amendment in order to eliminate the suspicion that the only reason why the amendment was proposed was to benefit the BNN broadcasting association. The same held for the case of Volkert van der G. Kuitenbrouwer concluded in this respect: "General rules must not be inspired by the issue of the day."[688]

Legal certainty

The argument that the legislature had violated the principle of legal certainty was expressed most clearly in the cases of the Licensing of Dredging Act and the Regulation on permanent camera surveillance. In that context, it has been said that the legislature creates uncertainty if it either deviates from the general rules for the sake of one case or suddenly changes the general rules as such. Remarkably, the BNN Act was not criticized from the angle of the legal certainty principle. The reason could be that this Act was mainly aimed to benefit, not to damage or punish.

The method of enactment

The last critical argument, which was put forward only in the case of the Regulation on permanent camera surveillance, concerned the method of enactment of the new rules. Their controversial nature forced the Minister to both circumvent the usual procedures concerning, for example, consultation on the draft, and embed it in a regulation where it did not belong.

In conclusion, the cases of ad hoc legislation generated three types of criticism. The first focused on the irrationality of legislative actions, the second addressed the violation of several principles of the rule of law, and the third concerned the unusual method of the enactment. This criticism was fundamental and it left almost no room for possible justification of legislative intervention in specific cases.

688 Kuitenbrouwer (2002).

Chapter 2

THE REQUIREMENT OF GENERALITY

Introduction

The most noticeable point of criticism that can be observed in the three cases discussed in the first chapter was the fact that the laws were not general in the sense of general applicability, the motives of the legislature, and the general, public interest that laws should serve. Although the critics were convinced of the existence of a general principle of the generality of laws, its meaning in Dutch constitutional law can be questioned. As will be shown below, the discussion of the generality of laws in the Netherlands centers on the concept of laws in the formal and in the material sense and the concept of general, public interest which the laws are deemed to serve. Project laws deserve special attention here as well, since they represent a new development in the use of special laws for individual, mostly infrastructural, projects. Although they do not have the typical characteristics of general legislative acts, they have nevertheless been accepted in Dutch legislative practice in the past few years. Given the choice made in the Dutch Constitution for the concept of legislation in the formal sense, they formally do not violate the Constitution on this point.

2.1. Two concepts of laws: Laws in the formal and laws in the material sense

The Dutch doctrine of the formal and material concepts of legislation (*formeel* and *materieel wetsbegrip*) is traditionally based on the German doctrine representing the same concepts. It was the German scholar Laband and his ideas about the notion of a legislative act that inspired Dutch scholars.[689] In the Netherlands, therefore, as well as in Germany, the *formeel* concept of legislation addresses the procedural aspects of legislation, while the material concept focuses on the content of legislation and its characteristics.

With respect to the formal concept of legislation, the Dutch Constitution (*Grondwet*) provides the procedure to be followed to enact valid legislation. Art. 81 states that legislation must be enacted by the two houses of Parliament jointly with the government.

[689] Ruiter suggests that this concept of legislation, being a distinction between the formal and material elements, is part of the constitutional law of all democratic constitutional states in Europe, D.W.P. Ruiter, *Bestuursrechtelijke wetgevingsleer*, Assen: Van Gorcum 1987, p. 6.

Several requirements have been formulated for the material concept of legislation. A law in the material sense must usually meet the following criteria. Firstly, the law must have external effect ("*naar buiten werkend*"). Logemann explains that this criterion means that the rules must be directed toward those who are "outside:" "So the upshot of this is that the term 'with external effect' only means 'aimed at,' namely, at those who are 'external'."[690] This implies that provisions that have only internal effect (like organizational laws attributing competences to specific institutions, laws approving international agreements) cannot be called law in the material sense.[691] Secondly, rules having external effect must be general.[692] The two components of generality are: 1) generality *sensu stricto*, which means that the law must be aimed at an indefinite group of persons, and 2) generality in the sense of the abstract application of rules. In other words, the first element deals with the law's addressees (generality regarding the subjects) and the second with the repeatable application of the law in similar cases (generality regarding the objects, situations).[693]

The development of the doctrine of formal and material concepts of legislation, including the clarification of the element of generality, does not answer the question which is most important for the legality of ad hoc laws: does the material concept of legislation bind the legislature and limit its power to the enactment of general laws only? In the literature, vigorous support for such a conclusion was given by Böhtlingk.

Most statutes enacted by the Dutch legislature are general, both as far as generality *sensu stricto* and generality within the meaning of the abstract application are concerned. This factual situation was not satisfying for Böhtlingk. He fiercely argued for the normative character of the material concept of legislation limiting the legislative power to general acts only:[694]

> A consequence of law and truth was that the legal rules of the law had to be *general* rules [...], whereby the concept 'general' had to be understood in its absolute meaning [...].

690 F.R. Böhtlingk & J.H.A. Logemann, *Het wetsbegrip in Nederland*, Alphen aan den Rijn: N. Samson 1966, p. 105.

691 Logemann stresses the importance of the classification "external effect," since only governmental rules which have external effect are subject to the legality principle. This means that internal rules of government are not required to have a legal basis in legislation stemming from Parliament, Böhtlingk & Logemann (1966), p. 81. See also the judgment of the Dutch Supreme Court, HR June 10, 1919, *NJ* 1919/647. For more case law references on the concept of law, see the final report of the Legislative Studies Commission (*Commissie voor Wetgevingsvraagstukken*), *Orde in regelgeving*, The Hague 1985, p. 14.

692 The element of generality of laws as a component of the material concept of legislation is uncontroversial among legal scholars. Duk, for example, has vigorously argued that provisions directed to a closed group of individuals cannot be seen as legal norms. They are simply individual orders, permissions, grants, or licenses, W. Duk, *Recht en slecht*, Nijmegen: Ars Aequi Libri 1999, pp. 32–33.

693 Ruiter (1987), p. 7. See also F.R. Böhtlingk & J.F. Glastra van Loon, "Het begrip rechtsregel," *RMThemis* 1959, p. 11 and P.W. Brouwer, *Samenhang in recht*, Groningen: Wolters-Noordhoff 1990, p. 164, who tried to answer the question of what laws are indeed general.

694 Böhtlingk & Logemann (1966), p. 30. For an overview of Böthlingk's ideas, see R. van den Berg, *Vormen van begrip van wet en wetgeving. Wetsbegrippen in de Staatsrechtsgeleerdheid in Duitsland en Nederland in de negentiende en twintigste eeuw*, The Hague: Boom Juridische uitgevers 2003, pp. 310ff.

> The generality of the law remains valuable in every respect, even if the law is of a bad quality: a general legal rule does not side with or against certain persons and treats everyone whom it deems equal in the same way. The generality of a legal provision is therefore also 'das allgemeine, logische, unumgängliche Minimum' that is still firmly embedded in the constitutional provisions on equality before the law, human rights and the separation of powers.

And:

> Generality is, however, still a strict requirement with respect to the person having legal rights at whom the legal rule is aimed. No longer in the sense that the rule must be binding on all and therefore must not distinguish between groups of persons, but in the sense that the legislature may never individualize, must treat equal persons in the same way and unequal persons in a different way and may not create inequalities or equalities that are not objectively relevant […].
> Finally, the requirement of generality is also important for the legal fact covered by the legal rule. Not in the sense that this fact must be able to occur always and everywhere […]. But it must be a repeatable fact, since there are no unique situations from a legal equality point of view. And for the same reason, this fact, as before, may not […] be bound to the existence of individually identifiable persons.

Although Böhtlingk believes that every piece of legislation expresses the will of the legislature, he argues that this does not mean that its will is unlimited. In his plea for generality of legislation, he clearly refers to the concept of equality and the separation of powers as preventing the legislature from acting arbitrarily and discriminatorily. In his opinion, these concepts force the legislature to enact general acts only.

Böhtlingk's opponent was Logemann. He could not agree with Böhtlingk's ideas on the concept of legislation, as Böhtlingk concluded from Art. 119 of the Dutch Constitution of 1956. Although Logemann acknowledged that in the Dutch Constitution, the term "law" usually refers to the concept of law as a general rule, he disputed Böhtlingk's conclusion that it also limits the legislative power to the enactment of general rules only. Logemann interpreted the material concept of legislation, including the requirement of legislation's generality, as a postulate in the sphere of law and politics rather than as a logical category:[695]

> It is to this rule that the attributes of 'external effect' and 'generality' must be added to achieve the material concept of legislation of a state under the rule of law. This concept of legislation is therefore not a logical category, but a legal-political postulate, as is the further requirement of the state under the rule of law that making this law should be the monopoly of an authority especially qualified to do so: the legislature.

[695] Böhtlingk & Logemann (1966), p. 111.

In his view, the Dutch Constitution does not require legislative acts to be general. Accordingly, every legislative act, irrespective of its content, is a legitimate one:[696] "I cannot see that the Constitution says, or can be interpreted to say, that a law for an individual case – however seldom it may be justified – must be unlawful."

An interesting interpretation of the theory of the generality of laws was later given by Van der Vlies. In her dissertation, she criticizes the idea of the material concept of legislation as restricting the legislative power to the enactment of general rules and explains the possible paradox of such a restriction. She considers the legislature as the only State body that is competent to take the most important and far-reaching decisions. To illustrate this thesis, she uses the example of a parliamentary endorsement of a declaration of war. She concludes:[697]

> There is very little point in generally excluding the legislature from making orders. This argument is stronger if it is assumed that the legislature must make the radical decisions. Restricting the legislature's competence to legislating by general rules only entails that the legislature cannot make orders involving radical decisions. Since it is the legislature's exclusive competence to make radical decisions, not one single body would be competent to make orders involving radical decisions. The result would be a legislative vacuum.

Continuing in her line of reasoning, one can say that the exceptional position of the legislature, which is responsible for making the most important and far-reaching choices in the country, can in certain circumstances even compel the legislature to enact specific acts.

As far as Dutch contemporary positive constitutional law is concerned, the conclusion must be that the legislature is not required to adopt only general legislation. During the general revision of the Dutch Constitution in 1983, Parliament took a clear standpoint on the constitutional concept of legislation. Despite the academic defense of the material concept of legislation including the generality of laws as a limitation of the legislature's power, the 1983 Constitution clearly chose the formal concept of legislation.[698] This implies that, according to Art. 81, every act of the legislature which is enacted in a democratic procedure as provided in Arts. 81–88 of the Constitution must be considered a legitimate piece of legislation regardless of its content.[699] Art. 81 reads: "Acts of Parliament shall be enacted jointly by the Government and the States General."

[696] *Ibid.*, p. 126.

[697] I.C. van der Vlies, *Het wetsbegrip en beginselen van behoorlijke regelgeving*, The Hague: VUGA 1984, p. 119.

[698] See the explanation and the commentary on the new Art. 81 in: C.A.J.M. Kortmann, *De Grondwetsherziening 1983*, Deventer: Kluwer 1983, pp. 239ff. The concept of legislation in the material sense can be found in the Directives on Legislation, but it is not intended to limit the legislature as to the content of statutes; see (*Aanwijzingen voor de regelgeving*), *Stcrt.* 1992, 230 as revised. On the nature and the status of the Directives, see J.M. Bonnes, *Aard en omvang van de Aanwijzingen voor de regelgeving*, *RegelMaat* 2005–1, pp. 9–13.

[699] Despite the clear choice in the new Constitution of 1983, several authors nevertheless argue for generality of laws as a limitation of the legislative power. See, for example, M. Scheltema, "De partijdige wetgever," Deventer: Kluwer 1984, p. 9.

2.2. Special laws: Individual laws and project laws

2.2.1. Individual laws and the Dutch Constitution

As stated above, the Dutch Constitution does not require every statute enacted by Parliament to be general. Nevertheless, statutes that apply to only one case are rare.[700] The Constitution sometimes requires such specific statutes. It does so in situations in which the legislature must enact specific laws regulating only one specific case and/or person, especially the Dutch Royal House. Pursuant to Article 28 (3) of the Constitution, for example, Parliament needs to give permission for the King's (or the heir to the throne's) marriage by a statute, while the legislature must also appoint a regent by legislative act for the period that the King is unable to reign (Article 37 [2]). Budgetary laws are another well-known example of non-general laws (Article 104). In the past, naturalization of individual persons and some types of individual expropriation also took place by means of legislative acts. These last types of individual acts were nevertheless based on general laws.[701]

Situations in which a specific case *inspired* the legislature to enact or change a general law are more common. In the case of the BNN broadcasting association, for example, the government sternly argued that the fact that BNN would not reach the number of members required to join the public broadcasting system was a strong impetus for the government to reconsider the system of the Media Act and lower the applicable requirements.

2.2.2. Project laws

In the previous section, it was said that the Dutch legislature, despite the formal concept of legislation which allows it to do so, rarely acts by means of legislation in specific cases. This indeed holds true for individual legislation for specific individuals. Since the beginning of the 1990s, however, the Dutch legislature has been enacting specific project

[700] As far as legislation for specific individuals is concerned, two examples can be given. The legislature once considered taking away the pension rights of widow Rost van Tonningen (see Chapter IV.4.1 for a detailed description), *Kamerstukken II* 1986/1987, 19 783. Although the public commotion was enormous, Parliament eventually decided not to act in that one specific case. Another, much older example of a legislative act for specific individuals (which was indeed enacted) is the pension law for the daughters of the Dutch politician Thorbecke, *Stb.* 1872, 117. As far as legislation for specific cases in the sense of (infrastructural) projects is concerned, more examples can be given; see Chapter IV.2.2.2. At the decentralized level of the municipalities, "general" rules concerning licensing of gambling which allowed gambling in only one or two specific buildings have also been seen as case-specific legislation, *CBb* October 3, 1989, *AB* 1990/398, *CBb* March 6, 1990, *AB* 1990/399, and *CBb* January 26, 2000, *AB* 2000/372.

[701] The Netherlands Citizenship and Residence in the Netherlands Act (*Wet op het Nederlanderschap en het ingezetenschap*) of 1892 (*Stb.* 1892, 268) made it possible for the legislature to grant Dutch citizenship to specific individuals. This practice had been abandoned in 1984 (Stb. 1984, 628). Expropriation for public use (a so-called *nutswet*) could be found in the Expropriation Act (*Onteigeningswet*) of 1851 (*Stb.* 1851, 125). Nowadays, no such laws are required anymore (*Stb.* 2005, 282).

laws which, in departure from general rules, create their own regime for one specific project. The most common project laws pertain to infrastructural projects.[702]

Infrastructural project laws

The first distinct project law, dating from the beginning of the 1990s, concerns the dike improvement subsequent to the great floods that the Netherlands was faced with in 1993 and 1995. These exceptional circumstances forced the government to propose a bill, the Delta (Major Rivers) Act (*Deltawet Grote Rivieren*)[703] which made dike improvement in the region of the Rhine and Meuse rivers possible within a short period of time. Given this emergency situation, the Dutch Parliament did not hesitate to approve the bill, even though it declared the usual procedures and substantive (environmental) requirements for such operations inapplicable to that specific project.

After that, several new projects were governed by special legislation, for example the famous project in the Western Scheldt River (*Vergunningwet Westerschelde*), the construction of the fifth runway at Schiphol Airport (*Wet procedures vijfde baan Schiphol*, popularly known as the Schiphol Act[704]) and the widening of several specific roads in order to diminish the build-up of traffic, the Road Widening Emergency Act (*Spoedwet wegverbreding*[705]). The above-mentioned pieces of legislation, like the Delta (Major Rivers) Act, were intended to accelerate the execution of significant infrastructural projects. To achieve that goal, the guarantees of legal protection, such as those laid down in the Dutch General Administrative Law Act (*Algemene wet bestuursrecht*),[706] were diminished: either the general time limits for individuals to challenge the administrative decisions on the projects were shortened or certain stages of the standard appeal procedures were eliminated. Moreover, two of the Acts, namely, the Delta (Major Rivers) Act and the Licensing of Dredging Act, departed not only from the procedural requirement concerning individual legal protection, but also from the substantive requirements as laid down in (environmental) legislation.[707] These project laws could be called special accelerating legislation.

702 See also a distinction between legal norms and plans, as made in the final report, *Orde in regelgeving* (1985), pp. 28ff. The report states that a fundamental difference between a legal norm and a plan is the generality of the norm and the fact that it treats equal cases equally, whereas a plan is strongly purpose oriented. Cf. the German discussion on special measure laws in Chapter III.2.2.2.

703 *Stb.* 1995, 210.

704 *Stb.* 1999, 17.

705 *Stb.* 2003, 256.

706 *Stb.* 1993, 693 as subsequently amended.

707 The government appears to find this legislative technique of declaring substantive legislative requirements inapplicable to some infrastructural projects quite attractive. See the statute on national roads, *Stb.* 2009, 189. The government based its proposal for the statute on the report by the Elverding Commission, which argued that the modification of existing laws is necessary to accelerate the execution of infrastructural projects, Advies Commissie Versnelling Besluitvorming Infrastructurele Projecten, *Sneller en beter*, 2008 at <http://snellerenbeter.nl/upload/files/Advies%20Commissie%20Versnelling%20Besluitvorming%20Intrastructurele%20Projecten.pdf> (last accessed on June 12, 2011). See also (a temporary) *Crisis- en herstelwet*, Stb. 2010, 136, and a new accelerating bill, *Wijziging*

Other project laws

Besides *infrastructural* project laws, a few other legislative proposals have been classified as project laws in the literature.[708] Well-known examples concern two bills which eventually became the so-called Rotterdam Act (*Wet bijzondere maatregelen grootstedelijke problematiek*)[709] and the EK Act (*Wijziging van de Gemeentewet ter verbetering van de mogelijkheden tot bestrijding van grootschalige verstoringen van de openbare orde*).[710] The Rotterdam Act created an exceptional legal regime for a number of bigger cities in the Netherlands in order to implement several plans dealing with their economic and social improvement. Even though the Act was inspired by the specific situation of Rotterdam, the government decided to extend its application to other big cities as well, because it was afraid the bill would otherwise be viewed as ad hoc legislation, which arouses negative feelings in the Netherlands. The same held for the EK Act. The parliamentary records reveal that the Act was proposed in view of the coming European Football Championship and the expected disturbances. The EK Act was meant to prevent hooliganism by creating far-reaching powers of preventive detention for the city mayor during this specific event. To avoid criticism of the specific character of the law, however, the legislature chose to draft it in general terms and make it (potentially) applicable in future situations as well.

Criticism

Generally, the Dutch government is a proponent of the use of specific project laws that create a distinct legal regime for individual infrastructural projects, but only when exceptional circumstances justify their use.[711] The government took this position on the basis of the academic report,[712] which mapped out the potential disadvantages of the use of specific infrastructural project laws. In particular, the problem of diminished legal protection was emphasized. In the author's view, individuals must have a possibility to challenge decisions included in a specific project law in judicial proceedings, even though they were made by Parliament. The current Art. 120 of the Dutch Constitution, which prevents the courts from reviewing the constitutionality of parliamentary legislation, irrespective of its contents (general or specific rules), could, however, be problematic in this respect.[713] In its legislative advice on several (infrastructural) project laws, the Dutch

van de Tracéwet met het oog op de versnelling en verbetering van besluitvorming over infrastructurele projecten, *Kamerstukken II* 2009/2010, 32 337.

708 See Verschuuren (1998), pp. 361–367 and Eijlander (2004), pp. 484–491.

709 *Stb.* 2005, 726.

710 *Stb.* 2000, 175.

711 Stroink also argued for a sparse use of project laws. In his view, only extremely exceptional situations could justify them, F.A.M. Stroink, "Complexe besluitvorming: een opgave voor burger, bestuur en rechter," in: H. Heida, F.A.M. Stroink & P.C.E. van Wijmen, *Complexe besluitvorming*, Alphen aan den Rijn: Samson 1998, p. 77.

712 The study on the benefits and disadvantages of special infrastructural project laws was carried out by Lubach and Heuvelhof. It clearly illustrated the relative benefits of such individual laws and particularly their disadvantages, *Kamerstukken II* 1996/1997, 24 690, no. 5.

713 *Kamerstukken II* 1996/1997, 24 690, no. 5, p. 2.

Council of State also stressed the problem of diminished legal protection. Moreover, the Council of State questioned the practice of project laws in general in light of the principle of legal certainty. Individuals' legitimate expectations regarding the applicability of existing general rules are frustrated when a divergent legal regime is created for one specific project. The Council of State argued for a more profound explanation of the exceptional circumstances that justify project laws:[714]

> Again, the acceleration is achieved mainly by shortening the time limits for legal protection. Against this background, the fundamental question arises on the basis of what arguments sidelining the normally applicable legislation can be justified. Replacing existing legislation by project legislation from time to time on the basis of incidental arguments may involve elements of arbitrariness. In the current opinion, the Dutch legislative tradition primarily involves the making of generally binding rules. In the proposed project law [...], this was not the case, or only to a very limited extent. This belies the expectations of the people subject to this jurisdiction that are based on the application of general rules.

It can be noted, however, that the Council of State's opinion on project laws such as the Schiphol Act is somewhat less negative than it was in the case of the Licensing of Dredging Act. In that case, the problem was even greater: the legislature fully eliminated any possibility of administrative judicial review by de facto executing the general laws in one specific case itself, by granting one general license for dredging works in the Western Scheldt (River). In that case, the argument addressing legal certainty and the requirement of the generality of legislation was explicitly put forward.

Another point of criticism regarding the use of project laws focuses on the diminished value of legislation as such when the legislature, instead of creating stable rules based on moral principles, applies legislative acts purely as instruments, as measures to achieve the goals of governmental policy. This argument was expressly put forward in the case of the Licensing of Dredging Act.[715]

The next point of criticism, which could only be found in the case of the Rotterdam Act and the EK Act, concerns their general character. Given the fact that the EK Act created far-reaching powers of preventive detention and the Rotterdam Act set substantive legislation aside, some Parliament members argued fervently to limit the application of the Acts to the event of the European Football Championship 2000 and the city of Rotterdam, respectively.[716] In summary, a special instead of a general character of the proposed legislation could be viewed in these two cases as a protection of individuals and

714 The Council of State's advice on the Schiphol Bill, *Kamerstukken II* 1998/1999, 25 863, B, p. 1.

715 Tak (1997), p. 9.

716 See, in particular, the arguments of Witteveen, who does not automatically reject laws that apply to specific cases, situations, or events. He rather argues for a careful preparation, balanced legislative policy, and a solid parliamentary debate on special laws and criticizes ad hoc legislation enacted on the sly, *Handelingen I* 2000, no. 25, pp. 1182–1183. See also the opinion of Meindertsma arguing for the specific focus of the Rotterdam Act on the city of Rotterdam and its adequate evaluation: *Handelingen I* 2005, no. 13, p. 640.

as a guarantee that these far-reaching powers would be exercised only once, namely during the European Football Championship 2000.[717]

Finally, special project laws have also been discussed from the point of view of public administration. The criticism concerning the use of project laws was especially directed at the risks of short-term policy thinking and unequal treatment, the unintended use of project laws and the complexity of legal rules as a result of a large number of exceptions.[718]

Remarkably perhaps, unlike the other infrastructural project laws, the Delta (Major Rivers) Act was applauded rather than criticized, despite the fact that it deviated from the general rules and reduced the guarantee of individual legal protection. This can probably be explained by the emergency situation caused by the flooding, which required immediate government action.

2.3. General interest requirement

The case of the BNN Act in particular touches upon the question whether the legislature is allowed to enact laws for the purpose of benefiting a special group of individuals. The opponents of the Act argued that, by amending the Media Act and relaxing the strict rules on the number of members required to join the public broadcasting system, the legislature did not serve the general interest.[719] Instead, the legislative intention was directed at the special interest of one young broadcasting association, namely, BNN, according to the critics. As far as the other cases of ad hoc legislation are concerned, it is also fair to question whether the legislature enacted them with a view to the general, public interest. Is the Dutch Parliament therefore obliged and limited to designing rules for the general, public interest?

It has been argued that the notion of the general, public interest indirectly ensues from Art. 50 of the Dutch Constitution, which prescribes that Parliament shall represent the entire people of the Netherlands.[720] Even though this is anything but a clear and enforceable requirement, it can be stated that it is a generally accepted idea in the Netherlands that the legislature's task is to serve and protect the general interest. The actual meaning of the ideal of the general interest, however, is somewhat unclear. Various legal scholars even seriously questioned the value of this concept for jurisprudence, seeing it as a vague and elusive ideal dependent on a changing political and social context. Polak described the concept as:[721]

> so 'general', so vague and indeterminate, so broad and elastic, so dependent on time and place, on constantly changing circumstances and on ever-changing political and social opinions

717 See also Eijlander (2004), p. 487.

718 J. Koppenjan & H. Hufen, "Nieuwe mechanismen voor probleemoplossing," *Bestuurswetenschappen* 1997-6, pp. 360–373.

719 The terms "general interest" and "public interest" are used here interchangeably.

720 Kortmann (1983), pp. 185–186 and W. Witteveen, "De nuttige fictie van het algemene belang," *Feit & Fictie* 1997, Vol. III, pp. 15ff.

721 C.H.F. Polak, *Het begrip 'algemeen belang' in de verschillende onderdelen van het administratieve recht*, VAR pre-advies, Haarlem: Tjeenk Willink 1950, p. 40.

> that it seems useless as a legal concept, and every attempt at its further definition appears to be doomed to failure.

Van Wijmen, among other authors, attempted to specify the meaning of "general interest" by defining it as "an interest of such a supra-individual character and so worthy of protection that the legislature takes on its protection and promotion. Put differently, the (theoretical) interest becomes a public interest because the legislative authorities consider it worth protecting."[722] Van Wijmen therefore argues that an interest is general if it concerns more than only one or a several persons and goes beyond the sphere of particular interests of individual persons. He positions the generality of the interest as the opposite of special, particular, and individual interests.[723] Having said that, he is aware of the fact that the general interest is not always what the majority of the people wish or think it is. In this respect, he mentions the interests of ethnic or linguistic minorities.

Despite the indefinite character of the concept of general interest, several authors indicated how the legislature should go about fulfilling its basic task. According to Tak, the legislature must first identify what interests belong in the category of the general, public interest. The subsequent task of the legislature is then to weigh diverse public interests that can even conflict with each other.[724] Moreover, other authors state that the legislature, being objective and impartial, must take account of private interests of individual groups as well and balance them against public interests.[725] Hirsch Ballin and Eijlander add that the balancing by the legislature of interests involved must be done from the general perspective: "The law provides the norm in abstracto and does not make any statements on what is the law in a concrete case. It is a democratically legitimized weighing of interests from general perspectives."[726]

In summary, it has been argued in the Dutch literature that a fundamental role of the legislature is to serve the general interest.[727] The authors seem to conceive this role at the same time as a limitation of legislative power. Polak, despite his doubts about the precise

722 P.C.E. van Wijmen, *Recht, belang en rechtsbescherming*, The Hague: Vuga 1981, p. 281. See also the distinction between individual, collective. and general, public interests proposed by Van Gestel and De Poorter with regard to environmental law and spatial planning in: R.A.J. van Gestel & J.C.A. de Poorter, "'Je maintiendrai'. Naar een prominentere rol van burgers en milieuorganisaties bij de handhaving van het omgevingsrecht?," *Tijdschrift voor omgevingsrecht* 2002, pp. 84–95.

723 Van Wijmen (1981), p. 293.

724 A.Q.C. Tak, *Overheidsbestuur en* privaatrecht, Alphen aan den Rijn: Samson 1978, p. 89. See also Schlössels' differentiation between the procedural and substantive criteria, which can both be used to determine the meaning of the concept of the general, public interest, R. Schlössels, *Het specialiteitsbeginsel. Over de structuur van bestuursbevoegdheden, wetmatigheid van bestuur en beleidsvrijheid*, The Hague: Sdu Uitgevers 1998, p. 78.

725 See, for example, Schlössels (1998), p. 78.

726 Ph. Eijlander, *De verbindende wetgever. Over de verhouding tussen staat, markt en* samenleving, The Hague: Boom Juridische uitgevers 2000, p. 20. See also E.M.H. Hirsch Ballin, *Het grondrecht op vrijheid en de wet*, Alphen aan den Rijn: Tjeenk Willink 1989, p. 58.

727 De Moor-van Vugt goes even further by classifying the State obligation to balance the interests involved as a principle of the rule of law, A. de Moor-van Vugt, *Maten en gewichten. Het evenredigheidsbeginsel in Europees perspectief*, Zwolle: Tjeenk Willink 1995, pp. 10–11.

meaning of the general, public interest notion, did not hesitate to explicitly proclaim its normative character:[728]

> Each observation on the "public interest" as a legal concept may be based on the proposition that the only task of the government in a country like ours is protecting the public interest and that all government powers, excepting those of the judiciary, may be used for the performance of that task only.

And:

> For instance, no legal provision will be proposed, challenged, or defended unless motives based on the public interest are put forward. As a result, it will be hard to find an Explanatory Memorandum that does not contain the expression 'public interest'. Whether invoking this concept is justified, whether the public interest truly makes the proposed regulations desirable, is to be decided by the legislative branch and no one else.

Polak treats the general interest notion as an absolute requirement and justification for every legislative act.[729] In his view, however, it is the legislature itself that determines the content of the general interest in different situations.[730]

Besides Art. 50, the Dutch Constitution, as fundamentally amended in 1983, contains a few provisions that directly refer to the concept of public interest. These are Arts. 14 (1), 132 (4), 133 (3) and 134 (3). Art. 14 (1) deals with expropriation and allows it only when a solid basis of the general interest is present. Arts. 132–134 concern government control with regard to bodies belonging to the decentralized government, including a possibility of annulment of their decisions by the central government if they conflict with the general interest. Some other provisions do not use the words "public interest," but simply list several concrete interests that determine the content of that concept, which is usual for constitutional provisions addressing the limitations of civil rights. The Constitution allows civil rights limitations as long as they are required by interests including health protection, the prevention of disorder (Arts. 6, 8, 9), and the protection of public decency (Art. 7).

It appears to be a generally accepted principle that the Dutch legislature serves the general interest instead of the special interests of various groups and individuals. It is therefore rather improbable that the State Secretary would ever admit that the BNN Act was enacted to benefit one broadcasting association. The State Secretary insisted that the lowering of the membership requirements in the Media Act was justified by the general interest of legitimacy, diversity, openness, and modernization of the media scenery.

728 Polak (1950), p. 43.

729 For the normative meaning of the general interest notion from a philosophical perspective, see also H.H.H. van Erp, *Political Reason and Interest. A Philosophical Legitimation of the Political Order in a Pluralistic Society*, Aldershot: Ashgate 2000, pp. 36ff.

730 See also, e.g., Van Wijmen's view, who also left a great margin of appreciation for the legislature to decide what the general interest is, Van Wijmen (1981), p. 281.

2.4. Conclusion

The most important criticism expressed in cases of ad hoc legislation as described in the first chapter concerned its specific focus and consequently the violation of the principle of the generality of laws. The legal discussion on this point in Dutch constitutional law centers on the distinction between legislation in the formal and in the material sense, the more frequent use of special laws for (infrastructural) projects, and the concept of general interest. It should be noted that despite the fact that case-oriented motives of the legislature were invoked and criticized during the general discussion of the three high-profile cases referred to in Chapter IV.1, the legal doctrines do not consider the motives of the legislature decisive for the question of generality. What counts, especially in light of the concept of legislation in the material sense, is its specific or general *scope* of application. If a law is not addressed to specific individuals and can repeatedly be applied to future cases as well, it will be seen as a general law within the concept of laws in the material sense, notwithstanding the case-specific motives of the legislature.

It can be concluded that, despite the fact that the Dutch Constitution does not require all laws to be general, laws that apply to specific individuals are rare. The more frequent use of project laws shows, however, that the legislature views laws that apply to specific projects as less problematic. These project laws are still criticized, but, in contrast to laws that affect specific individuals, the criticism is more often directed at the effect such laws have on the principle of legal certainty and diminished legal protection rather than its project-specific orientation.

A similar conclusion can be drawn with respect to the limitation of the legislature's power to enact rules which serve the general interest. Since this idea is generally accepted in Dutch constitutional law and politics the legislature would have a particularly hard job to explain legislation which serves merely special interests, instead of the general, public interest.

Chapter 3

EQUAL TREATMENT

Introduction

When legislatures draft exceptional rules for specific cases, concerns regarding the principle of equal treatment can arise. As regards the Dutch situation, such concerns were expressed in the Licensing of Dredging Act case. In this chapter, the principle of equal treatment as interpreted and applied in Dutch constitutional law will be discussed from the viewpoint of the possible limitation on the legislature to adopt ad hoc laws. Attention will therefore be paid to relevant (international) provisions in Dutch law and the test used to determine whether the right of equal treatment has been violated.

3.1. The principle of equal treatment in Dutch law

The general (written) constitutional principle of equal treatment was introduced in Art. 1 of the Dutch Constitution during its general review in 1983.[731] The Supreme Court, however, explicitly stated that, even before that time, the principle of equal treatment containing the requirement for the State to treat equal cases equally was a living principle of unwritten constitutional law.[732] Art. 1 reads: "All persons in the Netherlands shall be treated equally in equal circumstances. Discrimination on the grounds of religion, belief, political opinion, race or sex or on any other grounds whatsoever shall not be permitted." The General Equal Treatment Act (*Algemene wet gelijke behandeling*)[733] elaborates on Art. 1 and is generally intended to prevent discrimination among citizens (as opposed to between the government and citizens), for example, alleged discrimination of employees in labor relations between employees and the employer.[734] Besides the national legal provisions on equal treatment, the principle of equal treatment binds the Dutch legislature

731 Art. 3 of the Constitution also deals with equality, but it is restricted to the specific area of appointment to public service.

732 HR December 1, 1993, *BNB* 1994/64.

733 *Stb.* 1993, 690 as later amended.

734 See, however, Articles 5, 7, and 7a of the General Equal Treatment Act. Cf. P.J.J. Zoontjens, "Eenzijdig overheidshandelen," in: P.J.J. Zoontjens & M.L.M. Hertogh (eds.), *Gelijke behandeling: principes en praktijken*, Nijmegen: Wolf Legal Publishers 2006, p. 174.

at European and international levels. As far as European law is concerned,[735] a general anti-discrimination provision can be found in Art. 10 of the new Treaty on the Functioning of the European Union (former TEC) and in Articles 20 and 21 of the Charter of fundamental rights of the European Union.[736] There are specific provisions, however, on, for example the prohibition of discrimination on the basis of nationality (Art. 18, former Art. 12 TEC) and respect for the principle of equal pay for male and female workers for equal work or work of equal value (Art. 157, former Art. 141 TEC). At the international level, the most important equal treatment provisions having direct effect in the Dutch legal order through Art. 94 of the Dutch Constitution, are Art. 26 of the International Covenant on Civil and Political Rights (ICCPR),[737] Art. 14 of the European Convention on Human Rights (ECHR),[738] and Protocol no. 12 to the ECHR which contains a general right of non-discrimination.[739] Art. 14 of the ECHR is not independent since it can only be invoked in combination with any other substantive right as incorporated in the ECHR's provisions.[740] The right of equal treatment thus concerns only equal treatment of rights incorporated in the Convention, which limits its independent meaning for the practice of equal treatment. The same holds for Art. 1 of the Dutch Constitution: its significance appears to be limited as well. The reason is that Art. 120 of the Constitution prevents Dutch courts from testing the compatibility of Acts of Parliament against any provision of the Constitution.[741] Protocol no. 12 took effect on April 1, 2005, and its real impact cannot yet be assessed.

The prohibition of constitutional review with regard to the national Constitution and the accessory nature of Art. 14 ECHR contributed to the growing importance of Art. 26 of the ICCPR in Dutch law. This Article is independent of other rights and can be directly invoked and applied in the course of judicial proceedings.[742] The added value of this provision is that it applies to legislative acts as well. Art. 26 provides:

> All persons are equal before the law and are entitled without any discrimination to the equal protection of the law. In this respect, the law shall prohibit any discrimination and guarantee to all persons equal and effective protection against discrimination on any ground such as

735 The equality principle in European Law as applied by the European Court of Justice will not be discussed in this chapter. For a detailed description of the European equality principle, see J.H. Gerards, *Rechterlijke toetsing aan het gelijkheidsbeginsel*, The Hague: SDU 2002, pp. 221ff.

736 The Consolidated version of the Treaty on the functioning of the European Union, C 115/49, at <http://eur-lex.europa.eu/LexUriServ/LexUriServ.do?uri=OJ:C:2010:083:0001:0012:EN:PDF> The Charter can be found at < http://eur-lex.europa.eu/LexUriServ/LexUriServ.do?uri=OJ:C:2010:083:0389:0403:EN:PDF> (both last accessed on June 12, 2011).

737 To be found at <www2.ohchr.org/english/law/ccpr.htm> (last accessed on June 12, 2011).

738 To be found at <http://conventions.coe.int/treaty/en/Treaties/Html/005.htm> (last accessed on June 12, 2011).

739 To be found at <www.humanrights.coe.int/Prot12/Protocol%2012%20and%20Exp%20Rep.htm> (last accessed on June 12, 2011).

740 J. Vande Lanotte & Y. Haeck (eds.), *Handboek EVRM*, Vol. II, Part. 2, Antwerpen: Intersentia 2004, p. 135.

741 In the same sense, Gerards (2002), p. 514.

742 HR September 27, 1989, *NJ* 1990/449.

race, colour, sex, language, religion, political or other opinion, national or social origin, property, birth or other status.

Art. 26 ICCPR has great practical relevance in Dutch positive law. Its violation can be invoked not only in situations where equal cases are not treated equally as prescribed by the legislation involved (execution of laws), but also in situations where legislation as such treats similar cases differently. Accordingly, the equal protection clause in Art. 26 ICCPR pertains to both equality before the law and equality through the law. This far-reaching effect of Art. 26 has also been accepted by the Dutch government, and the courts apply it directly to legislative acts.[743] The focus in the following sections will therefore be on Art. 26 ICCPR.

3.2. Unequal treatment vs. discrimination

Art. 26 ICCPR is formulated in absolute terms. Its text, if taken literally, prohibits any kind of unequal treatment. This, however, was not the original purpose of Art. 26. Only unequal treatment that can be classified as discrimination is prohibited. It should be noted here that some Dutch courts explain the prohibition of unequal treatment in relation to personal characteristics only, while others read any form of unequal treatment of individuals into Art. 26 ICCPR.[744] The Human Rights Committee,[745] which is competent to assess individual claims within the scope of the ICCPR, has clarified the meaning of Art. 26 on repeated occasions. Most recently, in a Dutch case, it stressed again that "the Covenant does not require parties to proceedings to be placed in an identical formal position, but rather that such distinctions as may be made are based upon reasonable and objective grounds."[746] So not every form of unequal treatment of equal cases is prohibited. Consequently, Art. 26 is not violated if the legislature can prove the reasonableness and objectivity of the distinctions it made.[747] Dutch courts apply this criterion automatically when they are confronted with individual claims alleging violation of Art. 26.[748] In answering the justification question, they sometimes apply the proportionality test, which includes the question whether the legislation challenged on the basis of unequal treatment serves a legitimate purpose and whether there is a

743 A. J.Th. Woltjer, *Wetgever, rechter en het primaat van de gelijkheid*, The Hague: Boom Juridische uitgevers 2002, p. 155.

744 Gerards (2002), p. 536 with references.

745 Information about the Committee can be found at <www2.ohchr.org/english/bodies/hrc/> (last accessed on June 12, 2011).

746 *Gangadin v. The Netherlands*, April 4, 2007, Communication no. 1451/2006. This explanation was first formulated in the case of *Broeks v. The Netherlands*, April 9, 1987, Communication no. 172/1984, and *Danning v. The Netherlands*, April 9, 1987, Communication no. 180/1984.

747 A similar justification criterion in connection to the proportionality test is applied by the European Court of Human Rights. For the origins, see *Case "Relating to certain aspects of the laws on the use of languages in education in Belgium" v. Belgium* (Appl. nos. 1474/62, 1677/62, 1691/62, 1769/63, 1994/63, 2126/64) (1968) Series A, no. 6.

748 See, for example, HR May 7, 1993, *NJ* 1995/259, ABRvS March 3, 1994, *AB* 1995/85, and CRvB September 3, 2002, *AB* 2003/69.

proportional relation between that purpose and the means chosen.[749] Sometimes the suitability of the means chosen to achieve a specific purpose is examined.[750] The legitimacy of the State purpose as such, however, does not immediately justify every distinction made by the legislature to achieve that purpose, according to the Dutch Supreme Court.[751] In its decision concerning legislative changes in an employed person's tax reduction case (*Arbeidskostenforfaitarrest*),[752] for example, the Supreme Court decided that the governmental purpose of stimulating unemployed persons to find work by providing tax benefits for those who are employed can generally be viewed as a legitimate State purpose. But the inequality within the group of employed persons created by the legislation was disproportionate to that purpose and lacked any reasonable and objective grounds for justification.[753] The courts usually construe the purpose of a legislative act from its legislative history as provided by the official explanatory memorandum attached to every bill when they assess the legitimacy of the purpose.[754] They do not look for the real motives of the legislature, which can be problematic in light of ad hoc legislation, where it is most unlikely that the legislature will explicitly admit that the legislation's only purpose was to touch one specific case.

Principally, the courts leave the legislature a margin of appreciation to decide which cases are equal and whether a distinction can be based on objective and reasonable grounds. This holds even truer in tax cases.[755] This margin is smaller if a fundamental right is at issue, whereas the legislature has more freedom in making differentiations based on technical grounds, according to Happé.[756] His study shows that fundamental rights, such as access to a court,[757] carry a lot of weight, even if the financial burdens imposed on individuals treated unequally are negligible.[758] Mere financial interest of the State cannot as such justify unequal treatment.[759]

749 The proportionality test plays an important role especially in tax law. See, for example, HR November 12, 1997, *BNB* 1998/22.

750 HR May 7, 1993, *AB* 1993/440, *NJ* 1995/259 and CRvB June 26, 2001, *AB* 2001/277. The proportionality test was developed by the European Court of Justice in cases where the equal protection right stemming from the European Union law was invoked.

751 An interesting aspect is the doctrine of *détournement de pouvoir* (misuse of power), which prohibits administrative bodies from using their powers for other purposes. If these bodies misuse their power, the purpose of their action will be found unlawful, Gerards (2002), p. 597. It should be stressed, however, that the doctrine of *détournement de pouvoir* is one of the instruments limiting executive rather than legislative power. Cf. Tak (1997), pp. 7–9, who nevertheless addressed this doctrine in relation to parliamentary legislation in the particular case of the Licensing of Dredging Act.

752 HR May 12, 1999, *VN* 1999/24.3. See also HR July 15, 1998, *BNB* 1998/293 (*Autokostenforfaitarrest*).

753 HR May 12, 1999, *VN* 1999/24.3, Sec. 3.10 and 3.11. See also HR May 7, 1993, *AB* 1993/440, *NJ* 1995/259, Sec. 3.3.

754 Gerards (2002), p. 655.

755 Art. 26 ICCPR extends to tax legislation as well, HR November 17, 1993, *BNB* 1994/36 (*Studeerkamerarrest*).

756 R.H. Happé, *Schuivende machten. Over trias politica en het gelijkheidsbeginsel in het belastingrecht*, Deventer: Kluwer 1999, p. 32.

757 HR September 29, 1989, *BNB* 1990/61 (*Tandartsvrouwarrest*).

758 HR September 30, 1992, *BNB* 1993/30 (*Griffierechtarrest*). See also J.W. Zwemmer, "Schurende machten," *ArsAequi* 1999–9, pp. 668ff, who argues that the Supreme Court should always look at the heaviness of burdens imposed by the legislation.

759 HR June 15, 1995, *BNB* 1995/252.

3.3. Equal treatment and beneficial legislation

Art. 26 ICCPR applies not only to legislation that imposes burdens on individuals and is therefore disadvantageous. It can also restrict the legislature when it yields to the pressure of lobby groups, arbitrarily benefiting one or a few companies of the same kind. In a case concerning tax privileges for panel truck owners, as an exception, the Supreme Court considered the real intention of the new piece of legislation as enacted in 1993.

To prevent private owners of panel trucks from abusing the advantageous tax regime which was originally meant for owners using panel trucks for their occupation, the legislature changed the statutory concept of a "panel truck" in 1993 and imposed several new requirements for its equipment in order to be classified as a "panel truck" deserving such an advantageous tax regime. Pursuant to the new Act, cars that used to be considered panel trucks are now in the category of passenger cars, which made their owners pay more tax. The original bill was, however, slightly amended and the ultimate Act exempted big companies using such cars from the new rules. For them, the legislature created advantageous transitional rules so they could still enjoy the lower tax rate. During the parliamentary debates over the bill, the State Secretary for Finance already expressed his doubts and pointed out the violation of the equality principle if only big companies using trucks, such as the Dutch Automobile Association (*ANWB*), would enjoy tax privileges.[760] Nevertheless, the amendment was adopted.[761]

After the Act was challenged on the ground that it created unjustified inequality among panel truck owners, the Supreme Court elaborated on the exceptional treatment the Act gives to companies owning a large number of such cars. The Court supported the State Secretary's position and decided that there were no reasonable and objective grounds to justify the favorable treatment of big companies using panel trucks:[762]

> These financial consequences apply similarly to all cases. The legislator cannot reasonably consider the owners of a sizeable fleet of cars unequal to the other owners. The circumstance that the financial consequences weigh heavier in absolute terms if the owners have more motor vehicles that are affected by the regulations cannot [...] be deemed an objective and reasonable justification to treat owners of a sizeable fleet of cars more favorably than the other owners of similar motor vehicles.

Consequently, "[t]he exception in the transitional arrangement [...] made for entrepreneurs and institutions with a sizeable fleet of cars therefore cannot be perceived as anything but arbitrarily favoring that group of taxpayers." The Supreme Court thus clearly related the absence of any reasonable and objective ground for justification to the arbitrariness of the statute.[763]

760 *Kamerstukken II* 1993/1994, 23 215, no. 5, p. 3.

761 *Stb.* 1993, 673.

762 HR August 17, 1998, *BNB* 1999/122c, Sec. 3.6. See also Happé (1999), p. 29.

763 An interesting interpretation of the equality principle as a prohibition of arbitrariness by the government was given by Van Ommeren. In this context, he distinguishes a principle of consistency, including the equality principle with legal certainty as part of it, as a constitutional principle. In his view, the government has to act in a consistent manner. However, it seems that in his interpretation, this principle

3.4. Conclusion

The equality principle in Dutch constitutional law, which applies to unequal treatment resulting from parliamentary legislation, does not absolutely prohibit the legislature from treating similar cases differently.[764] Such differentiation violates the equality principle only when it is not based on objective and reasonable grounds. This criterion appears to be relevant and workable for ad hoc legislation that affects specific individuals because of who they are and not because they represent certain objective qualities. Moreover, the proportionality test, including the question whether the means applied (contested legislation) are suitable to achieve the legislation's purpose, could be useful in order to reveal the "true" legislative motives. The means are most likely unsuitable if the real purpose of the ad hoc legislation is different from the officially acceptable purpose as stated in the explanatory memorandum to a bill.

applies to the execution of legal rules by administrative bodies rather than their creation by the parliamentary legislature. He finds support for the consistency principle in, for example the case law of the Supreme Court, which found the unequal treatment of two applicants by an executive body of a municipality inconsistent and thus incompatible with the principle of equality, HR March 22, 1991, *AB* 1991/446 in: Van Ommeren (1996), pp. 318ff. Pauwels also admits that consistent operation by the government (he includes the legislature as well) is in aid of the principle of equal treatment, with which, as a general truth, I readily agree. He suggests that the legislature should act consistently by choosing the appropriate system of transitional rules. He underpins this conclusion by pointing out two decisions of the Central Appeals Tribunal for the public service and for social security matters (*Centrale Raad van Beroep*) which, in his eyes, apply the principle of consistency. In my opinion, these decisions are of much lesser importance and clarity on this point than Pauwels suggests. See CRvB June 18, 2004, *AB* 2004/296 and CRvB October 23, 1980, *AB* 1981/137, M.R.T. Pauwels, *Terugwerkende kracht van belastingwetgeving: gewikt en gewogen*, Tilburg 2009, p. 275.

764 It should be noted, however, that Dutch courts have not yet been confronted with a claim that an Act of Parliament violated the equality principle because it was not general. By contrast, such a claim was raised before the ECtHR in the *Asmundsson* case. Nevertheless, any meaningful elaboration of the Court on this point is lacking, *Asmundsson v. Iceland*, (Appl. no. 60669/00) ECHR 2004-IX.

Chapter 4

LEGAL CERTAINTY

Introduction

Ad hoc changes in general legislation can lead to problems with the principle of legal certainty. This type of criticism was put forth in all three cases described in Chapter IV.1. In the Western Scheldt (River) case, the ad hoc exceptions to the general rules were seen as problematic, whereas the case of Volkert van der G. generated criticism of the rash pace of the law's change. In the view of one legal commentator, this new development was tantamount to the conclusion that "what was the law yesterday may no longer be law today." The issue of the durability and stability of legislation plays a crucial role here. The same holds for impulsive changes in the general Media Act (the BNN case) just two years after the structural reform of the entire public broadcasting association system. The problem of legal certainty can also play a part in cases of *retroactive* expediency-driven legislation enacted or amended for the purpose of one case. In this chapter, the principle of legal certainty will be described as interpreted and explained in the Netherlands. First, its meaning as a limitation for the legislature on impulsively and *prospectively* changing the rules for one case will be discussed (Chapter IV.4.1). Next, I will devote attention to legal certainty as a limitation on retroactive legislation (Chapter IV.4.2). Conclusions about the meaning of the principle of legal certainty for ad hoc legislation will round off this chapter.

4.1. Prospective amendments

The constitutional principle of legal certainty is widely accepted in the Netherlands as one of the core elements of the rule of law. Its meaning, however, depends on its various facets. Oldenziel divided them into nine categories: 1) durability and stability, 2) application of legislation, 3) clarity of individuals' legal position, 4) administrative decision-making within a reasonable time, 5) foreseeability of administrative acts, 6) law's accessibility, 7) legal protection, 8) protection of legitimate expectations, and 9) prohibition of retroactive legislation.[765] As regards non-retroactive, unexpected and

[765] H.A. Oldenziel, *Wetgeving en rechtszekerheid*, Deventer: Kluwer 1998, pp. 14ff.

impulsive changes in legislation,[766] the aspects of a) durability and stability, and b) protection of legitimate expectations are particularly important.

The importance of stability of legal rules has regularly been stressed in the literature. Frequent legislative changes and ad hoc deviations from the general system of legal rules in a specific area can undermine the authority of these rules.[767] In this respect, Eijlander and Voermans mention the stability and durability of legislation as a necessary element for the good quality and the intrinsic value of legislation.[768]

When amending or repealing existing legislation, the legislature is also obliged to take the legitimate expectations of individuals into account. This view has been voiced by both the Dutch Supreme Court and the Dutch Council of State in its advisory function with respect to legislation. The Council of State addressed this aspect most explicitly in its advice concerning the lowering of the retirement age for university professors to 65 (the retirement age had first been fixed at 70). Despite the government's explanation that this legislative operation was necessary to improve both the dynamics in the academic working environment and the difficult financial conditions at universities and colleges, the Council of State pointed out a possible violation of the principle of legal certainty. The Council doubted whether the bill took the legitimate expectations of professors into account who, at the time of their appointment, not only believed but also had a right to believe that they could remain professors until the age of 70. In addition, notwithstanding this criticism, the Council of State underlined that this principle did not mean that existing legislation could never be amended or repealed. In doing so, the legislature must only respect individuals' legitimate expectations. Only compelling reasons of public interests can frustrate such expectations.[769]

A few years later, on the occasion of parliamentary debates on the controversial case of Mrs. Rost van Tonningen, the principle of legal certainty was used to prevent Parliament from acting arbitrarily by yielding to impulsive demands of public opinion. Since 1950, in accordance with the general legislation at that time, Mrs. Rost van Tonningen had received a state pension because her late husband had been a member of the Dutch Parliament before the Second World War. Mr. Rost van Tonningen had been known for his radical anti-Semitic ideas and collaboration with the Nazi regime. She advocated the same views on Jews, which she publicly acknowledged. Her outspoken view and distribution of discriminating writings eventually resulted in a conviction in 1985, which received a great deal of publicity. Moreover, the fact that she had received a state pension for as long as 36 years became public and was fiercely debated. Under public pressure, the Dutch Parliament debated the single case of Mrs. Rost van Tonningen and considered the possibilities of depriving the widow of her right to a pension. The principle of legal certainty eventually proved to be an obstacle. Several members of Parliament criticized

766 In this context, a distinction between legislation which is enacted for the purpose of one specific case and is also applicable to that single case only and legislation which is aimed at one specific case but does not exclude similar future cases from its application is irrelevant.

767 G. Knigge, *Verandering van wetgeving*, Arnhem: Gouda Quint 1984, p. 139.

768 Ph. Eijlander & W. Voermans, *Wetgevingsleer*, The Hague: Boom Juridische uitgevers 2000, pp. 55–56.

769 *Kamerstukken II* 1981/1982, 17 544, A-C, p. 5. For a recent legislative advice by the Council of State, where the Council deemed the principle of legal certainty to be a fundamental obstacle for the legislative plans, see, for example *Kamerstukken II* 2006/2007, 30 962, no. 4, pp. 25–26.

any possible interference by the legislature as arbitrary. The fact that Mrs. Rost van Tonningen had received the pension since 1950, and could therefore reasonably expect that she would continue to receive it, stood in the way of any legislation to discontinue pension payments to her. Moreover, the original purpose of the legislation on which her pension was based was precisely to provide the widows of Dutch Parliament members with state pensions, regardless of their husbands' ideology:[770]

> Justice with respect to Mrs. Rost van Tonningen must be achieved here in a criminal court, not by taking away long-standing pension rights through ad hoc legislation because that would violate one of the essential principles of our legal system: legal certainty. Legal security is not an impassive, legal concept, but is part of the legacy of the rule of law [...]. Partly or completely taking away a pension right that has existed and had been protected for so long is the first step toward ad hoc legislation, that is to say, legislation inspired by opportunistic considerations that seem important today. Furthermore, it is about legislation that is to the detriment of the addressee, what is more to the detriment of one identifiable individual or possibly two individuals. Must we turn the rule of law upside down just for one or two people?

And:[771]

> Whereas other pension laws, those for civil servants, Cabinet Ministers, State Secretaries, i.e., the special pensions, contain provisions on the extinction or non-existence of pension rights due to behavior that is reprehensible from the point of view of the Dutch State, such provisions cannot be found in the pension legislation that applies to members of Parliament. There is a reason for this: the independence of parliamentarians must be guaranteed.

The principle of legal certainty also plays an important role for the judiciary. Although no Dutch court has constitutional authority to review parliamentary legislation for compatibility with the Dutch Constitution, the Dutch Supreme Court once delivered a famous judgment strongly criticizing a new piece of legislation in light of the principle of legal certainty. The Harmonization Act (*Harmonisatiewet*[772]) shortened the period in which students who had started a second study were entitled to a financial grant from the Dutch State. The Supreme Court could not resist concluding that the Act violated the principle of legal certainty by thwarting the legitimate expectations of those students of receiving the grants at the time they decided to take a second subject.[773] The principle of legal certainty could be applied effectively to restrict the legislature if it changes the law unexpectedly and with immediate effect. The non-binding character of the recommendations of the Council of State and the prohibition of constitutional review of

770 *Handelingen II* 1986, no. 29, p. 1630.

771 *Handelingen II* 1986, no. 29, p.1629.

772 Act of July 7, 1988, *Stb.* 1988, 334.

773 HR April 14, 1989, *AB* 1989/207. For an assessment of prospective city ordinances in light of the legal certainty principle, including the requirement to respect individuals' legitimate expectations, see, for example, *HR* May 12, 1999, no. 33.320.

legislation, however, mean that they are not a solid, enforceable guarantee against arbitrary legislation.

4.2. Retroactive legislation

The presumption against the retroactivity of laws is one of the basic principles of Dutch constitutional law. The basic rule is that new legislation applies to situations and legal relationships that exist at the time that new provisions are enacted. This is so-called "immediate effect" (*onmiddellijke werking*).[774] Concerning retroactive legislation, Art. 4 of the General Provisions (Kingdom Legislation) Act,[775] for example, codifies the principle of legal certainty and prohibits retroactive legislation. On first thought, it seems as if retroactive legislation is absolutely banned. The Dutch Supreme Court, however, interpreted this provision as an instruction to executive bodies and courts not to apply legislation retroactively if the legislature has not explicitly expressed such an intention.[776] This would mean that, theoretically, the legislature is allowed to draft and adopt laws that have retroactive effect.

But there are some exceptional situations where retroactive laws are absolutely prohibited. Article 16 of the Dutch Constitution – with reference to Article 1 of the Dutch Criminal Code (*Wetboek van Strafrecht*) – prohibits the legislature from giving retroactive effect to criminal law provisions. This prohibition is also regulated in Article 7 of the European Convention on Human Rights and Article 15 of the International Covenant on Civil and Political Rights, which have both been ratified by the Netherlands.

The problem of the retroactivity of statutory provisions that place burdens on legal and natural persons can frequently be observed in the field of tax law.[777] This eventually led to some general policy guidelines for the legislature prescribing how to deal with the necessity and permissibility of the retroactivity of legal provisions.[778] These guidelines were structured on the basis of the advice on legislative drafts given by the Council of State and relevant case law of the Dutch Supreme Court in particular.[779] Despite the fact that the guidelines directly pertain to tax law, the Directives on Legislation declare them applicable to other fields of law as well.[780] According to these guidelines, changes in law that are to take effect before they are enacted must satisfy two requirements in order to be permissible: 1) there should be sufficient justification for introducing these retroactive

[774] Directive 166 of the Directives on Legislation.

[775] General Provisions (Kingdom Legislation) Act (*Wet Algemene Bepalingen*) of May 15, 1829, *Stb.* 1829, 28, as amended by *Stb.* 2008, 70.

[776] HR October 26, 1951, *NJ* 1954/756.

[777] Some publications in this field are: E. Thomas, *Terugwerkende kracht (on) toelaatbaar?*, *Weekblad Fiscaal Recht* 2005-6614, pp. 326–333, and M. Bravenboer & A.O. Lubbers, *Tijd voor uitbreiding van de Notitie terugwerkende kracht en eerbiedigende werking*, *Weekblad Fiscaal Recht* 2005-6631, pp. 964–971.

[778] *Kamerstukken II* 1996/1997, 25 212, no. 1. See also an additional letter from the State Secretary for Finance, 1996/1997, *Kamerstukken II* 1996/1997, 25 212, no. 2.

[779] See, for example the judgments of the Supreme Court (HR) of October 24, 1984, *BNB* 1985/59, and of March 7, 1979, *BNB* 1979/125 in which retroactive changes in law were deemed to be foreseeable to the appellant and therefore permissible.

[780] See the explanation to Directive 167.

changes;[781] and 2) the new law should have been foreseeable for the legal and natural persons affected by it.[782]

The legislative recommendations of the Council of State contain indications of possible grounds for justification of an immediate response by the legislature to enact laws with retroactive effect. The most important justifications are: 1) prevention of the abuse of existing law by affected persons; 2) omissions in existing law that have unintended effects such as loss of the right to file financial claims;[783] or 3) extreme consequences for the State budget and difficulties in the execution of existing law. In the last case, when mere State financial interest is involved, the State indeed has to come up with extremely exceptional arguments to justify cuts in existing financial claims of individuals against the State. The Council was therefore extremely critical of a bill which was aimed to reduce tax privileges of individuals who had already made investments and expected that they would receive a tax cut on that ground. In that case, the legislation involved could only be justified by the emergency situation.[784] As far as the second element – foreseeable changes in law – is concerned, a new law may have retroactive effect only from the time that the affected persons could foresee that the law would change. Changes in law are in any event foreseeable when they have been announced by the legislature or the government.[785]

4.2.1. *Retroactive legislation and the ECHR*

In giving advice on new legislation, the Council of State requires a bill's sponsors to give exceptional reasons that could justify the retroactive effect of new provisions. The European Court of Human Rights basically requires the same in its judgments based on the European Convention on Human Rights, which the national courts normally follow. In this context, the Court will also ask whether there is a "reasonable relationship of proportionality between the means employed and the aim sought to be reali[z]ed by any

781 Directive 167 requires "exceptional circumstances" as a possible justification of retroactivity.

782 For case law references, see H.D. van Wijk, W. Konijnenbelt & R. van Male, *Hoofdstukken van bestuursrecht*, The Hague: Elsevier juridisch 2005, pp. 313–316.

783 Curative retroactive (ad hoc) legislation that corrects errors in earlier legislation will therefore be upheld. In Belgium, there is a comparable phenomenon called "validating legislation" to remedy faults in administrative acts only. See P. Popelier, *Toepassing van de wet in de tijd*, Antwerpen: Kluwer 1999, pp. 135ff, and P. Popelier, "Legislatieve 'validatie': een kwestie van wetgevingstechniek," in: M. Adams & L.J. Wintgens (eds.), *Wetgeving in theorie en praktijk*, Antwerpen: Maklu 1994, pp. 77ff. In the Netherlands, examples of laws that retroactively validate administrative decisions are also known. One example is the Legal Effect (Green Space Structure Plan) Act (*Wet rechtskracht Structuurschema groene ruimte*) *Stb.* 2004, 99, which retroactively gave legal effect to a document comprising the government's policy on nature and spatial planning (Green Space Structure plan), after the Council of State had decided that it was no longer effective after 2000, because the government had failed to prolong its validity. Another example is a legislative amendment to the Land Use Act (*Landinrichtingswet*), *Stb.* 2004, 223 which validated all administrative decisions of a special commission implementing this law, including those which had been invalidated in court due to the lack of legal authority to issue these decisions.

784 *Kamerstukken II* 1990/1991, 21 842, B. See also a decision of the Supreme Court in that case, HR June 11, 1997, *BNB* 1997/396.

785 *Kamerstukken II* 1994/1995, 24 172, A.

measure depriving a person of his possession." One of the crucial judgments in which the Court investigated the facts to answer this question was given in a Belgian case, *Pressos Compania Naveira SA and Others v. Belgium*,[786] in which the legislature had attempted to retroactively neutralize a specific judicial decision, thereby depriving individuals of financial claims against the State arising from its unlawful acts. The Belgian government invoked the great financial effects of the judgment on the State finances as well as the intention to harmonize its own legislation on this point with that of the neighboring states as a justification of retroactivity. The Court investigated the facts of the case and concluded that the reasons mentioned above would justify *prospective* legislation. These reasons were thus insufficient to justify the law's retroactivity. Moreover, depriving the claimants of their right of financial claims against the State without offering any compensation was simply disproportional.[787] This shows that the Court requires exceptional circumstances to justify retroactive laws. An important justification can, in any event, be found in the correction of legislative errors. Curing technical errors, which does justice to the original and evident intention of the legislature, justifies the retroactivity, in the ECtHR's view (see Chapter IV.5.2.2).[788]

4.3. Conclusion

The principle of legal certainty in Dutch law can restrain the legislature if it unexpectedly changes rules for present, future, and past situations. As far as prospective and immediate changes are concerned, the element of stability of legal rules (a principle of good quality of legislation) and the protection of legitimate expectations play an important part. As far as retroactive legislation is concerned that deliberately attaches legal consequences to closed cases or to events decided before the law's enactment, the principle of legal certainty requiring a strong and sustainable justification for the retroactivity can be invoked as a constitutional limitation on the legislature. The requirements for the permissibility of retroactive legislation as construed by the courts (including the ECtHR) and the Dutch Council of State in its advisory function show that there must be a very special reason to justify retroactivity, especially if the new rules create obligations for or place burdens on the affected persons.

It should be noted that all examples of ad hoc legislation as described in Chapter IV.1 are in the category of laws having immediate effect. They represent unexpected or sometimes impulsive changes of legislation and are intended to be directly applied to specific, predetermined cases. Although they affect past events, in the Netherlands they are generally seen as non-retroactive laws. On the one hand, the principle of legal certainty in the sense of the law's stability is the most useful in this context. On the other hand, it appears that this interpretation has mainly academic value. In the courts, the

786 *Pressos Compania Naviera S.A. and Others v. Belgium*, (Appl. no. 38/1994/485/567) (1995) Series A no. 332.

787 *Pressos Compania Naviera S.A. and Others v. Belgium*, par. 43.

788 *National & Provincial Building Society, Leeds Permanent Building Society and Yorkshire Building Society v. the United Kingdom*, (Appl. nos. 117/1996/736/933–935) ECHR 1997-VII. The same element as a possible justification of retroactivity can be found in the advices of the Dutch Council of State.

principle of legal certainty in the sense of protection of legitimate expectations seems rather to be an enforceable norm.

In the Netherlands, hardly any examples can be given of truly retroactive laws which were enacted for one specific, predetermined case. To my knowledge, the Dutch legislature has hitherto never interfered with specific cases in a formally retroactive manner. The examples given concern rather obviously general laws. The expectation is, however, that in future cases of legislation deliberately enacted for one specific case, the legislature will try to avoid criticism and controversy by justifying the retroactivity as necessary to cure the technical legislative errors, as in the German case of the Lex Schörner and the English case of the Building Societies (for a detailed description, see Chapter IV.5.2.2).

Chapter 5

AD HOC LEGISLATION, THE DUTCH CONSTITUTIONAL PRINCIPLE OF THE SEPARATION OF POWERS, AND THE RIGHT TO A FAIR TRIAL

Introduction

Ad hoc legislation in the Netherlands, and particularly the Licensing of Dredging Act, received criticism from the separation of powers point of view. Both the relationship between the legislature and the judiciary, and the relationship between the legislature and the executive were at stake. In this chapter, I will therefore devote attention to the principle of the separation of powers in the Netherlands, to the extent relevant to ad hoc legislation. Furthermore, in the absence of Dutch doctrine, I will discuss the case law of the European Court of Human Rights[789] on expediency-driven laws interfering in judicial proceedings for the purpose of influencing their outcome. I will show that the ECtHR reviews such interference in light of the right to a fair trial in Art. 6 ECHR. Because Art. 6 ECHR includes 'the right to a court' as well, it can also be invoked when the legislature undermines access to a court by granting a specific environmental license by an ad hoc legislative act, an activity that is normally among the powers of the executive. This was clearly the case in the Western Scheldt (River) affair.

5.1. Ad hoc laws and the separation of powers between the legislature and the executive

It can generally be said that the Dutch principle of the separation of powers is based on Montesquieu's and Locke's ideals. Although the Dutch Constitution does not expressly articulate the separation of powers, it provides for a division of functions: Chapter 5 of the Constitution deals with the legislative function and the administration, while Chapter 6 regulates the administration of justice.

Dutch constitutional law operates within a system of checks and balances rather than a strict separation of State powers.[790] This is particularly true for the relationship between

[789] By ratifying the European Convention on Human Rights, the Netherlands committed itself to respecting fundamental rights included in the Convention, including their interpretation by the ECtHR.

[790] Kortmann observes that strict separation of powers, and lack of mutual control and cooperation leads to absolute power; the prevention of absolutism was exactly the purpose of the separation of powers

the executive branch and the legislative branch, especially with regard to lawmaking.[791] This can be illustrated by the fact that, in the Dutch Constitution, an important role is given to the executive in the process of lawmaking. Art. 81 of the Constitution provides that legislation must be enacted jointly by Parliament and the government. In practice, it is the government which introduces the bills, whereas the members of Parliament hardly use their right of legislative initiative. The strong influence of the government on the legislative process has even resulted in claims that the Dutch Parliament does not operate independently, but merely provides the instruments to realize the government's policy.[792]

Despite this close relationship between the legislative and the administrative powers in the lawmaking process, the National Commission for Water Legislation drew a sharp line between the legislature and the executive in the case of the dredging operations in the Western Scheldt (River). The position of the Commission therefore suggests that its point of reference was a strict separation rather than a balance between the State powers. This is not an established interpretation; thus it does not make other, opposite views less important. Van Buuren, for example, did not find any violation of a firm rule of constitutional law in the case of the Licensing of Dredging Act.[793]

5.2. Legislative intervention in pending court proceedings: The ECHR[794]

Dutch doctrine and case law lack any clear standpoint on the permissibility of legislative interventions in pending court proceedings for the specific purpose of influencing outcomes in these cases.[795] Such interfering ad hoc legislation has, however, already been observed in other countries and reviewed by the ECtHR in light of the ECHR. The

idea; Kortmann (2008), p. 49. Bovend' Eert, on the other hand, argued that the system of "checks and balances" can, in certain circumstances, upset the balance between the State powers, P.P.T. Bovend' Eert, "Het rechtsbeginsel van de machtenscheiding," in: R.J.N. Schlössels et al. (eds.), *In beginsel. Over aard, inhoud en samenhang van rechtsbeginselen in het bestuursrecht*, Deventer: Kluwer 2004, pp. 243–265. See also W.J. Witteveen, *Evenwicht van machten*, Zwolle: Tjeenk Willink 1991.

791 This interpretation was put forward during the preparatory works for the 1983 revision of the Constitution, *Kamerstukken II* 1980/1981, 16 035, no. 8, p. 4.

792 Scheltema (1984), p. 11.

793 Van Buuren (1997), pp. 122ff.

794 See also my publication: A. Jasiak, "Changing the rules mid-game. Legislative interference in specific pending cases: separation of powers and fair trial. A comparison between the European Court of Human Rights and the U.S. Supreme Court's views," *Vienna Online Journal on Int. Const. L.* Vol. 4, 1/2010, pp. 20–36.

795 Dutch law and the discussion of the separation of powers with a focus on the independence of the courts concentrate mostly on institutional independence. See, for example, J.B.J.M. ten Berge, "Organisatie en individuele rechter in balans," in: J.B.J.M. ten Berge & A.M. Hol (eds.), *De onafhankelijke rechter*, The Hague: Boom Juridische uitgevers 2007, pp. 11–29. See also R. de Lange & P.A.M. Mevis, "Constitutional Guarantees for the Independence of the Judiciary," in: J.H.M. van Erp & L.P.W. van Vliet (eds.), *Netherlands Reports to the Seventeenth International Congress of Comparative* Law, Antwerp, Oxford: Intersentia 2006, p. 327 for an excellent description of the constitutional rules governing the (institutional) independence of the judiciary in the Netherlands.

Court's judgment on this point has become part of the Convention and thus constitutes a standard for Dutch courts.[796]

Although, at first sight, this type of legislation causes problems with the separation of the legislative and judicial branches, the ECtHR reviews the impugned ad hoc legislation within the framework of Art. 6 ECHR which includes a right to a fair trial: "In the determination of his civil rights and obligations [...], everyone is entitled to a fair and public hearing within a reasonable time by an independent and impartial tribunal established by law." This is in line with the individual fundamental rights approach of the Convention. The principle of the separation of powers does not appear as such in the fundamental rights catalog.

Three key judgments show the development of the Court's view: *Stran Greek Refineries and Stratis Andreadis v. Greece (Stran Greek Refineries)*,[797] the *National & Provincial Building Society, the Leeds Permanent Building Society and the Yorkshire Building Society v. the United Kingdom (Building Societies)*,[798] and *Zielinski and Pradal and Gonzales and Others v. France (Zielinski)*.[799]

5.2.1. *The* Stran Greek Refineries *case*

In 1972, Mr. Andreadis signed a contract with the Greek State, which was governed by a military junta at that time. The contract allowed Mr. Andreadis and his company, Stran Greek Refineries, to build an oil refinery near Athens. However, a few years later, the military regime was succeeded by a democratic government that endeavored to cancel the agreement and made it impossible to continue the work.

Stran sued the State for failing to comply with the contract and claimed considerable financial compensation. Time after time, Stran Greek Refineries was successful in its proceedings. At some point, the State requested postponement of the scheduled court hearing. In the meantime, it prepared a new piece of legislation that was enacted a week before the hearing[800] and dealt with "the compulsory participation of the State in private undertakings [...] and the redemption of shares."[801] The Act declared claims against the State time-barred. It thereby de facto determined the outcome of the pending case of *Stran Greek Refineries* and saw to it that the State party would win the case.

Mr. Andreadis complained in Strasbourg that the new law deprived him of the possibility of a fair trial by making it impossible for the courts to decide the case in his favor. The Court looked pragmatically at the challenged law and explicitly concluded that the new piece of legislation, and in particular Article 12, "was in reality aimed at the

796 Kuijer sought the answers for the Dutch situation in the ECtHR's doctrine as well, M. Kuijer, *The Blindfold of Lady Justice – Judicial Independence and Impartiality in Light of the Requirements of Article 6 ECHR*, Nijmegen: Wolf Legal Publishers 2004.

797 *Stran Greek Refineries and Stratis Andreadis v. Greece*, (Appl. no. 13427/87) (1994) Series A no. 301.

798 *National & Provincial Building Society, Leeds Permanent Building Society and Yorkshire Building Society v. the United Kingdom*, (Appl. nos. 117/1996/736/933–935) ECHR 1997-VII.

799 *Zielinski and Pradal and Gonzales and Others v. France* (Appl. nos. 24846/94 and 34165/96 to 34173/96) ECHR 1999-VII.

800 Law No. 1701/1987.

801 *Stran Greek Refineries*, para. 20.

applicant company – although the latter was not mentioned by name."[802] The Court reached this conclusion on the basis of the *timing* and the *manner* of the adoption of the new provision.[803] The ECtHR emphatically rejected such legislative action, stating that:[804]

> [t]he principle of the rule of law and the notion of fair trial enshrined in Article 6 preclude *any interference* by the legislature with the administration of justice designed to influence the judicial determination of the dispute. The wording of paragraphs 1 and 2 of Article 12 taken together excluded any meaningful examination of the case.

This exceptionally strict application of the principle of a fair trial was elaborated in the *Building Societies* decision.

5.2.2. The **Building Societies** *case*

In the second case, which was decided three years after the case of Stran Greek Refineries, the ECtHR made an exception to its first rigorous statement on the permissibility of legislative interventions in pending cases. The *Building Societies* case centered on the payment of tax on interest income to the Inland Revenue by building societies in order to discharge their investors' liability for income tax at the basic rate.[805] Such payment was based on voluntary agreements between the building societies and the Inland Revenue, and had to be made for a period equal to the period of one fiscal year (the payment times differed for each building society). In order to harmonize the taxation of building societies and banks, the government had proposed new legislation which established a new taxation schedule and was not meant to increase taxes. In practice, however, the new law created a taxation gap period for the building societies.[806] The State attempted to correct this technical error to prevent the building societies from receiving an unintended financial windfall. Several pieces of legislation were enacted, also while the judicial proceedings of the Provincial Building Societies and other building societies were pending. The last piece of legislation corrected the previous legislative errors in such a way that it was pointless for the building societies to continue the proceedings for the restitution of the tax that they had paid in the gap period.

The applicant societies complained before the Commission[807] and the ECtHR. Unlike the Commission, which followed the Court's judgment in *Stran Greek Refineries*,[808] the Court ruled that, while it was true that the new pieces of legislation affected the outcome of the judicial proceedings of the three building societies, it was still essential to answer the question whether such legislative action had a legitimate aim and was not

802 *Stran Greek Refineries*, para. 47.
803 See also, *Papageorgiou v. Greece*, (Appl. no. 97/1996/716/913) ECHR 1997-VI.
804 *Stran Greek Refineries*, para. 49, emphasis added.
805 *Building Societies*, para. 8.
806 *Building Societies*, paras. 16–17.
807 The European Commission of Human Rights (E.Com.H.R.).
808 *Building Societies*, para. 106. The Commission also invoked a decision of the ECtHR in *Pressos Compania Naviera S.A. and Others v. Belgium*. (Appl. no. 38/1994/485/567) (1995) Series A no. 332.

disproportional.[809] The Court issued its decision in light of the circumstances in which the legislative measures had been taken. The most important findings were: 1) the legislative measures were taken in order to remedy the technical errors in the previous legislation; 2) the building societies could have known that the legislature would try to remedy such errors to comply with the legislative aim of the original legislation; 3) two new pieces of legislation were introduced without regard to the specific pending legal proceedings: it applied to all building societies that were in the same situation.[810] The Court reiterated that justification of legislative intervention in pending judicial proceedings to make them impossible to win should be treated with "the greatest possible degree of circumspection."[811] However, the Court rules that *not every* intervention is prohibited. In this specific case, the *compelling general interest* of creating legal certainty and repairing pure technical faults in order to comply with the general intention of Parliament justified legislative intervention in pending cases. In sum, legislation that repairs technical errors in previous regulations to remove unintentional effects does not violate the right to a fair trial set out in Article 6.

5.2.3. *The* Zielinski *case*

As has been shown above, the ECtHR in the *Building Societies* case prudently introduced a criterion of *a compelling general interest* as a possible justification for legislative interference with pending cases. In *Zielinski*, the Court clearly refined the formula again. This last refinement eventually became the standard point of reference for future cases.

The *Zielinski* case[812] dealt with the retroactive interference of the French legislature in pending cases of the same sort, where the interpretation of a collective agreement in the sphere of social security was at issue. This agreement had been applied differently by French courts in various districts (in some districts more favorably for the applicants than in others). In light of ongoing litigation concerning the interpretation of the agreement which had led to conflicting outcomes, and during the considerations on an unrelated public health bill, the French Parliament adopted an amendment that was meant to set a uniform standard for its interpretation.[813] This standard was much less favorable than the standards that had been applied by some courts. The new law was retroactive and was meant to be applied by the courts in proceedings that were still pending. The law did not order the reopening of final judicial decisions.

Zielinski and Gonzales, whose cases were still pending, argued before the ECtHR that they had been deprived of a fair trial since the State was aiming to direct the outcome of pending cases; the outcome would be favorable for the State party as a result.[814] The government, on the other hand, argued that the law had been enacted in the general

809 With reference to *Stubbings and Others v. United Kingdom* (Appl. nos. 36–37/1995/542–543/628–629) ECHR 1996-IV, para. 72.

810 *Building Societies*, paras. 109–111.

811 *Ibid.*, para. 112 quoting *Stran Greek Refineries.*

812 See also Van Gestel (2004), pp. 1667ff., in which attention is paid to this case as well.

813 Sec. 85 of Law No 94–43.

814 *Zielinski*, para. 51.

interest and had a legitimate aim.[815] The compelling general interest lay in the fact that the original standard as set out in the agreement would impose a heavy financial burden on the State and a reduction of the social security bodies' budget.

In its analysis, the ECtHR first argued that, in principle, the legislature may enact retrospective civil legislation in order to "regulate rights arising under existing laws."[816] Nevertheless,[817]

> the principle of the rule of law and the notion of fair trial enshrined in Article 6 preclude any interference by the legislature – *other than on compelling grounds of the general interest* – with the administration of justice designed to influence the judicial determination of a dispute.

The Court was clear: sometimes *a compelling general interest* will allow or even force the legislature to intervene in pending cases.

Applying this general formula to the *Zielinski* case, the Court found that the primary intention of the French legislature had been to influence the outcome of several pending cases and that the amendment had not been enacted after careful preparation. The Court considered the circumstances in which the law had been enacted and examined the effect, timing, and manner of its adoption. It observed that the new law had been enacted shortly after the Besançon Court of Appeal had rendered a decision favorable to Zielinski and Gonzales.[818] Moreover, the law had been enacted in a suspicious manner: the amendment had been drafted on impulse during the considerations on a public health bill.[819] It was therefore clear to the Court that the law was more an ad hoc piece of legislation that had been passed by Parliament as a reaction to the judicial decision to influence the outcome of the final judgment in that and in other similar cases, rather than a general policy law that was required by the general interest. The financial risk that the government used as a possible justification for the legislative intervention in pending cases was not a compelling general interest, in the Court's view. Furthermore, the Court endorsed the arguments of claimants that a judiciary system where different courts may reach divergent opinions in similar cases does not in itself justify legislative interference in pending cases.

5.2.4. The ECtHR's guidelines

All three decisions have been crucial in developing the current case law on legislative intervention in pending judicial proceedings aimed at influencing the outcome. The case law centers on the right to a fair trial, including the rights of equality of arms and of access to courts. These decisions as well as subsequent decisions seem to point to two tests used by the ECtHR, which will be referred to here as the procedural test and the substantive test.

[815] *Ibid.*, para. 53.
[816] *Ibid.*, para. 57.
[817] *Ibid.*, emphasis added.
[818] *Ibid.*, para. 58.
[819] *Ibid.*

Procedural test: Legislative intention

Applying the first test, the ECtHR considers whether or not the legislature *intended* to interfere in pending cases ("manifest object"). The Court answers this query pragmatically: it is not the legislature's explanation that matters, but the *circumstances* in which the contested legislation was introduced and passed. The Court establishes legislative intent on the basis of *the timing* and *the manner* of the new law's enactment. The *effect* of the impugned legislation is often put forward as a third element.[820] Using these elements, the Court deliberates on whether the new piece of legislation was adopted ad hoc while judicial proceedings against the State were pending.

If this question is answered in the affirmative, the ECtHR will often examine the *timing* of the legislation's enactment in relation to the stage of the proceedings: an enforceable judgment can more readily justify the conclusion that the interfering legislation violates Art. 6 than proceedings that have just been instituted.[821] If the legislation was enacted ad hoc shortly before scheduled hearings in the proceedings to which the State is a party, this can also indicate that the legislature's object was to influence the outcome of proceedings. Additionally, if a new piece of legislation was hurriedly enacted before the highest national court could deliver a judgment which, on the basis of the settled case law of that court, would be unfavorable for the State as a litigating party, the ECtHR will interpret this as a deliberate attempt to influence the outcome of proceedings.

Addressing *the manner* in which the interfering piece of legislation was adopted, the ECtHR examines whether it was prepared in a scrupulous legislative process or whether it was impulsively attached to a bill in which it in fact did not belong. In *Zielinski*, for example, the Court explicitly discussed the questionable adoption procedure of the controversial provision: "[S]ection 85 was part of an Act on 'public health and social welfare.' [...] It was only in the course of the parliamentary debates and shortly after the delivery of [...] the Besançon Court of Appeal's judgment that an amendment on the *IDP* was tabled."[822]

In terms of its *effect*, the interfering legislation must be able to have a *decisive* influence on the proceedings. In other words, it must be clear that continuing the judicial proceedings would have been pointless as the applicants would have had no chance of winning the case against the State,[823] even if the dismissal of the case "was based even subsidiarily on the impugned statute."[824]

820 See, e.g., *Stran Greek Refineries*, *Zielinski*, *Scordino v. Italy* (Appl. no. 36813/97) ECHR 29 March 2006, *Smokovitis and Others v. Greece* (Appl. no. 46356/99) ECHR 11 April 2002, and *Gorraiz Lizarraga and Others v. Spain* (Appl. no. 62543/00) ECHR 2004-III. For the observations on the legislative motive requirement in light of the *Zielinski* case, see M. de Werd, "Beïnvloeding van rechtspraak door de wetgever," *NJCM-Bulletin* 2001–3, pp. 348–353.

821 *Building Societies*, para. 111.

822 *Zielinski*, para. 57.

823 See, e.g., *Building Societies*, para. 107; *Anagnostopoulos and Others v. Greece* (Appl. no. 39374/98) ECHR 2000-XII, para. 20; *Smokovitis and Others v. Greece*, para. 26; and *Papageorgiou v. Greece*, para. 38.

824 *Anagnostopoulos and Others v. Greece*, para. 21.

Substantive test: Compelling general interest

Using the second test, the Court examines whether the legislature had good reasons to interfere in pending proceedings. The ECtHR will justify such interference on one condition only: the interfering legislation must have been inspired by compelling grounds of the general interest.

What does the ECtHR consider to be compelling grounds of the general interest? The Court's approach differs from the procedural test method. No subquestions or criteria are formulated in order to answer the question of possible justification. It seems as if the ECtHR uses two casuistic and extendable lists, one stating what the compelling general interest is and the other specifying what in any event it is not. Regarding the first, positive list, what interests can justify legislative interference in pending cases?

Firstly, the Court accepted legislative intervention when the new legislation was intended to remedy technical errors in the original legislation or to fill a legal gap, thereby effectuating the real intention of the legislature. In such cases, the legislature interfered to prevent some individuals or companies from unintentionally benefiting from technical errors.[825] Secondly, the contested law was not seen as contrary to Art. 6 even though it interfered with pending proceedings, because the law settled conflicts that had arisen after the reunification of West and East Germany in a general way. The law was not adopted ad hoc to influence pending proceedings; it was enacted to ensure enduring peace and legal certainty in Germany, according to the ECtHR in the *Forrer-Niedenthal* case.[826]

As for the second list, no compelling general interest justifying legislative interference in pending cases could be found in the legislature's intention to implement a political program centered on budgetary considerations, as the Court argued in the *Scordino* case.[827] Furthermore, neither a financial risk for the government nor conflicting decisions of different national courts could justify legislative intervention in judicial proceedings.[828]

The relationship between the two tests

The relationship between the procedural test and the substantive test is not entirely clear. Sometimes the ECtHR discussed legislative intervention in light of both the procedural test and the substantive test to eventually conclude that compelling grounds of general interest were absent.[829] The violation of the right to a fair trial is then based on the first test. In other cases, the ECtHR did not even ask whether the legislation was inspired by a compelling general interest. Then the procedural test appears to predominate.[830]

825 See the description of the *National Building Societies* case and *Ogis Institut Stanislas, Ogec St. Pie X et Blanche de Castille et Autres c. France* (Appl. nos. 42219/98 and 54563/00) ECHR 27 May 2004, para. 71.

826 *Forrer-Niedenthal c. Allemagne* (Appl. no. 47316/99) ECHR 20 February 2003, para. 64. See also the comment by P. Popelier, "Behoorlijke wetgeving in de rechtspraak van het Europees Hof voor de Rechten van de Mens," *Tijdschrift voor Wetgeving* 2004-6, p. 131.

827 *Scordino v. Italy*, para. 132.

828 *Zielinski*, para. 59.

829 *Zielinski* and *Scordino v. Italy*.

830 See, e.g., *Anagnostopoulos and Others v. Greece* and *Smokovitis v. Greece*.

Finally, when the ECtHR decided that the legislature had a compelling general interest in enacting the interfering legislation, it did not always pay attention to the first test.[831]

It is worthwhile noting that the ECtHR's review of legislative interference in pending cases appears to differ from its usual approach to the limitation of the right to a fair trial. Normally, the ECtHR seeks answers to the following two questions: 1) Does the limitation (by the State) have a legitimate aim? 2) Is there "a reasonable relationship of proportionality between the means employed and the aim sought to be achieved"?[832] The ECtHR referred to this test in *Building Societies*, but it appears to be the only case concerning legislative interference in pending cases where the Court explicitly invoked this proportionality test. It could be argued, however, that the ECtHR implicitly finds the law disproportional if 1) the only reason why the law is enacted is to influence the outcome of pending cases, and 2) the impugned law makes the continuation of the proceedings pointless.

The nature of the right breached

In *Gorraiz Lizarraga and Others*, the ECtHR emphasized the importance of the nature of the violated right for the assessment of legislative interference. The inhabitants of a small village in Spain had protested against a governmental dam-building project. After the national courts had upheld their claims and had ordered the work to be stopped, the legislature enacted a law sanctioning continued construction, although it was formulated in general terms. Consequently, the final judicial decision could not be enforced.

The Court distinguished the legislative intervention in this case from those in *Zielinski* and *Stran Greek Refineries*. In *Gorraiz Lizarraga and Others*, the challenged legislation concerned regional development plans, "a sphere in which an amendment or change to legislation following a judicial decision is generally accepted and practised." The Court found that the nature of the rights impaired in the sphere of environmental planning were different (i.e., less weighty) than those violated in, for instance, *Zielinski* or *Stran Greek Refineries* ("personal rights to receive payment"). The Court viewed the urban and regional policies as:[833]

> spheres (*par excellence*) in which the State intervenes, particularly through control of property in the general and public interest. In such circumstances, where the community's general interest is pre-eminent, the Court takes the view that the State's margin of appreciation is greater than when exclusively civil rights are at stake.

The Court's message is clear: environmental rights are of a different nature than traditional civil rights, and the legislature therefore has more freedom to change environmental policy even if it does so by interfering in the administration of justice.

831 See, e.g., *Forrer-Niedenthal c. Allemagne*.

832 P. van Dijk et.al., *Theory and Practice of the European Convention on Human Rights*, Antwerp: Intersentia 2006, p. 573.

833 *Gorraiz Lizarraga and Others v. Spain*, para. 70 with reference to *James and Others v. the United Kingdom* (Appl. no. 8793/79) (1986) Series A no. 98, para. 46; *Mellacher and Others v. Austria* (Appl. nos. 10522/83; 11011/84; 11070/84) (1989) Series A no. 169, para. 55; and *Chapman v. the United Kingdom* (Appl. no. 27238/95) ECHR 2001-I, para. 104.

The Court also emphasized the legislature's intent: it was not directed at influencing the outcome of a case to which the State was a party and the legislature therefore did not aim to circumvent the rule of law.[834]

Interference by a general or by a specific law

Does the ECtHR's doctrine on legislative interference in pending cases apply equally to specific legislation designed to influence one particular case and to general legislation affecting a large group of similar cases? In this respect, the cases of *Anagnostopoulos*[835] and *Scordino*[836] are illustrative examples. In these two cases, the ECtHR showed that the establishment of a violation of Article 6 does not require the legislative intention to have been aimed at influencing *one particular case*. The objective to influence the judicial process in a manner favorable for the State in a number of cases of *the same type* can be sufficient to declare the law incompatible with the rule of law and the fair trial principle in particular.[837] In the *Scordino* case, the Court formulated this idea as follows:[838]

> Although the Government submitted that the legislative provision was not aimed specifically at the present dispute, or any other dispute in particular, the Court considers that as it was immediately applicable, it had the effect of frustrating proceedings then in progress of the type brought by the applicants. The manifest object, and the effect, of the impugned provision was in any event to modify the applicable rules relating to compensation, including in the case of judicial proceedings then in progress to which the State was a party.

Nonetheless, the ECtHR sometimes stresses the general or specific nature of the legislation concerned. In *Stran Greek Refineries*, the contested piece of legislation was ruled to have been intended specifically to influence the outcome of that case. This ruling contributed significantly to the conclusion that, given the first procedural test, the right to a fair trial had been violated.

By contrast, the ECtHR has occasionally concluded that interfering legislation served the general interest precisely because of its *general* character. The ECtHR thus connects generality in terms of the law's addressees with generality in terms of the general interest when it applies the second substantive test.[839] Although it will often be true that general laws serve the general interest, situations in which specific laws, especially specific project laws, serve the general interest and those in which general laws do not, are conceivable.[840]

834 *Gorraiz Lizarraga and Others v. Spain*, para. 96.
835 *Anagnostopoulos and Others v. Greece.*
836 *Scordino v. Italy.*
837 *Scordino v. Italy*, para. 130. See also *Adamogiannis v. Greece* (Appl. no. 47734/9) ECHR 14 March 2002.
838 *Scordino v. Italy*, para 130.
839 *Forrer-Niedenthal c. Allemagne*, para. 64.
840 See, for example, the Delta (Major Rivers) Act, an example given in: A. Jasiak, "Gelegenheidswetgeving en beïnvloeding van rechterlijke procedures in het licht van het EVRM," in: J. Schooten & R. Gestel (eds.), *Europa en de toekomst van de nationale wetgever*, Nijmegen: Wolf Legal Publishers 2008, p. 108.

5.3. Overruling of judicial decisions by the legislature

In the Netherlands, it is not unusual for the legislature to respond to specific court judgments by either overruling them for future cases by a prospective piece of legislation or correcting technical errors in legislation as suggested by a judicial decision, including those from the past. The first situation is especially common in the field of taxation,[841] where the legislature tends to annul judicial decisions that have far-reaching effects on State finances in the future. The legislature obviously wishes to prevent individuals from enjoying considerable tax privileges as a result of judicial interpretation of legal provisions.[842] Such overruling legislation is seen as a type of democratic check on the judiciary.[843]

The second situation, which is rather more correctly referred to as a legislative response to specific court decisions than as overruling legislation, can be best illustrated by the reparation of the formal deficiencies in the Immigration Act. In December 1988, the Supreme Court decided in three identical cases that keeping persons seeking political asylum who were not admitted to the Netherlands in a locked building at Schiphol Airport must be classified as detention in the meaning of Art. 15 of the Dutch Constitution and Art. 5 (1) of the European Convention on Human Rights, which required a basis in an Act of Parliament. The Supreme Court was of the opinion that the Immigration Act contained no provision on which that type of detention could be based. To remedy this deficiency, the Dutch government prepared a bill within a few days that complemented the Immigration Act.[844] The bill proposed a new provision to provide the required basis.[845] It was sharply criticized in Parliament itself and by legal scholars. Remarkably, the criticism concentrated not on a violation of the separation of powers principle by overruling a specific judicial decision, but rather on the unusual and hurried way in which it had been prepared and adopted. Some members of Parliament sarcastically commented on the Act having been introduced with a speed greater than the speed of

841 See, however, among other overruling pieces of legislation, the amendment to the General Administrative Law Act (*Stb.* 2002, 55), which is a response to the decision of the Supreme Court, HR February 20, 1998, *BNB* 1998/207. In that decision, the Court gave a broad (in the eyes of the Parliament, too broad) interpretation of the tort liability of administrative bodies. The legislative amendment overruled this interpretation.

842 See also Visser's study on legislation overruling judicial decisions, N.B. Visser, "Het overrulen van jurisprudentie door de wetgever," *RegelMaat* 1987, pp. 22ff.

843 C.A. Groenendijk, "Parlementaire reacties op rechterlijke uitspraken: democratische controle op aanvullende regelgevers," in: G.C.J.J. van den Bergh e.a., *Met hoofd en hart*, Zwolle: Tjeenk Willink 1991, pp. 67ff.

844 The Bill was prospective and did not affect the specific cases decided by the Supreme Court. As a direct result of the Supreme Court's judgment, individuals seeking asylum were directly admitted to Dutch territory, *Kamerstukken I* 1988/1989, 20 972, no. 113b, p. 11. It eventually became a law and was published in *Stb.* 1989, 6.

845 There are many examples of laws that repair laws which in the court's view violated, for example, the international principle of equality. See, for example, HR July 15, 1998, *BNB* 1998/293 (*Autokostenforfait*), HR September 30, 1992, *BNB* 1993/30 (*Griffierecht*), and HR May 12, 1999, *BNB* 1999/271c (*Arbeidskostenforfait*).

light.[846] Notwithstanding the fast adoption, the Act could be considered a legitimate response of the legislature to the court decision which noted errors in the legislation. The legislature simply did what the Court had in fact advised: it repaired the faults for now and for the future.

The Licensing of Dredging Act and legislation preventing the enforcement of a final judicial decision

The neutralizing effect of the Licensing of Dredging Act on the decision of the highest administrative Court in the Netherlands, the Council of State, in the specific case of the dredging operations in the Western Scheldt River is quite remarkable. On the one hand, the Act had been enacted for the purpose of having immediate effect. Strictly speaking, it did not retrospectively overrule a court decision nor did it direct the reopening of a specific, finally decided case concerning the dredging operations in the Western Scheldt River. On the other hand, it clearly affected the outcome of this case by rendering the specific Council decision ineffective. It appears that legislation which, with immediate effect,[847] changes the outcome of a judicial decision where prospective relief (including periodical allowances) has been granted is generally less problematic than retroactive legislation which prevents the execution of a final court decision in the period before the law's enactment. Although it is hard to identify any established, typically Dutch doctrine on this point, this conclusion follows from the recommendations of the Council of State. The Council's advice on the Amendment to the Victims of Persecution (1940–1945) Benefits Act (*Wet uitkeringen vervolgingsslachtoffers 1940–1945*) is particularly significant in this respect. In 1981, the government proposed legislation which overruled an interpretation of the Victims of Persecution (1940–1945) Benefits Act by the Central Appeals Tribunal for the public service and for social security matters in its 1977 decisions in individual cases. These decisions were particularly favorable to specific individuals and entitled them to increased allowances. The government argued that such increases would have extreme financial consequences for the State. The government therefore proposed a bill which would make the enforcement of the court decisions impossible, not only from the year 1981 onwards, but also for the period beginning in 1977, the year in which the decisions had been issued. The Council of State sharply criticized the bill, stating that:[848]

> it is hardly possible to accept that their claims can be reduced retroactively by the legislature to a lower level than that to which they are entitled according to the interpretation of the Central Appeals Tribunal, and over time periods which are already past.

846 *Handelingen II* 1988/1989, no. 36, p. 2137. For a detailed discussion of the legislation and for criticism, see L.J.A. Damen, "Na 'confectierechtspraak' nu ook 'confectiewetgeving'?," *NJB* 1989-5, pp. 145–153.

847 New legislation, however, mostly contains rules for the transition from the old to the new legal regime. See A. Weggeman, "Het vormgeven van overgangsrecht," in: F.H. van der Burg & A. Weggeman, *Overgangsrecht*, The Hague 2001, pp. 41–88, and B.C. de Die, "Overgangsrecht – een herwaardering na vijftig jaar," *RMThemis* 1979, pp. 253ff.

848 *Kamerstukken II* 1980/1981, 16 833, B, pp. 3–4.

And:

> In sum, the Council is of the opinion that insufficient motivation is provided in the Explanatory Memorandum for the retroactive effect referred to in Article III, that this Article will lead to hardly acceptable legal consequences in a number of cases, and that the arrangement provided for in Article II detracts from the principle that, in a state under the rule of law, judicial decisions are respected. If the legislator thinks, for whatever reason – for example, for reasons of legal equality – that the effects of such decisions must be undone as much as possible, this may be done only in a responsible fashion for the future, so applying to time periods after the relevant legal provisions have taken effect.

During the parliamentary debates, the bill had even been compared to the English concept of "contempt of Court."[849] This type of retroactive legislation is highly unusual in the Netherlands. The Dutch legislature normally respects decisions that have become final, as evidenced, for example, by the case of the curative legislation in the field of social security, which was enacted as a response to the specific 1997 judgment of the Supreme Court.[850]

The ECtHR's case law

Dutch practice is in line with the ECtHR's case law, which takes the finality of final judicial decisions as a point of departure. In the ECtHR's view, judicial decisions which have become final may only be reopened if "circumstances of a substantial and compelling character,"[851] such as correction of "miscarriages of justice" or judicial errors require this. The Court bases this view on the principle of the rule of law, including the principle of legal certainty (not the separation of powers): "One of the fundamental aspects of the rule of law is the principle of legal certainty, which requires, among other things, that where the courts have finally determined an issue, their ruling should not be called into question."[852] It should be stressed, however, that the Court does not maintain that the law on which a final decision is based may never be changed and in that way affect the final decision: "It is conceivable that a judgment loses its legal force when the legislative framework changes."[853] The State, however, "cannot interfere with the process of adjudication in an arbitrary manner,"[854] which means that it is not allowed to change the underlying law merely to win a case it already lost in court.

Consequently, the relevant question in the Western Scheldt case is whether the legislature acted arbitrarily. Why did Parliament adopt such a far-reaching legislative

849 *Kamerstukken I* 1982/1983, 16 833, no. 11a, p. 2.

850 *Wet verduidelijking verzekerings- en premieplicht, Stb.* 1998, 267.

851 *Ryabykh v. Russia* (Appl. no. 52854/99) ECHR 2003-IX, para. 52.

852 *Ryabykh v. Russia*, paras. 51–52. See also *Pravednaya v. Russia* (Appl. no. 69529/01) ECHR 18 November 2004, paras. 31–32, *Brumarescu v. Romania* (Appl. no. 28342/95) ECHR 1999-VII, para. 62,.

853 See also the case of *Gorraiz Lizzaraga* discussed above, in which the ECtHR agreed that the final judicial decision blocking the construction of a national dam could not be enforced because of a subsequent law.

854 *Bulgakova v. Russia* (Appl. no. 69524/01) ECHR 18 January 2007, paras. 41–42.

measure? Was the only reason to reverse the Council of State's judgment so it could still win the case, or were there special reasons that could serve as a justification for the law's enactment? The argument that the Council of State's decision prevented fulfillment of the international obligations towards the Flemish region could indicate that the purpose of the bill was not merely to win the case already lost before the Council of State.

Assessment framework: Limiting constitutional principles

It can be said that in the Netherlands, overruling laws as referred to above are not usually analyzed within the context of a possible violation of the principle of the separation of powers.[855] It is rather the principle of legal certainty (also in Art. 6 ECHR), including individuals' legitimate expectations, which can serve as a review framework. Laws that overrule judicial decisions retroactively will be reviewed pursuant to the doctrine on the retroactivity of laws and the presumption against retroactivity (see particularly Chapter IV.4.2.1 on retroactive curative legislation).

5.4. The right to a court

One of the substantial points of criticism with regard to ad hoc legislation concerned the fact that the legislature opportunistically chose the instrument of a legislative act for a subject that was normally the province of administrative organs in order to avoid severe administrative and judicial review. This technique was clearly applied by the Dutch legislature in the dredging operations in the Western Scheldt (River) case. The Licensing of Dredging Act differed substantially from other project laws, which normally do not practically eliminate the possibility of administrative and judicial review, but shorten the administrative and judicial procedures. The Council of State[856] therefore argued that the Act violated the Netherlands' international obligations ensuing from the ECHR, namely, Art. 6 ECHR, including the right to a fair trial, "the right to a court" being part of it, as decided in the *Golder* case:[857]

> It would be inconceivable, in the opinion of the Court, that Article 6 para. 1 (art. 6-1) should describe in detail the procedural guarantees afforded to parties in a pending lawsuit and

855 Cf., however, Vlemminx's and Wattel's comment on the Victims of Persecution (1940–1945) Benefits Act, *Stb.* 1998, 267, as discussed earlier. Despite the fact that the law did not affect final cases, Vlemminx and Wattel still question the Act in light of the separation of powers principle between the legislature and the judiciary: F.M.C. Vlemminx, "Een grondwetswijziging onder het motto 'Verdeel en heers'?," in: J.L.W. Broeksteeg et al., *De Nederlandse Grondwet en de Europese Unie*, Deventer: Kluwer 2003, p. 94 and the Opinion of the Advocate General of the Supreme Court, HR February 28, 2001, *BNB* 2001/198c.

856 The Council of State apparently did not consider the possibility of judicial review of the Licensing of Dredging Act by a civil court as a serious alternative to administrative review. It simply concluded that no possibilities of legal protection were available, *Kamerstukken II* 1996/1997, 25 187, A, p. 5. See also Van Buuren (1997), p. 124, for his critical remarks on the relative superficiality of judicial review by civil courts.

857 *Golder v. United Kingdom* (Appl. no. 4451/70) (1975) ECHR Series A no. 18, par. 35.

> should not first protect that which alone makes it in fact possible to benefit from such guarantees, that is, access to a court. The fair, public and expeditious characteristics of judicial proceedings are of no value at all if there are no judicial proceedings.

Once the ECtHR acknowledged that the right to a fair trial includes the right of access to a court, it stressed that this right is not absolute:[858]

> The Court reiterates that the "right to a court," of which the right of access is one aspect, is not absolute; it is subject to limitations permitted by implication, in particular where the conditions of admissibility of an appeal are concerned, since by its very nature it calls for regulation by the State, which enjoys a certain margin of appreciation in this regard. However, these limitations must not restrict or reduce a person's access in such a way or to such an extent that the very essence of the right is impaired; lastly, such limitations will not be compatible with Article 6 §1 if they do not pursue a legitimate aim or if there is not a reasonable relationship of proportionality between the means employed and the aim sought to be achieved.

Assuming that Art. 6 ECHR is applicable to the Western Scheldt case,[859] it can seriously be questioned whether the Licensing of Dredging Act is in accordance with the ECHR's right to a fair trial, given the ECtHR's guidelines. The deciding factor will be whether the State had a legitimate aim and did not act disproportionally by eliminating the possibility of administrative judicial review.

5.5. Conclusion

The criticism regarding the violation of the separation of powers principle could especially be heard in the case of the Licensing of Dredging Act. In that case, the argument concerned two aspects of the separation of powers principle. On the one hand, according to the National Commission for Water Legislation, the legislature violated the separation of powers between the legislative and administrative functions because it granted administrative licenses for the specific project in the Western Scheldt (River), whereas the legislature most likely violated the separation of powers principle between the legislative and judicial branches by overruling the final decision of the Council of State in the Western Scheldt case.

Although the Commission's conclusion is rather outspoken, it is not based on any clear doctrinal ground in the Netherlands. First of all, the Dutch model of the division of State power does not prescribe any strict separation of powers, at least not in the relationship between the executive and the legislature. Moreover, the interpretation and specific meaning of this principle with regard to various types of relations between the three State powers remain unclear and underdeveloped. Instead of the separation of powers, the right to a fair trial in Art. 6 ECHR and the doctrine of legal certainty,

858 *Brualla Gomez de la Torre v. Spain* (Appl. no. 155/1996/774/975) ECHR 1997-VIII, para. 33 with reference to *Levages Prestations Services v. France* (Appl. no. 51/1995/557/643) ECHR 1996-V, para. 40.

859 The right to a fair trial, including "the right to a court" applies only to cases dealing with the determination of individuals' civil rights and obligations.

including the presumption against the retroactivity of laws, are used as a meaningful review framework. The case law of the European Court of Human Rights on Art. 6 is highly developed and offers practicable guidelines for the Dutch courts and the Dutch Council of State. This includes useful tools for situations like legislative intervention in pending cases, with which neither the Dutch courts nor the Dutch Council of State have so far been confronted.

IN SUM

The phenomenon of ad hoc legislation, the controversy it generates, and the possible role of constitutional principles in limiting the legislature in the Netherlands prompt the following conclusions.

Phenomenon of ad hoc legislation

It is interesting to mention that the three cases, which are the most explicit examples of legislative intervention in specific cases, are relatively new. They date especially from the 90s and afterwards. The Dutch Council of State points out in this respect the changing culture within the legislative body. In its annual report from 2003, it discusses the new possibilities the constituents have to contact their representatives, the disappearance of political ideologies, and the changed attitude of legislators, who follow the daily trends and are nowadays more likely to respond to incidents as blown up by the media than they used to be:[860]

> The stream of information addressed to the Lower House on a daily basis and direct access to individual members of parliament have increased tremendously. Possibilities to filter and select information have decreased. Political ideologies hardly offer a frame of reference anymore and the institutional filters no longer work. MPs are hardly given time to think: they must respond instantly. Political control has become dependent on the media and their priorities. Journalists are perceived as the voice of dissatisfied citizens; interested participants rather than critical observers. They dictate the political agenda and (subsequently) the focus of government action. Incidentalism is on the increase, stimulated by the way in which Article 68 of the Constitution (obligation to provide information) is applied. Incidentalism also entails arbitrariness. Those who are not in the spotlight (of the cameras) go unnoticed. The focus is on the incident, to the detriment of the parliamentary focus on legislation.

860 The Annual Report 2003 of the Dutch Council of State, p. 18 at <www.raadvanstate.nl/publicaties/jaarverslagen/> (last accessed on June 12, 2011). See also the criticism by the Parliament members themselves of the functioning of Parliament and the increased focus of the attention of members of Parliament on single incidents instead of the long-term vision, Parliamentary Report, *Vertrouwen en zelfvertrouwen. Parlementaire zelfreflectie*, The Lower House of Parliament, March 2009, pp. 43ff.

However, the focus on specific incidents, as the Council of State suggests, does not automatically imply that the Dutch Parliament regularly enacts laws that can be applied in only one specific case. Two of the three examples described in detail in Chapter V.1 were criticized for being enacted for the purpose of one predetermined case, although they concerned the general modification of applicable rules.

Constitutional principles and limitations

Part IV, in which the criticism of ad hoc legislation and the possible constitutional limitations of the legislature in this context have been explored, shows a discrepancy. On the one hand, the legislature received broad and far-reaching criticism for acting in specific cases, which suggests that the role of the legislature is basically seen as that of creating a system of general statutes. On the other hand, the criticism appeared not to be founded on any clear national principles of constitutional law derived from the Dutch Constitution. To begin with, the Dutch Constitution did not embrace the concept of legislation in the material sense, which has been advocated in the academic literature. Consequently, a choice for the concept of legislation in the formal sense allows the legislature to adopt case-specific laws without violating the national Constitution. The constitutional limitations must therefore be sought in other principles. The most effective constitutional principle in this regard appears to be the principle of legal certainty. Although it is not laid down as such in the Dutch Constitution, the courts stressed its importance as that of the rule of law. The principle of legal certainty also plays an important part in the advisory role of the Council of State. As far as other constitutional principles in Dutch constitutional law are concerned, the prospects are not encouraging. For example, the principle of the separation of powers, which in other jurisdictions appears to be particularly important as regards ad hoc legislation, is not clearly defined in the Netherlands and provides rather little practical protection against an arbitrary legislature.

Notwithstanding the lack of strong constitutional limitations and effective enforcement mechanisms (judicial constitutional review of legislation is impossible pursuant to Art. 120 of the Constitution and the advisory opinions of the Council of State are not legally binding on the legislature), the fact that the Netherlands is one of the Contracting States to the European Convention on Human Rights and International Covenant on Civil and Political Rights ensures that the Dutch legislature can still be limited when it acts arbitrarily in specific cases. Art. 6 ECHR appears to have the leading role in the context of ad hoc legislation. It can obviously be enforced by the European Court of Human Rights, and, by virtue of Art. 94 of the Dutch Constitution, directly applied by the national courts. Hitherto, the Court developed a meaningful view on legislative intervention in pending cases, stipulating that all circumstances in which an impugned piece of legislation has been enacted must be taken into consideration. It showed that ad hoc legislation is a special phenomenon that demands special treatment. This, however, does not mean that all laws designed for specific cases are invalid. Neutral classifications and (compelling) grounds of general, public interest have often been stated as a possible justification.

PART V

COMPARISON AND ANALYSIS

INTRODUCTION

In Chapter I.3, the central research question was posed. It reads:

When do laws enacted to deal with a specific case draw constitutional criticism in the United States, Germany, and the Netherlands, and what constitutional rules and principles primarily determine the legality of such laws?

To answer this question a number of sub-questions have been formulated:
1. What types of ad hoc laws can be distinguished? 2. What constitutional principles and norms come to the fore in case law and in the legal literature as regards different types of ad hoc legislation? 3. Do these constitutional rules and principles leave any margin for justification of ad hoc legislation?

In Part V these questions will be answered and a balanced view on the practicability of various constitutional principles for the assessment of ad hoc legislation will be given. These principles have primarily been identified on the basis of the discussion of ad hoc laws in the United States, Germany, and the Netherlands. It will be shown that a number of these principles apply to ad hoc laws in general (ChapterV.1), whereas some of the them depend on a particular type of ad hoc legislation (Chapter V.2). In Chapter V.2 my own typology of ad hoc legislation will be presented. It is based on different functions that ad hoc laws can fulfill, as observed in practice in the United States, Germany, and the Netherlands.

In order to show to what extent these principles can actually limit a legislature that enacts ad hoc laws, the manner of their application in the constitutional law of the three studied countries will be compared and analyzed. Some repetition of what has already been said in the American, German, and Dutch parts of this book is therefore unavoidable. Eventually, it will be concluded that there is a striking discrepancy between the potential significance of these principles for the assessment of the constitutionality of ad hoc laws and their practical meaning. Although these principles are not always effectively applied by the courts, they still draw a line that no legislature is allowed to cross, no matter how good the reasons for ad hoc legislation it thinks it has.

Chapter 1

CONSTITUTIONAL LIMITATIONS IN GENERAL

Introduction

In this chapter the focus will be on principles and norms that have been found in all three jurisdictions and which apply to ad hoc laws, regardless of the function these laws fulfill (for applicable principles and norms which depend on the function of ad hoc legislation, see the next chapter). First, the principle of the generality of laws will be described (Chapter V.1.1). Interestingly, it appears that the arguments for the generality of laws which can be found in the literature on both legal philosophy and constitutional law are less obvious in the positive constitutional law of the United States, Germany, and the Netherlands. Neither the Constitutions of the Netherlands and Germany nor the federal Constitution of the United States require that laws always be general, suggesting that not every law which is case-specific is objectionable. Other possible limitations on the adoption of ad hoc laws by the legislative branch are the principles of equality (Chapter V.1.2), legal certainty (Chapter V.1.3), proportionality (Chapter V.1.4), and transparency in lawmaking (Chapter V.1.5). These are all constitutional principles, with the exception of the principle of transparency. In the literature, it has been argued that the transparency principle involves constitutional aspects as well as those of democracy. It is the practice of legislative riders in U.S. Congress that particularly comes into conflict with principles of democracy.

1.1. Generality of laws...

Ad hoc laws have been defined as laws that are unexpectedly and sometimes impulsively enacted for specific, preselected cases. The primary criticism many of them have received involved the argument of the violation of the generality of laws as a constitutional principle that restrains the legislature's power. Apparently, the critics presupposed that the principle of the generality of laws is a strong constitutional guarantee against a legislature that interferes in specific cases. Before reflecting on the practical meaning, including the possibilities to enforce this principle in the constitutional law approaches in the United States, Germany, and the Netherlands, I will elaborate on the principle of the generality of laws, which has most often been discussed from a political and philosophy of law point of view rather than from a pure legal perspective. For this purpose, a selection has been made of the views of a few authors.

1.1.1. ... *in the philosophy of law*

In the opinion of the political and legal philosophers, the principle of the generality of laws is one of the most essential elements of the rule of law, "the central idea of the liberal legal system."[861] The purpose of this principle is to guarantee and secure the freedom of the people and to protect them against an arbitrary State. This aim can only be achieved if the rules meet at least three conditions: "[t]hey are that the laws must be general, equal and certain," according to Hayek.[862] Raz and Fuller complemented the list of these indispensable conditions by requiring that laws also be prospective (presumption against retroactivity), public, clear, stable, consistent, not contradictory, and reasonable: they should not require the impossible.[863] In connecting the requirement of the generality of laws and the liberty of the people, Hayek, for example, states that:[864]

> The conception of freedom under the law [...] rests on the contention that when we obey laws, in the sense of general abstract rules laid down irrespective of their application to us, we are not subject to another man's will and are therefore free. It is because the lawgiver does not know the particular cases to which his rules will apply and it is because the judge who applies them has no choice in drawing the conclusions that follow from the existing body of rules and the particular facts of the case, that it can be said that laws and not men rule. Because the rule is laid down in ignorance of the particular case and no man's will decides the coercion used to enforce it, the law is not arbitrary. This, however, is true only if by "law" we mean the general rules that apply equally to everybody. This generality is probably the most important aspect of that attribute of law which we have called its "abstractness." As a true law should not name any particulars, so it should especially not single out any specific persons or group of persons.

This quote shows that Hayek connects the generality (impersonality of rules) and abstractness of rules (recurrent application) with equality and legal certainty. General laws guarantee that their application in a particular case is predictable and that people can anticipate the rules and thus predict on their own what consequences their behavior will have if certain abstract conditions are fulfilled.[865] This view of legal certainty can be positioned within a broader concept of the orderliness of social activity, consistency, and constancy.[866]

As Tamanaha observes, Hayek based his ideas on the generality of laws and the distinction between a law and an order on Rousseau's conception of law. The generality of laws also means for Rousseau that "the law considers all subjects collectively and all

861 Neumann (1986), p. 212.

862 Hayek (1955), p. 34.

863 Raz (1979), 214 and L. Fuller (1974), pp. 46ff as discussed in: B. Tamanaha, *On the rule of law. History, Politics, Theory*, Cambridge: Cambridge University Press 2004, p. 93.

864 F. Hayek, *The Constitution of Liberty*, London, New York: Routledge Classics 2006, pp. 134–135. See also Hayek (1976), p. 57: "General rules, genuine laws as distinguished from specific orders, must therefore be intended to operate in circumstances which cannot be foreseen in detail, and, therefore, their effect on particular ends or particular people cannot be known beforehand."

865 See Tamanaha (2004) on Hayek's generality.

866 Hayek (2006) p. 140 with citations.

actions in the abstract; it does not consider any individual man or any specific action."[867] According to Rousseau, laws may determine that there will be some privileges, but it is not allowed to attribute them to specific individuals mentioned by name. This can be seen as Rousseau's reaction to the Ancient Regime in France, a system based on individual privileges.[868] A similar reasoning applies to laws dealing, for instance, with succession to the throne: they are allowed to provide general and abstract rules on this specific subject, whereas the legislature is prohibited from making a choice of a specific successor or a specific royal family.[869] Rousseau associates the generality of laws in the sense of their general subject matter and abstractness with the general will of a sovereign people and the furtherance of the common, public good. Neumann objected to this connection by arguing that, in exceptional circumstances, furtherance of the common good can be independent of the generality of laws.[870] Apparently, even specific laws may thus serve the common good. Neumann may be right. Particularly in cases of ad hoc infrastructural laws, the legislatures appealed to the common good or general, public interest, which in their view justified making exceptions to general administrative, environmental, and other laws for the purpose of one specific project. On the one hand, resulting individual project laws can be seen as laws enacted for the common good. On the other hand, common good is also expressed in the legislature's respect for the previously established legal order and the system of general laws. The ultimate question is whether the legislature had convincingly concluded that the common good or general, public interest served by the contested ad hoc law weighed more heavily than the general, public interest served by the legislature's deference to its previous legislative choices as laid down in general rules. Because legislative exceptions to general rules for specific cases undermine the stability and continuity of laws, and diminish the legal protection of individuals, one should not easily be satisfied with the legislature's explanation to deviate from the general rules. It is fair to argue that only a compelling general interest may be considered as an interest that prevails. There appears to be no such compelling interest that justifies either the legislature singling out one predetermined person for oppressive treatment or imposing criminal punishment retroactively.

The generality of laws can also be positioned within the ideal of the separation of powers, according to Montesquieu[871] and Hayek.[872] The generality principle is important for making a distinction between the three State powers and guarantees an independent judiciary. According to Hayek,[873]

867 J.J. Rousseau, *The Social Contract*, Middlesex: Penguin 1968, p. 82.

868 See, for example, W.R. Brubaker, "The French Revolution and the Invention of Citizenship," *French Politics and Society*, Vol. 7 (1989), pp. 30ff.

869 Rousseau (1968), p. 82.

870 Neumann (1986), p. 132.

871 Ch. de Secondat Montesquieu (1977), Book XI, Ch. 6. See also Neumann (1986), pp. 213ff. on the generality of laws in the theory of Montesquieu. While Rousseau considered the generality of laws from the ethical perspective and attached to it a moral value of equality, Montesquieu saw it rather in the context of a formal distinction between the State powers.

872 Hayek (1955), pp. 37ff.

873 Hayek (1955), p. 37.

> [t]he significance of the demand for the separation of powers is fairly clear in so far as the relation between legislature and judicature is concerned. The principle that the general rules should be laid down apart from their application to particular instances almost requires that these distinct functions should also be performed by distinct groups of people. This is perhaps not the only conceivable but almost certainly the only practicable safeguard that the rules are not made to fit particular instances but because of their general significance.

And:

> it would seem necessary that their [the general rules] application should be left to an independent authority.

Neumann rightly concludes that the independent character of the judiciary can be seriously questioned when the legislature issues specific orders including, for example, for confiscation of property or detention of a specific individual. A judge who is only expected to enforce such orders "becomes a mere bailiff, a mere policeman."[874]

I repeat: the concept of the generality of laws as presented above encompasses two aspects of generality: 1) generality in the sense of the impersonality and abstractness of laws, and 2) generality in the sense of the general, public interest laws should serve. Besides these two aspects, a third understanding of the generality of laws from the philosophy of law perspective has been put forward in the literature.[875] It refers to the motives of the legislature. As argued by Westerman, it is neither the impersonal character of laws nor the fact that they abstract from specific situations and are fit for repeated application, but the fact that they abstract from the specific intentions with which they were enacted that makes them general. If I understand Westerman correctly, she argues that the intrinsic value of law lies only in laws which are not designed to reach a particular, predefined result.[876]

Regardless of the uncertainty about the distinction between motives, intentions and purposes, it should be borne in mind that nowadays most of the laws are enacted to achieve a particular purpose, since the concept of legislation has undergone changes. Nowadays, legislation does not only order society, but increasingly modifies and steers it in a certain direction: "Das Zeitalter stabilisierender Kodifikationen ist abgelöst worden durch eine Periode mehr oder weniger planvoller legislatorischen Aushilfen und Kurskorrekturen,"[877] or as Koopmans argued for the Dutch situation: "The legislature's aspiration is no longer *codification* but *modification*."[878] The German academic discussion addressed these new developments and the changing function of legislation by

874 Neumann (1986), p. 257.

875 However, as explained by Westerman during her inaugural lecture, legal philosophers and practitioners of legal theory are still discussing the true meaning of these terms and their mutual relationship, P. Westerman, *Twee pleidooien voor formalisering*, The Hague: Boom Juridische uitgevers 2003, pp. 9ff.

876 Westerman (2003), p. 23.

877 Schneider (2002), p. 143.

878 T. Koopmans, *De rol van de wetgever*, Zwolle: Tjeenk Willink 1970, p. 3, my own translation. See also M. Adams, *Recht en democratie ter discussie*, Leuven: Leuven University Press 2006, pp. 145ff and B. van Klink, *De wet als symbol*, Deventer: Tjeenk Willink 1998, pp. 48ff & pp. 118ff. on legislative

distinguishing between the concept of *klassiches Rechtsgesetz* and *Maßnahmegesetz* (see particularly Chapter III.2.2.2).[879] The Federal Constitutional Court has already decided that *Maßnahmengesetze* (special measure laws), a new type of laws designed to achieve a particular purpose agreed beforehand, are irrelevant from a constitutional law point of view. In the United States, Tamanaha argued that legal instrumentalism has evolved into a concept in which "the law is becoming a means pure and simple, with the ends up for grabs."[880]

In the next section, I will show that even if the legislative intention appears to be directed at a particular result in one specific, predetermined case, the courts find it risky to involve it in their review of the contested law in the context of these constitutional provisions which require the generality of laws. The fact that the legislature might have had case-specific motives appears insufficient to declare the statute unconstitutional (Chapter V.1.1.2.3).

1.1.2. ... in constitutional law

All three aspects of generality regarding: 1) the scope of the law's application: impersonality and abstractness, 2) the general, public interest that laws should serve, and 3) the legislative motives, play a part within the concept of ad hoc legislation. The relevant constitutional provisions, doctrines, case law, and literature on the meaning of the principle of the generality of laws in the constitutional law of the United States, Germany, and the Netherlands that have been previously studied complement the rough ideas discussed above on generality in political and legal philosophy, and show the practical meaning and workability of this principle in constitutional law.

1.1.2.1. An absolute requirement of the generality of laws

First and foremost, I need to clarify that neither in the United States (at the federal level), in Germany, nor in the Netherlands, can a constitutional provision be found that limits the power of the legislature to enactment of general laws only. In other words, no absolute requirement of generality that would have consequences for the law's constitutionality could be identified in these countries.[881] Exceptionally, most of the state constitutions in the United States do explicitly prohibit special (individual) and local laws on several matters, such as divorce, crime and punishment, or granting privileges to a private corporation. The farthest-reaching requirement of generality observed in the state

instrumentalism. Veerman, however, argues that codification has a modifying function as well, Veerman (2007), p. 42.

879 See F. Reimer, "Das Parlementsgesetz als Steuerungsmittel und Kontrollmaßtab," in: W. Hoffmann-Riem, E. Schmidt-Aßmann & A. Voßkuhle (eds.), *Grundlagen des Verwaltungsrechts*, Vol. 1, München: C.H. Beck 2006, pp. 550ff.

880 Tamanaha (2006), p. 4. A vigorous opponent of instrumentalism in the United States was the legal philosopher Lon Fuller.

881 By overruling its judgment in *Morey v. Doud*, 354 U.S. 457 (1957), the U.S. Supreme Court even explicitly indicated that the mere fact that a law is case-specific does not suffice to declare it unconstitutional, *City of New Orleans v. Dukes*, 427 U.S. 297 (1976).

constitutions can be found in a prohibition of special laws in situations where a general law can be made applicable.[882] The ban on special laws was meant to change the legislative practice in the nineteenth century and combat the risks of arbitrary special legislation resulting from a short distance between the local legislature and the constituents. Although the nature of the federal legislature theoretically keeping more distance from its constituents is different from the situation at the state level, the examples of Congressional ad hoc laws that serve special interests show that this distance actually proves to be smaller than it seemed to be.

The same lack of a general requirement of the generality of laws can be found in the national constitutions of Germany and the Netherlands. Neither of them describes the legislative function as that of creating general laws only. What is more, both constitutions have explicitly chosen the concept of legislation in the formal sense, which means that every law enacted by Parliament in a constitutionally prescribed procedure must be as such considered a valid law. On the contrary, constitutional scholars in these countries strongly emphasized the importance of the concept of legislation in the material sense including the generality of legal norms in preventing the State from acting arbitrarily. Apparently, the constitutional legislator refused to see the generality of laws principle as a *conditio sine qua non* for the guarantee against government arbitrariness. Nevertheless, one type of case-specific legislation is always seen as problematic. Case-specific laws that single out one specific individual or an easily identifiable group of individuals to impose punishment on them are prohibited (U.S. Bill of Attainder Clause) as are those that restrict basic rights (Art. 19GG). The Dutch Constitution does not contain any comparable provision, although Art. 1 of the Dutch Criminal Code requires that no act is criminal, unless on the basis of prior legislation. Legislation in this context is commonly understood as generally applicable legislation.

In summary, the (federal) Constitutions of the United States, Germany, and the Netherlands do not formally oblige the legislatures to design general laws only. It can be said, however, that in the Netherlands and Germany most laws are general. This ensues from the legal tradition these countries share. They both have a civil law tradition characterized by a general and abstract manner of legislating. Continental statutes form part of a large and coherent system of general legal rules enacted for the general public. The United States' legal tradition, on the other hand, is that of common law. Although statutes in the United States are now more important that they used to be, they are still not intended to form a coherent system of general laws. They are rather fact-oriented and are often the legislature's response to particular situations, cases or court judgments. The long tradition of private bills also shows that individual laws are not objectionable in advance. The difference between the focus on general and abstract situations in Germany as a civil law country and the case-oriented approach in the United States, which has a common law tradition, has been illustrated by Lepsius in an interesting way:[883]

882 See Chapter II.2.2.1.

883 O. Lepsius, "Was kann die deutsche Staatsrechtslehre von der amerikanischen Rechtswissenschaft lernen," in: H. Schulze-Fielitz (ed.), *Staatsrechtslehre als Wissenschaft*, Berlin: Duncker & Humblot 2007, p. 328. See also P.G. Stein, "Roman Law, Common Law, and Civil Law," 66 *Tul. L. Rev.* 1591, 1594ff (1992).

> Im amerikanischen Rechtsdenken unterentwickelt ist im übrigen auch die soziale Kehrseite des juristischen Systembegriffs, nämlich die Orientierung des Rechts auf die Gesellschaft. Es ist eher der Einzelne, auf den Recht bezogen ist, als die Gemeinschaft. Hier manifestiert sich erneut die Abneigung gegen großflächige, artifizielle Konstrukte im Rechtsdenken. Individuen mit ihren Interessen sind in den USA viel eher der Bezugspunkt einer sich sozial informiert gebenden Rechtswissenschaft als ein überindividuelles Konstrukt namens „Gesellschaft."

The fact that the individual occupies center stage in American law does not, of course, mean that all statutes are intended to achieve a particular result in a specific case. This approach merely suggests that statutes enacted for the purpose of one specific case, company, etc. are not rejected in principle as contrary to the agreed legal system.

1.1.2.2. Generality of laws: General scope of application

The doctrine of special and local laws, the Bills of Attainder Clause, the *Einzelfallgesetzverbot*, and the concept of legislation in the material sense reflect a sophisticated view on the generality of laws. The main question to determine whether a law is general is: do the law's provisions qualify for future, repeatable application[884] in new cases.[885] To my mind, this question should be answered on the basis of facts rather than on the basis of fictitious distinctions. In line with the U.S. Supreme Court (Bill of Attainder Clause), the ECtHR (fair trial, Art. 6 ECHR), and the state courts in the United States (prohibition of special and local laws), the *circumstances* in which the law in question has been enacted and the actual *effects* of the law should be taken into consideration. This approach is essential; otherwise these constitutional provisions that prohibit certain case-specific laws regarding scope are ineffective. The *Bundesverfassungsgericht*'s interpretation of Art. 19 (1) GG shows the merely theoretical meaning of this provision. The Court is satisfied when the contested statute had been phrased in general terms and thus theoretically allows its application to future cases as well. By now it has become evident, however, that the legislatures (or more precisely: the bill sponsors, including the government in the Netherlands and Germany) are quite inventive and provide seemingly general rules for one specific case. The narrowly tailored conditions that must be fulfilled for the law's application often reveal the specific focus of the law. Such a law is practically inapplicable to future cases, in contrast to laws representing "a class of one."[886]

884 The *Bundesverfassungsgericht* is often interested in the aspect of indefiniteness ("Eine Norm hat den Charakter eines für eine unbestimmte Vielzahl von Fällen geltenden generellen Rechtssatzes – und ist also kein Einzelfallgesetz –, wenn sich wegen der abstrakten Fassung des gesetzlichen Tatbestandes nicht genau übersehen läßt, auf wieviele und welche Fälle das Gesetz Anwendung findet," BVerfGE 25, 371 (396)), which relates to the central question posed above.

885 In the Netherlands, this conclusion is based on the literature in the field of constitutional law, because 1) the Dutch Constitution does not have any provision on the general application of laws and 2) even if it did, the Dutch courts are prevented from reviewing the compatibility of Acts of Parliament with the Constitution, as provided in Art. 120.

886 See Chapter II.3.1.1.

The above has consequences for situations in which the legislature designs a law that has a general scope – it is indeed applicable to future cases as well – but the circumstances in which it was enacted justify the conclusion that the legislature's intention was to affect the outcome of one particular case. This brings us to the next aspect of the generality of laws as put forth in the theoretical debate on the principle of the generality of laws: generality in the sense of the general motives of the legislature.

1.1.2.3. Generality of laws: Legislative motives

In the broad criticism of ad hoc legislation, frequent reference is made to the specific motives of the legislature, which allegedly "wanted" to influence a predetermined case. Ad hoc laws are then classified as individual because of the case-specific motives of the legislature. This argument was most prominent in the Dutch case of the permanent camera surveillance of Volkert van der G. It should be borne in mind, however, that although the first case to which the amended regulation applied was Volkert van der. G.'s case, the rules were evidently formulated in a general manner and were therefore applicable in other, future cases as well.

As already said in Chapter V.1.1.1, case-specific motives of the legislature have limited significance in determining whether a law is an individual ad hoc law from the point of view of constitutional law. Initially, the *Bundesverfassungsgericht* seemed to recognize the importance of this aspect in determining whether contested laws are in fact "disguised" ad hoc laws, when deciding on the Platow Amnesty Act in 1959:[887]

> Von einem solchen ["getarntes Individualgesetz"] kann nur dann gesprochen werden, wenn der Gesetzgeber ausschließlich einen bestimmten Einzelfall oder eine bestimmte Gruppe von Einzelfällen regeln will und zur Verdeckung dieser Absicht generell formulierte Tatbestandsmerkmale dergestalt in einer Norm zusammenfaßt, daß diese nur auf jene konkreten Sachverhalte Anwendung finden kann, die dem Gesetzgeber vorschwebten und auf die die Norm zugeschnitten ist.

Remarkably, the Federal Constitutional Court neutralized this firm language and it in fact declared the "motive criterion" of little use. Deciding on the constitutionality of the Platow Amnesty Act, the Court eventually refused to take the motives of the German Parliament into account. Because the Platow Amnesty Act was formulated in general terms, it was general, according to the Court. In later judgments, the *Bundesverfassungsgericht* systematically avoided the application of the "motive test" to decide on the implicitly individual character of a law under attack. Instead, it has continued to test the phrasing of the law. This Court concludes on a regular basis that even if the legislature had one specific case in mind when designing the law, the general formulation of the law prevents it from being in conflict with the constitutional prohibition of *Einzelfallgesetzverbot*. Such general laws possibly enacted with one case in mind belong in the unproblematic category of *Anlassgesetze* (case-generated laws) and

[887] See the *Bundesverfassungsgericht*'s judgment in the *Platow Amnesty* case, BVerfGE 10, 234 (244). See also Chapter III.2.

not to the group of *Einzelfallgesetze* (case-specific laws). This interpretation of generality in Art. 19 (1) GG explains why the *Bundesverfassungsgericht* has not yet come to the point of declaring a law an unconstitutional *Einzelfallgesetz*.

In the United States, on the other hand, this "motive test" has more significance and is one of the instruments used by the American courts within the framework of the Bills of Attainder Clause. According to this Clause, a statute must be classified as a prohibited bill of attainder if it is both case-specific and designed to punish. However, the "motive test" is used as a helpful[888] tool in determining the punishment question, not the generality question. This test gives judges an opportunity to consult the congressional record while searching for statements of Congressmen disclosing the legislature's will to punish a specific individual.

By and large, the courts are rather reluctant to investigate the motives of the legislature and attach any legal consequences to them. The ECtHR maps out a more progressive route. Reviewing the compatibility of legislative interventions with the administration of justice with the right to a fair trial under Art. 6 of the European Convention on Human Rights, it employs two tests: the "motive test" and the "justification test" in order to find out whether the only motives of the legislature were to influence the judicial process or whether the law was motivated by compelling grounds of the general, public interest. Only in obviously arbitrary situations will the Court conclude that the legislature's only motives were to influence the judicial process, thereby violating Art. 6.

On the one hand, the courts' reluctance to discover the real motives of the legislature and their refusal to invalidate ad hoc legislation solely on the basis of the "true motives" of the legislature appears understandable.[889] The law is ultimately about objective situations and facts rather than about subjective intentions and speculations. In most of the cases, it will also be difficult to unanimously decide what the "real motives" of the legislature were at a certain time.[890] It can be argued that the explanatory memoranda

[888] The motive test is indeed helpful, but not decisive. Other tests used to determine whether the contested law is punishing are the functional and the historical tests. These tests carry more weight than the motive test. See Chapter II.3.1 on the three tests.

[889] See, for example, a sharp statement by the Supreme Court in *United States v. O'Brien*, 391 U.S. 367, 383–384 (1968): "It is a familiar principle of constitutional law that this Court will not strike down an otherwise constitutional statute on the basis of an alleged illicit legislative motive" and further: "Inquiries into congressional motives or purposes are a hazardous matter. When the issue is simply the interpretation of legislation, the Court will look to statements by legislators for guidance as to the purpose of the legislature, because the benefit to sound decision-making in this circumstance is thought sufficient to risk the possibility of misreading Congress' purpose. It is entirely a different matter when we are asked to void a statute that is, under well-settled criteria, constitutional on its face, on the basis of what fewer than a handful of Congressmen said about it. What motivates one legislator to make a speech about a statute is not necessarily what motivates scores of others to enact it, and the stakes are sufficiently high for us to eschew guesswork. We decline to void essentially on the ground that it is unwise legislation which Congress had the undoubted power to enact and which could be reenacted in its exact form if the same or another legislator made a 'wiser' speech about it," internal references omitted.

[890] On methodological problems concerning the determination of the "true motives" of the legislature in the context of statutory interpretation and with regard to the constitutional intention of the Framers, see R. Dworkin, *A Matter of Principle*, Cambridge and London: Harvard University Press 1985, pp. 43ff and 319ff.

accompanying legislative bills could be helpful in finding out the reasons for the law's enactment. This part of a bill could shed more light on the legislative intentions. A pragmatic approach, however, compels the conclusion that such a document would often have little value for the review of ad hoc legislation, because the authors will not be frank about the real motives for influencing (usually unfavorably) one targeted case. Realizing that ad hoc legislation appears at least as suspicious to the public and regularly generates a great deal of criticism and fierce debates, the legislature would not easily acknowledge its true intent. A general obligation to officially justify the proposal (as far as this is not an obligation already), giving the reasons for its enactment, does not seem to be a workable solution, either: the bill's sponsors can be obligated to justify the bill, but they cannot be obligated to tell the truth.

On the other hand, the court's reluctance to attach legal consequences to legislative motives in terms of the law's invalidation from a constitutional law point of view can be problematic and can conflict with our sense of justice in a particular case.[891] The case of colored workers in a salmon packing factory who had been discriminated against, as described in Chapter II.4, is most striking. There could be no reasonable doubt that Congress discriminatorily exempted their single pending case against their employer from the rules of the 1991 Civil Rights Act, which were otherwise favorable to them. By so doing, Congress complied with the company's request and sanctioned its expensive lobby in this specific case. The Court of Appeals was aware of the circumstances in which the Act had been enacted and of the statements by some congressmen complaining about this unjust deal, but it refused to take the true legislative motives into account in the assessment of the provision. On the contrary, it was satisfied with an invented story on the part of the government and accepted it as a plausible justification of the exemption.

This example shows that the courts' ignorance in assessing the motives of the legislature creates an artificial reality: the courts pretend to be blind by refusing to take notice of the circumstances in which the legislature initiated the contested law. This, as Shaman observes, may be especially problematic in high-profile cases which receive a great deal of media coverage. The motives of the legislature are then evident and are thoroughly known to the public.[892] The credibility of and the trust in the judiciary may consequently suffer damage.

I do agree that the courts' competence to declare a law unconstitutional solely on the basis of the legislature's subjective motives would often go quite far. But it would not be unreasonable to at least take the legislative motives into account. They can be reconstructed on the basis of the external circumstances in which the legislature acted.[893] As Shaman quite convincingly proposed, the party who challenges the law

[891] In a similar key, J.M. Shaman, *Constitutional Interpretation. Illusion and Reality*, Westport: Greenwood Press 2001, pp. 143ff.

[892] Shaman (2001), p. 155.

[893] There should not be any fear of the activism of the courts if they are encouraged to consider the legislative motives in their review. Even the European Court of Human Rights is not such a crusader in this respect as is sometimes assumed. Although it explicitly applies the motive test when it reviews the compatibility of laws with the right to a fair trial of Art. 6 ECHR, it would only find a violation of Art. 6 when the law is evidently arbitrary and clearly designed to influence the outcome of judicial proceedings. For a very clear example, see the judgment in *Stran Greek Refineries and Stratis Andreadis v. Greece.*

should be the one to prove that the legislature's motive was improper. The government would then always have the possibility to come up with a plausible counter-explanation based on facts. This approach can be successful only if the courts apply the standard of plausibility seriously and in a meaningful way: they should look critically into any after-the-fact explanation.

1.1.2.4. Generality of laws: The general, public interest

The third element of the principle of the generality of laws that plays a part both within the theoretical concept of the generality of laws and the discussion on ad hoc legislation at the more practical level refers to the general, public interest that laws are expected to serve.

Ad hoc laws that benefit specific individuals are criticized because they favor the individual private interests of these persons rather than the general, public interest. The opponents of ad hoc legislation clearly relate the case-specific character of a law (as regards the specific legislative motives, the specific scope of application, or both) to the generality of the interest served by the law. In other words, they argue that case-specificity of the law suggests that the law serves special interests instead of a general, public one. This criticism has been articulated most explicitly in the Dutch case involving the BNN Act. The argument applies also to other cases, such as the case of the northern spotted owl in the United States. Let us first examine case-specificity and the general, public interest and subsequently the meaning of the requirement of serving the general, public interest in the constitutional law practice in the United States, Germany, and the Netherlands.

It can fairly be argued that the contested statute serves special private interests instead of the general, public interest if the evident and *only* purpose of a law is to benefit one specific individual or legal person. However, if the factual benefits are only a *side-effect* or just a *means* for setting higher goals, it could reasonably be argued that the law serves the common good, as defined in the political process. The boundary between the two situations is, however, relatively thin, as the case of the Amendment to the Dutch Media Act illustrates.[894] Did the government propose to change the Media Act, easing the requirements for joining the public broadcasting system merely to benefit the young, innovative association BNN, or was the purpose of this change to achieve the general,

Cases in which the U.S. Supreme Court and the *Bundesverfassungsgericht* paid attention to arbitrary motives of the legislature are also quite obvious ones. See, for example, *Stone v. Graham*, 449 U.S. 39 (1980), *Board of Education v. Pico*, 475 U.S. 871 (1982) and BVerfGE 17, 306. For more references in U.S. case law, including the classification of constitutional rights, where the courts demonstrate a willingness to take the legislative motives into account, see J.H. Ely, "Legislative and Administrative Motivation in Constitutional Law," 79 *Yale L. Journal* 1205, 1969–1970, J.M. Clark, "Legislative Motivation and Fundamental Rights in Constitutional Law," 15 *San Diego L. Rev.* 953 (1977–1978), and Shaman (2001), pp. 155ff.

894 Chapter IV.1.2.

public interest of programming diversity within the public broadcasting system?[895] Two answers are possible.

It seems to be convincing, too, to argue that laws which create an open group of beneficiaries and base the conditions they need to meet in order to receive advantages on relevant and neutral grounds are more likely to avoid being attacked as serving special private interests. The same can be said of specific (infrastructural) project laws. In many cases, the legislature's explanation that by creating an exceptional, less stringent legal regime for one concrete infrastructural project, it aims to serve the general, public interest (economic growth, fulfillment of international agreements, the interest of good relations with neighboring states) will sound plausible.[896] Another question is, however, whether the legislature properly balanced all interests involved when it made the law (both private interests and other public interests such as the interests of environmental protection, effective legal protection, and the balance between the three branches of government when the legislature overrules a judicial decision or grants administrative licenses on its own initiative; see above Chapter V.1.1.1).

The next essential question concerns the practical significance of the requirement of serving the general, public interest (or public purpose and common good; terms used more often in the United States) including its enforceability at law. It follows from the description in Parts II, III, and IV that all three constitutions require the interest served by legislation to be general in certain situations. A provision that frequently occurs in this context concerns expropriation. Property may only be expropriated for a public purpose. Art. I, Section 8, Clause 1 of the U.S. Constitution requires that laws in the field of spending and taxation be limited laws serving the general welfare. But as long as courts, including the Supreme Court, are reluctant to enforce this provision effectively, the amount of special interest legislation, pork barrel legislation, and legislative earmarks will grow.[897] In addition, the warmly embraced public choice theory, which pictures Congress as a battlefield for various special interest groups, does not contribute to Congress' image as a guardian of the general, public interest.

With the exception of particular matters such as expropriation, neither the Dutch nor the German constitutions restrict the legislature in so many words to creating laws which serve the general interest only.[898] Surprisingly, in these countries, the idea of restricting the legislative power to making only this kind of law has nevertheless often been discussed in a normative sense in the academic literature. This indicates that such a requirement is more or less commonly accepted. The Federal Constitutional Court in

895 U.S. and German case law has recognized that laws which benefit one industry do not necessarily contradict the general, public interest. Consequently, laws which provide financial privileges to companies and thereby serve the higher purpose of promoting employment and economic growth may be upheld. See BVerfGE 59, 216 (229) and *Common Cause v. State of Maine*, 455 A.2d 1, 20 (1983).

896 Classical examples are special emergency laws, such as the Dutch Delta Major Rivers Act (*Deltawet Grote Rivieren, Stb.* 1995, no. 210). This piece of project legislation allowed the dykes to be strengthened quickly after the serious flooding in specific territories; see Chapter IV.2.2.2.

897 See, e.g., *South Dakota v. Dole*, 483 U.S. 203 (1987), where the Supreme Court seriously questioned the usefulness of the General Welfare Clause for positive constitutional law. See Chapter II.2.3.2.

898 See, however, my comment on Art. 50 of the Dutch Constitution in Chapter IV.2.3.

Germany also decided that the notion of the general interest (*Gemeinwohl*) is strongly related to the concept of human rights and the *Rechtsstaat*. By stating that "[e]s obliegt allerdings in erster Linie dem Gesetzgeber, zu entscheiden, ob eine bestimmte normative Ausgestaltung eines Lebenssachverhalts im Interesse des gemeinen Wohls liegt," it moreover suggested that the notion of the general interest may have an even broader meaning. Nevertheless, the Court acknowledges that it is primarily a political duty of the legislature to decide what the general, public interest is.

1.1.2.5. Concluding remarks

The principle of the generality of laws within the framework of constitutional provisions which, at least in the United States and Germany, prohibit Bills of Attainder and *Einzelfallgesetze*, is similarly interpreted by the courts and in the literature. Within the scope of these provisions, the generality of laws is understood in terms of the laws' scope of application. This implies that laws will not be struck down as violating the Bill of Attainder Clause or the *Einzelfallgesetzverbot* from Art. 19 (1) GG on the sole basis that the legislature's motives were case-specific. The same holds for the Dutch discussion in the academic literature, where the concept of generality concerns the general applicability of laws.[899] In this context, although Westerman's statement that laws are truly general when the legislature's motives are general is valuable and illustrates the ideal situation, it must be concluded that it has little practical meaning in positive constitutional law. On the one hand, this is understandable: the courts will not always find it easy to determine the "true" motives of the legislature, and they will probably consider it improper toward the legislature to make such an inquiry. On the other hand, such limited effect of the legislative motive criterion in positive constitutional law is especially troublesome as regards ad hoc legislation, because of the risks it generates. In particular, when the officially announced reasons for the enactment of the contested ad hoc law, given the circumstance under which it was enacted, prove to be false, and the law seems to be unable to achieve the officially stated purpose, the courts should be distrustful.

As far as the requirement of the generality of interest is concerned, it can be concluded that the quality aspect of this requirement as a limitation of the legislative power is generally recognized.[900] In general, however, it can be maintained that there is little chance that the courts will strike down a law only because it has been enacted for special, private interests. For the reasons I have discussed, prospects for eliminating ad hoc legislation on the basis of the generality of laws principle are rather dim.

1.2. Equality

At least theoretically, the equality of laws principle seems to offer better perspectives for the review of ad hoc legislation, even though the interpretation of this constitutional principle in the United States, Germany, and the Netherlands does not mean that all laws

899 Despite the popular criticism of Dutch cases of ad hoc laws as described in Chapter IV.1 where it was often concluded that a law was case-specific because the legislature's motives were case-specific.

900 In the Netherlands and Germany even more than in the United States.

that are case-specific automatically violate the equality principle. This has often been contended in the discussion and criticism of high-profile cases of ad hoc legislation and suggested in the more philosophical debate on the generality of laws. It is more accurate to say that case-specific legislation is likely to *jeopardize* the principle of equal treatment. The Equal Protection Clause from the Fourteenth (state) and Fifth (federal) Amendments to the U.S. Constitution, Art. 3 of the German Basic Law, and Art. 26 of the International Covenant on Civil and Political Rights (ICCPR) – the most meaningful provision guaranteeing equal treatment in the Netherlands – all allow legislatures to make classifications and distinctions. This is acceptable and even unavoidable. Categorizing is sometimes recommended, or even required, as different conditions apply to various groups, all of which have different needs.[901] There can be rules for educators, doctors, special governmental bodies, etc. In general, such classifications are not problematic, unless they are discriminatory in the sense of being arbitrary. What does this mean in the context of ad hoc legislation?

With the exception of the federal Act for the Relief of the parents of Teresa Marie Schiavo, the Northwest Timber Compromise, and the Lex Stendal, which were all literally limited to three specific cases, the legislatures consciously avoid using any names of addressees when passing ad hoc law. They rather choose to describe these particular cases in seemingly general, though very narrowly-tailored, terms. They thereby ostensibly provide general classifications, which are relevant for judicial review within the equality principle.[902]

The "European" approach to the constitutional guarantee of equal treatment by the legislature requires objective and reasonable grounds for legislative classifications;[903] in the words of the German Federal Constitutional Court "[…] ein vernünftiger, sich aus der Natur der Sache ergebender oder sonstwie sachlich einleuchtender Grund für die gesetzliche Differenzierung oder Gleichbehandlung."[904] In short, the legislature is not allowed to provide a divergent regime for X only because X is X, but because X possesses certain objective qualities. The American approach as developed by the U.S. Supreme Court basically includes a strongly comparable, though not the same, criterion. Using its "rational basis test," the Court asks whether there is a rational basis for the classifications made or, in other words, whether there is a substantial relationship between the classifications and a legitimate purpose of the act; whether the classifications are relevant to achieve the law's purpose.[905]

On the one hand, both criteria form a basis for the invalidation of *clearly* arbitrary ad hoc laws where the exceptions made by a legislature that acts impulsively or emotionally lack any neutral and relevant basis. On the other hand, one should realize that it is not

901 See the clear statement of the U.S. Supreme Court in *Personnel Adm'r of Massachusetts v. Feeney*, 442 U.S. 256, 271–272 (1979).

902 The term "classification" should be taken quite broadly. The case of a single individual who does not belong to any class will be treated within the scope of the Equal Protection Clause as well. See *Village of Willowbrook v. Olech*, 528 U.S. 562, 564 (2000).

903 Art. 26 of the International Covenant on Civil and Political Rights (ICCPR) also requires a legitimate aim and proportionality in the limitation of the right to equal protection.

904 BVerfGE 1, 14 (52). See also Chapter III.3.1.

905 Seidman (2003), p. 29.

always easy to determine whether such objective or relevant grounds are present. In the case of Ferdinand Schörner, did the German Parliament retroactively correct mistakes in disciplinary legislation after the case of Ferdinand Schörner laid them bare? Or did Parliament retroactively change the law only for the purpose of depriving unpopular Schörner of his right to a state pension, as public opinion demanded? The *Bundesverfassungsgericht* followed the first line of reasoning. I am still in doubt.

1.2.1. Low scrutiny vs. strict scrutiny

The above-mentioned tests represent a minimal standard for the review of ad hoc laws within the framework of equal protection. In general, the requirements are easy to meet, as painfully illustrated above by the case of colored workers in a salmon cannery who had been treated unequally. In that case, the U.S. Court of Appeal emphasized the very low scrutiny of the rational basis test by accepting highly dubious reasons for the challenged exemption. In addition, these tests apply to most ad hoc laws, because most of them do not provide classifications which are based on, e.g., race or sex. If they do, the courts *in all three* countries will perform a more rigorous review. Both the *Bundesverfassungsgericht* and the U.S. Supreme Court developed stringent *justification* tests for this purpose: the U.S. Congress will have to explain whether the law under attack is "narrowly tailored to serve a compelling governmental interest,"[906] while the German legislature will have to show that the distinctions are based on such important grounds that any unequal treatment is justified.[907] Although the Dutch courts have not developed any special strict scrutiny test, they tend to be particularly critical about the objectivity and reasonableness of grounds on which cases have been treated unequally if the distinction is not based on merely technical grounds.[908]

1.2.2. Consistency and stability of legal rules

Inconsistency is often a problem in the context of ad hoc legislation. Legislatures act inconsistently with the previously adopted rules in both situations: 1) when they exempt one specific case from their application, and 2) when they change the general system of laws in a certain area in order to ensure a particular, politically desired outcome in a specific case. The Terri Schiavo Law in the United States, the Lex Stendal in Germany, and the Licensing of Dredging Act in the Netherlands illustrate the first situation. The Dutch Modification of the Media Act, the so-called BNN Act, best illustrates the second situation.[909]

First and foremost, it must be said that consistency of legislative choices de facto relates to the stability of a legal system, which is generally seen as an element of the

[906] See the "strict scrutiny test," Chapter II.4.2.
[907] See "*die neue Formel*," Chapter II.3.2.
[908] Chapter IV.3.2.
[909] For a detailed argument, see Chapter IV.1.2.2.1.

principle of legal certainty.[910] Even though legal certainty in this sense has been acknowledged in the Dutch literature, its practical significance remains limited. Notwithstanding the fact that the Dutch courts are prevented from reviewing the constitutionality of Acts of Parliament, it appears unlikely that, if they had such a possibility, they would ever declare a law unconstitutional due to a violation of anything like a principle of legislative consistency.[911] Such a constitutional principle was not applied in the United States either. In fact, it has even been explicitly rejected:[912]

> [Congress] is bound by no obligation of consistency over time or loyalty to precedent. Just like raising the jurisdictional limit for federal question or diversity jurisdiction, Congress can say, we used to allow more suits than we are going to henceforward. On what premise however, does the Court make that statement? It is not master of its own jurisdiction; Congress is.

In contrast to the Netherlands and the United States, the German Federal Constitutional Court did recognize that there is something in the nature of a constitutional principle of legislative consistency (*Systemgerechtigkeit*). It relates to both situations described above: legislative exemptions for a specific case and modification of general rules for a specific case. Interestingly enough, and highly disappointing to authors who argue for the rationalization of legislative choices, the Federal Constitutional Court refused to attribute any independent meaning to it. Consequently, this Court will not strike down any law which is alien to the general system of previously enacted rules on the sole basis that it is inconsistent. In principle, however, it will consider the legislative inconsistency within the limits of the equality Art. 3 of the Basic Law: legislative inconsistency may indicate that Art. 3 has been violated.[913]

The Court's reluctance to recognize the principle of inconsistency as an independent touchstone for reviewing the compatibility of laws with the Constitution is understandable and even arguable if the principle of a consistent system of laws is perceived as one of the principles of good quality legislation, although not a principle of constitutional law. From this perspective, it can justifiably be stated that judging the quality of legislation is not the primary function of constitutional courts. In spite of the fact that there is undoubtedly a need for the pursuit of good quality legislation, poor quality cannot be put on a par

910 In Fuller's opinion, the principle of the stability of laws belongs to the internal morality of law, Fuller (1974), pp. 79ff.

911 See, however, the examples of court decisions with regard to executive orders given by Van Ommeren (1996), pp. 318ff.

912 T. Campbell, *Separation of Powers in Practice*, Stanford: Stanford University Press 2004, p. 58. See also the Supreme Court judgment in *I.N.S. v. Chadha*, where the Court concluded that Congress is not bound by its own laws: "Unlike the judiciary or an administrative agency, Congress is not bound by established substantive rules," 462 U.S. 919, 966. See also *United States v. Lopez Andino*, 831 F.2d 1164, 1172–1173 (1987): "Under well-established constitutional precedent, [...] an act of Congress [...] does not bind future Congresses. Like any other act of Congress it may be repealed, modified, or amended at the unilateral will of future Congresses" (concurring opinion of Torruella, J.), and *Cmty. Serv. Broad. Of Mid-America, Inc. v. FCC*, 593 F2d.1102, 1113 (1978): "To be sure, Congress is generally free to change its mind; in amending legislation Congress is not bound by the intent of an earlier body. But it is bound by the Constitution."

913 BVerfGE 81, 156 (207).

with the classification of unconstitutionality. The courts realize this, and, as evidenced by the legislative inconsistency case of the German Federal Constitutional Court, only inconsistent legislation which is arbitrary in the meaning of the Basic Law at the same time will be declared constitutionally invalid.

1.2.3. Concluding remarks

At first sight, the constitutional right of equal treatment through legislation appears to offer more possibilities, for uncovering as well as penalizing legislative arbitrariness. The constitutional practice in the United States, Germany, and the Netherlands shows, however, that its practical meaning is less far-reaching. First of all, no piece of legislation will be invalidated merely because it unexpectedly or even impulsively changed the rules. The often applied low standard of rational basis or neutrality allows the invalidation of only extremely and most obviously discriminatory ad hoc laws. The principle of legal certainty seems to offer better protection, at least in the Netherlands and Germany, as will be shown below.

1.3. Legal certainty

Uncertainty is inherent to changing legislation. The uncertainty can even be greater, however, when the legislature unexpectedly or even impulsively amends its own general laws, which were first adopted in a long and careful process. Besides the element of consistency and stability of legal rules, which has been treated above, the principle of legal certainty in the sense of protecting the legitimate expectations of individuals who are confronted with such unexpected changes is particularly important in relation to ad hoc legislation.

1.3.1. Individuals' expectations

The protection of the legitimate expectations of individuals who are confronted with legislative changes as an element of the principle of legal certainty applies to legislation that is retroactive in the strict sense (in Germany referred to as legislation having *echte Rückwirkung*), which will be discussed below in the context of curative laws in Chapter V.2.1, as well as to legislation applicable to currently existing legal relations and status. Although such legislation is called 'pseudo-retroactive' in Germany (*unechte Rückwirkung*), it does not basically qualify as retroactive in the United States and the Netherlands. The U.S. Supreme Court ruled in this respect: "[a] statute does not operate 'retrospectively' merely because it is applied in a case arising from conduct antedating the statute's enactment […], or upsets expectations based in prior law. Rather, the court must ask whether the new provision attaches new legal consequences to events completed before its enactment."[914] In the Netherlands, the classification "immediate effect"[915] is used as a default rule when laws change.[916] In other words, changing laws are normally immediately applicable to cases which, at the moment of the law's enactment and in the future, meet certain abstract and general conditions.[917] Such immediate effect is not analyzed in terms of retroactivity, although even laws with immediate effect may affect past situations and refer to past facts.[918] It should be noted that much ad hoc legislation belongs in the latter category. The federal Terri Schiavo Act, the Elisabeth Morgan Act, the Northwest Timber Compromise, the BNN Act, and the Regulation on permanent camera surveillance in the case of Volkert van der G., were all enacted (some more hastily than the other ones) in order to be immediately applicable in these specific cases. Elements of retroactivity can be identified in all of these cases, even though the laws in question were not deemed retroactive.

A relevant question in the context of laws having immediate effect is whether the principle of legal certainty enables individuals to oppose immediate changes in law. First and foremost, it should be stressed that, in all three countries, a general and broad right of the legislature to make laws and change policy is recognized. The effect of the principle of legal certainty does not go so far as to frustrate the legislative process. The U.S. Supreme Court is very clear in this respect:[919]

> Even uncontroversially prospective statutes may unsettle expectations and impose burdens on past conduct: a new property tax or zoning regulation may upset the reasonable expectations that prompted those affected to acquire property; a new law banning gambling harms the person who had begun to construct a casino before the law's enactment or spent his life learning to count cards,

and (quoting Fuller): "If every time a man relied on existing law in arranging his affairs, he were made secure any change in legal rules, the whole body of our law would be ossified forever." Although immediate legislative changes are in principle viewed as

914 *Landgraf v. USI Film Products*, 511 U.S. 244, 269–270 (1994). This definition resembles the German definition of real retroactive laws. However, the U.S. Supreme Court admitted that it is not always easy to apply this definition and mechanically decide on the retroactive character of a contested law: "The conclusion that a particular rule operates 'retroactively' comes at the end of a process of judgment concerning the nature and extent of the change in the law and the degree of connection between the operation of the new rule and a relevant past event. Any test of retroactivity will leave room for disagreement in hard cases, and is unlikely to classify the enormous variety of legal changes with perfect philosophical clarity," *Landgraf v. USI Film Products*, 511 U.S. 244, 270 (1994). On the difficulty of the distinction between retrospective and prospective laws, see also Troy (1998), pp. 4ff, who nevertheless distinguishes between retroactive and retrospective laws. In practice, these two terms are used interchangeably.

915 The principle of "immediate effect" is comparable to the German notion of pseudo retroactivity.

916 See Directive 166 of the Directives on Legislation.

917 F.H. van der Burg, "Overgangsrecht," in: J.A. van Schagen (ed.), *Overgangsrecht*, Vereniging voor wetgeving en wetgevingsbeleid, SDU: Den Haag 2001, p. 20. Transitional rules are conceivable as well.

918 Sometimes the term "substantive retroactivity" is used, but it is generally seen as a vague and misleading term. Cf. Pauwels, who nevertheless sees its advantages, Pauwels (2009), pp. 105ff.

919 *Landgraf v. USI Film Products*, 511 U.S. 244, 270 (1994) quoting Fuller (1974), p. 60. See also Weggeman (2001), p. 58.

unproblematic, the German Federal Constitutional Court is willing to uphold individuals' legitimate expectations that the law will not change in exceptional circumstances. It then conducts a balancing of interests test. In the Netherlands, a similar or even stricter[920] assessment of immediately changing legislation can be observed. The strength of the principle of legal certainty became clear when the Dutch Parliament proved able to resist public emotions and refused to act arbitrarily in the specific case of Mrs. Rost van Tonningen. By appealing to the principle of legal certainty, the legislature imposed restrictions on itself and showed that the principles of the rule of law and not public emotions dominate the legislative process.[921] The principle of legal certainty, if reasonably applied, can be seen as an effective tool for the review of ad hoc legislation. Deciding questions are 1) whether those who are negatively affected by new ad hoc law had legitimate expectations that the law would not change and, if so, 2) whether the public interest in changing the law may legitimately frustrate such expectations.

1.3.2. Legal certainty in the United States, Germany, and the Netherlands

It is striking that in the description of constitutional principles that set the boundaries of legislative power in the field of ad hoc legislation in Parts II, III, and IV, the principle of legal certainty as such did not receive any separate treatment in the United States Part (II) of this study. The absence of such a description corresponds to the actual lack of explicit discussion on the principle of legal certainty in the United States in this context. This became even clearer after the research on ad hoc legislation showed that the principle of legal certainty cannot be left out of the consideration in the Netherlands and Germany with regard to legislative changes. How can this difference be explained?

The principle of legal certainty has repeatedly been mentioned as one of the elements of the rule of law. It is generally accepted and effectively applied not only by the European courts, such as the European Court of Justice (ECJ) and the European Court of Human Rights (ECtHR),[922] but also by most European countries. In the Netherlands, it is applied as the concept of *rechtszekerheid*,[923] while in Germany it is called *Rechtssicherheit*. The German Federal Constitutional Court has decided on a regular basis that the principle of legal certainty is part of the notion of the *Rechtstaat* as formulated in Art. 20 of the Basic Law. It is not, however, merely a theoretical concept. If confronted with a claim concerning (a violation of) the principle of legal certainty, the courts will actively consider the law in

920 See the attitude of the Dutch Council of State that requires "compelling grounds of general interest" as a justification for frustrating individuals' legitimate expectations by changing law, *Kamerstukken II* 1981/82, 17 544, A-C, p. 5. In Belgium, for example, the courts have already decided that objective and reasonable justification suffices: "The law maker cannot harm a subject of law in its interest to foresee the legal consequences of its action, unless an objective and reasonable justification exists," P. Popelier, *Legal Certainty and Principles of Proper Law Making*, 2 *Eur. J.L. Reform* 321, 328 (2000) with references.

921 For a detailed description of the case, see Chapter IV.4.1.

922 See also P. Popelier, "The Role of the Belgian Constitutional Court in the Legislative Process," 26 *Statute Law Review* 22 (2005).

923 The most famous judgment, in which the Dutch Supreme Court invoked the principle of legal certainty to express its serious dissatisfaction with the parliamentary legislation frustrating students' legitimate expectation is the *Harmonisatiewetarrest*, HR April 14, 1989, *AB* 1989/207, Chapter IV.4.1.

the context of this principle. The principle of legal certainty is not mentioned in the Netherlands Constitution. It was nevertheless developed under the influence of European law and the case law of the ECJ and the ECtHR. It has also been mentioned as one of the principles of sound legislation, which is applied in the process of drafting legislation by the competent government department as well as by the Dutch Council of State, Legislation Division, in its advisory function.

A famous American creed revealing the American attitude toward the principle of legal certainty is: "We are all realists now."[924] The notion of certainty of law had already largely been abandoned in the United States at the beginning of the twentieth century. The idea that a law can be certain and provide foreseeable results was then criticized for being illusory and naive: "[O]nly ordinary citizens, some jurisprudes, and first year law students have a working conception of law as determinate."[925] Maxeiner also concluded that "[m]any American jurists regard legal certainty as a chimera, an infantile longing, a childhood belief, that one gets over, just as one gets over belief in Santa Claus or the Wizard of Oz."[926] This explains why the principle of legal certainty as such has not been invoked in the context of ad hoc laws. Does this mean that, in the United States, ad hoc laws can never be challenged for unsettling settled expectations or creating instability and inconsistency in the law system? Complaints about frustration of settled expectations are likely to be discussed within the constitutionally guaranteed right of due process and the protection of settled expectations and vested rights, particularly in relation to retroactive legislation.[927] Constitutional claims as to the violation of the Constitution by the instability and inconsistency of a law are most likely to be dismissed in the U.S. courts.

1.4. Proportionality

Nowadays, the principle of proportionality is one of the essential elements of constitutional adjudication and, as Cohen-Eliya and Porat argue, its tremendous influence cannot be overstated.[928] The reason why this principle was dealt with in more detail in the German part of this book has to do with the prominent role it plays in German constitutional law and its significance by spreading to other (European) countries.[929] Moreover, it is often assumed that the German invention and interpretation of this principle served as a model

924 J.R. Maxeiner, "Legal Certainty: A European Alternative to American Legal Indeterminacy?," 15 *Tul. J. Int'l. & Comp. L.* 541, 543 (2007).

925 J.L. Coleman & B. Leiter, "Determinacy, Objectivity, and Authority," 142 *U. Pa. L. Rev.* 549, 549, n. 54 (1993), quoted in: Maxeiner (2007), pp. 543–544.

926 Maxeiner (2007), pp. 543–544 with reference to C.M. Bradley, "The Uncertainty Principle in the Supreme Court," 1986 *Duke L.J.* 1, 63 (1986).

927 See, e.g., *Rivers v. Roadway Express,* 511 U.S. 298 (1994). See also Chapter II.5 on the due process requirement in the United States.

928 M. Cohen-Eliya & I. Porat, "The Hidden Foreign Law Debate in *Heller*: The Proportionality Approach in American Constitutional Law" at <http://ssrn.com/abstract=1317833> (last accessed on June 12, 2011).

929 Grimm (2007), p. 84.

for European Community Law and case law of the European Court of Justice.[930] The method applied by the European Court of Human Rights in deciding on whether any interference with rights protected by the Convention is justified is comparable on certain points to the German approach as well. Through the ECtHR's case law, the principle of proportionality gained ground in Dutch law, most prominently during the assessment of the compatibility of Dutch legislation with the Convention. By contrast, the proportionality principle as such does not belong to established principles of American constitutional law, even though the term "proportionality" has been used in several judgments of the U.S. Supreme Court.[931] Tushnet claims that "the US Supreme Court, which has not adopted any general test of proportionality, is the origin of the phrase 'less restrictive means.'"[932] What then is the proportionality principle about and what relevance does it have to the phenomenon of ad hoc legislation? A detailed description of this principle in Germany was given in Chapter III.5. Only general ideas will be presented here.

First of all, it should be borne in mind that, in constitutional adjudication, the principle of proportionality has a narrower meaning than it normally has in common usage. The Dutch Council of State, for example, also takes the proportionality issue into account within its policy-oriented assessment framework. In examining the effects of proposed legislation, the Council poses the question whether they are disproportional in relation to, for instance, the costs which must be borne by the (administrative) bodies responsible for implementation of the law in question.[933] For the purposes of constitutional law, such a broad interpretation does indeed go too far. In constitutional adjudication, only laws (and State action in general) that *limit fundamental rights and liberties* of individuals are subject to proportionality assessment.[934] Consequently, this principle has a limited effect on ad hoc laws which do not directly limit such rights. The evidence can be given by, for example, the German Lex Naumann (see Chapter III.2.2.1.2), where rules were changed for one person. Even though this "general" change obviously smacked of abuse of legislative power for improper, individual purposes, the facts that the change concerned legislation of general application to future cases as well (Art. 19 [1]GG did not apply) and the law did not directly limit fundamental rights and individual freedoms

930 J.H. Jans, R. de Lange et al, *Europeanisation of Public Law*, Groningen: Europa Law Publishing 2007, p. 144.

931 See, e.g., *City of Boerne v. Flores*, 521 U.S. 507, 508 (1997): "While preventive rules are sometimes appropriate remedial measures, there must be a congruence between the means used and the ends to be achieved. The appropriateness of remedial measures must be considered in light of the evil presented," and *Bartnicki v. Vopper*, 532 U.S. 514, 529 (2001): "[Bu]t it by no means follows that punishing disclosures of lawfully obtained information of public interest by one not involved in the initial illegality is an acceptable means of serving those ends."

932 Tushnet (2006), p. 1252, with reference to *Shelton v. Tucker*, 364 U.S. 479 (1960).

933 On the use of the proportionality principle by the Dutch Council of State in its recommendations on legislative proposals both within the frameworks of policy analysis and legality, see J.L.W. Broeksteeg et al., *Zicht op wetgevingskwaliteit. Een onderzoek naar de wetgevingsadvisering van de Raad van State*, The Hague: WODC 2005, pp. 321ff.

934 On the meaning of the proportionality principle in the context of federalism, see V. C. Jackson, "Ambivalent Resistance and Comparative Constitutionalism: Opening up the Conversation on "Proportionality," Rights and Federalism," 1 *U. Pa. J. Const. L.* 583, 623ff. (1999).

made this irrelevant for the purposes of constitutional law and for the application of the proportionality principle in particular.

The principle of proportionality is about the relationship between the ends sought by the law in question and the means adopted once it has been concluded that this purpose is legitimate. This relationship must be proportional. In most cases, the requirement of "legitimate purpose" will not cause problems, since the courts generally rely on general, public interest purposes as officially presented by the legislature. Other elements, often mentioned in proportionality tests are 1) "the suitability of the means chosen," an element particularly used in the *Bundesverfassungsgericht*'s adjudication, 2) "the availability of less restrictive means," and 3) "strict proportionality." The latter element concerns a "cost-benefit analysis."[935] It is about the balance between the seriousness of the violation and the importance of the law's objective. A fair balance must be struck. "Strict proportionality" strongly depends on the context, the facts, and the law's actual effects on fundamental freedoms, whereas the other elements concern an abstract assessment. All three elements are extremely important for the assessment of ad hoc laws as they are for every regular, general piece of legislation. The first and third elements, however, appear to have additional value in relation to ad hoc legislation.

1.4.1. Suitability of means

Although, to my knowledge, the *Bundesverfassungsgericht* expressly unmasked the true motives of the legislature by applying "the suitability of means test" only once, it revealed the potential of this test for the phenomenon of ad hoc laws. In the case of private transportation agencies (Chapter III.2.3), it decided that the means applied by the German Parliament were unsuitable to achieve the official and as such legitimate public interest. Nevertheless, the means proved suitable to reveal the true purpose, which was controversial and therefore concealed by the legislature.[936] The "suitability of means test" appears to be an objective manner to disclose the true motives of the legislature. Despite the U.S. courts' reluctance to look at the real motives of the legislature,[937] it could also work in the United States:[938] the main, objective question is, after all, not of the legislative

935 Grimm (2007), p. 387.

936 BVerfGE 17, 306.

937 Especially when economic and social welfare legislation is questioned, the U.S. Supreme Court refuses to investigate the true motives of the legislature: "Moreover, because we never require a legislature to articulate its reasons for enacting a statute, it is entirely irrelevant for constitutional purposes whether the conceived reason for the challenged distinction actually motivated the legislature," *FCC v. Beach Communications, Inc.*, 508 U.S. 307, 315 (1993). For the same deference of the U.S. Supreme Court, see *Central State University v. American Association of University Professors*, 526 U.S. 124 (1999). Only in a narrowly limited group of situations, such as certain free speech cases, or cases in which race/gender issues are involved has the U.S. Supreme Court paid attention to the legislative motives. For more on this subject, see Shaman (2001), pp. 144ff. See also Chapter V.2.1.1.2, where attention has also been paid to legislative motives of the legislature.

938 In the framework of the ECHR, the ECtHR does not apply any clear, separate "suitability test." Any relevant considerations on this aspect are rather involved in the concrete fair balance test. See, e.g., ECtHR *Ásmundsson v. Iceland* (Appl. no. 60669/00) ECHR 2004-IX, para. 43, where the ECtHR decided that discontinuing the payment of disability pensions of just a small group of such pensioners was

intention, but of the suitability of means. The "suitability of means test" interestingly shows how laws which cannot achieve their purpose (efficiency aspect) can be in conflict with constitutional law (lawfulness aspect).[939]

1.4.2. Fair balance

The question in respect of the third element is whether the violation or burden imposed by the law is excessive in relation to the end which the law is meant to serve. In other words, there must be a fair balance between the ends pursued and the means chosen. This element is extremely important in the constitutional adjudication of the German Federal Constitutional Court and the European Court of Human Rights, where contested laws suffer most from this strict proportionality assessment. Likewise, in the United States, the concerns about the excessiveness of state action (including the legislature's) in relation to the purpose sought can be perceived in areas of equal protection, due process, and free speech.[940] But, as Jackson illustrates with free speech cases, the U.S. Supreme Court relies on its precedent and formal distinctions in determining proportionality rather than on contextual analysis and balancing. Nevertheless and notwithstanding the arguments in favor of the U.S. Supreme Court's approach to the stability and legitimacy of judicial review, in my opinion, a meaningful review of ad hoc laws can benefit only from effective consideration of all relevant facts, factors, and circumstances, which is allowed within the fair balance test.

One of the elements that could save a challenged law within the proportionality test is compensation offered by the legislature. With regard to ad hoc laws, particularly infrastructural project laws that diminish individuals' rights to administrative and judicial review, the question whether individuals had sufficient opportunity to respond to the plans during the legislative procedure will then be especially important. It is also conceivable that the case-specific character of the legislation in question plays an important part. The case-specific application of laws may indicate their excessiveness, whereas laws that restrict individuals' rights and are limited to only one specific event may be assessed positively. If a law seriously restricts fundamental rights, it should be "narrowly tailored," to use American terminology. Accordingly, the Dutch government should not have yielded to public opinion and the criticism from some political parties in Parliament who asserted that abuse of legislative power would have been involved if the proposed legislation had applied only to the European Football Championship in 2000 (Chapter IV.2.2.2). On the other hand, it could plausibly be argued that it was exactly such specific application that was in line with the requirements of the proportionality principle.

unlikely to solve the (in itself legitimate) purpose of resolving the financial difficulties of the Pension Fund.

939 In this context, De Lange concluded that the criteria of lawfulness can, in some cases, require maximal efficiency, R. de Lange, *Publiekrechtelijke rechtsvinding*, Zwolle: W.E.J. Tjeenk Willink 1991, p. 181.

940 See Chapters II.4 and II.5. See also Jackson (1999), p. 609 and V.C. Jackson, "Being Proportional about Proportionality," 21 *Const. Comment.* 803 (2004) for an excellent analysis and response to Beatty's ideas on the universality of the principle of proportionality.

1.5. Transparency in lawmaking

The concept of transparency appears to be useful in many different areas, for example public disclosure in financial institutions, contract law, and government rulemaking. More specifically, in the field of lawmaking, transparency can require that 1) parliamentary debates are public, 2) the activities of special and public interest groups are registered and made public, 3) laws are published, and 4) legislative texts are clear and definite.[941] Within the context of ad hoc legislation, however, the principle of transparency would be most meaningful in the context of two problems other than those just roughly sketched.

1.5.1. Transparency of legislative choices

First, a lack of transparency occurs when the legislature does not make known in advance which public interests it considered and weighed against each other in deciding on the adoption of ad hoc legislation. It could be argued that transparency in this sense is appropriate for lawmaking of any kind, whether it concerns ad hoc legislation or not. In general, this is true. But it seems justified to treat ad hoc legislation with increased scrutiny. Transparency of the legislature's choice with regard to ad hoc legislation appears to be even more important. As the criticism shows, this has to do with possible conflicts with or even violation of various constitutional principles, including the separation of powers and equal treatment. It can hardly be denied that by making the process of lawmaking transparent, the legislature would enhance the quality of the legislation and make it easier for the courts to discover its line of reasoning. The question here is whether transparency in this sense has more far-reaching significance in constitutional law. Is transparency of legislative choices an autonomous constitutional principle able to limit the legislature when it enacts ad hoc laws?

In view of the national Constitutions of the United States, Germany, and the Netherlands, the answer to this question is simply no. None of these documents[942] expressly requires the legislature to explain why and how it decided to adopt (ad hoc) laws.[943] Constitutional courts are also basically hesitant to put such an obligation on the

941 For a discussion of the transparency principle as a concept of an open government and its positive and negative consequences, see, for example, M. Fenster, "The Opacity of Transparency," 91 *Iowa L. Rev.* 885 (2006).

942 The U.S. Constitution is a doubtful case in this respect. Art. I, Sec. 5 provides that "[e]ach House shall keep a journal of its proceedings, and from time to time publish the same, excepting such parts as may in their judgment require secrecy; and the yeas and nays of the members of either House on any question shall, at the desire of one fifth of those present, be entered on the journal." On the one hand, it could be argued that Sec. 5 entails a kind of transparency principle. On the other hand, Sec. 5 only prescribes that what has been said during the parliamentary debates be written down and made public, not more than that. See also Art. XIX of the Dutch Constitution formally prescribing what a preamble to a statute must contain. One of the elements requires reasons for the enactment. In practice, this is just a formal prescription.

943 See, however, other procedural requirements of transparency in the German Basic Law. They address various aspects of parliamentary publicity, the publicity of parliamentary debates being the most explicit (Art. 42 (1) GG). See J. Bröhmer, *Transparenz als Verfassungsprinzip. Grundgesetz und*

legislature. It is highly unlikely that they will ever strike down a statute only because the legislature did not explicitly underpin its choices in advance.[944]

Despite the fact that the national Constitutions of the United States, Germany, and the Netherlands do not oblige the legislature to be transparent in the sense referred to above, arguments have been raised in the literature in favor of a transparency principle in the form of a constitutional principle of an *obligation to provide grounds*. This is especially true for Germany and the Netherlands, where attempts have been made to rationalize the lawmaking process and the discussion of the quality of legislation has intensified over the years. Academics have argued that such an obligation (*motiveringsplicht* in the Netherlands and *Begründungspflicht* in Germany[945]) exists as an unwritten constitutional principle of sound legislation, even though it is as such judicially unenforceable.[946] Besides the academic defense of such a principle, in the Netherlands, several provisions of the Directives on Legislation refer to such an obligation. Although they are not legally binding, government officials normally follow them when drafting bills and the Council of States indirectly involves them in its recommendations on legislative proposals.[947] These Directives require legislative proposals to be accompanied by an explanation indicating why State intervention is necessary, whether the problem can be dealt with through the already existing instruments (in this case, the general rules), and whether all interests involved have been weighed against each other, etc.[948] In the context of ad hoc legislation, Directive 49 is the most relevant and explicit. It emphasizes that departure from the general rules by means of a *lex specialis* is only allowed if necessary. In addition, such a departure must be explicitly underpinned in an explanatory memorandum to a new bill. The Dutch Council of State, which advises on legislative proposals, also requires the government to provide solid substantiation of the

Europäische Union, Tübingen: Mohr Siebeck 2004, pp. 97ff. See also the Dutch Publication Act (*Bekendmakingswet*), *Stb.* 1988, 18.

944 The German Federal Constitutional Court, for example, is even hesitant to effectively apply those provisions of the Basic Law which explicitly require transparency in the legislative process (see previous note). As Eckert concludes, the *Bundesverfassungsgericht* will strike down a statute on the basis that it violates constitutional provisions of a procedural nature only when the law in question would otherwise not be enacted [BVerfGE 44, 308 (313)]. Eckert therefore has little trust in effective judicial control and suggests that the people who democratically choose the legislature are in a better position to enforce the transparency requirement: "Die gerichtliche Kontrolle der Gesetzgebung stellt deshalb kein wirksames Instrument zur Garantie des Transparenzgebot dar," and "Verstöße gegen das Transparenzgebot durch die politische Staatsleitung sollten in der Demokratie Meinungskampfes gerügt werden," Ch. Eckert, Transparenz im Gesetzgebungsprozess. Das Prinzip der Öffentlichkeit staatslenkender Entscheidungen zwischen Anspruch der Rechtsordnung und Realität, Hamburg: Verlag Dr. Kova 2004, pp. 308–309, with references.

945 See Brandner (2004), pp. 351ff. and Meßerschmidt (2000), pp. 920ff., both with references.

946 In the Netherlands, the obligation to provide grounds for legislative choices has also been interpreted as a supplement to the constitutional provisions regulating the procedure of lawmaking in Articles 81 et seq. For a compilation of the views on this obligation in the Dutch literature, see K. Waaldijk, *Motiveringsplichten van de wetgever*, Lelystad: Vermande 1994, pp. 281ff., who is an ardent advocate of such a principle.

947 See Broeksteeg et al. (2005).

948 Directives 6 to 18, 47 to 49 and 212. These requirements can also be found in Stoter's model for the assessment of the weighing of interests by the legislature, W.S.R. Stoter, *Belangenafweging door de wetgever*, The Hague: Boom Juridische uitgevers 2000, Chapter 6.

necessity of a new statute. This is a strict requirement, particularly when the proposed bill adversely affects rights, liberties, or interests. This is often the case, for example with regard to retroactive legislation.[949]

I believe that, although it is not a judicially enforceable constitutional principle, an obligation to provide grounds is highly important. It not only enhances the quality of legislation and helps the judiciary to understand the legislature better,[950] as stated above, but it also reduces the chances of the legislature for acting arbitrarily. This is particularly important in the case of ad hoc laws, given the dangers they create, and is even truer for countries such as the Netherlands, where the courts are not allowed to review the constitutionality of parliamentary legislation. The obligation to provide grounds means that the legislature must explain what exceptional reasons justify the enactment of ad hoc laws. A more pragmatic perspective, however, prompts the inevitable question as to the actual significance and enforceability of such an obligation. Being aware of the controversy surrounding ad hoc laws (which is clearly evident from the descriptions in Chapters II.1, III.1, and IV.1 of ad hoc laws and the criticism they received), the legislature would be likely to prepare a deceptive explanation,[951] ostensibly based on relevant and neutral grounds, just to avoid criticism.[952] If the legislature is unwilling to provide the true reasons, the obligation to give reasons unfortunately loses its meaning (Chapter V.1.1.2).

1.5.2. Transparency as a limitation on legislative riders

The principle of transparency applies to another aspect of ad hoc laws as well. It concerns the practice of legislative riders in the United States, which make it easier to adopt ad hoc laws than in the Netherlands and Germany. The examples of high-profile ad hoc laws at the federal level as given primarily in Chapter II.1 illustrate that the possibility of attaching a small rider to an omnibus spending bill became an attractive tool for legislators to ensure the passage of ad hoc laws. Of the three examples of highly controversial ad hoc laws discussed in detail above, two were passed as riders. Besides the criticism addressing the policy and quality of legislation aspects, legislative riders were

949 See Chapter IV.4.2.

950 Other advantages mentioned in the literature concern the limitation of the courts' and administrative bodies' freedom to reconstruct the law's purpose and the explanation's ability to convince the political opponents of the bill; see R.M. van Male, "Geen wetgeving zonder motivering," in: *Recht doen door wetgeving*, Zwolle: W.E.J. Tjeenk Willink 1990, pp. 282ff.

951 Unlike with respect to beneficial or harmful ad hoc laws for specific individuals, the legislature is expected to have less trouble in explaining the necessity of ad hoc infrastructural project laws.

952 On a similar note, Waaldijk: "Law-making is only one tool for a legislature to exert political power. Giving reasons for the law-making can be used as a separate tool for influencing citizens, judges, etcetera. Therefore, legislatures may be tempted to put forward other than their actual reasons, or at least to tailor their reasoning to other political aims than supporting the enactment concerned." Other difficulties regarding the obligation to give reasons which he mentions include "the collective, political, unlimited, clustered, and continuous character of legislative decisions," K. Waaldijk, "Can we Require Legislatures to State the Reasons for their Legislative Decisions?," in: F. van Eemeren et al. (eds.), *Argumentation: Analysis and Practices. Proceedings of the Conference on Argumentation 1986*, Dordrecht: Foris Publications Holland 1986, p. 113.

often considered to contradict the principle of transparency. This is shown by the fact that they can be effectively hidden in an omnibus spending bill. Consequently, they are hardly ever exposed to an open and extensive Congressional debate. This is vital, since legislative riders not only bestow privileges, but may also negatively affect civil rights and liberties, as illustrated by the Elisabeth Morgan Act. In an attempt to avoid too much repetition (for a detailed description see Chapter II.6), I will confine myself to the observation that the transparency principle in the context of legislative riders is seen as a principle of democratic government rather than as an element of constitutional law. Legislative riders particularly jeopardize the ideal of deliberative democracy, but this ideal cannot be enforced through constitutional law: "The Constitution does not and cannot guarantee that legislators will carefully scrutinize legislation and deliberate before acting. In a democracy it is the electorate that holds the legislators accountable for the wisdom of their choices."[953] Constitutional review thus does not offer many options. It is the people who enforce transparency through democratic election. In addition, a stricter enforcement of the internal rules of Congress, which formally do limit the possibility of attaching legislative riders to the appropriations bills, would help to combat this excessive backdoor practice.[954]

953 In the words of Justice White, dissenting, in *INS v. Chadha*, 462 U.S. 919, 997 (1983).

954 See Chapter II.6.1. The significant rules are House Rule XXI(2) and Rule XVI (4) of the Standing Rules of the Senate which can both be found at <www.gpoaccess.gov/hrm/index.html>.

Chapter 2

CONSTITUTIONAL LIMITATIONS AND TYPOLOGY OF AD HOC LEGISLATION

Introduction

The constitutional principles of sound legislation as described in the previous chapter appear to apply to ad hoc laws regardless of their function. Apart from that, as follows from the study on constitutional law in the context in the United States, Germany, and the Netherlands, other constitutional principles apply more prominently to one type of ad hoc legislation than to another. The focus is then on the function of ad hoc laws rather than on their case-specific nature or the way they were enacted. It can be concluded, for example, that the principle of legal certainty and presumption of non-retroactivity is most jeopardized by ad hoc laws the function of which is to cure legislative errors. Ad hoc laws that interfere with pending proceedings are most problematic from the viewpoint of the separation of powers and fair trial. This relationship will be demonstrated below. The extent to which these constitutional principles can exercise restraint on the legislature will be shown on the basis of doctrine and case law on curative legislation (Chapter V.2.1), interfering legislation (Chapter V.2.2), overruling legislation (Chapter V.2.3), and accelerating legislation (Chapter V.2.4). It is important to note, however, that this distinction between the different functions ad hoc laws can fulfill will not always be strict. It is conceivable that some of them fulfill two or more functions simultaneously, which means that they can be placed in a number of categories.

2.1. Curative legislation: Legal certainty and the presumption against retroactivity

Responding to the criticism directed at the ad hoc character of legislation, including the fact that the legislature's only reason to change the law was to affect the outcome of one specific case,[955] the State, by way of the legislature, regularly argued that the legislation was curative. In other words, the argument was that the outcome of a specific case made the legislature realize that the general legislation as applied in that case contained errors that needed to be corrected or deficiencies that had to be remedied.[956] This argument was

955 Even though the law was written in general terms, which is usually the case.

956 Cf. curative legislation that validates administrative decisions, Popelier (1994), pp. 77ff.

put forward most explicitly in the case of Ferdinand Schörner. By (clearly) retroactively changing a disciplinary statute by the so-called Lex Schörner, the German Parliament ensured that Schörner lost his pension rights, which was exactly the wish of the general public. In the proceedings before the Federal Constitutional Court, the state justified the amendment, and its retroactive character in particular, by stating that its only purpose was to cure legislative errors in general disciplinary legislation.[957]

Since curative laws in this sense basically operate retroactively, which means that they attach legal consequences to facts and events that happened and were closed before the law's enactment, they may jeopardize the principle of legal certainty, including the general presumption against the retroactivity of laws. Although, in the United States, unlike in the Netherlands and Germany, the principle of legal certainty is not directly invoked in this context, a general presumption against the retroactivity of laws does exist there as well.[958] The U.S. Supreme Court has repeatedly acknowledged:[959]

> [T]he presumption against retroactive legislation is deeply rooted in our jurisprudence, and embodies a legal doctrine centuries older than our Republic. Elementary considerations of fairness dictate that individuals should have an opportunity to know what the law is and to conform their conduct accordingly; settled expectations should not be lightly disrupted.

In the Netherlands, not only the courts, but also the Council of State, Legislation Division, strongly emphasizes that laws must operate prospectively, unless there are exceptional and compelling grounds that justify retroactivity. In Germany, a similar approach can be found in the case law of the Federal Constitutional Court. This Court has adopted an even more fundamental position by prohibiting retroactive laws in principle unless, again, they can be justified by special reasons.[960]

Interestingly, there are few differences in the way retroactive curative laws are treated in the United States, Germany, and the Netherlands. It can be concluded that such laws will be upheld in most cases, because they represent a compelling general interest (or a "legitimate interest" as required in the due process analysis of curative laws in the United States). This interest can be found in the legislature's will to remove unintended flaws and to clarify the meaning of a statute, giving full effect to the original intention of the legislature. In such situations, individuals have little chance to effectively oppose the retroactivity, especially if it is clear that they attempted to take advantage of statutory errors, while they could reasonably expect that the legislature would seek to correct them.[961] Although it could be argued that curative laws shift the legislature's responsibility to adopt correct legislation onto citizens, there is a case for accepting such laws, unless they have particularly unfair effects on individuals.

957 See Chapter III.1.1.2.2.

958 On the adoption of this principle in American law, see Troy (1998), pp. 27ff.

959 *Landgraf v. USI Film Products*, 511 U.S. 244, 264 (1994) with references.

960 The term "retroactive legislation" is used here in the meaning of *echte rückwirkung* in the *Bundesverfassungsgericht's* classification (Chapter III.4.1).

961 See also a clear statement by the European Court of Human Rights in the *Building Societies* case as described in Chapter IV.5.2.2.

Curative laws should be narrowly defined. In the words of the German Federal Constitutional Court, only laws that correct legislative errors *and* are in harmony with the entire system of the law can be classified as curative laws in the pure meaning. Laws that are ostensibly meant to repair flaws in existing laws, but in fact create a completely new, alien rule, cannot be viewed as constitutionally unproblematic curative laws.[962] Moreover, only gaps that can be objectively identified can be retroactively repaired by the legislature without violating the presumption against the retroactivity of laws.[963]

Although these guidelines seem to be a useful tool to decide which ad hoc laws are permissible, their effectiveness strongly depends on the manner in which they are applied. As regards the legality of ad hoc laws which the legislature presents as curative laws, the decisive factor will be whether the contested ad hoc law is truly curative. Again, ad hoc laws that only purport to cure legislative errors, but actually enact new retroactive rules for one specific case, should be subject to a more severe review. The only problem is that this distinction will not always be easy to make. The case of Lex Schörner illustrates this strikingly.

2.2. Interfering legislation: Separation of powers and fair trial

Within the general group of ad hoc laws, a clear category of interfering ad hoc laws can be distinguished. Their function is to interfere with judicial proceedings, pending cases to, as the argument often goes, secure a certain politically attractive and desired outcome. Research in the United States, Germany, and the Netherlands on this point shows that this category of laws occurs most often in the United States. One of the American cases of high political moment concerns legislative interference with the pending environmental cases of the Audubon Societies.[964] In Germany, Parliament once interfered in the criminal proceedings in the so-called Platow Affair,[965] but it in fact realized itself how bizarre this move was. In the Netherlands, to my knowledge, Parliament has not yet interfered in specific pending cases.

The legal doctrine on the limits of the legislative power in this specific area is best developed in the United States. It is essentially based on the distinction between "legislative changes of general rules" (a permissible exercise of the legislative power) and "a legislative direction of a rule of decision" (constitutionally prohibited action of the legislature)[966] within the framework of the constitutional principle of the separation of powers. In Germany, the doctrine concentrating on the independent judiciary (as an element of the separation of powers principle) in the context of legislation interfering with pending cases occupies a humble place. In the Netherlands, however, there is no clear case law or doctrine as a consequence of Art. 120 of the Dutch Constitution which prohibits the constitutional review of legislation by courts and the fact that interfering

962 BVerfGE 7, 129 (151).
963 BVerfGE 13, 261 (273).
964 The Northwest Timber Compromise affair, treated in detail in Chapter II.1.3.
965 Chapter III.6.2.
966 See *United States v. Klein*, 80 U.S. (13 Wall) 128 (1871) and *Pennsylvania v. Wheeling & Belmont Bridge Co.*, 59 U.S. 421 (1855).

legislation is highly unusual. Meaningful guidelines for the assessment of such a type of ad hoc legislation in the future can be found in the case law of the ECtHR. In the past, this Court was confronted with individual claims from various jurisdictions, including such countries as Greece (*Stran Greek Refineries*), the United Kingdom (*Building Societies*), and France (*Zielinski*). These three cases were discussed in Chapter IV.5. Here it suffices to recall that they led to the development of the doctrine on the limits of a legislature interfering in either specific, identified cases (*Stran Greek Refineries*) or a class of pending cases (*Zielinski, Building Societies*). At its heart is the following formula:[967]

> The principle of the rule of law and the notion of fair trial enshrined in Article 6 preclude any interference by the legislature – *other than on compelling grounds of the general interest* – with the administration of justice designed to influence the judicial determination of a dispute.

For the purposes of comparison and analysis, the positions of the U.S. Supreme Court and the ECtHR will be discussed. Both Courts have developed a test to assess legislative interference in pending cases from the perspective of the rule of law. But the method used and thus the severity of the approaches in Europe and in the United States differ significantly.

2.2.1. *Rule of law: Separation of powers vs. fundamental right to a fair trial*

Both Courts assess legislative interference in pending cases in light of the rule of law, but they use different elements of the rule of law. While the Supreme Court analyzes legislative intervention in pending cases from the perspective of the separation of powers principle, the central question in the ECtHR's analysis is whether the State violated the claimant's fundamental right to a fair trial, including the right of access to a court and equality of arms under Art. 6 of the ECHR. The ECtHR's position is determined by the ECtHR's mandate, which is to review the contracting states' actions in light of the fundamental rights enshrined in the Convention. By contrast, the U.S. Supreme Court concentrates on the strict separation between the legislative and the judicial powers. It appears that this Court is convinced that the true purpose of the separation of powers principle can only be achieved by a strict separation between these two powers, which is characteristic of the formalist approach. Even if this is the case, the Supreme Court's reluctance to take the principle of the generality of laws and all relevant facts accompanying the enactment of the challenged statute into account appears to impede the full achievement of the separation of powers, let alone in its strictest meaning. In other words, the Supreme Court takes strict separation as a point of departure, but it in fact gives the legislature much freedom to interfere in pending proceedings without violating the separation of powers principle. Strict separation then becomes illusory.

967 *Zielinski* case, par. 57, emphasis added.

2.2.2. The purpose of the separation of powers principle

In the previous section, I stated that the U.S. Supreme Court appears not to be able to achieve the full meaning of the separation of powers principle. What then is the purpose of the separation of powers the U.S. Supreme Court ought to consider? In the United States, the foundations of this constitutional principle can already be found in the Federalist Papers.[968] The Federalists were inspired by Montesquieu's body of thought. The purposes of the separation of powers principle have regularly been examined in the academic literature. Gerangelos mentions: "The maintenance of the rule of law and its progeny, an independent judiciary, and the maintenance of public confidence in the courts and the accountability of the non-judicial branches to the constitution." He elaborates further: "This means that the judiciary must be protected from legislative and executive pressure or interference; protected to decide cases and declare the law independently, of the interests of faction and government, and in order to maintain its independence generally so as to contribute to public confidence in the administration of justice."[969] It should not be forgotten, however, that judicial independence in turn serves a higher purpose and that there is more than just public confidence involved. The prevention of the *arbitrary* exercise of State power (legislative power in this case) and consequently the protection of *civil liberties* are ultimately the reasons for the separation of powers.[970] One may doubt whether these objectives can be achieved if the courts refuse to consider the obvious facts and circumstances in which the legislature decided to intervene in pending cases.

2.2.3. Factual vs. fictitious approach

A striking difference between the ECtHR's and the U.S. Supreme Court's attitudes towards interfering legislation is the very factual assessment by the ECtHR as opposed to the Supreme Court's fictitious assessment.[971] The ECtHR sees its role as providing *effective* protection of fundamental rights against the State's arbitrary actions toward individuals. The Court has repeatedly ruled that "the convention [ECHR] is intended to guarantee not rights that are theoretical or illusory but rights that are practical and effective."[972] To be able to provide effective protection, the ECtHR devotes a great deal of attention to the facts of the case and the circumstances in which the interfering legislation was adopted. For this purpose, the ECtHR has developed a procedural test – focusing on the *timing*, *manner*, and *effect* of the law's adoption – to decide whether the actual legislative intent was to influence the outcome of pending proceedings in such a way as to benefit the State.

968 See particularly Papers 47, 48, and 51 (Madison).

969 Gerangelos (2009), pp. 36–37.

970 In fact, the U.S. Supreme Court arrived at this conclusion itself; see *Mistretta v. United States*, 488 U.S. 361, 380 (1989).

971 The following two sections were first published in Jasiak (2010).

972 *Multiplex v. Croatia* (Appl. no. 58112/00) ECHR 10 July 2003, para. 44.

This factual approach is not at the forefront of the U.S. Supreme Court's decisions regarding legislative intervention in pending cases. *Robertson v. Seattle Audubon Society* is a case in point. The Supreme Court based its judgment on a vague distinction between "changing the general rules" and "directing a rule of decision."[973] Using this test, the Court allows the legislature quite a bit of latitude in taking the law into its own hands. In its review of interfering legislation, the Supreme Court does not investigate the real reasons for the adoption of a law, nor whether the courts, not only in theory but also in practice, could have decided the case themselves, i.e., within their discretionary powers and without being directed by the legislature. This question was not raised by the Supreme Court in the *Robertson v. Seattle Audubon Society* case. The Court did not consider the fact that the law had been enacted and initiated by the Congressmen from Oregon and Washington who had been approached by the timber industry from these two states when the proceedings were pending. Moreover, the Court found nothing suspicious in the fact that the law mentioned the cases by name and caption number, despite the fact that it was obvious that the law had been drafted to ensure that these two cases would be decided in favor of the State and thus indirectly in favor of the timber industry.

2.2.4. The importance of the generality of laws

It appears that the principle of the generality of laws can have an important role in the Supreme Court's review of interfering legislation. It can be argued that, in answering the question whether the interfering legislation constituted a general change rather than a specific instruction directing a rule of decision, the Supreme Court should take its specificity or generality into account. The essential factor should then be whether the law applies to an open group of cases and therefore constitutes a general change of law, or to a limited and specifically identifiable number of cases, and therefore de facto prescribes a rule of decision. This approach, however, requires a method in which facts play a central part. In Germany, the same approach was followed in the assessment of legislative interference in pending cases. In both the literature and case law of the Federal Constitutional Court, it has been contended that judicial independence is jeopardized in any event if the law is directed at a specific case.[974]

Unlike the Supreme Court, the ECtHR does sometimes stress the nature of interfering legislation in its analysis. In doing so, the ECtHR distinguishes two types of generality: generality in the sense of the general interest served by the legislation and generality in the sense of the addressees of the law. Although the Court has clearly stated that laws intended to influence the outcome of one specific case as well as general laws can violate the right to a fair trial, it appears that the ECtHR treats laws that affect single cases even more stringently. As evidenced by *Stran Greek Refineries*, the case-specific character of legislation can be a compelling reason for the Court to find a violation of Art. 6 ECHR. Conversely, the Court may be of the opinion that the general nature of the contested law

973 See P. Gerangelos, "The Separation of Powers and Legislative Interference in Pending Cases," 30 *Sydney Law Review* 61, 89ff (2008), who proposes a more precise interpretation of that criterion in the U.S. and Australia.

974 See Chapter III.6.2.

can indicate that the law served a compelling general interest, and is therefore justified (*Forrer-Niedenthal*). It is, however, fair to question whether a law's specificity automatically leads to the conclusion that it was not enacted in the general interest. The conclusion that, when a law is general, it must have been enacted in the general interest does not always hold true, either. Despite these inconsistencies, the ECtHR's characteristically practical approach to legislation designed to influence the outcome of pending proceedings can in general be applauded, because it seems to protect individual rights more effectively. Perhaps the U.S. Supreme Court will one day come to appreciate the merits and potential of this approach.

2.2.5. *Concluding remarks*

The permissibility of legislation interfering in pending cases can best be assessed against the background of circumstances that accompanied its enactment. The effective assessment method appears to be the factual one, as employed by the ECtHR. The core of the ECtHR's assessment is the following: the more suspicious the circumstances and the more doubts there are as to the legislature's reasons to enact the law, the greater the risk that the individual right to a fair trial has been violated. True ad hoc laws which are tailored for one specific case must be treated with great caution. In contrast to general legislation that interferes with a general class of cases, case-specific laws are less likely to be justified by compelling grounds of the general interest, because of the risk of legislative arbitrariness.[975]

Besides the right to a fair trial, the separation of powers as applied by the U.S. Courts in the pending case scenario can also be seen as a limitation on the legislative branch in this respect. One could, however, argue that it can only serve its higher purpose and protect its values if applied effectively or rigorously.[976] This means that, in answering the question whether the legislature gave the court a rule of decision, the courts will have to examine the nature of the contested law. If it is case-specific, it seems reasonable to conclude that it therefore gives the court a rule of decision.

2.3. Overruling legislation: Separation of powers, fair trial, and retroactivity

Closely related to the category of ad hoc legislation interfering with pending cases is legislation that has the function of overruling judicial decisions. In general, the legislature may use various methods to set aside a judicial decision. The proper way for the legislature

975 Cf. my earlier comments on the case-specific character of legislation within the framework of the proportionality principle, Chapter V.2.1.4.

976 On a similar note, see Gerangelos (2009), p. 189: "The maintenance of a strong direction principle therefore ensures, in part, the continuing efficacy of the separation of powers as an entrenched constitutional rule, but also the other fundamental pillars of the liberal democratic polity, representative government. On the one hand, it insists that an amendment to the law be applied by the courts. […] On the other hand, the direction principle will not permit an interference with the decisional independence of the judicial branch if it is in fact a direction under the guise of legislation. Applied in this way, an entrenched separation of powers can provide a surer protection to branch integrity than it might if it remained as a convention, albeit one with significant normative influence."

to show its dissatisfaction with judicial decisions is to overrule them for future cases, leaving the cases already decided untouched. This would be the case if a court interprets the law in a manner which is politically controversial and thwarts the legislative policy, as a result of which the legislature decides to act. This type of overruling legislation, the general nature and prospective effect of which can hardly be disputed, can be considered to be a healthy, democratic check of the legislative branch of government on the judiciary. It can be justly defended as a form of dialog and mutual control.

The situation is different, however, if the legislature deliberately modifies the outcomes of specific definitively adjudicated cases. This was clearly what the Dutch Parliament (or in fact the government who proposed the bill) did in the case of the dredging operations in the Western Scheldt (River). Similarly, the U.S. Congress intervened in the Terri Schiavo case by creating a new court procedure and legislatively instructing the federal judges to ignore the final decision of the Florida Supreme Court. If it wants to overrule final court decisions, the legislature has at least three different operating procedures at its disposal. The legislature may 1) direct the reopening of the case, 2) retroactively change the law underlying finally decided cases, thereby reviewing these decisions, or 3) block the effectuation of a specific judicial decision by changing its underlying laws with immediate effect.

2.3.1. *Reopening a case*

Situations in which the legislature orders courts to open specific finally decided cases are highly unusual. If the legislature decides to take this course of action, it will most likely direct the reopening of a neutrally defined class of cases of a certain type rather than specific cases. For the purposes of this comparative analysis, it is again useful to examine the approaches of the U.S. Supreme Court and the European Court of Human Rights, as these courts have developed clear views on situations of this nature. In doing so, they used the principle of the separation of powers and the Art. 6 ECHR right to a fair trial (including equality of arms), respectively, as a review framework.

It can be observed that the U.S. Supreme Court's manner of applying this principle to situations of reopening finally decided cases is characterized by the same rigorous point of departure as that applied to legislative interference in pending cases. This time, however, the Court practices what it preaches.[977] The Court indeed adopts a strict separation of powers, irrespective of the consequences such strict application has for the individual rights of those whose cases are to be reopened. This is illustrated by the *Plaut* decision. In that case, the Court invalidated a piece of legislation which directed the courts to reopen finally decided cases, even though the challenged law was evidently advantageous to individuals. The Supreme Court decided that Congress had violated the principle of the separation of powers "to the extent that it required federal courts to

[977] The Court departs from the same strict separation of powers approach in the context of legislative interference with pending cases. It appears, however, that the separation of powers can indeed be called strict only when the Court decides on the violation of the separation of powers by legislation that reopens finally decided cases. As regards legislative interference in pending cases, the strict separation is less strict in practice than it was intended to be; see Chapter V.2.2.1.

reopen final judgments entered before its enactment." Justice Scalia, writing for the Court, explained the working of this principle in the following way:[978]

> Ultimately, the concurrence agrees with our judgment only "[b]ecause the law before us embodies risks of the very sort that our Constitution's 'separation of powers' prohibition seeks to avoid." But the doctrine of separation of powers is a *structural safeguard* rather than a remedy to be applied only when specific harm, or risk of specific harm, can be identified. In its major features (of which the conclusiveness of judicial judgments is assuredly one) it is a prophylactic device, establishing high walls and clear distinctions because low walls and vague distinctions will not be judicially defensible in the heat of interbranch conflict. [...] The delphic alternative suggested by the concurrence (the setting aside of judgments is all right so long as Congress does not "impermissibly tr[y] to *apply,* as well as *make,* the law,") simply prolongs doubt and multiplies confrontation. Separation of powers, a distinctively American political doctrine, profits from the advice authored by a distinctively American poet: Good fences make good neighbors.

This radical approach can be best elucidated by the American history of the seventeenth and eighteenth centuries, when it was common practice in the English colonies that colonial legislative assemblies reviewed judicial determinations in specific cases by special bills.[979] It was this practice that motivated the Framers of the U.S. Constitution to formulate Art. III on the separation of government powers. In reaching its decision in *Plaut*, Scalia reasoned from these events and the Framers' stringent position on this legislative practice:[980]

> It is not true [...] that the parliament of Great Britain, or the legislatures of the particular States, can rectify the exceptionable decisions of their respective courts, in any other sense than might be done by a future legislature of the United States. The theory, neither of the British, nor the State constitutions, authorizes the revisal of a judicial sentence by a legislative act [...]. A legislature, without exceeding its province, cannot reverse a determination once made in a particular case; though it may prescribe a new rule for future cases.

It is important to emphasize that it is reopening by the *legislature* which is absolutely forbidden. By contrast, U.S. federal law allows the *courts* to reopen cases when compelling grounds require them to do so. Deciding on the reopening of final cases by the judiciary is therefore viewed in principle as constitutionally unproblematic.[981] Likewise, the

978 *Plaut v. Spendthrift Farm, Inc.*, 514 U.S. 211, 239 (1995), internal references omitted. See also Chapter II.3.4.1.

979 *Plaut v. Spendthrift Farm, Inc.*, 514 U.S. 211, 219ff. (1995) with references. The State Constitutions therefore introduced prohibition on special and local laws as stated in Chapter II.2.3.1.

980 The Federalist No. 81, p. 483, in: C. Rossiter (ed.), *The Federalist Papers*, New York: A Signet Classic 2003.

981 See Rules 59–61 of Federal Rules of Civil Procedure, version of December 1, 2009, at <www.uscourts.gov/uscourts/RulesAndPolicies/rules/CV2009.pdf> (last accessed on June 12, 2011). Rule 60, for example, reads:
(b) GROUNDS FOR RELIEF FROM A FINAL JUDGMENT, ORDER, OR

ECtHR allows the reopening of finally decided cases in the context of Art. 6 ECHR only when compelling grounds of general interest allow this. In this context, the ECtHR is not interested in the relations between the government branches, which is clearly the focus of the American doctrine, but the Court's point of departure is the protection of individuals' human rights:[982]

> Legal certainty presupposes respect for the principle of *res judicata* [..], that is the principle of the finality of judgments. This principle underlines that no party is entitled to seek a review of a final and binding judgment merely for the purpose of obtaining a rehearing and a fresh determination of the case. Higher courts' power of review should be exercised to correct judicial errors and miscarriages of justice, but not to carry out a fresh examination. The review should not be treated as an appeal in disguise, and the mere possibility of there being two views on the subject is not a ground for re-examination. A departure from that principle is justified only when made necessary by circumstances of a substantial and compelling character.

It should be borne in mind that neither Court pays extraordinary attention to the specific character of legislation. The U.S. Supreme Court in fact decided that it does not matter whether the challenged law is general or case-specific. It appears that the severity with which these Courts, and the U.S. Supreme Court in particular, approach the reopening of finally decided cases place an additional focus on case-specificity otiose.

2.3.2. *Retroactive review*

A slightly different situation is presented by laws that do not actually direct the courts to reopen finally decided cases, but retroactively review final court judgments. In other words, it is conceivable that the legislature might adopt a retroactive piece of legislation that changes past law, nullifying or reviewing the final judicial decisions which were based on the original law. Like the first category of overruling legislation, this is a peculiar phenomenon. Normally legislatures respect final judicial decision when the law operates retroactively. In Germany, for example, "the angle of a decided case" approach (*der Gesichtspunkt der 'entschiedenen Sache'*) of the Federal Constitutional Court is important.[983]

PROCEEDING. On motion and just terms, the court may relieve a party or its legal representative from a final judgment, order, or proceeding for the following reasons:
(1) mistake, inadvertence, surprise, or excusable neglect;
(2) newly discovered evidence that, with reasonable diligence, could not have been discovered in time to move for a new trial under Rule 59(b);
(3) fraud (whether previously called intrinsic or extrinsic), misrepresentation, or misconduct by an opposing party;
(4) the judgment is void;
(5) the judgment has been satisfied, released, or discharged; it is based on an earlier judgment that has been reversed or vacated; or applying it prospectively is no longer equitable; or
(6) any other reason that justifies relief.

982 *Ryabykh v. Russia* (Appl. no. 52854/99) ECHR 2003-IX, para. 52.

983 See for example BVerfGE 15, 167 (205ff.), BVerfGE 48, 1 (22), BVerfGE 72, 302. For more details, see Chapter III.4.1.3.

With regard to constitutional principles which apply to this particular type of retroactive legislation, the presumption of non-retroactivity seems to constitute the most meaningful framework for review.[984] For the ECtHR, Art. 6, guaranteeing the right to a fair trial, is an obvious point of reference. In Germany,[985] the Federal Constitutional Court suggested that retroactive legislation that violates the *res judicata* principle may also be problematic in light of the principle of the separation of powers, without further elaborating on this idea. Finally, in the *Plaut* decision, the U.S. Supreme Court took a fundamental view of the legislation that overruled the final court decision. Although the challenged legislation in that case concerned the reopening of final judicial decisions, the Court's view appears to have broader implications. Strict application of the principle of the separation of powers results in the invalidation of any retroactive legislation that reviews final court judgments:[986]

> Having achieved finality, however, a judicial decision becomes the last word of the judicial department with regard to a particular case or controversy, and Congress may not declare by retroactive legislation that the law applicable *to that very case* was something other than what the courts said it was.

The U.S. case law on the finality of judicial decisions shows that the separation of powers principle is the most obvious tool for the review of overruling retroactive laws. If the retroactive legislation imposes criminal punishment at the same time, a possible violation of the Ex Post Facto Clause may be investigated.

2.3.3. *Rendering the judgment impracticable*

The fact that examples of the two above mentioned types of overruling legislation could barely be given demonstrates that the method of reopening final court decisions or reversing them retroactively is not particularly popular. This is not surprising, because laws of these types are controversial and evidently conflict with the principles of the rule of law, including the principle of the separation of powers and the presumption against the retroactivity of laws. The legislatures' reluctance to employ these methods to show their dissatisfaction with specific court judgments is therefore understandable. Consequently, legislatures prefer to apply a less suspicious method: by amending the relevant statutory provisions with immediate effect, the legislature de facto prevents the final court decision from being enforced.[987] Cases in point are the Dutch Licensing of Dredging Act and the Tellico Dam case. In both cases, the legislature did not directly and retroactively *sensu stricto* attack the final court decision. Instead, it enacted a special

[984] For one example of a case in which the Dutch Parliament considered, but eventually decided not to yield to public pressure, see Chapter IV.5.4.

[985] See Chapter III.4.1.3.

[986] *Plaut v. Spendthrift Farm, Inc.*, 514 U.S. 211, 227 (1995).

[987] Cf. H.L.A. Hart, *The Concept of Law*, Oxford: Clarendon Press 1994, p. 146: "[...] the result of the consequent decision in a particular case cannot, because of the rules as to the finality of decisions, be counteracted except by legislation which concedes its validity though not its correctness."

law with immediate effect in such a manner that the final court decision could not be enforced. This meant, specifically, that the dredging operations in the Western Scheldt (River) and the construction of the Tellico Dam could proceed, despite the final court decisions that blocked the projects.

Although the legislature de facto overrules final judicial decisions by this clever method, the principle of the separation of powers as interpreted by the U.S. courts and the right to a fair trial which is most relevant to the Netherlands and Germany seem not to apply as rigorously as in cases of other truly retroactive overruling legislation. In general, it can be said that both Courts accept that a judicial decision in which a prospective injunction instead of monetary damages has been awarded cannot be enforced if a newly enacted statute blocks this enforcement.[988]

The ECtHR has adopted a similar attitude toward this type of overruling legislation. In particular, the ECtHR grants the contracting states a broad margin of appreciation in the field of environmental planning. In that field, the Courts seems to assume that immediate changes of legislative policy *serve the general, public interest* and do not affect civil rights, such as rights to receive payments. Moreover, the Court pays attention to the nature of the contested legislation. If it is general, and therefore not *directed at any specific person (or company)*, the law is more likely to be compatible with Art 6. ECHR.[989]

In essence, the general presumption appears logical that the legislature is permitted to change the law rendering the enforcement of a court decision impossible in the light of the separation of powers and the right to a fair trial, as argued by the U.S. Supreme Court and the ECtHR. The separation of powers principle, however, as interpreted by the U.S. Supreme Court in this respect once again seems not to sufficiently eliminate the risk of legislative arbitrariness. In my view, the additional questions as posed by the ECtHR can be helpful on this point. Consequently, no arbitrariness would be found if 1) the law applies to a general neutrally defined class of persons, 2) it is enacted to serve the general, public interest, and 3) it does not affect civil rights, such as a right to damages.

2.3.4. *Concluding remarks*

Legislative overruling of final court decisions remains problematic. First, it seriously jeopardizes the independent position of the judiciary vis-à-vis the legislature. Second, it may be contrary to the constitutional presumption against retroactive legislation, which expresses the general principle of legal certainty and protection of legitimate expectations of individuals that have obtained a final enforceable judgment. Third, and related to the

[988] See *Miller v. French*, 530 U.S. 327, 347 (2000): "The provision of prospective relief is subject to the continuing supervisory jurisdiction of the court, and therefore may be altered according to subsequent changes in the law" with reference to *Plaut*, 514 U.S. 211, 227 (1995), and *Rufo v. Inmates of Suffolk County Jail*, 502 U.S. 367, 388 (1992). See also ECtHR *Bulgakova v. Russia* (Appl. no. 69524/01) ECHR 18 January 2007, paras. 41–42 with reference to *Sukhobokov v. Russia* (Appl. no. 75470/01) ECHR 13 April 2006, para. 26.

[989] The ECtHR distinguished the case of *Gorraiz Lizzaraga* from the case of *Ruiz Mateos v. Spain* (Appl. no. 12952/87) ECHR 23 June 1993, where the legislature deliberately expropriated the company Rumasa S.A. by a formal law. Cf. the case law of the German Federal Constitutional Court on legislative expropriations, which are allowed in extraordinary situations, BVerfGE 24, 367.

second point, it questions the fairness of the judicial procedure involving the element of the finality of court decisions. In the United States, the principle of the separation of powers is applied to define the boundaries of the legislative branch in this respect. The two other principles are more often used in the Netherlands and might be used in Germany (also through the ECHR) as the review framework. Although truly retroactive laws, which either annul final judicial decisions or direct the reopening of closed cases, are particularly rare, the legislature indirectly tends to adopt overruling legislation that renders final court decisions impracticable. It appears that the constitutional principles referred to above can only offer effective protection against arbitrary ad hoc legislation if they entail objective justification of the compelling general, public interest of the legislation in question. It can be argued fairly that overruling ad hoc laws that focus on specific cases of specific individuals would be less likely to fulfill the justification requirement, especially when they single out specific individuals for oppressive treatment. Ad hoc infrastructural project laws that set inconvenient court decisions aside appear to have more chances to pass constitutional muster. Such laws do not deliberately target individuals and the argument that they serve the general, public interest is often plausible.[990]

2.4. Accelerating legislation: Access to a court, separation of powers

The last function of ad hoc laws which comes to the fore is that of accelerating the execution of specific projects, mostly infrastructural or related to other construction. Resulting ad hoc project laws[991] are triggered by the attractiveness of achieving quick results by setting demanding and complex pre-existing general rules of both a procedural and substantive nature aside. In the Dutch and German cases of the Licensing of Dredging Act and the Lex Stendal, respectively, the governments sponsoring the bill explicitly justified the choice of divergent legal regimes for these concrete infrastructural projects by referring to a possible gain in time.[992] In the United States, the situation is slightly different. Although the gain in time sometimes explicitly played a part in past Congressional decisions to deviate from the general rules for one specific project,[993] it

990 However, such infrastructural project laws must also be in harmony with other principles that apply to all types of ad hoc legislation, as described in Chapter V.1. The principle of proportionality is particularly important.

991 On project laws, see Chapter V.1.3.3.

992 The opponents may argue, however, that "gaining time" was just a cover used by the government to push the project through, despite the blocking decision of the Administrative Jurisdiction Division of the Council of State. In response to this claim, it can be stated that the obstacles suggested by the Council of State were just of a procedural nature and could be removed. Such removal meant in practice that new administrative decisions needed to be taken. Because this process is extremely time-consuming, the Licensing of Dredging Act was promulgated instead.
Perhaps a more accurate example of a Dutch ad hoc project law is the Delta (Major Rivers) Act. It was a response to the flood in the 90s, not a response to any uncomfortable court decision.

993 In the case of the construction of the World War II Memorial at the National Mall, the argument of gaining time was used during the Congressional debate as a reason for exempting the World War II Memorial project from the applicable general rules, including the National Environmental Policy Act: "Eight years after Congress authorized the construction of this memorial, and six years from the first of

appears that Congress' main motivation was often to simply execute specific projects that had been countermanded by any earlier administrative or court decision or that were expected to perish if the general relevant law provisions were applied. In such situations, Congress tends to use the magic "notwithstanding clause" to help the project get executed. By means of this clause the legislature exempts one specific project from the application of existing general rules that are expected to either delay or even block the project.[994] Besides the already mentioned example of the Tellico Dam project and the corresponding legislation, this famous clause has also been used with regard to projects such as the Three Sisters Bridge, the Potomac River Freeway, the Center Leg of the Inner Loop, the East Leg of the Inner Loop at the Potomac River in the District of Colombia, and with regard to the Second World II Memorial Site at the National Mall. In the two statutes, this clause reads respectively:[995, 996]

> Notwithstanding any other provision of law, or any court decision or administrative action to the contrary, the Secretary of Transportation and the government of the District of Columbia shall [...] construct all routes on the Interstate System within the District of Columbia as set forth in the document entitled '1968 Estimate of the Cost of Completion of the National System of Interstate and Defense Highways in the District of Columbia' [...],

And:

> Notwithstanding any other provision of law, the World War II memorial [...] shall be constructed expeditiously at the dedicated Rainbow Pool site in the District of Columbia.

As follows from the description of the criticism of ad hoc infrastructural project laws in Part II, III, and IV, the separation of powers doctrine and legal protection, including the constitutional guarantee of a right to a court, are at issue. Can they indeed effectively limit the legislative branch with respect to project laws?

2.4.1. Separation of powers

If the legislature decides to accelerate the execution of a specific infrastructural project, it can do two things: 1) it can either design an exceptional legal regime for a specific project instructing the administrative bodies of the executive branch to implement them for that specific project or 2) it can issue specific administrative decisions, including

the 22 public hearings on its site and design, the memorial's construction remains delayed by a procedural issue involving the National Capital Planning Commission (NCPC), one of the agencies required by law to approve the memorial, and a lawsuit filed by a small group of opponents. This legislation would remove those obstacles and require the construction process to promptly go forward," 147 CONG. REC. S 5261 (May 21, 2001), cited in *National Coalition to Save Our Mall v. Norton*, 161 F.Supp. 2d 14 (2001).

994 See Chapter II.2.3.1.2.

995 Pub. L. 90–495, Sec. 23.

996 Pub. L. 107–11.

necessary licenses in the field of planning, on its own. The second appears to be more problematic, because of possible conflict with the constitutional principle of the separation of powers between the legislative and executive branches.

In deciding on specific projects, the U.S. legislature tends to choose the first method of giving instructions to the executive on how it should act with respect to a specific project. In such a situation, Congress presents the new rules as a change of law rather than as an execution or interpretation of its own previous laws in a specific case. The first option is permitted while the second results in violation of the separation of powers between the legislature and the executive, as appears from the case law.[997] This test is a clear guide for the legislature on how to avoid constitutional challenges based on violation of the separation of powers doctrine by usurping executive powers. The only thing Congress has to do is to write the rules in such a way that they resemble an exemption from rather than an interpretation of preexisting rules for a specific project. Anyhow, it seems always to be possible for the legislature to achieve its desired result, since the most important role is reserved for the staffs writing the legislative drafts. The correct formulation of the terms of ad hoc project laws can work miracles.[998]

Even more clearly than U.S. Congress, the Dutch and German Parliaments also choose to apply the first method. They tend to change the general rules to gain time with respect to particular infrastructural projects. The favored method includes shortening both the fixed terms for decision-making procedures and the course of judicial proceedings. Since the changed rules are obviously general in nature, they usually do not attract criticism from the perspective of the principle of the separation of powers between the legislature and the executive. Only sporadically has such a violation been contended, for example, when the German and Dutch legislatures explicitly took over the executive function to decide on specific infrastructural projects. In the German case of the Südumfahrung Stendal, the *Bundesverfassungsgericht* confirmed that Parliament had encroached on the powers of the executive branch, but since this encroachment could be justified by good reasons of the general interest resulting from the reunification of the eastern and the western parts of Germany, no violation of the separation of powers principle was found. In the Netherlands, the absence of a constitutional court is significant for the underdevelopment of the interpretation of the principle of the separation of powers. It is true that the Royal Commission on Water Legislation concluded that by granting a specific license for the dredging operations in the Western Scheldt (River), the legislature had violated the separation of powers principle. This statement, however, was not based on any established interpretation in terms of strict separation. The opposite seems to be true. During the preparatory works on the 1983 review of the Constitution, the absence of a strict separation between the legislature and the executive was acknowledged.[999]

Comparing the American and the German positions on project laws within the context of the separation of powers, I can state that the U.S. courts mainly depart from

997 See Chapter II.3.5 for references.

998 See, for example, the case of Congress' intervention in the pending case on the construction of the interstate highway H-3 in Hawaii as described in Chapter II.3.5.

999 *Kamerstukken II*, 1980/1981, 16 035, no. 8, p. 4.

the strict separation of powers between the legislature and the executive. By contrast, the German Constitutional Court sees the separation in this context rather as a distribution of functions which must be performed by those branches which are best equipped to do so. Such a position allows sporadic justifiable encroachments:[1000]

> Eine Entscheidung über eine konkrete Fachplanung ist nach den einschlägigen Fachplanungsgesetzen üblicherweise der Verwaltung vorbehalten, die dafür den erforderlichen Verwaltungsapparat und Sachverstand besitzt. Das Parlament darf durch Gesetz eine solche Entscheidung nur dann an sich ziehen, wenn hierfür im Einzelfall gute Gründe bestehen, etwa weil die schnelle Verwirklichung des Vorhabens von besonderer Bedeutung für das Gemeinwohl ist. Insofern steht dem Gesetzgeber ein Beurteilungs- und Einschätzungsspielraum zu.

In essence, these opposite approaches do not seem to lead to opposite results in practice in the context of ad hoc project laws. In general, it can be said that legislative encroachments on the province of the executive are in fact treated less stringently than legislative encroachments on the judiciary. This can be explained by the special position that an independent judiciary has always had within the separation of powers principle. This holds true for all three countries.[1001]

2.4.2. Legal protection: Access to a court

When the legislature shortens the normally applicable terms for decision-making procedures and the course of administrative and judicial proceedings to accelerate the execution of infrastructural projects, it risks criticism from a legal protection point of view. This criticism is particularly severe with regard to ad hoc project laws to which the second method is applied, namely, when the legislature issues administrative decisions by means of legislation. The argument is then that, once administrative decisions have been made by the legislature in the form of a law, they are exempted from the application of the general rules governing the possibilities of both administrative and judicial review, which would normally have been available if the decisions had been made by administrative bodies. In particular, this means that no extensive review involving procedural and substantive rules governing the subject of the decision can be effectuated. What usually remains is constitutional review, or, as argued with regard to the Licensing of Dredging Act, less demanding review by civil law courts. Diminished legal protection is the result.

The principle of effective legal protection is not absolute and therefore can only constrain the legislative branch to a certain extent in the context of project laws. As regards the Dutch situation, the absence of a clear view on this point forces us to turn to

1000 BVerfGE 95, 1 (17).

1001 In the Netherlands, the idea of a strict separation of powers between the executive and the legislature was abandoned during the preparatory works on the 1983 revision of the Constitution, as already stated above. The independent position of the judiciary, on the other hand, does require a strict separation of powers, *Kamerstukken II*, 1980/81, 16 035, no. 8, p. 4. See also Bovend'eert (2004), p. 249.

the European Convention on Human Rights (ECHR) for inspiration. Art. 6 ECHR, which prescribes the right to a fair trial, including the right of access to a court, is significant here. It is now established case law of the ECtHR that this right may be limited as long as the very essence of the right is not impaired and the (legislative) limitations serve a legitimate aim and are not disproportional to fulfill this purpose.[1002] At the center of the German Federal Constitutional Court's rulings lies a comparable approach: although the right of effective legal protection of Art. 19 (4) GG does not guarantee the best possible protection for individuals, the legislature may only limit it if there are exceptional reasons to do so and when it has carefully considered all public and private interests involved.[1003] Natural disasters are in any event among such exceptional reasons.[1004]

Lastly, in the United States, it is not unusual for legal protection to be diminished. As far as judicial review is concerned, it should be noted that Congress does not hesitate to preclude the judicial review of some decisions of administrative bodies. In the case of the World War II Memorial, referred to above, for example, Congress clearly decided that "[t]he decision to locate the memorial at the Rainbow Pool site in the District of Columbia and the actions of the Commission of Fine Arts [...], the actions by the National Capital Planning Commission [...], and the issuance of the special use permit identified in section 1 shall not be subject to judicial review."[1005] The courts accept such limitations of legal protection. When the legislative intention is clear, as was the case in the World War II Memorial affair, the courts will defer and refuse to consider claims on the subject matter of the law at stake. Nonetheless, constitutional claims with regard to such a limiting law remain possible. It is conceivable that a law eliminating judicial review may be in conflict with the constitutional right of due process in the Fifth and Fourteenth Amendments to the U.S. Constitution. The courts, however, are particularly reluctant to uphold such claims. Hitherto, they have recurrently rejected claims of this type. For instance, in 2005, Congress exempted manufacturers, importers, and distributors of firearms from civil liability actions in federal or state courts for injuries caused by third parties using non-defective firearms.[1006] The Act dismissed liability actions pending in the courts and precluded such actions in the future. Individuals who already had their cases pending argued that the Act deprived them of the due process of law, since it eliminated their cause of action based on the Strict Liability Act. In *District of Columbia v. Beretta U.S.A. Corp.*, the Court decided that 1) a cause of action in general "is not a vested property right

1002 See Chapter IV.5.5.

1003 BVerfGE 95, 1 (25).

1004 BVerfGE 24, 367 (403).

1005 Pub. L. 107–11.

1006 The Protection of Lawful Commerce in Arms Act, Pub. L. 109–92. As a result of the strong gun lobby, the Act was introduced one week after a young woman had been shot by her ex-husband during a Friday night service in a Baptist church in Kentucky. See K. Cordier Karnezis, "Validity, Construction, and Application of Protection of Lawful Commerce in Arms Act (PLCAA)," 17 A.L.R. Fed. 2d 167 (2007). See also T. Mowry, "The Protection of [Unlawful] Commerce in Arms Act-Does Congress Have the Power to Pass Special Legislation," 14 *Temp. Pol. & Civ. Rts. L. Rev.* 225 (2004).

until reduced to a final, unreviewable judgment," and "[a]ccordingly, a cause of action brought under the Strict Liability Act is not a vested property right protected by the Fifth Amendment, and 2) Congress had not "burdened or blocked Plaintiffs' right of access to the courts to seek enforcement of the law; rather [...] Congress has altered Plaintiff's prior rights and remedies."[1007] In conclusion, the American courts continue to uphold Congress' right to change the underlying laws and standards, even if individuals are deprived of effective legal protection. This is at least worrisome, because it gives the legislature much power to act as it sees fit, often under the pressure from lobby groups.

2.4.3. *Concluding remarks*

General rules which normally govern infrastructural projects are becoming more and more complex. They also set high standards and require time-consuming procedures before an infrastructural project can be executed. A favored method applied by the legislature is therefore to exempt specific projects from the application of such inconvenient general laws by means of specific infrastructural project laws. Such laws give rise to serious concerns regarding their constitutionality. Two constitutional principles are invoked: the separation of powers principle and the legal protection principle, including access to a court. Especially with regard to the latter, the Dutch and German approaches seem to differ essentially from the American approach. It could be argued that the U.S. legislature retains great latitude to restrict individuals' rights of legal protection, because their statutory rights to bring an action in court may easily be impaired without violating the Due Process Clause. Although laws limiting such a right may be subject to review in connection with such other constitutional principles as the presumption against retroactivity and the equal treatment principle, the low scrutiny standard that then applies casts doubts on their ability to eliminate arbitrary legislation. When legal protection, including access to courts, is at stake, the interests involved should be carefully considered. In my view, two questions should be decisive in this context: 1) Is the interest the legislature seeks to serve by adopting a specific infrastructural project law of such compelling importance that it justifies the limitation of individual legal protection? and 2) Did the legislature provide adequate compensation for diminished legal protection? A possibility of individuals' participation during the drafting process of a specific project law is certainly worth considering as an example of a compensating measure.

1007 *District of Columbia v. Beretta U.S.A. Corp.*, 2006 WL 1892023 (D.C. Super. Ct.), affirmed by *District of Columbia v. Beretta U.S.A. Corp.*, 940 A.2d. 163 (2008), cert. denied. The Court based its decision on extensive federal case law and, just like the District Court in New York, dismissed all constitutionality claims, *City of New York v. Beretta U.S.A. Corp.*, 401 F. Supp.2d 244, 291 (2005). The judgment of the District Court has been affirmed with respect to the constitutionality of the PLCAA by the U.S. Court of Appeals for the Second Circuit in 2008, *City of New York v. Beretta U.S.A. Corp.* 2008 U.S. App. LEXIS 9309 (2d Cir.), cert. denied.

The problems with accelerating infrastructural project laws mentioned above focused on constitutionality issues. It should be emphasized, however, that ad hoc deviations from general carefully enacted laws, such as general laws in the field of environmental policy, attract policy-oriented criticism as well. Infrastructural project laws guarantee quick results, but can be particularly damaging in the long run.

CONCLUSIONS

Introduction

Ad hoc legislation is a complex phenomenon. On the one hand, ad hoc laws can be viewed as a legislature's response to public outrage and demands of the public, a response to a superior force, such as a natural disaster, or a way to overcome a deadlock and thereby fulfill international obligations. In that case, they can be viewed as a quick and adequate response by the legislature to the will of the general public or to problems at hand. On the other hand, ad hoc laws can be the result of lobbying or strong and sometimes even irrational preferences of politicians. Regardless of the expediency-driven character of these laws and a hasty manner of their adoption, which is often the case, they are still products of a democratically chosen Parliament or Congress and must be respected as such even though their quality is not always high.

Nevertheless, even if they are products of a democratic process which, as illustrated by the practice of legislative riders in the United States is not all that democratic, they may be a serious threat to the agreed legal order. By unexpectedly or even impulsively deviating from the existing general rules *or* by amending these rules to achieve one politically desired outcome in a specific preselected case, the legislature breaches the general rules. By doing so, it may seriously jeopardize the rule of law, including several constitutional principles. In Chapters V.1 and V.2 above, the central research question was answered (although one page was not enough to answer this question) by comparing and analyzing the impact of constitutional principles on ad hoc legislation in general *and* with regard to various types of ad hoc laws. At this point, conclusions as to the capability of various constitutional principles to limit legislatures that interfere in specific cases will be offered. With the central research question in mind, I will determine the boundaries of the legislative branch in the context of ad hoc legislation. The central question is: *When do laws enacted to deal with a specific case draw constitutional criticism in the United States, Germany, and the Netherlands, and what constitutional rules and principles primarily determine the legality of such laws?*

Constitutional limitations

Democracy and the rule of law, including various constitutional principles, need each other to function properly.[1008] They may, however, also conflict with each other as evidenced by the examples of ad hoc laws. This study was based on a presumption that, in such a conflict situation, constitutional principles prevail and function as a restraint on the democratically operating legislature. The focus was thus on constitutional restraints on the legislature with regard to ad hoc legislation. The constitutional principles that have been identified as possible limitations on the legislative branch in the context of ad hoc legislation are:

- the (limited) generality of laws
- equality
- legal certainty, including the presumption against retroactivity
- proportionality
- the separation of powers
- legal protection, including access to courts
- fair trial

Transparency in lawmaking, which is particularly important in the context of legislative riders in the United States, eventually appeared to be one of the aspects of democracy rather than a principle of constitutional law.

The principles listed above and the corresponding tests used in American, German, and Dutch practice are varied, but the purpose they serve is the same. It is the prevention of arbitrary government actions toward citizens. In this sense, these principles have much potential to function as a review framework for ad hoc laws. Unfortunately, they are not always as effective as they seem to be.

First of all, these constitutional principles are unable to limit a legislature that could be accused of abusing the instrument of a legislative act but which nevertheless does not restrict individuals' rights or encroach on the domain of other government branches.

Second, the significance of these, at first sight strong, principles for the review of ad hoc legislation appears to be limited. The research shows that the principle of the generality of laws, which appeared to play the most important role in the context of ad hoc legislation, has a limited practical meaning in positive constitutional law. None of the national constitutions of the three studied countries empowers the courts to invalidate a law merely because it is not general. There must be always something more: punishment for the application of the Bill of Attainder Clause in the U.S. Constitution or a limitation of fundamental rights as required by Art. 19 (1) of the German Basic Law. Even when the generality question must be answered in the context of these provisions, it is not always answered in a meaningful way. The German *Bundesverfassungsgericht*, in particular, is easily satisfied with the general wording of the contested statutes. If a statute is written in general terms, the Court concludes that it is therefore general. But especially in the

[1008] On the relationship between democracy and the rule of law, see J.M. Maravall & A. Przeworski (eds.), *Democracy and the Rule of Law*, Cambridge: Cambridge University Press 2003.

context of ad hoc legislation, it is important to be particularly critical of laws enacted under suspect circumstances which, in view of their time, manner, and effect, strongly suggest that the law was enacted for only one case. It is not surprising that in such situations, the legislature will couch its intentions in a seemingly "general" law to avoid controversy. When answering the question whether the law is general, the courts should therefore take the facts and de facto effects of the law into account. Since most ad hoc laws are simply formulated in general terms, merely examining these terms is not enough, in my view. Most of the state constitutions in the United States are an exception. They prohibit special and local laws, and the principle of generality of laws is there particularly meaningful. This is reasoned by the colonial history of the American states. At that time acting by means of arbitrary case-specific laws was usual. The constitutional provisions which prohibit special and local laws were meant to stop this practice.

The same that has been said about the principle of the generality of laws in the national constitutions of the three countries holds true for other constitutional principles. As such, they have sufficient potential to constrain a legislature that enacts arbitrary ad hoc laws in relation to individuals. In my opinion, the manner in which they are actually applied, however, in many cases renders them less effective in the context of ad hoc laws. The tests developed in the framework of these principles often do not seem to apply in any special, exceptional, or more stringent way to ad hoc laws than they do in situations where usual, general legislation is reviewed. There can be two reasons for this: either the courts have not yet been confronted with claims concerning ad hoc legislation or they have simply refused to take the characteristics of ad hoc legislation into account in their review. I do not argue that any law intended for one specific case should be invalidated. But I do think that ad hoc laws deserve special treatment, because of the risks they entail. More precisely, the case-specific motives of the legislature, as long as they clearly appear from external circumstances, should at least be taken into account when the courts seek justification for a law's enactment. Courts should then be particularly critical as regards the question whether the legislature indeed designed the law to serve a legitimate general, public interest.

The more factual approach in reviewing ad hoc legislation as propounded above should not be feared. It is unlikely that the courts will go so far as to invalidate legislation in situations where they only have a slight suspicion that it was enacted for one specific case. The European Court of Human Rights, for example, is known for its particularly factual approach, as was demonstrated in previous paragraphs. Nevertheless, most decisions of this Court in which national legislation is invalidated do indeed concern serious violations of fundamental human rights. The courts cannot be expected either to allow the constitutionality of ad hoc laws to depend on aspects of their quality (in the sense of rationality). Although this study is not about the principles of good quality of laws in general,[1009] it confirms that the quality of legislation plays a marginal role, if any, in judicial constitutional review. The courts seem to be particularly aware of their role as guardians of constitutional principles and individuals' rights *vis-à-vis* the legislature, rather than as patrons of the quality of democratic acts of the legislature. Consequently, they will not easily encroach on the domain of a democratically chosen legislature just

[1009] See Chapter I.3.

because the law was, for example, hastily enacted and is inconsistent with the previously agreed rules. This does not mean that justified concerns about the quality of ad hoc legislation should be ignored. Attempts to enhance the quality of laws should also always be made, but it is unlikely that constitutional courts will blow the whistle on the legislature for its poor quality legislation.

Constraints on the legislative branch

Despite the fact that these constitutional principles are not always applied in such a way as to effectively limit the legislature in the context of ad hoc legislation, they still do set the boundaries of the legislative branch. In this respect, three categories of ad hoc laws can be distinguished: 1) ad hoc laws that are absolutely prohibited, 2) ad hoc laws that are not prohibited in advance, but which must comply with the requirements of the constitutional principles listed above, and 3) legislation that leaves much to be desired, but cannot be limited by principles of constitutional law.

1) Prohibited in principle

The lower limit set by the constitutional principles concerns in any event the following types of ad hoc laws.

a) Ad hoc laws that single out one particular individual or an easily defined group of persons and subject them to punishment (bills of attainder);
   In Germany, this category is even broader. According to Art. 19 (1) GG not only individual laws that punish, but laws that restrict fundamental rights in general are unconstitutional.
b) Retroactive ad hoc laws that impose punishment for acts that were not criminal when committed;
c) Ad hoc laws that overrule specific final judicial decisions and replace the court's final judgment, which was correct when rendered, by the legislature's own adjudication in that specific case;
d) Laws that interfere in pending cases for the sole purpose of influencing the outcome of a particular case, leaving the courts no freedom to decide the case independently;
e) Laws that direct the reopening of cases finally decided.

The last three categories follow from the special position the independent judiciary has in a state under the rule of law.

2) Sometimes problematic

There is a much larger group of ad hoc laws that cannot be classified in advance as prohibited ad hoc laws. The constitutionality of these laws must be examined anew in every single case. The decisive factor is whether they can meet the requirements set by these principles. In this context attention is paid to the nature of these laws (are they disadvantageous or do they provide benefits?), the nature and the seriousness of the infringement, and possible justification grounds. It is advisable that the general or individual character of the contested law and the legislature's motives which manifest themselves are taken into account, too.

3) Constitutionally unproblematic

As already indicated above, the constitutional principles discussed in Chapters V.1 and V.2 are not applicable to ad hoc laws where no encroachment upon fundamental rights or conflict with other government branches is at issue. A classical example is that of privileging Michael Naumann to become the *Staatsminister* for Culture. The German Parliament obviously used its power of legislation as a tool to effectuate the personal ambitions of two politicians. This is anything but elegant, but unproblematic from a strict constitutional point of view.

In conclusion, this study shows that constitutional principles provide only limited protection against every type of arbitrary ad hoc legislation. Although they mark the lower limit the legislature cannot exceed without acting arbitrarily in a constitutional sense, they rather ineffectively reckon with arbitrariness in the sense of the other aspects of legislative quality. A solid policy on legislative quality that helps to nip arbitrary elements of ad hoc legislation in the bud is therefore essential.

BIBLIOGRAPHY

A

Adams, M., *Recht en democratie ter discussie*, Leuven: Leuven University Press 2006
Aleinikoff, T.A., Martin, D.A. & Motomura, H., *Immigration and Citizenship: Process and Policy*, 4th ed., St. Paul, MN: West Publishing Co. 1998
Allen, M.P., "Congress and Terri Schiavo: A Primer on the American Constitutional Order?," 108 *W. Va.L. Rev.* 309 (2005)
Alstyne, W.W. van, "A Critical Guide to Ex Parte McCardle," 15 *Ariz. L. Rev.* 229 (1973)
Amar, A.R., "Attainder and Amendment 2: *Romer's* Rightness," 95 *Mich. L. Rev.* 203 (1996)
Ames, H., *The Proposed Amendments to the Constitution of the United States during the First Century of Its History*, New York: Burt Franklin 1970
Anderheiden, M., *Gemeinwohl in Republik und Union*, Tübingen: Mohr Siebeck 2006
Anderheiden, M., "Gemeinwohlförderung durch die Bereitstellung kollektiver Güter," in: Brugger, W., Kirste, S. & Anderheiden, M. (eds.), *Gemeinwohl in Deutschland, Europa und der Welt*, Baden-Baden: Nomos (2002), pp. 391ff.
Anderson, D.L., "The Sports Broadcasting Act: Calling it What It Is – Special Interest Legislation," 17 *Hastings Comm. & Ent. L. J.* 945 (1995)
Araiza, W.D., "Irrationality and Animus in Class-of-One Equal Protection Cases," 34 *Ecology L.Q.* 413 (2007)

B

Bacon, D.C., Davidson, R.H. & Keller, M., *The Encyclopedia of the United States Congress*, New York: Simon & Schuster 1995
Balla, S.J. et al., "Partisanship, Blame Avoidance, and the Distribution of Legislative Pork," *American Journal of Political Science*, 46 (3), July 2002, p. 515ff.
Bartholmes, Th., *Die "Flick-Affäre"-Verlauf und Folgen*, Speyer 2003
Battis, U., "Systemgerechtigkeit," in: Stödter, R. & Thieme, W. (eds.), *Hamburg, Deutschland, Europa. Festschrift für Hans Peter Ipsen*, Tübingen: J.C.B. Mohr 1977, p. 11ff.

Bauernfeind, H., "Zum Verbot von Einzelfallgesetzen gemäß Art. 19 I GG," *DVBl.* 1976, pp. 193ff.
Beermann, J.M., "Federal Court Self-Preservation and Terri Schiavo," 54 *Buff. L. Rev.* 553 (2006)
Beijerse, J. uit & Bos, W., "Camera's in de cel om het publiek gerust te stellen?," *NJB* 2002–29, pp. 1414ff.
Benda, E., Maihofer, W. & Vogel, H.J., *Handbuch des Verfassungsrechts der Bundesrepublik Deutschland*, Berlin, New York: Walter de Gruyter 1983
Berg, R. van den, *Vormen van begrip van wet en wetgeving. Wetsbegrippen in de Staatsrechtsgeleerdheid in Duitsland en Nederland in de negentiende en twintigste eeuw*, The Hague: Boom Juridische uitgevers 2003
Berge, J.B.J.M. ten, "Organisatie en individuele rechter in balans," in: Berge, J.B.J.M. ten & Hol, A.M. (eds.), *De onafhankelijke rechter*, Den Haag: Boom Juridische uitgevers 2007, pp. 11ff.
Berger, Th., *Zulässigkeit der Rückwirkung von Gesetzen*, Frankfurt am Main: Peter Lang 2002
Beth, R.S., "Trends in Activity on Private Legislation in Congress, 1949–1980," Washington, D.C.: Congressional Research Service (1982)
Bethge, H., "Art. 5," in: Sachs, M., *Grundgesetz. Kommentar*, München: C.H. Beck 2007, pp. 276ff.
Beyme, K. von, *Der Gesetzgeber: der Bundestag als Entscheidungszentrum*, Opladen: Westdeutscher Verlag 1997
Blümel, W., "Fachplanung durch Bundesgesetz (Legalplanung)," *DVBl.* 1997, pp. 205ff.
Blümel, W., *Verkehrswegeplanung in Deutschland*, Forschungsinstitut für öffentliche Verwaltung, Speyer 1991
Bonnes, J.M., *Aard en omvang van de Aanwijzingen voor de regelgeving, RegelMaat* 2005–1, pp. 9ff.
Bovend' Eert, P.P.T., "Het rechtsbeginsel van de machtenscheiding," in: Schlössels, R.J.N. et al. (eds.), *In beginsel. Over aard, inhoud en samenhang van rechtsbeginselen in het bestuursrecht*, Deventer: Kluwer 2004, pp. 243ff.
Böckenförde, E.W., *Gesetz und gesetzgebende Gewalt*, Berlin: Duncker und Humblot 1958
Böhler, B., *Crisis in de rechtsstaat*, Amsterdam: De Arbeiderspers 2004
Böhtlingk, F.R. & Glastra van Loon, J.F., "Het begrip rechtsregel," *RMThemis* 1959, pp. 11ff.
Böhtlingk, F.R. & Logemann, J.H.A., *Het wetsbegrip in Nederland*, Alphen aan den Rijn: N. Samson 1966
Bradley, C.M., "The Uncertainty Principle in the Supreme Court," 1986 *Duke L.J.* 1 (1986)
Brandner, Th., *Gesetzesänderung*, Berlin: Berliner Wissenschafts-Verlag 2004
Bravenboer, M. & Lubbers, A.O., *Tijd voor uitbreiding van de Notitie terugwerkende kracht en eerbiedigende werking, Weekblad Fiscaal Recht* 2005–6631, pp. 964ff.
Briffault, R. & Reynolds, L., *Cases and Materials on State and Local Government Law*, 6th ed., American Casebook Series, St. Paul, MN: Thomson West 2004

Broeksteeg, J.L.W. et al., *Zicht op wetgevingskwaliteit. Een onderzoek naar de wetgevingsadvisering van de Raad van State*, Den Haag: WODC 2005

Brohm, W., "Beschleunigung der Verwaltungsverfahren-Straffung oder konsensuales Verwaltungshandeln?," *NVwZ* 1991, pp. 1025ff.

Brouwer, P.W., *Samenhang in recht*, Groningen: Wolters-Noordhoff 1990

Bröhmer, J., *Transparenz als Verfassungsprinzip. Grundgesetz und Europäische Union*, Tübingen: Mohr Siebeck 2004

Brubaker, W.R., "The French Revolution and the Invention of Citizenship," *French Politics and Society*, Vol. 7 (1989)

Bruff, H.H., *Balance of Forces. Separation of Powers Law in the Administrative State*, Carolina Durham, North Carolina: Academic Press 2006

Brugger, W., "Gemeinwohl als Integrationskonzept von Rechtssicherheit, Legitimität und Zweckmäßigkeit," in: Brugger, W., Kirste, S. & Anderheiden, M. (eds.), *Gemeinwohl in Deutschland, Europa und der Welt*, Baden-Baden: Nomos (2002), pp. 17ff.

Burg, F.H. van der, "Overgangsrecht," in: Schagen, J.A. van (ed.), *Overgangsrecht*, Vereniging voor wetgeving en wetgevingsbeleid, SDU: Den Haag 2001

Burghart, A., *Die Pflicht zum guten Gesetz*, Berlin: Duncker & Humblot 1996

Buuren, P.J.J. van, "Vergunningwet Westerschelde niet voor herhaling vatbaar," *M&R* 1997-6, pp. 122ff.

Bücker, J, *Die Zulässigkeit von Individualgesetzen nach dem Grundgesetz*, Bonn: H. Bouvier u. Co. 1965

Butler, P., "Taking Lessons from Elizabeth Morgan. On Congressional Attitudes toward D.C. and the Rule of Law," *Legal Times*, week of June 8, 1998

C

Calabresi, S.G., "The Terri Schiavo Case: In Defense of the Special Law Enacted by Congress and President Bush," 100 *Nw. U.L. Rev.* 151 (2006)

Campbell, T., *Separation of Powers in Practice*, Stanford: Stanford University Press 2004

Claes, M., "Comparative Constitutional Law," in: Smits, J.M. (ed.), *Encyclopedia of Comparative Law*, Cheltenham: Edward Elgar 2006, pp. 187ff.

Claes, M. & Schyff, G. van der, "Towards judicial constitutional review in the Netherlands?," in: Schyff, G. van der (ed.), *Constitutionalism in the Netherlands and South Africa: A Comparative Study*, Nijmegen: Wolf Legal Publishers 2008, pp. 123ff.

Clark, J.M., "Legislative Motivation and Fundamental Rights in Constitutional Law," 15 *San Diego L. Rev.* 953 (1977–1978)

Cohen-Eliya, M. & Porat, I., "The Hidden Foreign Law Debate in *Heller*: The Proportionality Approach in American Constitutional Law" at <http://ssrn.com/abstract=1317833>

Coleman, J.L. & Leiter, B., "Determinacy, Objectivity, and Authority," 142 *U. Pa. L. Rev.* 549 (1993)

Cordier Karnezis, K., "Validity, Construction, and Application of Protection of Lawful Commerce in Arms Act (PLCAA)," 17 A.L.R. Fed. 2d 167 (2007)

Cowles, W.H. "The Distinction Between the Legislative and the Judicial Power," 40 *Am. L. Reg.* 433 (1892)

Crezelius, G., "Rechtsprechungüberholende Gesetzgebung und gesetzesüberholende Rechtsprechung," in: Carlé, D., Korn, K. & Stahl, R., *Herausforderungen-Steuerberatung im Spannungsfeld der Teilrechtsordnungen*, Köln: Otto Schmidt 1989, pp. 37ff.

D

Damen, L.J.A., "Na 'confectierechtspraak' nu ook 'confectiewetgeving'?," *NJB* 1989–5, pp. 145ff.

Dechsling, R., *Das Verhältnismäßigkeitsgebot*, München: Verlag Franz Vahlen 1989

Die, B.C. de, "Overgangsrecht – een herwaardering na vijftig jaar," *RMThemis* 1979, pp. 253ff.

Degenhart, Ch., "Gesetzgebung im Rechtsstaat," *DÖV* 1981, pp. 477ff.

Degenhart, Ch., *Staatsorganisationsrecht*, Heidelberg: Müller 2007

Degenhart, Ch., *Systemgerechtigkeit und Selbstbindung des Gesetzgebers als Verfassungspostulat*, München: C.H. Beck 1976

Die, B.C. de, "Overgangsrecht – een herwaardering na vijftig jaar," *RMThemis* 1979, pp. 253ff.

Dijk, P. van et al., *Theory and Practice of the European Convention on Human Rights*, Antwerp: Intersentia 2006

Donadio, R., "Death Ends Coma Case That Set Off Furor in Italy," *New York Times* February 9, 2009

Drupsteen, Th., "Kroniek van het milieurecht," *NJB* 1997, pp. 1492ff.

Duk, W., *Recht en slecht*, Nijmegen: Ars Aequi Libri 1999

Dürig, G., "Art. 3" in: Maunz Th., & Dürig, G., *Grundgesetz: Kommentar*, München: Beck 1958–2003, pp. 13ff.

Dworkin, R., *A Matter of Principle*, Cambridge and London: Harvard University Press 1985

Dworkin, R., *Laws Empire*, Cambridge, Massachusetts: Belknap Press 1986

E

Eckert, Ch., Transparenz im Gesetzgebungsprozess. Das Prinzip der Öffentlichkeit staatslenkender Entscheidungen zwischen Anspruch der Rechtsordnung und Realität, Hamburg: Verlag Dr. Kova 2004

Eijlander, Ph., *De verbindende wetgever. Over de verhouding tussen staat, markt en* samenleving, The Hague: Boom Juridische uitgevers 2000

Eijlander, Ph., "Gelegenheidswetgeving. Een rechtsstaat onwaardig," *Ars Aequi*, 2004, pp. 484ff.

Eijlander, Ph. & Voermans, W., *Wetgevingsleer*, Den Haag: Boom Juridische uitgevers 2000

Ely, J.H., "Legislative and Administrative Motivation in Constitutional Law," 79 *Yale L. Journal* 1205 (1969–1970)

Engstrom, D.F., "Drawing Lines Between Chevron and Pennhurst: A Functional Analysis of the Spending Power, Federalism and the Administrative State," 82 *Tex. L. Rev.* 1197 (2004)

Erp, H.H.H. van, *Political Reason and Interest. A Philosophical Legitimation of the Political Order in a Pluralistic Society*, Aldershot: Ashgate 2000

Eskridge, W.N. et al., *Cases and Materials on Legislation. Statutes and the Creation of Public Policy*, St. Paul, Minn.: West Group 2001

F

Fenster, M., "The Opacity of Transparency," 91 *Iowa L. Rev.* 885 (2006)

Ferejohn, J.A., *Pork Barrel Politics. Rivers and Harbors Legislation, 1947–1968*, Palo Alto, CA: Stanford University Press 1974

Figueiredo, J.M. de, & Silverman, B.S., "Academic Earmarks and the Returns to Lobbying," 49 *J.L. & Econ.* 597 (2006)

Fischkin, B., "He's the Mastermind behind Abscam," *Boston Globe*, February 12, 1980

Forsthoff, E., "Über Maßnahme=Gesetze," in: Forsthoff, E., *Rechtsstaat im Wandel*, Stuttgart: W. Kohlhammer Verlag 1964, pp. 78ff.

Frisch, S.A., *The Politics of Pork. A Study of Congressional Appropriation Earmarks*, New York: Garland Publishing, Inc. 1998

Fuller, L., *The Morality of Law*, New Haven: Yale University Press 1974

G

Galle, B., "Getting Spending: How to Replace Clear Statement Rules with Clear Thinking About Conditional Grants of Federal Funds," 37 *Conn. L. Rev.* 155 (2004)

George, A.L. & Bennett, A., *Case Studies and Theory Development in the Social Sciences*, Cambridge: MIT Press 2005

Gerangelos, P., *The Separation of Powers and Legislative Interference in Judicial Process. Constitutional Principles and Limitations*, Oxford and Portland: Hart Publishing 2009

Gerangelos, P., "The Separation of Powers and Legislative Interference in Pending Cases," 30 *Sydney Law Review* 61 (2008)

Gerards, J.H., *Rechterlijke toetsing aan het gelijkheidsbeginsel*, The Hague: SDU 2002

Gerhardt, R., "Veröffentlichung von Gesetzesvorhaben und Rückwirkung von Gesetzen," *ZRP* 1973, pp. 81ff.

Gestel, R.A.J. van, "De wetmatigheid van wetgeving," *RMThemis* 2005–6, pp. 282ff.

Gestel, R.A.J. van, "Incident- of gelegenheidswetgeving: balanceren op het smalle koord van de trias politica," *Tijdschrift voor privaatrecht* 2004, pp. 1667ff.

Gestel, R.A.J. van &. Poorter, J.C.A de, "'Je maintiendrai'. Naar een prominentere rol van burgers en milieuorganisaties bij de handhaving van het omgevingsrecht?," *Tijdschrift voor omgevingsrecht* 2002, pp. 84ff.

Gilette, C.P. & Baker, L.A., *Local Government Law. Cases and Materials*, 2nd ed., New York: Aspen Law & Business 1999
Gilmore, M.S., "Application of Statutory Changes to Cases in Progress: The Crossroads of the Legislative and Judicial Power – An Analysis of Federal and Idaho Law," 34 *Idaho L. Rev.* 571 (1998)
Goerlich, H., "Formenmißbrauch-Einzelfallgesetz-Gewaltenteilung," *DÖV* 1985, pp. 945ff.
Griffith, B., "Lobbying Reform: House – Cleaning or Window Dressing?," 75 *U. Cin. L. Rev.* 863 (2006)
Griffith, K.L., "Perfecting Public Immigration Legislation: Private Immigration Bills and Deportable Lawful Permanent Residents," 18 *Geo. Immigr. L. J.* 273 (2004)
Grimm, D., "Stufen der Rechtsstaatlichkeit," *JZ* 2009/12, pp. 596ff.
Grimm, D., "Proportionality in Canadian and German Constitutional Law," 57 *U. Toronto L.J.* 383 (2007)
Groenendijk, C.A., "Parlementaire reacties op rechterlijke uitspraken: democratische controle op aanvullende regelgevers," in: Van den Bergh, G.C.J.J. et al., *Met hoofd en hart*, Zwolle: Tjeenk Willink 1991, pp. 67ff.
Groner, J., "Custody Saga's Latest Twist. Bid to Aid Morgan Hits Home – Rule Snag," *Legal Times*, week of March 4, 1996
Grzeszick, B., "Art. 20, VII," in: Maunz, T., Dürig, G. & Herzog, R. (eds.), *Grundgesetz: Kommentar*, München: Beck 1958-(2006), pp. 39ff.
Grzeszick, B., "Art. 20, VI," in: Maunz, T., Dürig, G. & Herzog, R. (eds.), *Grundgesetz: Kommentar*, München: Beck 1958-(2007), pp. 54ff.
Guide to Congress, 5th ed., Vol. 1, Washington, D.C.: CQ Press 2000
Gutersohn, A., "Gruppeninteresse und Allgemeinwohl," in: Pleitner, H.J. & Schmidt, K.H., *Grundlagen und Grundfragen der gewerblichen Wirtschaft*, Berlin/München/St. Gallen: Duncker & Humblot 1984
Gross, W., "Die Entwicklung des öffentlichen Rechts," *DVBl.* 1955, pp. 390ff.
Gusy, Ch., "Das Grundgesetz als normative Gesetzgebungslehre," *ZRP* 1985–11, pp. 291ff.

H

Habscheid, W., "Urteilswirkungen und Gesetzänderungen," *ZZP* 1965–6, pp. 401ff.
Hall, Ch.W., "Rep. Wolf Fends Off Criticism after Intervening in Custody Battle," *Washington Post*, September 20, 1996
Happé, R.H., *Schuivende machten. Over trias politica en het gelijkheidsbeginsel in het belastingrecht*, Deventer: Kluwer 1999
Harper, E.J. & Chase, R.F., *Immigration Laws of the United States*, Indianapolis: Bobbs-Merrill 1975
Hart, H.L.A., *The Concept of Law*, Oxford: Clarendon Press 1994
Hayek, F., *The Constitution of Liberty*, London, New York: Routledge Classics 2006
Hayek, F., *The Political Ideal of the Rule of Law*, Cairo 1955, F. Hayek, *The Road to Serfdom*, London: Routledge & Kegan Paul 1976

Herzog, R., "Art. 19," in: Maunz, Th., Dürig G., *Grundgesetz. Kommentar*, Vol. III, München: C.H. Beck 1981, no. 27

Herzog, R., "Art. 97," in: Maunz, Th., Dürig, G. & Herzog, R., *Grundgesetzkommentar*, München: C.H. Beck 1997, pp. 11ff.

Hill, J.S. & Williams, K.C., "The Decline of Private Bills: Resource Allocation, Credit Claiming, and the Decision to Delegate," 37 *AJPS* 1008 (1993)

Hinds, A.C., *Hind's Precedents of the House of Representatives of the United States*, Vol. IV, Washington D.C.: Government Printing Office 1907

Hippel, E. von, "Machtmißbrauch der Lobby als Herausforderung," in: Brink, S. & Wolf, H.A., *Gemeinwohl und Verantwortung*, Berlin: Duncker & Humblot 2004

Hirsch Ballin, E.M.H., *Het grondrecht op vrijheid en de wet*, Alphen aan den Rijn: Tjeenk Willink 1989

Hochman, Ch.B., "The Supreme Court and the Constitutionality of Retroactive Legislation," 73 *Harv. L. Rev.* 692 (1960)

Hoffmann, G., "Das verfassungsrechtliche Gebot der Rationalität im Gesetzgebungsverfahren," *ZG* 1990–2, pp. 97ff.

Hofmann, H., "Der Postulat der Allgemeinheit des Gesetzes," in: Starck, Ch., *Die Allgemeinheit des Gesetzes*, Göttingen: Van Den Hoeck & Ruprecht 1987, pp. 9ff.

Hoffstadt, B.M., "Retaking the Field: The Constitutional Constraints on Federal Legislation that Displaces Consent Decrees," 77 *Wash. U. L. Q.* 53 (1999)

Hollmann, M. & Von Jena, K., *Die Kabinettsprotokolle der Bundesregierung*, Vol. 8, 1955, München: R. Oldenbourg Verlag 1997

Hopper, R. & Osuna, J.P., "Remedies of Last Resort: Private Bills and Deferred Action," *Immigration Briefings*, No. 97–6 (Federal Publications, Washington, D.C., June 1997)

Houck, O., "Unfinished Stories," 73 *U. Col. L. Rev.* 867 (2002)

Huber, K., *Maßnahmegesetz und Rechtsgesetz*, Berlin: Duncker & Humblot 1963

Huber, P.M., "Art. 19," in: Mangoldt, H. von, Klein, F. & Starck, Ch., *Kommentar zum Grundgesetz*, München: Franz Vahlen 2005, pp. 1719ff.

Hudson D.L. Jr., "Schiavo Law Prompts Constitutional Questions," 4 No. 12 *A.B.A. J. E-Report* 1 (2005)

Hufeld, U., "Anmerkung," *JZ* 1997, pp. 302ff.

I

Iliopoulos-Strangas, J., *Rückwirkung und Sofortwirkung von Gesetzen*, Baden-Baden: Nomos 1986

Ireland, R.M., "The Problem of Local, Private and Special Legislation in the Nineteenth Century United States," 46 *Am. J. Legal Hist.* 271 (2004)

J

Jackson, V.C., "Ambivalent Resistance and Comparative Constitutionalism: Opening up the Conversation on "Proportionality," Rights and Federalism," 1 *U. Pa. J. Const. L.* 583 (1999)

Jackson, V.C., "Being Proportional about Proportionality," 21 *Const. Comment.* 803 (2004)

Jans, J.H., Lange, R. de et al., *Europeanisation of Public Law*, Groningen: Europa Law Publishing 2007

Jarass, H. & Pieroth, B., *Grundgesetz für die Bundesrepublik Deutschland. Kommentar*, München: C.H. Beck 2006

Jasiak, A., "Changing the rules mid-game. Legislative interference in specific pending cases: separation of powers and fair trial. A comparison between the European Court of Human Rights and the U.S. Supreme Court's views," *Vienna Online Journal on Int. Const. L.* Vol. 4, 1/2010, pp. 20–36

Jasiak, A., "Gelegenheidswetgeving en beïnvloeding van rechterlijke procedures in het licht van het EVRM," in: Schooten, J. & Gestel, R. van (eds.), *Europa en de toekomst van de nationale wetgever*, Nijmegen: Wolf Legal Publishers 2008, pp. 91ff.

K

Kahn-Freund, O., "On Uses and Misuses of Comparative Law," 37 *Mod. L. Rev.* 1 (1974)

Kaltenegger, R., *Schörner. Feldmarschall der letzten Stunde. Biographie*, München, Berlin: Herbig 1994

Kaplin, W.A., *The Concepts and Methods of Constitutional Law*, Durham: Carolina Academic Press 1992

Katz, A., *Staatsrecht*, Heidelberg: C.F. Müller Verlag 2007

Kirchner, K.P., "Special Interests v. the Public Interest: Money Talks in Environmental Regulation," 25 *Ecology L. Q.* 665 (1999)

Kirchhof, G., *Die Allgemeinheit des Gesetzes*, Tübingen: Mohr Siebeck 2009

Klink, B. van, *De wet als symbool*, Deventer: Tjeenk Willink 1998

Knigge, G., *Verandering van wetgeving*, Arnhem: Gouda Quint 1984

Koekkoek, A.K., "Constitutionele toetsing door de Eerste Kamer," in: Rimanque, K. (ed.), *Het recht op veiligheid*, Antwerp-Apeldoorn: Maklu 2002, pp. 89ff.

Koller, P., "Das Konzept des Gemeinwohls," in: Brugger, W., Kirste, S. & Anderheiden, M. (eds.), *Gemeinwohl in Deutschland, Europa und der Welt*, Baden-Baden: Nomos 2002, pp. 41ff.

Koopmans, T., *Courts and Political Institutions. A Comparative View*, Cambridge: Cambridge University Press 2003

Koopmans, T., *De rol van de wetgever*, Zwolle: Tjeenk Willink 1970

Koppenjan, J. & Hufen, H., "Nieuwe mechanismen voor probleemoplossing," *Bestuurswetenschappen* 1997–6, pp. 360ff.

Kortmann, C.A.J.M., *De Grondwetsherziening 1983*, Deventer: Kluwer 1983

Krüger, H., Die Verfassungswidrigkeit der lex Schörner, *DVBl.* 1955, pp. 758ff.

Kuijer, M., *The Blindfold of Lady Justice - Judicial Independence and Impartiality in Light of the Requirements of Article 6 ECHR*, Nijmegen: Wolf Legal Publishers 2004

Kuitenbrouwer, F., "Gelegenheidswet voor Volkert van der G.," *NRC Handelsblad* July 9, 2002, p. 3

Kunig, P., "Einzelfallentscheidungen durch Gesetz," *Jura* 1993, pp. 308ff.

L

Laband, P., *Das Staatsrecht des Deutschen Reichs*, Tübingen: J.C.B. Mohr, Vol. 2, 5th ed. 1911

Lang, J., "Reaktion der Finanzverwaltung auf mißliebige Entscheidungen des Bundesfinanzhofs," *DRiZ* 1992–10, pp. 365ff.

Lange, R. de, *Publiekrechtelijke rechtsvinding*, Zwolle: W.E.J. Tjeenk Willink 1991

Lange, R. de & Mevis, P.A.M., "Constitutional Guarantees for the Independence of the Judiciary," in: Erp, J.H.M. van & Vliet, L.P.W. van (eds.), *Netherlands Reports to the Seventeenth International Congress of Comparative* Law, Antwerp, Oxford: Intersentia 2006, pp. 327ff.

Lange, R. de, "Constitutionele toetsing van wetgeving in Nederland," *RegelMaat* 2006–4/5, pp. 142ff.

Lanotte, J. Vande & Haeck, Y. (eds.), *Handboek EVRM*, Vol. II, Part. 2, Antwerpen: Intersentia 2004

Lazarus, R.J., "Congressional Descent: The Demise of Deliberative Democracy in Environmental Law," 94 *Georg. L. J.* 635 (2006)

Leif, Th. & Speth, R., *Die Stille Macht: Lobbyismus in Deutschland*, Wiesbaden: VS Verlag 2003

Lepsius, O., "Was kann die deutsche Staatsrechtslehre von der amerikanischen Rechtswissenschaft lernen," in: Schulze-Fielitz, H. (ed.), *Staatsrechtslehre als Wissenschaft*, Berlin: Duncker & Humblot 2007

Lerche, P., *Übermaß und Verfassungsrecht*, Goldbach: Keip Verlag 1999

Leyendecker, H., Stiller, M. & Prantl, H., *Helmut Kohl, die Macht und das Geld*, Göttingen: Steidl 2000

Lösche, P., "Demokratie braucht Lobbying," in: Leith, Th. & Speth, R., *Die fünfte Gewalt Lobbyismus in Deutschland*, Bonn: Bundeszentrale für politische Bildung 2006, pp. 53ff.

M

Maaß, A.R., "Die neuere Rechtsprechung des BVerfG zum allgemeinen Gleichheitssatz – Ein Neuansatz?," *NVwZ* 1988, pp. 14ff.

Maguire, B., *Immigration. Public Legislation and Private Bills*, Lanham: University Press of America 1997

Male, R.M. van, "Geen wetgeving zonder motivering," in: *Recht doen door wetgeving*, Zwolle: W.E.J. Tjeenk Willink 1990, pp. 279ff.

Manig, B.O., "Der Bluthund ist zurück," *Zeit Online*, no. 37, 2005 <www.zeit.de/2005/37/A-Sch_9arner_neu>
Mantel, M., "Private Bills and Private Laws," 99 *Law. Libr. J.* 87 (2007)
Maravall, J.M. & Przeworski, A. (eds.), *Democracy and the Rule of Law*, Cambridge: Cambridge University Press 2003
Marritz, D., "Making Equality Matter (Again): The Prohibition Against Special Laws in the Pennsylvania Constitution," 3 *Widener J. Pub. L.* 161 (1993)
Marks, T.C. Jr., "Terri Schiavo and the Law," 67 *Alb. L. Rev.* 843 (2004)
Mascott, J.L., "Recent Decisions of the United States Court of Appeals for the District of Columbia Circuit," 73 *Geo. Wash. L. Rev.* 802 (2005)
Maxeiner, J.R., "Legal Certainty: A European Alternative to American Legal Indeterminacy?," 15 *Tul. J. Int'l. & Comp. L.* 541 (2007)
Mayer, G., *Lehrbuch des deutschen Staatsrechts*, 1919, Berlin: Duncker & Humblot 2005
McCubbins, M.D. & Rodriguez, D.B., "Canonical Construction and Statutory Revisionism: The Strange Case of the Appropriations Canon," 14 J *Contemp. Legal Issues* 669 (2005)
Meessen, K.M., "Maßnahmegesetze, Individualgesetze und Vollziehungsgesetze," *DÖV* 1970, pp. 314ff.
Menger, Ch.F., *Das Gesetz als Norm und Maßnahme*, Berlin: Walter de Gruyter & Co. 1957
Meßerschmidt, K., *Gesetzgebungsermessen*, Berlin: Nomos 2000
Milbank, D., "Senate's Bold Proposal for Iraq: Sugar Beets and Rural Schools – in the U.S." *The Washington Post*, March 29, 2007, p. A2
Montesquieu, Ch. de Secondat, *The Spirit of the Laws*, Book XI, Ch. 6, Berkeley: University of California Press 1977
Moor-van Vugt, A. de, *Maten en gewichten. Het evenredigheidsbeginsel in Europees perspectief*, Zwolle: Tjeenk Willink 1995
Morehead, J., "Into the Hopper. Private Bills and Private Laws: A Guide to the Legislative Process," 9 *The Serials Librarian* no. 3, 115 (1985)
Mowry, T., "The Protection of [Unlawful] Commerce in Arms Act-Does Congress Have the Power to Pass Special Legislation," 14 *Temp. Pol. & Civ. Rts. L. Rev.* 225 (2004)

N

Neumann, F., *The Rule of Law. Political Theory and the Legal System in Modern Society*, Leamington Spa and Heidelberg: Berg 1986
Nowak, J.E. & Rotunda, R.D., *Constitutional Law*, St. Paul: Thomson West 2004

O

Oldenziel, H.A., *Wetgeving en rechtszekerheid*, Deventer: Kluwer 1998
Oldershaw, J.B. et al., "Persistent Vegetative State: Medical, Religious, Economic and Legal Perspectives," 1 *DePaul J. Health Care L.* 495 (1997)

Oleszek, W.J., *Congressional Procedures and the Policy Process*, 4th ed., Washington, D.C: CQ Press 1996

Ommeren, F.J. van, *De verplichting verankerd. De reikwijdte van het legaliteitsbeginsel en het materiële wetsbegrip*, Zwolle: W.E.J. Tjeenk Willink 1996

Ossenbühl, F., "Die Bindung der Verwaltung an die höchstrichterliche Rechtsprechung," *AöR* 1967–92, pp. 478ff.

Ossenbühl, F., "Der Grundsatz der Verhältnismäßigkeit (Übermaßverbot) in der Rechtsprechung der Verwaltungsgerichte," *JURA* 1997, pp. 617ff.

Osterloh, L., "Art. 3," in: Sachs, M., *Grundgesetz. Kommentar*, München: C.H. Beck 2007, pp. 183ff.

P

Pabst, H.J., "Das Investitionsmaßnahmegesetz 'Südumfahrung Stendal' vor dem BVerfG," *UPR* 1997, pp. 284ff.

Paetow, S., "Rechtsprechung zum Verkehrswegeplanungsbeschleunigungsgesetz," *DVBl.* 1994, pp. 94ff.

Pauwels, M.R.T., *Terugwerkende kracht van belastingwetgeving: gewikt en gewogen*, Tilburg 2009

Perris, E.L. & Dworin, Ch., "Private Immigration and Naturalization Bills – Equitable Safety Valves," 8 *U.C.D. L. Rev.* 263 (1975)

Pestalozza, Ch., *"Formenmißbrauch" des Staates*, München: C.H. Beck 1973

Philips, K.P., *Arrogant Capital: Washington, Wall Street, and the Frustration of American Politics*, Boston: Little, Brown and Co. 1994

Pieroth, B., "Die neuere Rechtsprechung des Bundesverfassungsgerichts zum Grundsatz des Vertrauensschutzes," *JZ* 1984, pp. 971ff.

Plater, Z.J.B., "The Snail Darter, the Tellico Dam, and Sustainable Democracy – Lessons for the Next President from a Classic Environmental Law Controversy," *Boston College Law School Lectures and Presentations* 2000, at <http://lsr.nellco.org/bc/bclslp/papers/4/>

Polak, C.H.F., *Het begrip 'algemeen belang' in de verschillende onderdelen van het administratieve recht*, VAR pre-advies, Haarlem: Tjeenk Willink 1950

Popelier, P., "Behoorlijke wetgeving in de rechtspraak van het Europees Hof voor de Rechten van de Mens," *Tijdschrift voor Wetgeving* 2004–6, pp. 126ff.

Popelier, P., *Legal Certainty and Principles of Proper Law Making*, 2 *Eur. J.L. Reform* 321 (2000)

Popelier, P., "Legislatieve 'validatie': een kwestie van wetgevingstechniek," in: Adams, M. & Wintgens, L.J. (eds.), *Wetgeving in theorie en praktijk*, Antwerpen: Maklu 1994, pp. 77ff.

Popelier, P., "The Role of the Belgian Constitutional Court in the Legislative Process," 26 *Statute Law Review* 22 (2005)

Popelier, P., *Toepassing van de wet in de tijd*, Antwerpen: Kluwer 1999

Popkin, W.D., *Materials on Legislation: Political Language and the Political Process*, Westbury, New York: The Foundation Press, Inc. 1997

Prakke, L. &. Kortmann, C.A.J.M (eds.), *Constitutional Law of 15 EU Member States*, Deventer: Kluwer 2004

Q

Quack, K., "Die Rückwirkung belastender Gesetze," *DVBl.* 1962, pp. 289ff.

R

Ramge, Th., *Die großen Polit-Skandale. Eine andere Geschichte der Bundesrepublik*, Frankfurt/New York: Campus 2003

Ransdell, J.E., "The High Cost of the Pork Barrel," *Annals of the American Academy of Political and Social Science*, Vol. 64, Public Administration and Partisan Politics (1916)

Raz, J., *The Rule of Law and Its Virtue*, in: Raz, J., *The Authority of Law*, Clarendon Press: Oxford 1979

Redish, M.H. & Pudelski, Ch.R., "Legislative Deception, Separation of Powers, and the Democratic Process: Harnessing the Political Theory of United States v. Klein," 100 *Nw. U. L. Rev.* 437 (2006)

Reimer, F., "Das Parlementsgesetz als Steuerungsmittel und Kontrollmaßtab," in: Hoffmann-Riem, W., Schmidt-Aßmann, E. & Voßkuhle, A. (eds.), *Grundlagen des Verwaltungsrechts*, Vol. 1, München: C.H. Beck 2006, pp. 533ff.

Reynolds, O.M., Jr., *Local Government Law*, 2nd ed., St. Paul, Minn: West Group 2001

Reynolds, J., "The Rule of Law and the Origins of the Bill of Attainder Clause," 18 *St. Thomas L. Rev.* 177 (2005)

Ricciardi, L. & Sinclair, M.B.W., "Retroactive Civil Legislation," 27 *U. Tol. L. Rev.* 301 (1996)

Ronellenfitsch, M., "Maßnahmegesetze zur Beschleunigung von Verkehrsprojekten," *DÖV* 1991, pp. 771ff.

Ronellenfitsch, M., "Neues Verkehrswegeplanungsrecht," *DVBl.* 1994, pp. 441ff.

Ronner, A.D., "Judicial Self-demise: The Test of When Congress Impermissibly Intrudes on Judicial Power After Robertson v. Seattle Audubon Society and the Federal Appellate Courts' Rejection of the Separation of Powers Challenges to the New Section of the Securities Exchange Act of 1934," 35 *Ariz. L. Rev.* 1037 (1993)

Rosenblatt-Hoffman, M., "The Schiavo Odyssey: A Tale of TWO Legislative Reprieves," 7 *Marq. Elder's Advisor* 357 (2006)

Rossiter, C. (ed.), *The Federalist Papers*, A Signet Classic: New York 2003

Rousseau, J.J., *The Social Contract*, Middlesex: Penguin 1968

Ruiter, D.W.P., *Bestuursrechtelijke wetgevingsleer*, Assen: Van Gorcum 1987

S

Safire, W., *Safire's Political Dictionary*, 3rd ed., New York: Ballantine 1978

Samaha, A.M., "Undue Process: Congressional Referral and Judicial Resistance in the Schiavo Controversy," 22 *Const. Comment.* 505 (2005)
Scalia, A., "The Doctrine of Standing as an Essential Element of the Separation of Powers," 17 *Suffolk U. L. Rev.* 881 (1983)
Schachtschneider, K.A., *Prinzipien des Rechtsstaates*, Berlin: Duncker & Humblot 2006
Scheerbarth, H.W., "Zur 'Rückwirkung' von Gesetzen, insbesondere der 'Lex Schörner'," *DVBl.* 1956, pp. 395ff.
Scheltema, M., "De partijdige wetgever," Deventer: Kluwer 1984
Schily, O., "Wie der Flick-Konzern in Bonn Politik machte," *Blätter für deutsche und internationale Politik* 1986–4, pp. 436ff.
Schlössels, R., *Het specialiteitsbeginsel. Over de structuur van bestuursbevoegdheden, wetmatigheid van bestuur en beleidsvrijheid*, The Hague: Sdu Uitgevers 1998
Schmidt, R., *Staatsorganisationsrecht*, Grasberg: Rolf Schmidt Verlag 2008
Schmidt-Aßmann, E., *Das allgemeine Verwaltungsrecht als Ordnungsidee*, Berlin, Heidelberg: Springer 2004
Schmitt, C., *Verfassungslehre*, München und Leipzig: Duncker & Humblot 1928
Schneller, Ch., "Gewaltenteilung und Rechtsschutz in der objektbezogen Legalplanung," *ZG* 1998, pp. 179ff.
Schneider, H., *Gesetzgebung*, Heidelberg: C.F. Müller Verlag 2002
Schneider, H., "Über Einzelfallgesetze," in: Barion, H., Forsthoff, E., & Weber, W., *Festschrift für Carl Schmitt*, Berlin: Duncker & Humblot 1959, pp. 159ff.
Schneider, H., "Der Niedergang des Gesetzgebungsverfahrens," in: Rittersbach, Th.& Geiger, W. (eds.), *Festschrift für Gebhard Müller*, Tübingen: J.C.B. Mohr 1970, pp. 421ff.
Schuijt, G., "Kroniek van het Nederlandse mediarecht 2001–2006," *Auteurs & Media* 2006–3, pp. 238ff.
Schultz, G., "Rundschau. Blick in die Zeit," *MDR* 1955, pp. 336ff.
Schulze-Fielitz, H., "Art. 20," in: Dreier, H., *Grundgesetz Kommentar*, Tübingen: Siebeck Mohr 2006, pp. 258ff.
Schulze-Fielitz, H., *Theorie und Praxis parlamentarischer Gesetzgebung*, Berlin: Duncker & Humblot 1988
Schulze-Fielitz, H., "Art. 97," in: Dreier, H., *Grundgesetzkommentar*, Tübingen: Mohr Siebeck 2000, pp. 490ff.
Schünemann, B., "Amnestie und Grundgesetz. Zur Verfassungswidrigkeit einer Amnestie in der Parteispendenaffäre," *ZRP* 1984–6, pp. 137ff.
Seidman, L.M., *Equal Protection of the Laws*, New York: Foundation Press 2003
Shaman, J.M., *Constitutional Interpretation. Illusion and Reality*, Westport: Greenwood Press 2001
Shepsle, K.A. & Weingast, B.R., "Political Preferences for the Pork Barrel: A Generalization," *American Journal of Political Science* 25 (1), February 1981, pp. 96ff.
Shimomura, F.D., "The History of Claims Against the United States: The Evolution from a Legislative toward a Judicial Model of Payment," 45 *La. L. Rev.* 625 (1985)
Skidmore, D., "Bill Would Let Morgan, Daughter Come Home. Congress OKs Special Custody Measure," *The Washington Times*, September 19, 1996

Starck, Ch., *Die Allgemeinheit des Gesetzes*, Göttingen: Van Den Hoeck & Ruprecht 1987

Starck, Ch., *Der Gesetzesbegriff des Grundgesetzes*, Baden-Baden: Nomos 1970

Starck, Ch., " Art. 3," in: Mangoldt H. von., Klein, F. & Starck, Ch., *Kommentar zum Grundgesetz*, München: Franz Vahlen 2005, pp. 307ff.

Stein, P.G., "Roman Law, Common Law, and Civil Law," 66 *Tul. L. Rev.* 1591 (1992)

Steinkamp, P., "Generalfeldmarschall Ferdinand Schörner," in: Ueberschär, G.R., *Hitlers militärische Elite. Bd. 2 Vom Kriegsbeginn bis zum Weltkriegsende*, Darmstadt: Primus Verlag 1998, pp. 236ff.

Stern, K., *Des Staatsrecht der Bundesrepublik Deutschland*, Vol. III/2, München: Beck 1994

Story, J., *Commentaries on the Constitution of the United States*, Durham Carolina Academic Press 1987

Stoter, W.S.R., *Belangenafweging door de wetgever*, The Hague: Boom Juridische Auteurs 2000

Strasser, M., "Ex Post Facto Laws, Bills of Attainder, and the Definition of Punishment: On DOMA, the Hawaii Amendment, and Federal Constitutional Constraints," 48 *Syracuse L.Rev.* 227 (1998)

Stroink, F.A.M., "Complexe besluitvorming: een opgave voor burger, bestuur en rechter," in: Heida, H., Stroink, F.A.M & Wijmen, P.C.E. van, *Complexe besluitvorming*, Alphen aan den Rijn: Samson 1998, pp. 7ff.

Sturm, G., "Art. 100," in: Sachs, M., *Grundgesetz. Kommentar*, München: C.H. Beck 2007

Stüer, B., "Investitionsmaßnahmegesetze als Verfassungsproblem," *DVBl.* 1991, pp. 1333ff.

T

Tak, A.Q.C., "Misbruik van wetgeving," *Openbaar bestuur* 1997–12, pp. 7ff.

Tak, A.Q.C., *Overheidsbestuur en privaatrecht*, Alphen aan den Rijn: Samson 1978

Tamanaha, B.Z., *Law as a Means to an End. Threat to the Rule of Law*, New York: Cambridge University Press 2006

Tamanaha, B.Z., *On the rule of law. History, Politics, Theory*, Cambridge: Cambridge University Press 2004

Thiele, W., "Vom Wandel des Gesetzesinhalts," *DVBl.* 1978, pp. 901ff.

Thomas, E., *Terugwerkende kracht (on) toelaatbaar?*, *Weekblad Fiscaal Recht* 2005–6614, pp. 326ff.

Tribe, L.H., *American Constitutional Law*, 2nd ed., New York: The Foundation Press 1988

Tribe, L.H., *American Constitutional Law*, 3rd ed., New York: The Foundation Press 2000

Troy, D.L., *Retroactive Legislation*, Washington D.C: The AEI Press 1998

Turley, J., "One American at a Time. Legislating by Bill of Attainder," *Legal Times*, week of February 26, 1996

Tushnet, M., "Comparative Constitutional Law," in: Reimann, M. & Zimmermann, R. (eds.), *The Oxford Handbook of Comparative Law*, Oxford: Oxford University Press 2006, pp. 1225ff.

U

Uerpmann, R., *Das öffentliche Interesse*, Tübingen: Mohr Siebeck 1999
Utt, R.D., "The Bridge to Nowhere: A National Embarrassment," October 20, 2005, at <www.heritage.org/Research/Budget/wm889.cfm?renderforprint=1>

V

Veerman, G.J., *Over wetgeving. Principes, paradoxen en praktische beschouwingen*, Den Haag: SDU Uitgevers 2007
Verschuuren, J., "De formele wetgever als uitvoerder: de Vergunningwet Westerschelde en het streven naar een integrale afweging," *Bouwrecht* 1998–5, pp. 361ff.
Visser, N.B., "Het overrulen van jurisprudentie door de wetgever," *RegelMaat* 1987, pp. 22ff.
Vlemminx, F.M.C., "Een grondwetswijziging onder het motto 'Verdeel en heers'?," in: Broeksteeg J.L.W. et al., *De Nederlandse Grondwet en de Europese Unie*, Deventer: Kluwer 2003, pp. 93ff.
Vlies, I.C. van der, *Het wetsbegrip en beginselen van behoorlijke regelgeving*, The Hague: Vuga 1984

W

Waaldijk, K., "Can we Require Legislatures to State the Reasons for their Legislative Decisions?," in: Eemeren, F. van et al. (eds.), *Argumentation: Analysis and Practices. Proceedings of the Conference on Argumentation 1986*, Dordrecht: Foris Publications Holland 1986, pp. 110ff.
Waaldijk, K., *Motiveringsplichten van de wetgever*, Lelystad: Vermande 1994
Weggeman, A., "Het vormgeven van overgangsrecht," in: Burg, F.H. van der & Weggeman, A., *Overgangsrecht*, Den Haag 2001, pp. 41ff.
Werd, M. de, "Beïnvloeding van rechtspraak door de wetgever," *NJCM-Bulletin* 2001–3, pp. 348ff.
Werthmüller, D., *Junge Wissenschaft. Schriften der Hochschule für Politik München*, Vol. 1, München: Ernst Vögel 1990
Westerholt, L. von, *Neugliederungsgesetze als Maßnahmegesetze und generelles Landesplanungsrecht in Nordrhein-Westfalen*, Münster 1976
Westerman, P., *Twee pleidooien voor formalisering*, Den Haag: Boom Juridische uitgevers 2003
Wijk, H.D. van, Konijnenbelt, W.& Van Male, R., *Hoofdstukken van bestuursrecht,* The Hague: Elsevier juridisch 2005
Wijmen, P.C.E. van, *Recht, belang en rechtsbescherming*, The Hague: Vuga 1981

Winters, J.M., "Classification of Municipalities," 57 *Nw. U.L.Rev.* 279 (1962)
Wise, Ch., *The Dynamics of Legislation*, San Francisco, Oxford: Jossey-Bass Publishers 1991
Witteveen, W.J., "De nuttige fictie van het algemene belang," *Feit & Fictie* 1997, Vol. III, pp. 15ff.
Witteveen, W.J., *Evenwicht van machten*, Zwolle: Tjeenk Willink 1991
Wolff, H.J., Bachof, O. & Stober, R., *Verwaltungsrecht*, Vol. 1, München: Beck 1999
Woltjer, A.J.Th., *Wetgever, rechter en het primaat van de gelijkheid*, Den Haag: Boom Juridische uitgevers 2002
Wormuth, F.D., "Legislative Disqualifications As Bills of Attainder," 4 *Vand. L. Rev.* 603 (1951)
Würtenberger, J., " 'Maßnahmegesetze' zur Beschleunigung der Verkehrsplanung?," *VBlBW* 1992, pp. 1ff.
Würtenberger, Th., "Legitimationsmuster von Herrschaft im Laufe der Geschichte," *JuS* 1986, pp. 344ff.

Y

Young, G.G., "Congressional Regulation of Federal Courts' Jurisdiction and Processes: *United States v. Klein* Revisited," 1981 *Wis. L. Rev.* 1189, 1243 (1981)

Z

Zahn, K.Ch., *Gesetz und Einzelakt*, Göttingen 1963
Zeidler, K., *Maßnahmegesetz und ‹‹klassisches›› Gesetz*, Karlsruhe: C.F. Müller 1961
Zelenak, L., "Are Rifle Shot Transition Rules and other Ad Hoc Tax Legislation Constitutional?," 44 *Tax L. Rev.* 563 (1989)
Zellmer, S.B., "Sacrificing Legislative Integrity on the Altar of Appropriations Riders: A Constitutional Crisis," 21 *Harv. Envtl. L. Rev.* 457 (1997)
Zoontjens, P.J.J., "Eenzijdig overheidshandelen," in: Zoontjens P.J.J. & Hertogh, M.L.M. (eds.), *Gelijke behandeling: principes en praktijken*, Nijmegen: Wolf Legal Publishers 2006, pp. 117ff.
Zweigert, K & Kötz, H., *An Introduction to Comparative Law*, Oxford: Clarendon Press 1998
Zwemmer, J.W., "Schurende machten," *AA* 1999-9, pp. 668ff.
Zywicki, T.J., "Senators and Special Interests: A Public Choice Analysis of the Seventeenth Amendment," 73 *Or. L. Rev.* 1007 (1994)

Notes

Comment, "The Distinction between Legislative and Judicial Courts," 43 *Yale L. J.* 316 (1933–1934)
Note, "The Court of Claims: Judicial Power and Congressional Review," 46 *Harv. L. Rev.* 677 (1932–1933)

Note, "The Constitutionality of Private Acts of Congress," 49 *Yale L. J.* 712 (1940)
Note, "Private Bills and the Immigration Law," 69 *Harv. L. Rev.* 1083 (1956)
Note, "The Bounds of the Legislative Specification: A Suggested Approach to the Bill of Attainder Clause," 72 *Yale L.J.* 330 (1962)
Note, "Private Bills in Congress," 79 *Harv. L. Rev.* 1684 (1966)

Reports

Commissie Versnelling Besluitvorming Infrastructurele Projecten, *Sneller en beter*, 2008, at <www.verkeerenwaterstaat.nl/Images/webversieRapportelverdingsnijtekenstijd1146_tcm195-219331.pdf>
Legislative Studies Commission (*Commissie voor Wetgevingsvraagstukken*), *Orde in regelgeving*, The Hague 1985
Parliamentary Report, *Vertrouwen en zelfvertrouwen. Parlementaire zelfreflectie*, The Lower House of the Parliament, March 2009
The Annual Report 2003 of the Dutch Council of State, at <www.nicis.nl/kenniscentrum/binaries/kcgs/bulk/nieuws/2004/4/193847.pdf>

Other

"Abscam Trial Opens for Rep. Kelly, First Republican to Face Charges," *New York Times*, December 5, 1980
"Camera blijft in cel V.d. G. via noodwet," *NRC Handelsblad* July 9, 2002, p. 1
"Flick – ein Mann kauft die Republik," *Der Spiegel* 1984–44, p. 26
"Ford to City: Drop Dead," *Daily News*, October 30, 1975
"Indictments Expected Soon in Abscam Case," *Boston Globe*, February 29, 1980
"Juristen: camera in cel Van der G. is onaanvaardbaar," *Volkskrant* July 10, 2002, p. 2

INDEX

References are to Sections

Beginning with
- I: Part I, Introduction
- II: Part II, The United States
- III: Part III, Germany
- IV: Part IV, The Netherlands
- V: Comparison and analysis

A

B

F

G

I

L

M

N

P

R

ABOUT THE AUTHOR

Anna Jasiak studied law at the University of Silesia in Poland and at Tilburg University in the Netherlands. In Tilburg she was in 2002 appointed assistant to A.K. Koekkoek, professor at the Department of Constitutional and Administrative Law. She worked there until she graduated in 2005 (cum laude – the highest honour in the Netherlands). In that same year she started her Ph.D. research program at Tilburg University on ad hoc legislation from a constitutional perspective. In June 2010 she obtained her doctorate.

While working on her Ph.D. she was a visiting researcher at Georgetown University Law Center in Washington D.C. (the United States) and at the Graduiertenkolleg "Verfassung jenseits des Staates" at Humboldt University in Berlin (Germany).

She is currently working at the Dutch Council of State in the Hague, advising the government and Parliament on legislation and doing constitutional law research.

IUS COMMUNE EUROPAEUM

A peer-reviewed book series in which the common foundations of the legal systems of the Member States of the European Community are the central focus.

The *Ius Commune Europaeum* series includes horizontal comparative legal studies as well as studies on the effect of treaties within the national legal systems. All the classic fields of law are covered. The books are published in various European languages under the auspices of METRO, the Institute for Transnational Legal Research at the Maastricht University.

Recently published:
Volume 85: *Fact-Finding in Civil Litigation. A Comparative Perspective*, R. Verkerk
Volume 86: *The Making of Chinese Condominium Law. A Comparative Perspective with American and South African Condominium Laws*, L. Chen
Volume 87: *Effective Criminal Defence in Europe*, Z. Namoradze, R. Smith, T. Spronken and E. Cape (eds.)
Volume 88: *Conflict of Laws and Laws of Conflict in Europe and Beyond. Patterns of Supranational and Transnational Juridification*, R. Nickel (ed.)
Volume 89: *The Regulation of Architects in Belgium and the Netherlands. A Comparative Analysis*, S. Schoenmaekers
Volume 90: *Evolutie van de basisbeginselen van het contractenrecht*, I. Samoy (red.)
Volume 91: *Recidive in België en Nederland. Een analyse van 200 jaar rechtspraak en rechtsleer*, M. Dams
Volume 92: *An EU-wide Letter of Rights. Towards Best Practice*, T. Spronken (ed.)
Volume 93: *The Costanzo Obligation. The Obligations of National Administrative Authorities in the Case of Incompatibility between National Law and European Law*, M. Verhoeven
Volume 94: *The Effect of a Change of Circumstances on the Binding Force of Contracts. Comparative Perspectives*, R. Momberg Uribe
Volume 95: *The Landscape of the Legal Professions in Europe and the USA: Continuity and Change*, A. Uzelac and C.H. van Rhee (eds.)